BENCHMARK SERIES

WORD 2013
MICROSOFT®

LEVEL 2

NITA RUTKOSKY
Pierce College Puyallup
Puyallup, Washington

AUDREY ROGGENKAMP
Pierce College Puyallup
Puyallup, Washington

IAN RUTKOSKY
Pierce College Puyallup
Puyallup, Washington

PARADIGM
EDUCATION SOLUTIONS

St. Paul

Director of Editorial	Christine Hurney
Director of Production	Timothy W. Larson
Production Editor	Sarah Kearin
Cover Designer	Leslie Anderson
Text Designers	Leslie Anderson and Jaana Bykonich
Copy Editor	Communicáto, Ltd.
Desktop Production	Jaana Bykonich, Julie Johnston, Valerie King, Timothy W. Larson, Jack Ross, and Sara Schmidt Boldon
Proofreader	Katherine Lee
Indexer	Terry Casey
VP & Director of Digital Projects	Chuck Bratton
Digital Projects Manager	Tom Modl

Acknowledgements: The authors, editors, and publisher thank the following instructors for their helpful suggestions during the planning and development of the books in the Benchmark Office 2013 Series: Olugbemiga Adekunle, Blue Ridge Community College, Harrisonburg, VA; Letty Barnes, Lake WA Institute of Technology, Kirkland, WA; Erika Nadas, Wilbur Wright College, Chicago, IL; Carolyn Walker, Greenville Technical College, Greenville, SC; Carla Anderson, National College, Lynchburg, VA; Judy A. McLaney, Lurleen B. Wallace Community College, Opp, AL; Sue Canter, Guilford Technical Community College, Jamestown, NC; Reuel Sample, National College, Knoxville, TN; Regina Young, Wiregrass Georgia Technical College, Valdosta, GA; William Roxbury, National College, Stow, OH; Charles Adams, II, Danville Community College, Danville, VA; Karen Spray, Northeast Community College, Norfolk, NE; Deborah Miller, Augusta Technical College, Augusta, GA; Wanda Stuparits, Lanier Technical College, Cumming, GA; Gale Wilson, Brookhaven College, Farmers Branch, TX; Jocelyn S. Pinkard, Arlington Career Institute, Grand Prairie, TX; Ann Blackman, Parkland College, Champaign, IL; Fathia Williams, Fletcher Technical Community College, Houma, LA; Leslie Martin, Gaston College, Dallas, NC; Tom Rose, Kellogg Community College, Battle Creek, MI; Casey Thompson, Wiregrass Georgia Technical College, Douglas, GA; Larry Bush, University of Cincinnati, Clermont College, Amelia, OH; Tim Ellis, Schoolcraft College, Liconia, MI; Miles Cannon, Lanier Technical College, Oakwood, GA; Irvin LaFleur, Lanier Technical College, Cumming, GA; Patricia Partyka, Schoolcraft College, Prudenville, MI.

The authors and publishing team also thanks the following individuals for their contributions to this project: checking the accuracy of the instruction and exercises—Brienna McWade, Traci Post, and Janet Blum, Fanshawe College, London, Ontario; creating annotated model answers and developing lesson plans—Ann Mills, Ivy Tech Community College, Evansville, Indiana; developing rubrics—Marjory Wooten, Laneir Techncial College, Cumming, Georgia.

Trademarks: Access, Excel, Internet Explorer, Microsoft, PowerPoint, and Windows are trademarks or registered trademarks of Microsoft Corporation in the United States and/or other countries. Some of the product names and company names included in this book have been used for identification purposes only and may be trademarks or registered trade names of their respective manufacturers and sellers. The authors, editors, and publisher disclaim any affiliation, association, or connection with, or sponsorship or endorsement by, such owners.

We have made every effort to trace the ownership of all copyrighted material and to secure permission from copyright holders. In the event of any question arising as to the use of any material, we will be pleased to make the necessary corrections in future printings. Thanks are due to the aforementioned authors, publishers, and agents for permission to use the materials indicated.

Paradigm Publishing is independent from Microsoft Corporation, and not affiliated with Microsoft in any manner. While this publication may be used in assisting individuals to prepare for a Microsoft Office Specialist certification exam, Microsoft, its designated program administrator, and Paradigm Publishing do not warrant that use of this publication will ensure passing a Microsoft Office Specialist certification exam.

ISBN 978-0-76385-345-7 (Text)
ISBN 978-0-76385-388-4 (Text + CD)
ISBN 978-0-76385-367-9 (eBook)

© 2014 by Paradigm Publishing, Inc.
875 Montreal Way
St. Paul, MN 55102
Email: educate@emcp.com
Website: www.emcp.com

Printed in the United States of America

23 22 21 20 19 18 17 16 15 14   3 4 5 6 7 8 9 10 11 12

Contents

Benchmark Series Microsoft Word 2013 is designed for students who want to learn how to use this powerful word processing program to create professional-looking documents for workplace, school, and personal communication needs. No prior knowledge of word processing is required. After successfully completing a course using this textbook, students will be able to

- Create and edit memos, letters, fliers, announcements, and reports of varying complexity
- Apply appropriate formatting elements and styles to a range of document types
- Add graphics and other visual elements to enhance written communication
- Plan, research, write, revise, and publish documents to meet specific information needs
- Given a workplace scenario requiring a written solution, assess the communication purpose and then prepare the materials that achieve the goal efficiently and effectively

In addition to mastering Word skills, students will learn to import and export files between Word and other programs in the Office 2013 suite. Upon completing the text, they can expect to be proficient in using Word to organize, analyze, and present information.

Well-designed textbook pedagogy is important, but students learn technology skills from practice and problem solving. Technology provides opportunities for interactive learning as well as excellent ways to quickly and accurately assess student performance. To this end, this textbook is supported with SNAP, Paradigm Publishing's web-based training and assessment learning management system. Details about SNAP as well as additional student courseware and instructor resources can be found on page xiv.

Achieving Proficiency in Word 2013 ■■■■■■■■

Since its inception several Office versions ago, the Benchmark Series has served as a standard of excellence in software instruction. Elements of the book function individually and collectively to create an inviting, comprehensive learning environment that produces successful computer users. The following visual tour highlights the text's features.

UNIT OPENERS display the unit's four chapter titles. Each level has two units, which conclude with a comprehensive unit performance assessment.

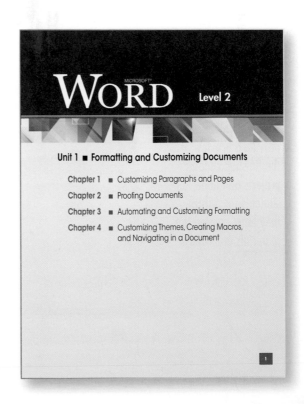

WORD Level 2

Unit 1 ■ Formatting and Customizing Documents

Chapter 1 ■ Customizing Paragraphs and Pages

Chapter 2 ■ Proofing Documents

Chapter 3 ■ Automating and Customizing Formatting

Chapter 4 ■ Customizing Themes, Creating Macros, and Navigating in a Document

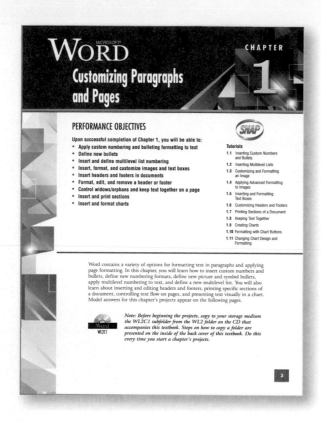

CHAPTER OPENERS present the performance objectives and an overview of the skills taught.

SNAP interactive tutorials are available to support chapter-specific skills at snap2013.emcp.com.

DATA FILES are provided for each chapter. A prominent note reminds students to copy the appropriate chapter data folder and make it active.

PROJECT APPROACH: Builds Skill Mastery within Realistic Context

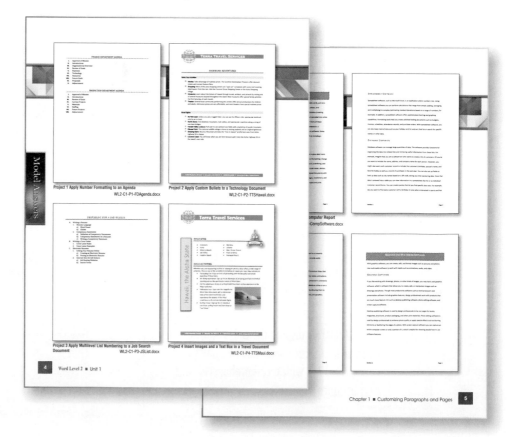

MODEL ANSWERS provide a preview of the finished chapter projects and allow students to confirm they have created the materials accurately.

MULTIPART PROJECTS provide a framework for the instruction and practice on software features. A project overview identifies tasks to accomplish and key features to use in completing the work.

STEP-BY-STEP INSTRUCTIONS guide students to the desired outcome for each project part. Screen captures illustrate what the student's screen should look like at key points.

MAGENTA TEXT identifies material to type.

Project 5 | **Insert Document Properties and Fields in an Agreement Document** | **3 Parts**

You will open a testing agreement document and then insert and update document properties and fields.

Inserting Document Properties

If you click the Quick Parts button on the INSERT tab and then point to *Document Property* at the drop-down list, a side menu displays with document property options. Click an option at this side menu and a document property placeholder is inserted in the document. Type the desired text in the placeholder.

If you insert a document property placeholder in multiple locations in a document, updating one of the placeholders will automatically update all occurrences of that placeholder in the document. For example, in Project 5a, you will insert a Company document property placeholder in six locations in a document. You will then change the content in the first occurrence of the placeholder and the remaining placeholders will update to reflect the change.

When you click the FILE tab, the Info backstage area displays containing information about the document. Document properties display at the right side of the Info backstage area and include information such as the document size, number of pages, title, and comments. Some of the document properties that you insert with the Quick Parts button will display at the Info backstage area.

Project 5a | **Inserting Document Property Placeholders** | **Part 1 of 3**

1. Open **TestAgrmnt.docx** and then save the document and name it **WL2-C3-P5-TestAgrmnt**.
2. Select the first occurrence of *FP* in the document (located in the first line of text after the title) and then insert a document property placeholder by completing the following steps:
   a. Click the INSERT tab, click the Quick Parts button in the Text group, point to *Document Property*, and then click *Company* at the side menu.
   b. Type **Frontier Productions** in the Company placeholder.
   c. Press the Right Arrow key to move the insertion point outside the Company placeholder.
3. Select each remaining occurrence of *FP* in the document (it appears five more times) and then insert the Company document property placeholder. (The company name, *Frontier Productions*, will automatically be inserted in the Company placeholder.)

---

4. Press Ctrl + End to move the insertion point to the end of the document and then insert a Comments document property placeholder by completing the following steps:
   a. Click the Quick Parts button, point to *Document Property*, and then click *Comments* at the side menu.
   b. Type **First Draft** in the Comments placeholder.
   c. Press the Right Arrow key.
   d. Press Shift + Enter.
5. Click the FILE tab, make sure the *Info* option is selected, and then notice that the comment you typed in the Comments document property placeholder displays at the right side of the backstage area. Click the Back button to display the document.
6. Save and then print **WL2-C3-P5-TestAgrmnt.docx**.
7. Click in the first occurrence of the company name *Frontier Productions* and then click the Company placeholder tab. (This selects the Company placeholder.)
8. Type **Frontier Video Productions**.
9. Press the Right Arrow key. (Notice that the other occurrences of the Company document property placeholder are automatically updated to reflect the new name.)
10. Save **WL2-C3-P5-TestAgrmnt.docx**.

Inserting Fields

▼ **Quick Steps**

Insert a Field
1. Click INSERT tab.
2. Click Quick Parts button.
3. Click *Field* at drop-down list.
4. Click desired field.
5. Click OK.

Fields are placeholders for data that varies and main documents that are merged with data source files. You have inserted fields in a main document, inserted the date and time field, inserted page numbering in a document, and so on. Word provides buttons for many of the types of fields that you may want to insert into a document as well as options at the Field dialog box, shown in Figure 3.9. This dialog box contains a list of all available fields. Just as the Building Blocks Organizer dialog box is a central location for building blocks, the Field dialog box is a central location for fields. To display the Field dialog box, click the INSERT tab, click the Quick Parts button in the Text group, and then click *Field* at the drop-down list. At the Field dialog box, click the desired field in the *Field names* list box and then click OK.

Typically, a file remains open throughout all parts of the project. Students save their work incrementally.

Between project parts, the text presents instruction on the features and skills necessary to accomplish the next section of the project.

QUICK STEPS provide feature summaries for reference and review.

HINTS provide useful tips on how to use features efficiently and effectively.

---

2. Print only page 1 of section 1 and page 1 of section 2 by completing the following steps:
   a. Click the FILE tab and then click the *Print* option.
   b. At the Print backstage area, click in the *Pages* text box in the *Settings* category and then type **p1s1,p1s2**.
   c. Click the Print button.
3. Save **WL2-C1-P5-CompSoftware .docx**.

Step 2a

Step 2c

Step 2b

Keeping Text Together ▪▪▪▪▪▪▪▪▪▪▪▪▪▪▪▪▪▪▪

♦ Quick Steps
Keep Text Together
1. Click Paragraph group dialog box launcher.
2. Click Line and Page Breaks tab.
3. Click *Keep with next*, *Keep lines together*, and/or *Page break before*.
4. Click OK.

HINT
Text formatted with Keep with next formatting is identified with a ▪ nonprinting character in the left margin.

In a multiple-page document, Word automatically inserts a soft page break, which is a page break that adjusts when you add or delete text from the document. A soft page break may occur in an undesirable location. For example, a soft page break may cause a heading to display at the bottom of a page while the text connected to the heading displays at the top of the next page. A soft page break may also create a *widow* or *orphan*. A widow is the last line of text in a paragraph that appears at the top of a page and an orphan is the first line of text in a paragraph that appears at the bottom of a page.

Use options at the Paragraph dialog box with the Line and Page Breaks tab selected, as shown in Figure 1.7, to control widows and orphans and keep a paragraph, group of paragraphs, or group of lines together. Display this dialog box by clicking the Paragraph group dialog box launcher on the HOME tab and then clicking the Line and Page Breaks tab at the dialog box.

By default, the *Widow/Orphan control* option is active and Word tries to avoid creating a widow or orphan when inserting a soft page break. The other three options in the *Pagination* section of the dialog box are not active by default. Use the *Keep with next* option if you want to keep a line together with the next line. This is useful for keeping a heading together with the first line below the heading. If you want to keep a group of selected lines together, use the *Keep lines together* option. Use the *Page break before* option to tell Word to insert a page break before selected text.

Figure 1.7 Paragraph Dialog Box with Line and Page Breaks Tab Selected

Use options in this section to control the locations of page breaks in a document.

Project 5g Keeping Text Together   Part 7 of 7

1. With **WL2-C1-P5-CompSoftware.docx** open, scroll through the document and notice that the *SPREADSHEET SOFTWARE* heading displays at the bottom of page 1 and the paragraph that follows it displays at the top of page 2. Keep the heading together with the paragraph of text by completing the following steps:
   a. Position the insertion point on any character in the heading *SPREADSHEET SOFTWARE*.
   b. Make sure the HOME tab is active and then click the Paragraph group dialog box launcher.
   c. At the Paragraph dialog box, click the Line and Page Breaks tab.
   d. Click the *Keep with next* check box to insert a check mark.
   e. Click OK to close the dialog box.

Step 1c

Step 1d

2. Scroll through the document and notice the heading *MULTIMEDIA SOFTWARE* that displays near the end of the document. Insert a soft page break at the beginning of the heading by completing the following steps:
   a. Move the insertion point to the beginning of the *MULTIMEDIA SOFTWARE* heading.
   b. Click the Paragraph group dialog box launcher.
   c. At the Paragraph dialog box with the Line and Page Breaks tab selected, click the *Page break before* check box to insert a check mark.
   d. Click OK to close the dialog box.
3. Save, print, and then close **WL2-C1-P5-CompSoftware.docx**.

At the end of the project, students save, print, and then close the file.

CHAPTER REVIEW ACTIVITIES: A Hierarchy of Learning Assessments

Chapter Summary

- You can sort text in paragraphs, columns, and tables and sort records in a data source file. You can also select specific records in a data source file for merging with a main document.
- Use the Sort button in the Paragraph group on the HOME tab to sort text in paragraphs, columns, and tables.
- When sorting text set in columns, Word considers the left margin *Field 1*, text typed at the first tab *Field 2*, and so on.
- Sort on more than one field with the *Sort by* and *Then by* options at the Sort dialog box.
- Use the *Header row* option in the *My list has* section in the Sort Text dialog box to sort all text in colum
- Sort records in a data s by clicking the column with the Sort Records
- Select specific records i dialog box with the Filt
- When nonbreaking spa words as one unit and text to the next line. I Ctrl + Shift + spaceba
- Use the Find and Repla nonprinting elements a
- Save a document as a t As dialog box to *Word* click the *Change File Ty* click the Save As butto Custom Office Templat
- Word adds the file exte
- Open a template locate the New backstage area desired template.
- Footnotes and endnotes are inserted and printed end of the document.
- By default, footnotes a numbered with lowerca
- Move, copy, or delete a all of the other footnot
- Delete a footnote or er pressing the Delete key
- Consider using in-text c citation and reference s Modern Language Asso

CHAPTER SUMMARY captures the purpose and execution of key features.

- Insert a citation using the Insert Citation button in the Citations & Bibliography group on the REFERENCES tab. Specify source information at the Create Source dialog box.
- Insert a citation placeholder in a document if you want to type the source information at a later time.
- Edit a source at the Edit Source dialog box. Display this dialog box by clicking the source citation in the document, clicking the Citation Options arrow, and then clicking *Edit Source* at the drop-down list. Another option is to display the Source Manage dialog box, click the source you want to edit, and then click the Edit button.
- Manage sources—such as copying, deleting, editing, and inserting a new source—with options at the Source Manager dialog box. Display this dialog box by clicking the Manage Sources button in the Citations and Bibliography group on the REFERENCES tab.
- Insert a sources list, such as a works cited page, references page, or bibliography at the end of the document on a separate page. To do so, use the Bibliography button in the Citations & Bibliography group on the REFERENCES tab.
- To update a sources list, click anywhere in list text and then click the Update Citations and Bibliography tab.
- Change the reference style with the *Style* option box in the Citations & Bibliography group on the REFERENCES tab.

Commands Review

COMMANDS REVIEW summarizes visually the major features and alternative methods of access.

FEATURE	RIBBON TAB, GROUP	BUTTON, OPTION	KEYBOARD SHORTCUT
bibliography	REFERENCES, Citations & Bibliography		
Create Source dialog box	REFERENCES, Citations & Bibliography		
Filter and Sort dialog box with Select Records tab selected	MAILINGS, Start Mail Merge	Filter	
Filter and Sort dialog box with Sort Records tab selected	MAILINGS, Start Mail Merge		
Find and Replace dialog box	HOME, Editing		
endnote	REFERENCES, Footn		
footnote	REFERENCES, Footn		
nonbreaking space			
Sort Options dialog box	HOME, Paragraph		
Sort Text dialog box	HOME, Paragraph		
Source Manager dialog box	REFERENCES, Citati		
style	REFERENCES, Citati		

Concepts Check Test Your Knowledge SNAP

Completion: In the space provided at the right, indicate the correct term, symbol, or command.

1. The Sort button is located in this group on the HOME tab.

2. When sorting text in columns, Word considers the first tab this field number.

3. Click this option at the Sort Text dialog box to tell Word not to include the column headings in the sort.

4. Click the <u>Filter</u> hyperlink at this dialog box to display the Filter and Sort dialog box with the Filter Records tab selected.

5. Use this keyboard shortcut to insert a nonbreaking space.

6. Click this button at the expanded Find and Replace dialog box to display a pop-up list of special characters and nonprinting elements.

7. Word saves template documents with this file extension.

8. Click this option at the New backstage area to display templates saved in the Custom Office Templates folder.

9. Word numbers footnotes with this type of number.

10. Word numbers endnotes with this type of number.

11. Three of the most popular reference styles are APA (American Psychological Association), Chicago (*Chicago Manual of Style*), and this.

12. Click this tab to display the Citations & Bibliography group.

13. Create a new source for a document with options at this dialog box.

14. Click this button in the Citations & Bibliography group to display the Source Manager dialog box.

15. To update a bibliography, click anywhere in the bibliography and then click this tab.

CONCEPTS CHECK questions assess knowledge recall. Students enrolled in SNAP can complete the Concepts Check online. SNAP automatically scores student work.

Skills Check Assess Your Performance

Assessment

1 CREATE AND APPLY CUSTOM THEMES TO A MEDICAL PLANS DOCUMENT

1. At a blank document, create custom theme colors named with your initials that make the following color changes:
   a. Change the Accent 1 color to *Dark Red* (the first option in the *Standard Colors* section).
   b. Change the Accent 5 color to *Gold, Accent 4, Darker 50%* (eighth column, bottom row in the *Theme Colors* section).
2. Create custom theme fonts named with your initials that change the heading font to Corbel and the body font to Garamond.
3. Click the Theme Effects button and then click *Top Shadow* at the drop-down gallery (first column, third row).
4. Save the custom theme and name it with your initials. *Hint: Do this with the* **Save Current Theme** *option at the* Themes *drop-down gallery*.
5. Close the document without saving the changes.
6. Open **KLHPlan.docx** and then save the document and name it **WL2-C4-A1-**
7. Make the foll
   a. Apply the
   b. With the i
      the title **K**
   c. Apply the
   d. Apply the
8. Move the ins
   insert a page
   Hint: Do this
9. Apply the cus
   Themes butt
10. Save, print, a
11. At a blank do
    initials, the c
    theme named

Assessment

2 RECORD AND RUN

1. Open **Macro**
   named *XXXT*
   the following
   a. Position th
      Title and th
   b. Press the F
   c. Click the C
   d. Change the

---

10. At the blank document, delete the macro buttons from the Quick Access toolbar and then delete the macros from the Macros dialog box.
11. Remove the DEVELOPER tab from the ribbon. (Do this by displaying the Word Options dialog box with *Customize Ribbon* selected in the left panel. Remove the check mark from the *Developer* check box, and then click OK to close the dialog box.)

Visual Benchmark Demonstrate Your Proficiency

INSERT SMARTART GRAPHICS IN A BUSINESS DOCUMENT

1. Open **DIRevenues.docx** and then save the document and name it **WL2-C4-VB-DIRevenues**.
2. Create the following custom theme colors named with your first and last names with the following changes:
   a. Change the Text/Background - Dark 2 color to *Orange, Accent 2, Darker 50%* (sixth column, last row in the *Theme Colors* section).
   b. Change the Accent 1 color to *Green, Accent 6, Darker 50%* (tenth column, last row in the *Theme Colors* section).
   c. Change the Accent 4 color to *Orange, Accent 2, Darker 50%*.
   d. Change the Acce
3. Create the followin
   with the following c
   a. Change the head
   b. Change the body
4. Apply the Riblet th
5. Save the custom th
   Do this with the Sa
   gallery.
6. Center the title and
7. Save, print, and the
8. Open **DICorporate**
   VB-DICorporate.
9. Apply the WL2C4
10. Center the title and
    page 171.
11. Save, print, and the
12. At a blank docume
    of the Theme Color
    display), a screen ca
    your custom theme
    Theme dialog box (
    screen capture imag
13. Save the document
14. Print and then clos
15. At a blank docume
    the custom font the

Case Study Apply Your Skills

Part 1

You work for Jackson Photography and want to create a new letterhead for the company. Open **JPLtrd.docx** and then customize the text and clip art to create an attractive and professional-looking letterhead. Save the completed letterhead with the same name (**JPLtrd.docx**). Create a building block with the letterhead.

Part 2

At a blank document, create and then save custom theme colors that match the letterhead you created in Part 1. Create and then save custom theme fonts that apply the Arial font to headings and the Constantia font to body text. Apply a custom theme effect of your choosing. Save the custom theme in the Save Current Theme dialog box and name it with your initials followed by *JP*.

Part 3

At a blank document, insert the company letterhead building block you created in Part 1, type the title **Photography Services**, and then insert a SmartArt graphic of your choosing that contains the following text:
   • Wedding Photography
   • Sports Portraits
   • Senior Portraits
   • Family Portraits
   • Processing

Apply a heading style to the *Photography Services* title, apply the custom theme to the document, and then save it and name it **WL2-C4-CS-JPServices**.

Part 4

Open **JPReport.docx** and then save the document and name it **WL2-C4-CS-JPReport**. Apply or insert the following in the document:
   • Apply your custom theme.
   • Apply the Intense Quote style to the quote at the beginning and the quote at the end of the document.
   • Insert a footer of your choosing in the document.

Apply any other enhancements to improve the appearance of the document. Save **WL2-C4-CS-JPReport.docx**.

Part 5

With **WL2-C4-CS-JPReport.docx** open, insert at the end of the third paragraph in the *Photography* section a hyperlink that links to the document **KodakHistory.docx** located in the WL2C4 folder on your storage medium. Using the Internet, research and locate at least one company that sells digital cameras. At the end of the document, insert text that tells the reader to click the hyperlink text to link to that particular site on the Internet and then insert the hyperlink to the website you found. Save, print, and close **WL2-C4-CS-JPReport.docx**.

SKILLS CHECK exercises ask students to create a variety of documents using multiple features without how-to directions. Versions of the activities marked with a SNAP Grade It icon are available for automatic scoring in SNAP.

VISUAL BENCHMARK assessments test students' problem-solving skills and mastery of program features.

CASE STUDY requires analyzing a workplace scenario and then planning and executing multipart projects.

Students search the Web and/or use the program's Help feature to locate additional information required to complete the Case Study.

UNIT PERFORMANCE ASSESSMENT: Cross-Disciplinary, Comprehensive Evaluation

UNIT 2

WORD
MICROSOFT®
Performance Assessment

Word
WL2U2

Note: Before beginning the unit assessments, copy to your storage medium the WL2U2 subfolder from the WL2 folder on the CD that accompanies this textbook and then make WL2U2 the active folder.

Assessing Proficiency ■■■■■■■■■

In this unit, you learned how to use features for citing sources in a document, such as footnotes, endnotes, in-text citations, and bibliographies; how to insert tables of contents, tables of figures, and indexes; and how to use features for sharing and distributing documents, such as inserting comments, tracking changes, comparing and combining documents, linking and embedding files between programs, and restricting access to documents.

Assessment 1 Sort Text

1. Open **SHSSort.docx** and then save the document and name it **WL2-U2-A01-SHSSort**.
2. Select the five clinic names, addresses, and telephone numbers below *SUMMIT HEALTH SERVICES* and then sort the text alphabetically in ascending order by clinic name.
3. Sort the three columns of text below *EXECUTIVE TEAM* by the extension number in ascending order.
4. Sort the text in the table in the *First Half Expenses* column numerically in descending order.
5. Save, print, and then close **WL2-U2-A01-SHSSort.docx**.

Assessment 2 Select Records and Create Mailing Labels

1. At a blank document, use the mail merge feature to create mailing labels with Avery US Letter, 5160 Easy Peel Address Labels and the **SHS.mdb** data source file (located in the WL2U2 folder). Before merging the data source file with the mailing labels document, sort the records alphabetically in ascending order by last name.
2. Merge the sorted data source file with the labels document.
3. Save the merged labels document and name it **WL2-U2-A02-Lbls1**.
4. Close the document and then close the labels main document without saving it.
5. Use the mail merge feature to create mailing labels using the **SHS.mdb** data source file (use the same label option as in Step 1). Select records from the data source file of clients living in the city of Greensboro and then merge those records with the labels document.

6. Save the document and then print only the document properties.
7. Inspect the document and remove any hidden text.
8. Save and then print **WL2-U2-A11-KLHPlan.docx**.
9. Assume that the document will be read by a colleague with Word 2003 and run the compatibility checker to determine what features are not supported by earlier versions of Word.
10. Save the document in the *Word 97-2003 Document (*.doc)* format and name it **WL2-U2-A11-KLHPlan-2003format**.
11. Save, print, and then close **WL2-U2-A11-KLHPlan-2003format.doc**.

Writing Activities ■■■■■■■■■

The following writing activities give you the opportunity to practice your writing skills and demonstrate an understanding of some of the important Word features you have mastered in this unit.

Activity 1 Prepare an APA Guidelines Document

You work for a psychiatric medical facility and many of the psychiatrists and psychiatric nurses you work with submit papers to journals that require formatting in APA style. Your supervisor has asked you to prepare a document that describes the APA guidelines and then provides the steps on how to format a Word document in APA style. Find a website that provides information on APA style and include the hyperlink in your document. (Consider websites for writing labs at colleges and universities.) Apply formatting to enhance the appearance of the document. Save the document and name it **WL2-U2-Act1-APA**. Print and then close **WL2-U2-Act1-APA.docx**.

Internet Research ■■■■■■■■■

Create a Job Search Report

Use a search engine to search for companies offering employment oppo[...] Search for companies offering jobs in a field in which you are interested in working. Locate at least three websites that interest you and then create a report in Word that includes the following information about the sites:

- Site name, address, and URL
- A brief description of the site
- Employment opportunities available at the site

Create a hyperlink from your report to each site and include any additional information pertinent to the site. Apply formatting to enhance the document. Save the document and name it **WL2-U2-Act3-JobSearch**. Print and then close **WL2-U2-Act3-JobSearch.docx**.

Job Study ■■■■■■■■■■■■■■■■■■■

Format a Guidelines Report

As a staff member of a computer e-tailer, you are required to maintain cutting-edge technology skills, including being well versed in the use of new software programs such as those in the Office 2013 suite. Recently, your supervisor asked you to develop and distribute a set of strategies for reading technical and computer manuals that the staff will use as they learn new programs. Use the concepts and techniques you learned in this unit to edit the guidelines report as follows:

1. Open **Strategies.docx** and then save the document and name it **WL2-U2-JS-Strategies**.
2. Turn on Track Changes and then make the following changes:
   a. Change all occurrences of *computer manuals* to *technical and computer manuals*.
   b. Format the document with appropriate heading styles.
   c. Insert at least two comments about the content and/or formatting of the document.
   d. Print the list of markup.
   e. Accept all of the tracked changes.
3. Turn off Track Changes.
4. Insert a table of contents.
5. Number the pages in the document.
6. Create a cover page.
7. Save, print, and then close **WL2-U2-JS-Strategies.docx**.

ASSESSING PROFICIENCY checks mastery of features.

WRITING ACTIVITIES involve applying program skills in a communication context.

INTERNET RESEARCH project reinforces research and word processing skills.

JOB STUDY at the end of Unit 2 presents a capstone assessment requiring critical thinking and problem solving.

Student Courseware

Student Resources CD Each Benchmark Series textbook is packaged with a Student Resources CD containing the data files required for completing the projects and assessments. A CD icon and folder name displayed on the opening page of chapters reminds students to copy a folder of files from the CD to the desired storage medium before beginning the project exercises. Directions for copying folders are printed on the inside back cover.

Internet Resource Center Additional learning tools and reference materials are available at the book-specific website at www.paradigmcollege.net/BenchmarkWord13. Students can access the same files that are on the Student Resources CD along with study tools, study quizzes, web links, and tips for using computers effectively in academic and workplace settings.

SNAP Training and Assessment Available at snap2013.emcp.com, SNAP is a web-based program offering an interactive venue for learning Microsoft Office 2013, Windows 8, and Internet Explorer 10. Along with a web-based learning management system, SNAP provides multimedia tutorials, performance skill items, Concepts Check matching activities, Grade It Skills Check Assessment activities, comprehensive performance evaluations, a concepts test bank, an online grade book, and a set of course planning tools. A CD of tutorials teaching the basics of Office, Windows, and Internet Explorer is also available if instructors wish to assign additional SNAP tutorial work without using the web-based SNAP program.

eBook For students who prefer studying with an eBook, the texts in the Benchmark Series are available in an electronic form. The web-based, password-protected eBooks feature dynamic navigation tools, including bookmarking, a linked table of contents, and the ability to jump to a specific page. The eBook format also supports helpful study tools, such as highlighting and note taking.

Instructor Resources

Instructor's Guide and Disc Instructor support for the Benchmark Series includes an *Instructor's Guide* and Instructor Resources Disc package. This resource includes course planning resources, such as Lesson Blueprints, teaching hints, and sample course syllabi; presentation resources, such as PowerPoint slide shows with lecture notes; and assessment resources, including an overview of available assessment venues, live model answers for chapter projects, and live and annotated PDF model answers for end-of-chapter exercises. Contents of the *Instructor's Guide* and Instructor Resources Disc package are also available on the password-protected section of the Internet Resource Center for this title at www.paradigmcollege.net/BenchmarkWord13.

Computerized Test Generator Instructors can use the ExamView® Assessment Suite and test banks of multiple-choice items to create customized web-based or print tests.

Blackboard Cartridge This set of files allows instructors to create a personalized Blackboard website for their course and provides course content, tests, and the mechanisms for establishing communication via e-discussions and online group conferences. Available content includes a syllabus, test banks, PowerPoint presentations, and supplementary course materials. Upon request, the files can be available within 24–48 hours. Hosting the site is the responsibility of the educational institution.

System Requirements ■■■■■■■■■■■■■■■■■■■■■■■■■■■■■

This text is designed for the student to complete projects and assessments on a computer running a standard installation of Microsoft Office Professional Plus 2013 and the Microsoft Windows 8 operating system. To effectively run this suite and operating system, your computer should be outfitted with the following:

- 1 gigahertz (GHz) processor or higher; 1 gigabyte (GB) of RAM (32 bit) or 2 GB of RAM (64 bit)
- 3 GB of available hard-disk space
- .NET version 3.5, 4.0, or 4.5
- DirectX 10 graphics card
- Minimum 1024 × 576 resolution (or 1366 × 768 to use Windows Snap feature)
- Computer mouse, multi-touch device, or other compatible pointing device

Office 2013 will also operate on computers running the Windows 7 operating system.

Screen captures in this book were created using a screen resolution display setting of 1600 × 900. Choose the resolution that best matches your computer; however, be aware that using a resolution other than 1600 × 900 means that your screens may not match the illustrations in this book.

About the Authors ■■■■■■■■■■■■■■■■■■■■■■■■■■■■■

Nita Rutkosky began teaching business education courses at Pierce College Puyallup, Washington, in 1978. Since then she has taught a variety of software applications to students in postsecondary Information Technology certificate and degree programs. In addition to *Benchmark Office 2013,* she has co-authored *Marquee Series: Microsoft Office 2013, 2010, 2007,* and *2003; Signature Series: Microsoft Word 2013, 2010, 2007,* and *2003; Using Computers in the Medical Office: Microsoft Word, Excel, and PowerPoint 2010, 2007* and *2003;* and *Computer and Internet Essentials: Preparing for IC³.* She has also authored textbooks on keyboarding, WordPerfect, desktop publishing, and voice recognition for Paradigm Publishing, Inc.

Audrey Roggenkamp has been teaching courses in the Business Information Technology department at Pierce College Puyallup since 2005. Her courses have included keyboarding, skill building, and Microsoft Office programs. In addition to this title, she has co-authored *Marquee Series: Microsoft Office 2013, 2010,* and *2007; Signature Series: Microsoft Word 2013, 2010,* and *2007; Using Computers in the Medical Office: Microsoft Word, Excel, and PowerPoint 2010, 2007,* and *2003;* and *Computer and Internet Essentials: Preparing for IC³* for Paradigm Publishing, Inc.

Ian Rutkosky teaches Business Technology courses at Pierce College Puyallup, Washington. In addition to this title, he has coauthored *Computer and Internet Essentials: Preparing for IC³, Marquee Series: Microsoft Office 2013,* and *Using Computers in the Medical Office: Microsoft Word, Excel, and PowerPoint 2010.* He is also a co-author and consultant for Paradigm's SNAP training and assessment software.

MICROSOFT WORD

Level 2

Unit 1 ■ Formatting and Customizing Documents

MICROSOFT WORD

CHAPTER 1

Customizing Paragraphs and Pages

PERFORMANCE OBJECTIVES

Upon successful completion of Chapter 1, you will be able to:

- Apply custom numbering and bulleting formatting to text
- Define new bullets
- Insert and define multilevel list numbering
- Insert, format, and customize images and text boxes
- Insert headers and footers in documents
- Format, edit, and remove a header or footer
- Insert and print sections
- Control widows/orphans and keep text together on a page
- Insert and format charts

Tutorials

1.1 Inserting Custom Numbers and Bullets
1.2 Inserting Multilevel Lists
1.3 Customizing and Formatting an Image
1.4 Applying Advanced Formatting to Images
1.5 Inserting and Formatting Text Boxes
1.6 Customizing Headers and Footers
1.7 Printing Sections of a Document
1.8 Keeping Text Together
1.9 Creating Charts
1.10 Formatting with Chart Buttons
1.11 Changing Chart Design and Formatting

Word contains a variety of options for formatting text in paragraphs and applying page formatting. In this chapter, you will learn how to insert custom numbers and bullets, define new numbering formats, define new picture and symbol bullets, apply multilevel numbering to text, and define a new multilevel list. You will also learn about inserting and editing headers and footers, printing specific sections of a document, controlling text flow on pages, and presenting text visually in a chart. Model answers for this chapter's projects appear on the following pages.

WL2C1

Note: Before beginning the projects, copy to your storage medium the WL2C1 subfolder from the WL2 folder on the CD that accompanies this textbook. Steps on how to copy a folder are presented on the inside of the back cover of this textbook. Do this every time you start a chapter's projects.

FINANCE DEPARTMENT AGENDA

I. Approval of Minutes
II. Introductions
III. Organizational Overview
IV. Review of Goals
V. Expenses
VI. Technology
VII. Resources
VIII. Future Goals
IX. Proposals
X. Adjournment

PRODUCTION DEPARTMENT AGENDA

I. Approval of Minutes
II. Introductions
III. Review of Goals
IV. Current Projects
V. Materials
VI. Staffing
VII. Future Projects
VIII. Adjournment

Project 1 Apply Number Formatting to an Agenda

WL2-C1-P1-FDAgenda.docx

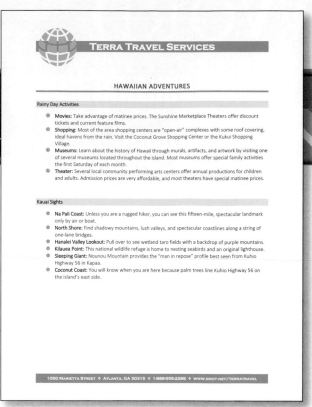

TERRA TRAVEL SERVICES

HAWAIIAN ADVENTURES

Rainy Day Activities

- **Movies:** Take advantage of matinee prices. The Sunshine Marketplace Theaters offer discount tickets and current feature films.
- **Shopping:** Most of the area shopping centers are "open-air" complexes with some roof covering, ideal havens from the rain. Visit the Coconut Grove Shopping Center or the Kukui Shopping Village.
- **Museums:** Learn about the history of Hawaii through murals, artifacts, and artwork by visiting one of several museums located throughout the island. Most museums offer special family activities the first Saturday of each month.
- **Theater:** Several local community performing arts centers offer annual productions for children and adults. Admission prices are very affordable, and most theaters have special matinee prices.

Kauai Sights

- **Na Pali Coast:** Unless you are a rugged hiker, you can see this fifteen-mile, spectacular landmark only by air or boat.
- **North Shore:** Find shadowy mountains, lush valleys, and spectacular coastlines along a string of one-lane bridges.
- **Hanalei Valley Lookout:** Pull over to see wetland taro fields with a backdrop of purple mountains.
- **Kilauea Point:** This national wildlife refuge is home to nesting seabirds and an original lighthouse.
- **Sleeping Giant:** Nounou Mountain provides the "man in repose" profile best seen from Kuhio Highway 56 in Kapaa.
- **Coconut Coast:** You will know when you are here because palm trees line Kuhio Highway 56 on the island's east side.

1050 MARIETTA STREET ❖ ATLANTA, GA 30315 ❖ 1-888-555-2288 ❖ WWW.EMCP.NET/TERRATRAVEL

Project 2 Apply Custom Bullets to a Technology Document

WL2-C1-P2-TTSHawaii.docx

PREPARING FOR A JOB SEARCH

A. Writing a Resume
   1. Resume Language
      a) Word Power
      b) Clichés
   2. Competency Statements
      a) Definition of Competency Statements
      b) Competency Statements on a Resume
      c) Writing a Competency Statement
B. Writing a Cover Letter
   1. Cover Letter Rules
   2. Cover Letter Examples
C. Electronic Resumes
   1. Getting Your Resume Online
      a) Creating an Electronic Resume
      b) Posting an Electronic Resume
   2. Internet Sites for Job Seekers
      a) Job Hunting Websites
      b) Search Terms

Project 3 Apply Multilevel List Numbering to a Job Search Document

WL2-C1-P3-JSList.docx

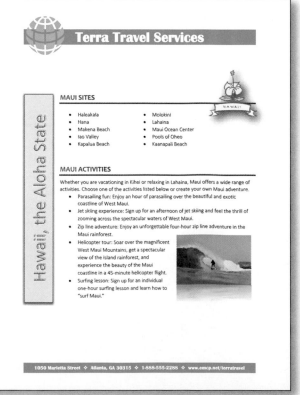

Terra Travel Services

MAUI SITES

- Haleakala
- Hana
- Makena Beach
- Iao Valley
- Kapalua Beach
- Molokini
- Lahaina
- Maui Ocean Center
- Pools of Oheo
- Kaanapali Beach

MAUI ACTIVITIES

Whether you are vacationing in Kihei or relaxing in Lahaina, Maui offers a wide range of activities. Choose one of the activities listed below or create your own Maui adventure.

- Parasailing fun: Enjoy an hour of parasailing over the beautiful and exotic coastline of West Maui.
- Jet skiing experience: Sign up for an afternoon of jet skiing and feel the thrill of zooming across the spectacular waters of West Maui.
- Zip line adventure: Enjoy an unforgettable four-hour zip line adventure in the Maui rainforest.
- Helicopter tour: Soar over the magnificent West Maui Mountains, get a spectacular view of the island rainforest, and experience the beauty of the Maui coastline in a 45-minute helicopter flight.
- Surfing lesson: Sign up for an individual one-hour surfing lesson and learn how to "surf Maui."

Hawaii, the Aloha State

1050 Marietta Street ❖ Atlanta, GA 30315 ❖ 1-888-555-2288 ❖ www.emcp.net/terratravel

Project 4 Insert Images and a Text Box in a Travel Document

WL2-C1-P4-TTSMaui.docx

PRODUCTIVITY SOFTWARE

Productivity software includes software that people typically use to complete work, such as a word processor (working with words), spreadsheet (working with data, numbers, and calculations), database (organizing and retrieving data records), and presentation (creating slideshows with text and graphics) programs. Productivity software is often compiled into suites of applications, such as Microsoft Office, because many people use two or more of these products to get their work completed. Office suites often include a word processor, a spreadsheet application, presentation software, and database management software. Suites also allow users to integrate content from one program into another, such as including a spreadsheet chart in a report created with a word processor.

WORD PROCESSING SOFTWARE

Word processor software certainly does "process" words, but today it does a great deal more. With a word processor you can create documents that include sophisticated formatting; change text fonts (styles applied to text); add special effects such as bold, italics, and underlining; add shadows, background colors, and other effects to text and objects; and include tables, photos, drawings, and links to online content. You can also use templates (predesigned documents with formatting and graphics already in place for you to fill in) to design web pages, newsletters, and more. A mail merge feature makes it easy to take a list of names and addresses and print personalized letters and envelopes or labels.

Section 1   Page 1

SPREADSHEET SOFTWARE

Spreadsheet software, such as Microsoft Excel, is an application where numbers rule. Using spreadsheet software you can perform calculations that range from simple (adding, averaging, and multiplying) to complex (estimating standard deviations based on a range of numbers, for example). In addition, spreadsheet software offers sophisticated charting and graphing capabilities. Formatting tools help you create polished looking documents such as budgets, invoices, schedules, attendance records, and purchase orders. With spreadsheet software, you can also keep track of data such as your holiday card list and sort that list or search for specific names or other data.

DATABASE SOFTWARE

Database software can manage large quantities of data. The software provides functions for organizing the data into related lists and retrieving useful information from these lists. For example, imagine that you are a salesperson who wants to create a list of customers. Of course you want to include the name, address, and company name for each person. However, you might also want each customer record to include the customer's birthday, spouse's name, and favorite hobby as well as a record of purchases in the past year. You can also set up fields to look up data such as city names based on a ZIP code, saving you time reentering data. Once that data is entered into a table you can view information in a spreadsheet-like list or as individual customer record forms. You can create queries that let you find specific data sets. For example, say you want to find every customer with a birthday in June who is interested in sports and has

Section 1   Page 2

Project 5 Insert Headers and Footers in a Computer Report

WL2-C1-P5-CompSoftware.docx

purchased at least $2,000 of products in the last year so you can invite them to a company sponsored sports event. With a database, you can generate a list of those records easily.

PRESENTATION SOFTWARE

Presentation software, such as Microsoft PowerPoint, uses the concept of individual slides that form a slideshow. Slides may contain bulleted lists of key concepts, graphics, tables, animations, hyperlinks to web pages, diagrams, and charts. A slideshow can support a presenter's comments during a talk, can run continuously on its own, or can be browsed by an individual online or on a computer. A presentation program can help users create attractive slides by allowing them to use background art from a template, placeholders for titles and bulleted lists, and graphics.

Section 1   Page 3

GRAPHICS AND MULTIMEDIA SOFTWARE

With graphics software, you can create, edit, and format images such as pictures and photos. Use multimedia software to work with media such as animations, audio, and video.

GRAPHICS SOFTWARE

If you like working with drawings, photos, or other kinds of images, you may have used graphics software, which is software that allows you to create, edit, or manipulate images such as drawings and photos. Though most productivity software such as word processors and presentation software include graphics features, design professionals work with products that are much more feature-rich such as desktop publishing software, photo editing software, and screen capture software.

Desktop publishing software is used by design professionals to lay out pages for books, magazines, brochures, product packaging, and other print materials. Photo editing software is used by design professionals to enhance photo quality or apply special effects such as blurring elements or feathering the edges of a photo. With screen capture software you can capture an entire computer screen or only a portion of it, which is helpful for showing people how to use software features.

Section 2   Page 1

MULTIMEDIA SOFTWARE

Use multimedia software to work with media such as animations, audio, and video. Animation software enables you to animate objects and create interactive content. Animations are sometimes combined with music or narration. Use audio software to work with music files and record and edit audio used for podcasts or as audio files to be shared with others. Create and edit video programs with video software. Videos might include an audio track with voice or music, or a variety of specific effects.

Section 2   Page 2

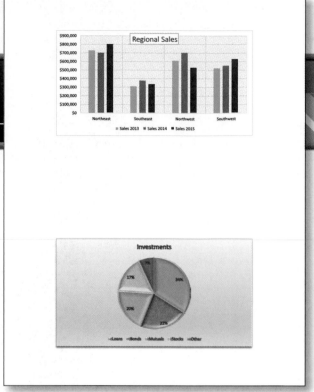

Project 6 Create and Format a Column Chart and Pie Chart
WL2-C1-P6-Charts.docx

Project **1** Apply Number Formatting to an Agenda   2 Parts

You will open an agenda document, apply formatting that includes number formatting, and then define and apply custom numbering.

Inserting Custom Numbers and Bullets ■■■■■■■■■■■■■

Numbering

Bullets

You can automatically number paragraphs or insert bullets before paragraphs using buttons in the Paragraph group on the HOME tab. Use the Numbering button to insert numbers before specific paragraphs and use the Bullets button to insert bullets. If you want to insert custom numbering or bullets, click the button arrow and then choose from the drop-down gallery that displays.

Inserting Custom Numbers

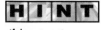

If the automatic numbering or bullets feature is on, press Shift + Enter to insert a line break without inserting a bullet or number.

You can insert numbers as you type text or select text and then apply a numbering format. If you type *1.* and then press the spacebar, Word indents the number approximately 0.25 inch. When you type text and then press Enter, Word indents all of the lines in the paragraph 0.5 inch from the left margin (called a *hanging indent*) and inserts the number 2 followed by a period 0.25 inch from the left margin at the beginning of the next paragraph. Continue typing items and Word adds successive numbers onto the list. To number existing paragraphs of text, select the paragraphs and then click the Numbering button in the Paragraph group on the HOME tab.

When you click the Numbering button in the Paragraph group, arabic numbers (1., 2., 3., etc.) are inserted in the document. You can change this default numbering by clicking the Numbering button arrow and then clicking the desired option at the Numbering drop-down gallery.

To change list levels, click the Numbering button arrow, point to the *Change List Level* option located toward the bottom of the drop-down gallery, and then click the desired list level at the side menu. You can set the numbering value with options at the Set Numbering Value dialog box. Display this dialog box by clicking the Numbering button arrow and then clicking the *Set Numbering Value* option at the bottom of the drop-down gallery.

Project 1a	Inserting Custom Numbers	Part 1 of 2

1. Open **FDAgenda.docx** and then save the document and name it **WL2-C1-P1-FDAgenda**.
2. Restart the list numbering at 1 by completing the following steps:
   a. Select the numbered paragraphs.
   b. Click the Numbering button arrow in the Paragraph group on the HOME tab and then click *Set Numbering Value* at the drop-down gallery.
   c. At the Set Numbering Value dialog box, select the number in the *Set value to* measurement box, type 1, and then press the Enter key.

Step 2c

3. Change the paragraph numbers to letters by completing the following steps:
   a. With the numbered paragraphs selected, click the Numbering button arrow.
   b. At the Numbering drop-down gallery, click the option that uses capital letters. (The location of the option may vary.)

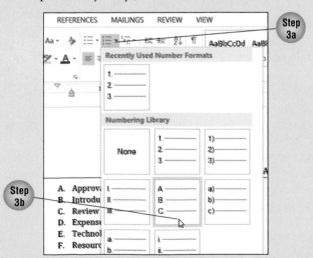

Step 3a

Step 3b

4. Add text to the agenda by positioning the insertion point immediately to the right of the text *Introductions*, pressing the Enter key, and then typing **Organizational Overview**.

5. Demote the lettered list by completing the following steps:
   a. Select the lettered paragraphs.
   b. Click the Numbering button arrow, point to the *Change List Level* option, and then click the *a.* option at the side menu (*Level 2*).
6. With the paragraphs still selected, promote the list by clicking the Decrease Indent button in the Paragraph group on the HOME tab. (The list changes back to capital letters.)
7. Move the insertion point to the end of the document and then type **The meeting will stop for lunch, which is catered and will be held in the main conference center from 12:15 to 1:30 p.m.**
8. Press the Enter key and then click the Numbering button.

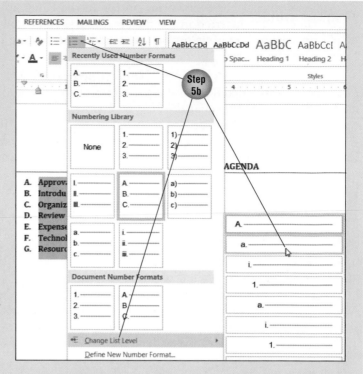

9. Click the AutoCorrect Options button that displays next to the *A.* inserted in the document and then click *Continue Numbering* at the drop-down list. (This changes the letter from *A.* to *H.*)

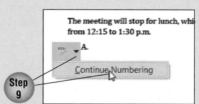

10. Type **Future Goals**, press the Enter key, type **Proposals**, press the Enter key, and then type **Adjournment**.
11. Press the Enter key and *K.* is inserted in the document. Turn off the list formatting by clicking the Numbering button arrow and then clicking the *None* option at the drop-down gallery.
12. Save and then print **WL2-C1-P1-FDAgenda.docx**.
13. Select and then delete the paragraph of text in the middle of the list (begins *The meeting will stop*). (All of the lettered items should be listed consecutively with the same spacing between them.)
14. Save **WL2-C1-P1-FDAgenda.docx**.

Defining Numbering Formatting

Along with default numbers and custom numbers, you can also define your own number format with options at the Define New Number Format dialog box, shown in Figure 1.1. Display this dialog box by clicking the Numbering button arrow and then clicking *Define New Number Format* at the drop-down gallery. Use options at the dialog box to specify the number style, font, and alignment. Preview the formatting in the *Preview* section.

Any number format that you create at the Define New Number Format dialog box is automatically included in the *Numbering Library* section of the Numbering button drop-down list. Remove a number format from the drop-down list by right-clicking the format and then clicking *Remove* at the shortcut menu.

▼ **Quick Steps**

Define New Number Format
1. Click Numbering button arrow.
2. Click *Define New Number Format*.
3. Specify desired format.
4. Click OK.

Figure 1.1 Define New Number Format Dialog Box

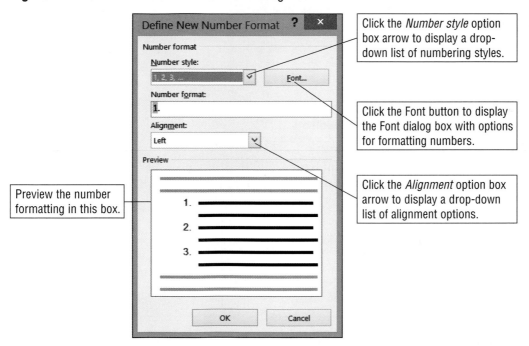

Click the *Number style* option box arrow to display a drop-down list of numbering styles.

Click the Font button to display the Font dialog box with options for formatting numbers.

Click the *Alignment* option box arrow to display a drop-down list of alignment options.

Preview the number formatting in this box.

Project 1b **Defining a Numbering Format**   **Part 2 of 2**

1. With **WL2-C1-P1-FDAgenda.docx** open, define a new number format by completing the following steps:
   a. With the insertion point positioned on any character in the numbered paragraphs, click the Numbering button arrow in the Paragraph group on the HOME tab.
   b. Click *Define New Number Format* at the drop-down list.
   c. At the Define New Number Format dialog box, click the down-pointing arrow at the right of the *Number style* option and then click the *I, II, III, ...* option.
   d. Click the Font button that displays at the right side of the *Number style* list box.

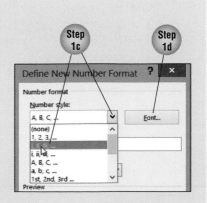

Step 1c

Step 1d

e. At the Font dialog box, scroll down the *Font* list box and then click *Calibri*.

f. Click *Bold* in the *Font style* list box.

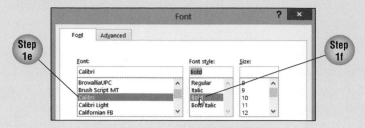

g. Click OK to close the Font dialog box.

h. Click the down-pointing arrow at the right of the *Alignment* option box and then click *Right* at the drop-down list.

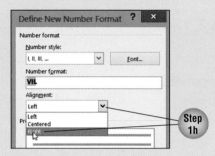

i. Click OK to close the Define New Number Format dialog box. (This applies the new formatting to the numbered paragraphs in the document.)

2. Insert a file into the current document by completing the following steps:

a. Press Ctrl + End to move the insertion point to the end of the document and then press the Enter key.

b. Click the INSERT tab.

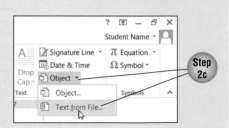

c. Click the Object button arrow in the Text group and then click *Text from File* at the drop-down list.

d. At the Insert File dialog box, navigate to the WL2C1 folder and then double-click **PDAgenda.docx**.

3. Select the text below the title *PRODUCTION DEPARTMENT AGENDA*, click the HOME tab, click the Numbering button arrow, and then click the roman numeral style that you created in Step 1.

4. Remove from the Numbering Library the number format you created by completing the following steps:

a. Click the Numbering button arrow.

b. In the *Numbering Library* section, right-click the roman numeral number format that you created.

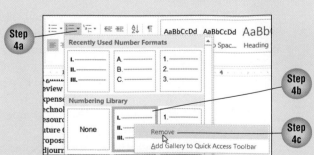

c. Click *Remove* at the shortcut menu.

5. Save, print, and then close **WL2-C1-P1-FDAgenda.docx**.

> You will open a travel document and then define and insert custom picture and symbol bullets.

Defining and Inserting Custom Bullets

When you click the Bullets button in the Paragraph group, a round bullet is inserted in the document. Insert custom bullets by clicking the Bullets button arrow and then clicking the desired bullet type at the drop-down gallery. This drop-down gallery displays the most recently used bullets along with an option for defining new bullets.

Click the *Define New Bullet* option and the Define New Bullet dialog box displays, as shown in Figure 1.2. From the options at the dialog box, you can choose a symbol or picture bullet, change the font size of the bullet, and specify the alignment of the bullet. When you choose a custom bullet, consider matching the theme or mood of the document to maintain a consistent look or creating a picture bullet to add visual interest.

A bullet that you create at the Define New Bullet dialog box is automatically included in the *Bullet Library* section of the Bullets button drop-down gallery. You can remove a bullet from the drop-down gallery by right-clicking the bullet and then clicking *Remove* at the shortcut menu.

As with a numbered list, you can change the level of a bulleted list. To do this, click the item or select the items you want to change, click the Bullets button arrow, and then point to *Change List Level*. At the side menu of bullet options that displays, click the desired bullet. If you want to insert a line break in the list while the automatic bullets feature is on without inserting a bullet, press Shift + Enter. (You can also insert a line break in a numbered list without inserting a number by pressing Shift + Enter.)

▼ **Quick Steps**

Define a Custom Bullet
1. Click Bullets button arrow.
2. Click *Define New Bullet* at drop-down gallery.
3. Click Symbol button or Picture button.
4. Click desired symbol or picture.
5. Click OK.
6. Click OK.

Create a picture bullet to add visual interest to a document.

Figure 1.2 Define New Bullet Dialog Box

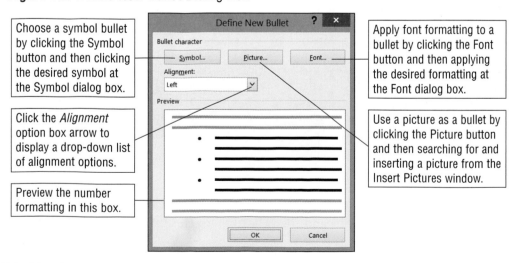

Choose a symbol bullet by clicking the Symbol button and then clicking the desired symbol at the Symbol dialog box.

Click the *Alignment* option box arrow to display a drop-down list of alignment options.

Preview the number formatting in this box.

Apply font formatting to a bullet by clicking the Font button and then applying the desired formatting at the Font dialog box.

Use a picture as a bullet by clicking the Picture button and then searching for and inserting a picture from the Insert Pictures window.

1. Open **TTSHawaii.docx** and then save the document and name it **WL2-C1-P2-TTSHawaii**.

2. Define and insert a picture bullet by completing the following steps:

   a. Select the four paragraphs of text below the heading *Rainy Day Activities*.

   b. Click the Bullets button arrow in the Paragraph group on the HOME tab and then click *Define New Bullet* at the drop-down gallery.

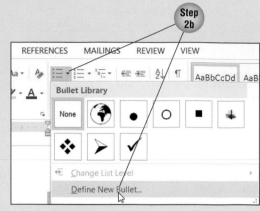

   c. At the Define New Bullet dialog box, click the Picture button.

   d. At the Insert Pictures window, click in the *Office.com Clip Art* text box, type **green flower**, and then press Enter.

   e. Double-click the green flower image shown at the right.

   f. Click OK to close the Define New Bullet dialog box. (The new bullet is applied to the selected paragraphs.)

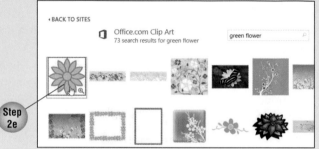

3. Define and insert a symbol bullet by completing the following steps:

   a. Select the six paragraphs below the heading *Kauai Sights*.

   b. Click the Bullets button arrow and then click *Define New Bullet* at the drop-down gallery.

   c. At the Define New Bullet dialog box, click the Symbol button.

   d. At the Symbol dialog box, click the down-pointing arrow at the right of the *Font* option, scroll down the drop-down list, and then click *Wingdings*.

   e. Click the flower symbol shown at the right.

   f. Click OK to close the Symbol dialog box.

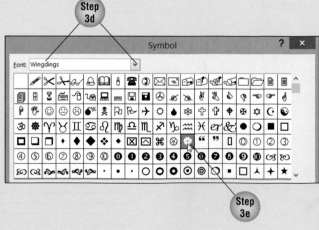

   g. At the Define New Bullet dialog box, click the Font button.

   h. At the Font dialog box, click *11* in the *Size* list box.

   i. Click the down-pointing arrow at the right of the *Font color* option box and then click the *Green, Accent 5, Darker 25%* color option (ninth column, fifth row in the *Theme Colors* section).

   j. Click OK to close the Font dialog box and then click OK to close the Define New Bullet dialog box.

4. Remove the two bullets you defined from the *Bullet Library* section by completing the following steps:
   a. Click the Bullets button arrow.
   b. Right-click the green flower picture bullet in the *Bullet Library* section and then click *Remove* at the shortcut menu.
   c. Click the Bullets button arrow.
   d. Right-click the green symbol bullet in the *Bullet Library* section and then click *Remove* at the shortcut menu.
5. Save, print, and then close **WL2-C1-P2-TTSHawaii.docx**.

Project **3** **Apply Multilevel List Numbering to a Job Search Document** **2 Parts**

You will open a document containing a list of job search terms, apply multilevel list numbering to the text, and then define and apply a new multilevel list numbering style.

Inserting Multilevel List Numbering ■■■■■■■■■■■■■■

Use the Multilevel List button in the Paragraph group on the HOME tab to specify the type of numbering for paragraphs of text at the left margin, first tab, second tab, and so on. To apply predesigned multilevel numbering to text in a document, click the Multilevel List button and then click the desired numbering style at the drop-down gallery.

Some options at the Multilevel List drop-down gallery display with *Heading 1*, *Heading 2*, and so on after the number. Click one of these options and Word inserts the numbering and applies the heading styles to the text.

▼ **Quick Steps**

Insert Multilevel List Numbering
1. Click Multilevel List button.
2. Click desired style at drop-down gallery.

Multilevel List

Project 3a **Inserting Multilevel List Numbering** **Part 1 of 2**

1. Open **JSList.docx** and then save the document and name it **WL2-C1-P3-JSList**.
2. Select the paragraphs of text below the title and then apply multilevel list numbers by completing the following steps:
   a. Click the Multilevel List button in the Paragraph group on the HOME tab.
   b. At the drop-down gallery, click the middle option in the top row of the *List Library* section.
   c. Deselect the text.
3. Save and then print **WL2-C1-P3-JSList.docx**.

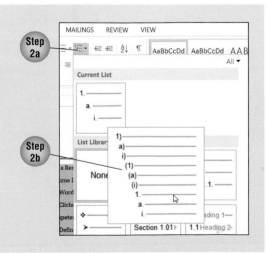

Defining a Multilevel List

▼ Quick Steps

Define a Multilevel List
1. Click Multilevel List button.
2. Click *Define New Multilevel List.*
3. Choose desired level, number format, and/or position.
4. Click OK.

The Multilevel List button drop-down gallery contains predesigned level numbering options. If the gallery does not contain the type of numbering you want, you can create your own. To do this, click the Multilevel List button and then click *Define New Multilevel List.* This displays the Define new Multilevel list dialog box, shown in Figure 1.3. At this dialog box, click a level in the *Click level to modify* list box and then specify the number format, style, position, and alignment.

Typing a Multilevel List

Select text and then apply a multilevel list or apply the list and then type the text. As you type text, press the Tab key to move to the next level or press Shift + Tab to move to the previous level.

When defining a multilevel list style, you can mix numbers and bullets in the same list.

Figure 1.3 Define New Multilevel List Dialog Box

Click a level in this list box and then specify the number format, style, position, and alignment.

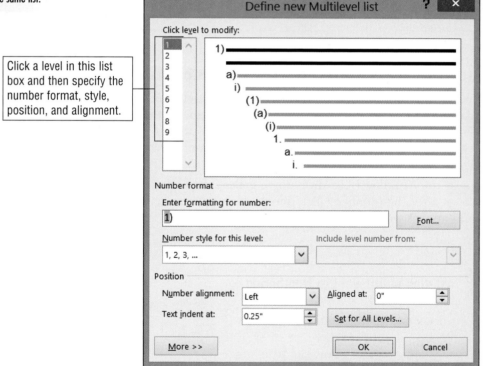

1. With **WL2-C1-P3-JSList.docx** open, select the paragraphs of text below the title.
2. Click the Multilevel List button in the Paragraph group on the HOME tab.
3. Click the *Define New Multilevel List* option at the drop-down gallery.
4. At the Define new Multilevel list dialog box, make sure *1* is selected in the *Click level to modify* list box.
5. Click the down-pointing arrow at the right side of the *Number style for this level* option box and then click *A, B, C, …* at the drop-down list.
6. Click in the *Enter formatting for number* text box, delete any text that displays after *A*, and then type a period (.). (The entry in the text box should now display as *A*.)

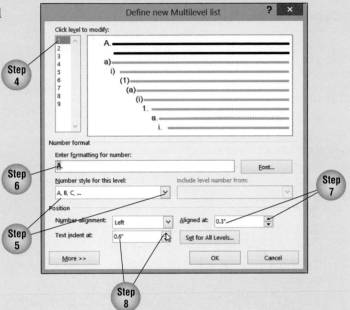

7. Click the up-pointing arrow at the right side of the *Aligned at* measurement box until *0.3"* displays in the measurement box.
8. Click the up-pointing arrow at the right side of the *Text indent at* measurement box until *0.6"* displays in the measurement box.
9. Click *2* in the *Click level to modify* list box.
10. Click the down-pointing arrow at the right side of the *Number style for this level* option box and then click *1, 2, 3, …* at the drop-down list.
11. Click in the *Enter formatting for number* text box, delete any text that displays after the *1*, and then type a period (.).

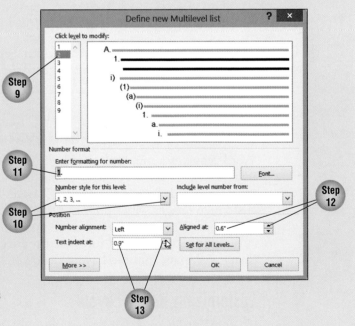

12. Click the up-pointing arrow at the right side of the *Aligned at* measurement box until *0.6"* displays in the measurement box.
13. Click the up-pointing arrow at the right side of the *Text indent at* measurement box until *0.9"* displays in the measurement box.

14. Click *3* in the *Click level to modify* list box.
15. Click the down-pointing arrow at the right side of the *Number style for this level* option box and then click *a, b, c, ...* at the drop-down list.
16. Make sure that *a)* displays in the *Enter formatting for number* text box. (If not, delete any text that displays after the *a* and then type a right parenthesis.)
17. Click the up-pointing arrow at the right side of the *Aligned at* measurement box until *0.9"* displays in the measurement box.
18. Click the up-pointing arrow at the right side of the *Text indent at* measurement box until *1.2"* displays in the measurement box.
19. Click OK to close the dialog box. (This applies the new multilevel list numbering to the selected text.)
20. Deselect the text.
21. Save, print, and then close **WL2-C1-P3-JSList.docx**.

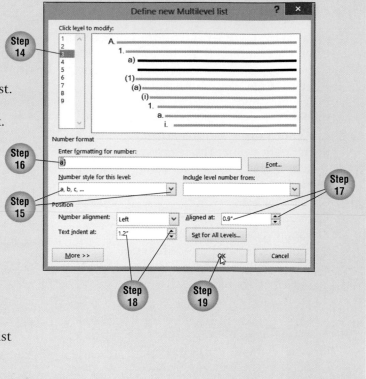

Project 4 Insert Images and a Text Box in a Travel Document   3 Parts

You will open a travel document on Maui, insert and customize a clip art image and photograph, and then insert and customize a text box.

Customizing Images and Text Boxes ■■■■■■■■■■■■■■

Word provides a number of methods for formatting and customizing graphic images such as pictures, clip art images, and text boxes. Format pictures and clip art images with buttons on the PICTURE TOOLS FORMAT tab and further customize images with options at the Format Picture task pane and the Layout dialog box. Use buttons on the DRAWING TOOLS FORMAT tab to format and customize text boxes and further customize text boxes with options at the Format Shape task pane and the Layout dialog box.

Customizing Image Layout

Customize the layout of images with options at the Layout dialog box. Display the Layout dialog box by clicking the Size group dialog box launcher on the PICTURE TOOLS FORMAT tab. The Layout dialog box contains three tabs. Click the Position tab and the dialog box displays as shown in Figure 1.4.

Figure 1.4 Layout Dialog Box with Position Tab Selected

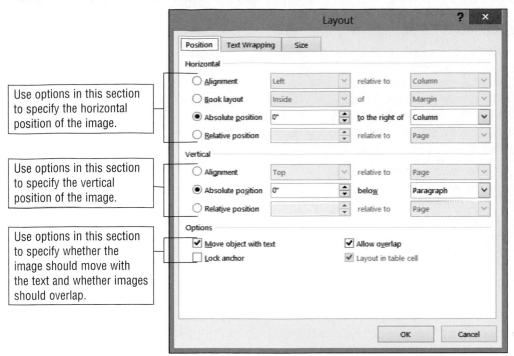

Use options in this section to specify the horizontal position of the image.

Use options in this section to specify the vertical position of the image.

Use options in this section to specify whether the image should move with the text and whether images should overlap.

Use options at the Layout dialog box with the Position tab selected to specify horizontal and vertical layout options. In the *Horizontal* section, choose the *Alignment* option to specify if you want the image horizontally left-, center-, or right-aligned relative to the margin, page, column, or character. Choose the *Book layout* option if you want to align the image with the inside or outside margins of the page. Use the *Absolute position* option to align the image horizontally with the specified amount of space between the left edge of the image and the left edge of the page, column, left margin, or character. In the *Vertical* section of the dialog box, use the *Alignment* option to align the image at the top, bottom, center, inside, or outside relative to the page, margin, or line. In the *Options* section, you can attach (anchor) the image to a paragraph so that the image and paragraph move together. Choose the *Move object with text* option if you want the image to move up or down on the page with the paragraph to which it is anchored. Keep the image anchored in the same place on the page by choosing the *Lock anchor* option. Choose the *Allow overlap* option if you want images with the same wrapping style to overlap.

Use options at the Layout dialog box with the Text Wrapping tab selected to specify the wrapping style for the image. You can also specify which sides of the image you want text to wrap around and the amount of space you want between the text and the top, bottom, left, and right edges of the image.

Click the Size tab at the Layout dialog box to display options for specifying the height and width of the image relative to the margin, page, top margin, bottom margin, inside margin, or outside margin. Use the *Rotation* option to rotate the image by degrees and use options in the *Scale* section to change the percentage of height and width scale. To reset the image size, click the Reset button in the lower right corner of the dialog box.

1. Open **TTSMaui.docx** and then save the document and name it **WL2-C1-P4-TTSMaui**.
2. Insert a clip art image by completing the following steps:
   a. Click the INSERT tab and then click the Online Pictures button in the Illustrations group.
   b. At the Insert Pictures window, click in the *Office.com Clip Art* text box, type **banners, Hawaii**, and then press the Enter key.
   c. Double-click the clip art image in the list box, as shown below.

3. Select the current measurement in the *Shape Height* measurement box in the Size group on the PICTURE TOOLS FORMAT tab, type 1.5, and then press Enter.
4. Click the *Beveled Matte, White* style thumbnail in the Picture Styles group (second thumbnail from the left).

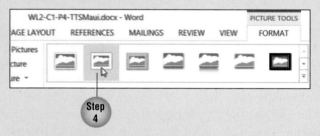

5. Click the Corrections button in the Adjust group and then click the *Brightness: –20% Contrast: +20%* option (second column, fourth row).
6. After looking at the image, you decide to reset it. Do this by clicking the Reset Picture button arrow in the Adjust group and then clicking *Reset Picture & Size* at the drop-down list.

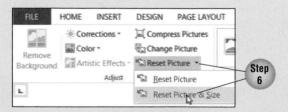

7. Select the current measurement in the *Shape Height* measurement box, type 1.3, and then press Enter.
8. Click the Wrap Text button in the Arrange group and then click *In Front of Text* at the drop-down list.

9. Position the clip art image precisely on the page by completing the following steps:
  a. With the image selected, click the Size group dialog box launcher.
  b. At the Layout dialog box, click the Position tab.
  c. Make sure the *Absolute position* option in the *Horizontal* section is selected.
  d. Press the Tab key twice and then type **6.2** in the *Absolute position* measurement box.
  e. Click the down-pointing arrow at the right of the *to the right of* option box and then click *Page* at the drop-down list.
  f. Click the *Absolute position* option in the *Vertical* section.

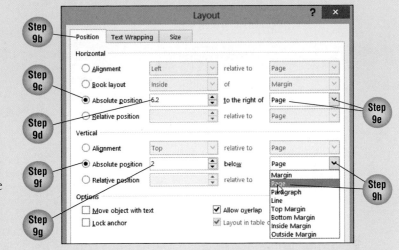

  g. Select the current measurement in the box to the right of the *Absolute position* option and then type **2**.
  h. Click the down-pointing arrow at the right of the *below* option box and then click *Page* at the drop-down list.
  i. Click OK to close the Layout dialog box.
10. Click the *Drop Shadow Rectangle* style thumbnail in the Picture Styles group (fourth thumbnail from the left).
11. Click the Color button in the Adjust group and then click the *Blue, Accent color 1 Light* option (second column, third row).
12. Compress the clip art image by clicking the Compress Pictures button in the Adjust group and then clicking OK at the Compress Pictures dialog box.
13. Click outside the clip art image to deselect it.
14. Save **WL2-C1-P4-TSSMaui.docx**.

Applying Formatting at the Format Picture Task Pane

Options for formatting an image are available at the Format Picture task pane, shown in Figure 1.5 on the next page. Display this task pane box by clicking the Picture Styles group task pane launcher on the PICTURE TOOLS FORMAT tab.

The options in the Format Picture task pane vary depending on the icon selected. You may need to display (expand) the formatting options within the icons. For example, click *SHADOW* in the task pane with the Effects icon selected to display options for applying shadow effects to an image. Many of the options available at the Format Picture task pane are also available on the PICTURE TOOLS FORMAT tab. The task pane is a central location for formatting options and also includes some additional advanced formatting options.

Figure 1.5 Format Picture Task Pane

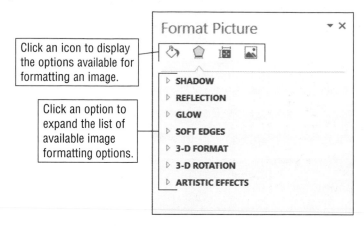

Click an icon to display the options available for formatting an image.

Click an option to expand the list of available image formatting options.

Applying Artistic Effects to Images

If you insert a picture or photograph into a document, the Artistic Effects button in the Adjust group on the PICTURE TOOLS FORMAT tab becomes active. Click this button and a drop-down gallery displays with effect options. Hover the mouse over an option in the drop-down gallery to see the effect applied to the selected picture or photograph. This button is not active when a clip art image is selected. You can also apply artistic effects at the Format Picture task pane with the Effects icon selected.

Project 4b   Inserting and Customizing a Photograph   **Part 2 of 3**

1. With **WL2-C1-P4-TTSMaui.docx** open, press Ctrl + End to move the insertion point to the end of the document and then insert a photograph by completing the following steps:
   a. Click the INSERT tab and then click the Online Pictures button in the Illustrations group.
   b. Type **surfer riding wave** in the *Office.com Clip Art* text box and then press the Enter key.
   c. Double-click the image in the list box, as shown below.

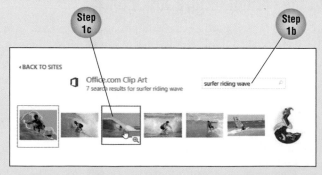

2. With the surfing photograph selected, click the Picture Effects button in the Picture Styles group, point to *Bevel*, and then click the *Circle* option (first option in the *Bevel* section).

3. Click the Artistic Effects button in the Adjust group and then click the *Cutout* option (first column, bottom row).

4. After looking at the formatting, you decide to remove it from the image by clicking the Reset Picture button in the Adjust group.

5. Select the current measurement in the *Shape Height* measurement box, type **1.4**, and then press Enter.

6. Format the photograph by completing the following steps:

   a. Click the Picture Styles group task pane launcher.

   b. At the Format Picture task pane, click *REFLECTION* to expand the reflection options in the task pane.

   c. Click the Presets button and then click the *Tight Reflection, touching* option (first option in the *Reflection Variations* section).

   d. Click *ARTISTIC EFFECTS* in the task pane to expand the artistic effect options.

   e. Click the Artistic Effects button and then click the *Paint Brush* option (third column, second row).

   f. Close the task pane by clicking the Close button located in the upper right corner of the task pane.

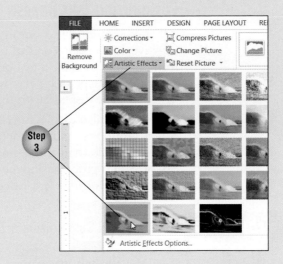

Step 3

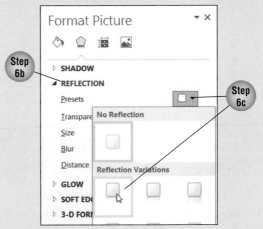

Step 6b

Step 6c

7. Click the Wrap Text button in the Arrange group on the PICTURE TOOLS FORMAT tab and then click *Tight* at the drop-down list.

8. Position the photograph precisely on the page by completing the following steps:

   a. With the photograph selected, click the Position button in the Arrange group and then click *More Layout Options* at the bottom of the drop-down gallery.

   b. At the Layout dialog box with the Position tab selected, select the current measurement in the *Absolute position* measurement box in the *Horizontal* section and then type **5.3**.

   c. Click the down-pointing arrow to the right of the *to the right of* option box and then click *Page* at the drop-down list.

   d. Select the current measurement in the *Absolute position* measurement box in the *Vertical* section and then type **6.6**.

   e. Click the down-pointing arrow at the right of the *below* option box and then click *Page* at the drop-down list.

   f. Click OK to close the Layout dialog box.

9. Click outside the photograph to deselect it.

10. Save **WL2-C1-P4-TTSMaui.docx**.

Customizing Text Boxes

When you insert a text box in a document, the DRAWING TOOLS FORMAT tab is active. Use options on this tab to format and customize a text box. You can also format and customize a text box with options at the Format Shape task pane. Display the Format Shape task pane by clicking the Shape Styles group task pane launcher. The task pane displays with three icons: Fill & Line, Effects, and Layout & Properties.

You can also display the Format Shape task pane by clicking the WordArt Styles group task pane launcher. The Format Shape task pane displays with different icons than the Format Shape task pane that displays when you click the Shape Styles group task pane launcher. The task pane displays with three icons: Text Fill & Outline, Text Effects, and Layout & Properties.

Project 4c **Inserting and Customizing a Text Box**   **Part 3 of 3**

1. With **WL2-C1-P4-TTSMaui.docx** open, insert a text box by completing the following steps:
   a. Click the INSERT tab, click the Text Box button in the Text group, and then click the *Draw Text Box* option at the drop-down list.
   b. Click above the heading *MAUI SITES* and then type **Hawaii, the Aloha State**.
2. Select the text box by clicking the border of the text box. (This changes the text box border from a dashed line to a solid line.)
3. Press Ctrl + E to center the text in the text box.
4. Click the Text Direction button in the Text group and then click *Rotate all text 270°* at the drop-down list.
5. Select the current measurement in the *Shape Height* measurement box, type **5.8**, and then press Enter.
6. Select the current measurement in the *Shape Width* measurement box, type **0.8**, and then press Enter.
7. Format the text box by completing the following steps:
   a. Click the Shape Styles group task pane launcher.
   b. At the Format Shape task pane with the Fill & Line icon selected, click *FILL* to expand the options.
   c. Click the Fill Color button (displays to the right of the *Color* option) and then click the *Blue, Accent 1, Lighter 80%* option (fifth column, second row).
   d. Click the Effects icon and then click *SHADOW* to expand the options.
   e. Click the Presets button and then click the *Offset Bottom* option (second column, first row in the *Outer* section).

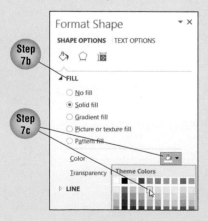
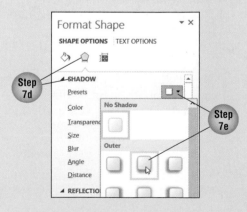

22   Word Level 2 ■ Unit 1

f. Scroll down the task pane and then click *GLOW* to display the glow options.

g. Click the Presets button in the *Glow* section and then click the *Blue, 5 pt glow, Accent color 1* option (first column, first row in the *Glow Variations* section).

h. Close the Format Shape task pane by clicking the Close button located in the upper right corner of the task pane.

8. Click the More button at the right side of the WordArt Styles thumbnails and then click the *Fill - Blue, Accent 1, Outline - Background 1, Hard Shadow - Accent 1* option (third column, third row).

9. Position the text box precisely on the page by completing the following steps:

a. With the text box selected, click the Size group dialog box launcher.

b. At the Layout dialog box, click the Position tab.

c. Select the current measurement in the *Absolute position* measurement box in the *Horizontal* section and then type 1.

d. Click the down-pointing arrow at the right of the *to the right of* option box and then click *Page* at the drop-down list.

e. Select the current measurement in the *Absolute position* measurement box in the *Vertical* section and then type 2.7.

f. Click the down-pointing arrow at the right of the *below* option box and then click *Page* at the drop-down list.

g. Click OK to close the Layout dialog box.

10. Click the HOME tab, click the Font Size button arrow, and then click *36* at the drop-down list.

11. Click outside the text box to deselect it.

12. Save, print, and then close **WL2-C1-P4-TTSMaui.docx**.

Project 5 Insert Headers and Footers in a Computer Software Report   7 Parts

You will open a report on productivity and graphics and multimedia software and then create and position headers and footers in the document. You will also create headers and footers for different pages in a document, divide a document into sections, and then create footers for specific sections.

Inserting Headers and Footers ■■■■■■■■■■■■■■■■■

Text that appears in the top margin of a page is called a ***header*** and text that appears in the bottom margin of a page is called a ***footer***. Headers and footers are commonly used in manuscripts, textbooks, reports, and other publications to display the page numbers and section or chapter titles. For example, see the footer at the bottom of this page.

You can insert a predesigned header by clicking the INSERT tab and then clicking the Header button. This displays a drop-down list of header choices. Click the predesigned header and the formatted header is inserted in the document. Complete similar steps to insert a predesigned footer.

One method for formatting a header or footer is to select the header or footer text and then use the options on the Mini toolbar.

Header   Footer

If the predesigned headers and footers do not meet your needs, you can create your own. To create a header, click the INSERT tab, click the Header button in the Header & Footer group, and then click *Edit Header* at the drop-down list. This displays a Header pane in the document and also displays the HEADER & FOOTER TOOLS DESIGN tab, as shown in Figure 1.6. Use options on this tab to insert elements such as page numbers, pictures, and clip art; navigate to other headers or footers in the document; and position headers and footers on different pages in a document.

Inserting Elements in Headers and Footers

Use buttons in the Insert group on the HEADER & FOOTER TOOLS DESIGN tab to insert elements into the header or footer, such as the date and time, Quick Parts, pictures, and images. Click the Date & Time button and the Date and Time dialog box displays with options for inserting the current date and current time. Click the Pictures button and the Insert Picture dialog box displays. At this dialog box, navigate to the desired folder and double-click the picture file. Click the Online Pictures button and the Insert Pictures window displays, where you can search for and then insert an image into the header or footer.

Figure 1.6 HEADER & FOOTER TOOLS DESIGN Tab

Project 5a   **Inserting Elements in a Header and Footer**   Part 1 of 7

1. Open **CompSoftware.docx** and then save the document and name it **WL2-C1-P5-CompSoftware**.
2. Insert a header by completing the following steps:
   a. Click the INSERT tab.
   b. Click the Header button in the Header & Footer group.
   c. Click *Edit Header* at the drop-down list.
   d. With the insertion point positioned in the Header pane, click the Pictures button in the Insert group on the HEADER & FOOTER TOOLS DESIGN tab.

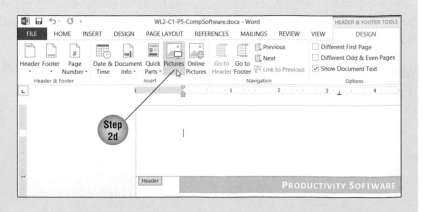

e. At the Insert Picture dialog box, navigate to the WL2C1 folder on your storage medium and then double-click *Worldwide.jpg*.

f. With the image selected, click in the *Shape Height* measurement box, type **0.6**, and then press Enter.

g. Click the Wrap Text button in the Arrange group and then click *Behind Text* at the drop-down list.

h. Drag the image up approximately one-third of an inch.

i. Click to the right of the image to deselect it.

j. Press the Tab key twice. (This moves the insertion point to the right margin.)

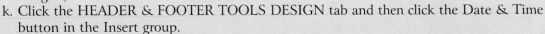

k. Click the HEADER & FOOTER TOOLS DESIGN tab and then click the Date & Time button in the Insert group.

l. At the Date and Time dialog box, click the twelfth option from the top (the option that displays the date in numbers and the time) and then click OK to close the dialog box.

m. Select the date and time text and then click the HOME tab. Click the Bold button in the Font group, click the Font Size button arrow, and then click *9* at the drop-down gallery.

n. Double-click in the document to make the document active and dim the header.

3. Save **WL2-C1-P5-CompSoftware.docx**.

Positioning Headers and Footers

Word inserts a header 0.5 inch from the top of the page and a footer 0.5 inch from the bottom of the page. You can change these default positions with buttons in the Position group on the HEADER & FOOTER TOOLS DESIGN tab. Use the *Header from Top* and *Footer from Bottom* measurement boxes to adjust the position of the header and the footer, respectively, on the page.

By default, headers and footers contain two tab settings. A center tab is set at 3.25 inches and a right tab is set at 6.5 inches. If the document contains default left and right margin settings of 1 inch, the center tab set at 3.25 inches is the center of the document and the right tab set at 6.5 inches is at the right margin. If you make changes to the default margins, you may need to move the default center tab before inserting header or footer text at the center tab. You can also set and position tabs with the Insert Alignment Tab button in the Position group. Click this button and the Alignment Tab dialog box displays. Use options at this dialog box to change tab alignment and set tabs with leaders.

Project 5b   **Positioning Headers and Footers**   **Part 2 of 7**

1. With **WL2-C1-P5-CompSoftware.docx** open, change the margins by completing the following steps:
   a. Click the PAGE LAYOUT tab, click the Margins button in the Page Setup group, and then click the *Custom Margins* option that displays at the bottom of the drop-down list.
   b. At the Page Setup dialog box with the Margins tab selected, select the measurement in the *Left* measurement box and then type **1.25**.

c. Select the measurement in the *Right* measurement box and then type **1.25**.

d. Click OK to close the dialog box.

2. Create a footer by completing the following steps:

   a. Click the INSERT tab.

   b. Click the Footer button in the Header & Footer group and then click *Edit Footer* at the drop-down list.

   c. With the insertion point positioned in the Footer pane, type your first and last names at the left margin.

   d. Press the Tab key. (This moves the insertion point to the center tab position.)

   e. Click the Page Number button in the Header & Footer group, point to *Current Position*, and then click *Accent Bar 2* at the drop-down list.

   f. Press the Tab key, click the Document Info button in the Insert group, and then click *File Name* at the drop-down list.

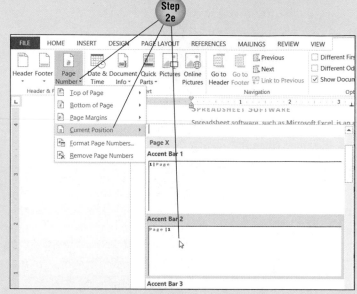

   g. You notice that the center tab and right tab are slightly off, because the left and right margins in the document are set at 1.25 inches instead of 1 inch. To align the tabs correctly, drag the center tab marker to the 3-inch mark on the horizontal ruler and drag the right tab marker to the 6-inch mark on the horizontal ruler.

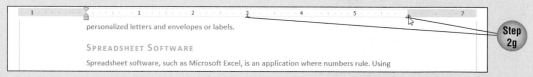

   h. Select all of the footer text and then change the font to 9-point Calibri bold.

3. Move the right tab in the header by completing the following steps:

   a. Click the HEADER & FOOTER TOOLS DESIGN tab.

   b. Click the Go to Header button in the Navigation group.

   c. Drag the right tab marker to the 6-inch mark on the horizontal ruler.

4. Change the position of the header and footer by completing the following steps:

   a. With the HEADER & FOOTER TOOLS DESIGN tab active, click the up-pointing arrow at the right side of the *Header from Top* measurement box until *0.8"* displays.

   b. Click in the *Footer from Bottom* measurement box, type **0.6**, and then press Enter.

   c. Click the Close Header and Footer button.

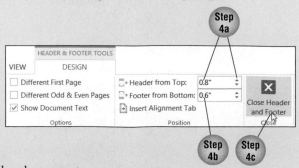

5. Save and then print the first two pages of the document.

Creating a Different First Page Header or Footer

When you insert a header or a footer in a document, Word will insert the header or footer on every page in the document by default. You can create different headers and footers within one document. For example, you can create a unique header or footer on the first page and insert a different header or footer on subsequent pages.

To create a different first page header, click the INSERT tab, click the Header button, and then click *Edit Header* at the drop-down list. Click the *Different First Page* check box to insert a check mark and the First Page Header pane displays with the insertion point inside. Insert elements or type text to create the first page header and then click the Next button in the Navigation group. This displays the Header pane with the insertion point positioned inside. Insert elements and/or type text to create the header. Complete similar steps to create a different first page footer.

In some situations, you may want the first page header or footer to be blank. This is particularly useful if a document contains a title page and you do not want the header or footer to print on this page.

▼ **Quick Steps**

Create a Different First Page Header or Footer
1. Click INSERT tab.
2. Click Header or Footer button.
3. Click *Edit Header* or *Edit Footer* at drop-down list.
4. Click *Different First Page* check box.
5. Insert desired elements and/or text.
6. Click Next button.
7. Insert desired elements and/or text.

Project 5c   **Creating a Header That Prints on All Pages Except the First Page**   Part 3 of 7

1. With **WL2-C1-P5-CompSoftware.docx** open, press Ctrl + A to select the entire document and then press Ctrl + 2 to change the line spacing to 2.
2. Remove the header and footer by completing the following steps:
   a. Click the INSERT tab.
   b. Click the Header button in the Header & Footer group and then click *Remove Header* at the drop-down list.
   c. Click the Footer button in the Header & Footer group and then click *Remove Footer* at the drop-down list.
3. Press Ctrl + Home and then create a header that prints on all pages except the first page by completing the following steps:
   a. With the INSERT tab active, click the Header button in the Header & Footer group.
   b. Click *Edit Header* at the drop-down list.
   c. Click the *Different First Page* check box located in the Options group on the HEADER & FOOTER TOOLS DESIGN tab.
   d. With the insertion point positioned in the First Page Header pane, click the Next button in the Navigation group. (This tells Word that you want the first page header to be blank.)
   e. With the insertion point positioned in the Header pane, click the Page Number button in the Header & Footer group, point to *Top of Page*, and then click *Accent Bar 2* at the drop-down gallery.
   f. Click the Close Header and Footer button.
4. Scroll through the document and notice that the header appears on the second, third, fourth, and fifth pages.
5. Save and then print the first two pages of **WL2-C1-P5-CompSoftware.docx**.

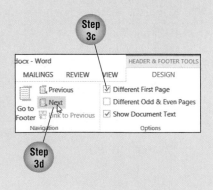

Step 3c

Step 3d

▼ Quick Steps

Create Odd and Even Page Headers or Footers

1. Click INSERT tab.
2. Click Header or Footer button.
3. Click *Edit Header* or *Edit Footer* at drop-down gallery.
4. Click *Different Odd & Even Pages* check box.
5. Insert desired elements and/or text.

Creating Odd and Even Page Headers or Footers

If your document will be read in book form, consider inserting odd and even page headers or footers. When presenting pages in a document in book form with facing pages, the outside margin is the left side of the left page and the right side of the right page. Also, when a document has facing pages, the page at the right side is generally numbered with an odd number and the page at the left side is generally numbered with an even number.

You can create even and odd headers or footers to insert this type of page numbering. Use the *Different Odd & Even Pages* check box in the Options group on the HEADER & FOOTER TOOLS DESIGN tab to create odd and even headers and/or footers.

Project 5d   **Creating Odd and Even Page Footers**   **Part 4 of 7**

1. With **WL2-C1-P5-CompSoftware.docx** open, remove the header from the document by completing the following steps:
   a. Click the INSERT tab.
   b. Click the Header button in the Header & Footer group and then click *Edit Header* at the drop-down list.
   c. Click the *Different First Page* check box in the Options group on the HEADER & FOOTER TOOLS DESIGN tab to remove the check mark.
   d. Click the Header button in the Header & Footer group and then click *Remove Header* at the drop-down list. (This displays the insertion point in an empty Header pane.)
2. Create one footer that prints on odd pages and another that prints on even pages by completing the following steps:
   a. Click the Go to Footer button in the Navigation group on the HEADER & FOOTER TOOLS DESIGN tab.
   b. Click the *Different Odd & Even Pages* check box in the Options group. (This displays the Odd Page Footer pane with the insertion point inside.)

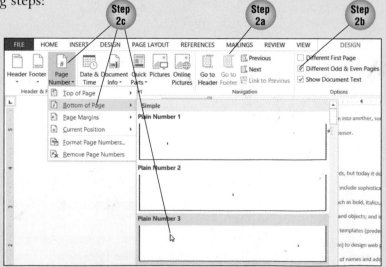

   c. Click the Page Number button in the Header & Footer group, point to *Bottom of Page*, and then click *Plain Number 3* at the drop-down list.
   d. Click the Next button in the Navigation group. (This displays the Even Page Footer pane with the insertion point inside.)

   e. Click the Page Number button in the Header & Footer group, point to *Current Position*, and then click *Plain Number 1* at the drop-down list.

   f. Click the Close Header and Footer button.

3. Scroll through the document and notice the page number at the right side of the odd page footer and the page number at the left side of the even page footer.

4. Save and then print the first two pages of **WL2-C1-P5-CompSoftware.docx**.

Creating Headers and Footers for Different Sections

You can divide a document into sections and then apply different formatting in each section. You can insert a section break that begins a new page or insert a continuous section break. You can also insert a section break that starts the new section on the next even-numbered page or a section break that starts the new section on the next odd-numbered page.

If you want different headers and/or footers for pages in a document, divide the document into sections. For example, if a document contains several chapters, you can create a section for each chapter and then create a different header and footer for each section. When dividing a document into sections by chapter, insert section breaks that also begin new pages.

When a header or footer is created for a specific section in a document, the header or footer can be created for all previous and next sections or just for next sections. If you want a header or footer to print on only those pages in a section and not the previous or next sections, you must deactivate the Link to Previous button. This tells Word not to print the header or footer on previous sections. Word will, however, print the header or footer on following sections. If you do not want the header or footer to print on following sections, create a blank header or footer at the next section. When creating a header or footer for a specific section in a document, preview the document to determine if the header or footer appears on the correct pages.

▼ Quick Steps

Create Headers or Footers for Different Sections
1. Insert section break in desired location.
2. Click INSERT tab.
3. Click Header or Footer button.
4. Click *Edit Header* or *Edit Footer* at drop-down list.
5. Click Link to Previous button to deactivate.
6. Insert desired elements and/or text.
7. Click Next button.
8. Insert desired elements and/or text.

Link to Previous

Project 5e	**Creating Footers for Different Sections**	**Part 5 of 7**

1. With **WL2-C1-P5-CompSoftware.docx** open, remove the odd and even page footers by completing the following steps:

   a. Click the INSERT tab.

   b. Click the Footer button in the Header & Footer group and then click *Edit Footer* at the drop-down list.

   c. Click the *Different Odd & Even Pages* check box in the Options group on the HEADER & FOOTER TOOLS DESIGN tab to remove the check mark.

   d. Click the Footer button in the Header & Footer group and then click *Remove Footer* at the drop-down list.

   e. Click the Close Header and Footer button.

2. Remove the page break before the second title in the document by completing the following steps:

   a. Move the insertion point immediately right of the period that ends the paragraph in the *PRESENTATION SOFTWARE* section (located near the top of page 3).

   b. Press the Delete key twice. (The title *GRAPHICS AND MULTIMEDIA SOFTWARE* should now display below the paragraph on the third page.)

3. Insert an odd page section break by completing the following steps:
   a. Position the insertion point at the beginning of the title GRAPHICS AND MULTIMEDIA SOFTWARE.
   b. Click the PAGE LAYOUT tab, click the Breaks button in the Page Setup group, and then click *Odd Page* at the drop-down list. (The section break takes the place of the hard page break.)

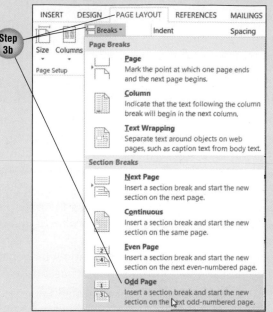

Step 3b

4. Create section titles and page numbering footers for the two sections by completing the following steps:
   a. Position the insertion point at the beginning of the document.
   b. Click the INSERT tab.
   c. Click the Footer button in the Header & Footer group and then click *Edit Footer* at the drop-down list.
   d. At the Footer - Section 1- pane, type **Section 1 Productivity Software** and then press the Tab key twice. (This moves the insertion point to the right margin.)
   e. Type **Page** and then press the spacebar.
   f. Click the Page Number button in the Header & Footer group, point to *Current Position*, and then click *Plain Number* at the side menu.
   g. Click the Next button in the Navigation group.
   h. Click the Link to Previous button to deactivate it. (This removes the message *Same as Previous* from the top right side of the footer pane.)

Step 4g

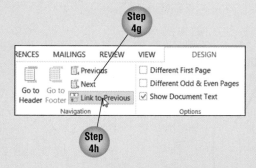

Step 4h

   i. Change the text *Section 1 Productivity Software* to *Section 2 Graphics and Multimedia Software* in the footer.
   j. Click the Close Header and Footer button.
5. Scroll through the document and notice the page numbering in the sections.
6. Save **WL2-C1-P5-CompSoftware.docx**.

Printing Sections ■■■■■■■■■■■■■■■■■■■■■■■■■■■■■■

Print specific pages in a document by inserting page numbers in the *Pages* text box at the Print backstage area. When entering page numbers in this text box, use a hyphen to indicate a range of consecutive pages for printing or a comma to specify nonconsecutive pages.

If a document contains sections, use the *Pages* text box at the Print backstage area to specify the section and pages within the section that you want printed. For example, if a document is divided into three sections and you want to print only section two, type *s2* in the *Pages* text box. If a document contains six sections and you want to print sections three through five, type *s3-s5* in the *Pages* text box. You can also identify specific pages within or between sections for printing. For example, to print pages 2 through 5 of section 4, type *p2s4-p5s4*; to print from page 3 of section 1 through page 5 of section 4, type *p3s1-p5s4*; to print page 1 of section 3, page 4 of section 5, and page 6 of section 8, type *p1s3,p4s5,p6s8*.

If you insert section breaks in a document and then insert a header and footer with page numbering for each section, the page numbering is sequential throughout the document. The **WL2-C1-P5-CompSoftware.docx** document has a section break but the pages are numbered sequentially. If you want page numbering in a section to start with a new number, such as 1, use the *Start at* option at the Page Number Format dialog box. Display this dialog box by clicking the Page Number button in the Header & Footer group on the HEADER & FOOTER TOOLS DESIGN tab and then clicking the *Format Page Numbers* option at the drop-down list. At the Page Number Format dialog box, click the *Start at* option. This inserts *1* in the text box. You can leave this number or type a different page number in the text box.

▼ **Quick Steps**

Print a Section
1. Click FILE tab.
2. Click *Print* option.
3. Click in *Pages* text box.
4. Type s followed by section number.
5. Click Print button.

Project 5f   Changing Section Numbering and Printing Section Pages   Part 6 of 7

1. With **WL2-C1-P5-CompSoftware.docx** open, change the starting page number to *1* for section 2 by completing the following steps:
   a. Click the INSERT tab, click the Footer button in the Header & Footer group, and then click *Edit Footer* at the drop-down list.
   b. At the *Footer - Section 1-* footer pane, click the Next button in the Navigation group on the HEADER & FOOTER TOOLS DESIGN tab.
   c. At the *Footer - Section 2-* footer pane, click the Page Number button in the Header & Footer group and then click the *Format Page Numbers* option at the drop-down list.
   d. At the Page Number Format dialog box, click the *Start at* option. (This inserts *1* in the text box.)
   e. Click OK to close the dialog box.
   f. Click the Close Header and Footer button.

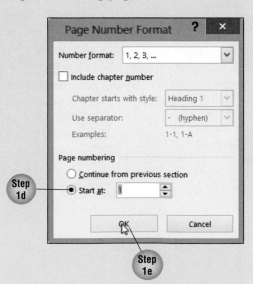

---

2. Print only page 1 of section 1 and page 1 of section 2 by completing the following steps:
   a. Click the FILE tab and then click the *Print* option.
   b. At the Print backstage area, click in the *Pages* text box in the *Settings* category and then type **p1s1,p1s2**.
   c. Click the Print button.
3. Save **WL2-C1-P5-CompSoftware .docx**.

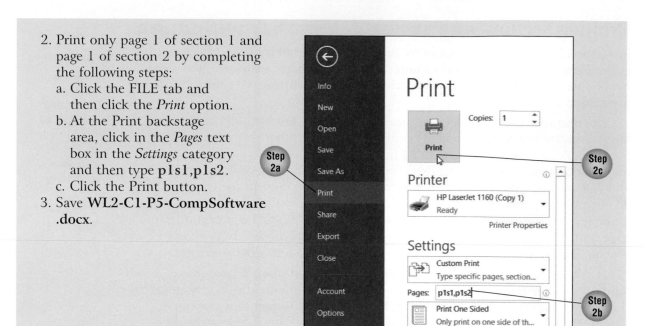

Keeping Text Together ■■■■■■■■■■■■■■■■■■■■■■

 **Quick Steps**

Keep Text Together
1. Click Paragraph group dialog box launcher.
2. Click Line and Page Breaks tab.
3. Click *Keep with next, Keep lines together,* and/or *Page break before.*
4. Click OK.

HINT

Text formatted with Keep with next formatting is identified with a ■ nonprinting character in the left margin.

In a multiple-page document, Word automatically inserts a soft page break, which is a page break that adjusts when you add or delete text from the document. A soft page break may occur in an undesirable location. For example, a soft page break may cause a heading to display at the bottom of a page while the text connected to the heading displays at the top of the next page. A soft page break may also create a ***widow*** or ***orphan***. A widow is the last line of text in a paragraph that appears at the top of a page and an orphan is the first line of text in a paragraph that appears at the bottom of a page.

Use options at the Paragraph dialog box with the Line and Page Breaks tab selected, as shown in Figure 1.7, to control widows and orphans and keep a paragraph, group of paragraphs, or group of lines together. Display this dialog box by clicking the Paragraph group dialog box launcher on the HOME tab and then clicking the Line and Page Breaks tab at the dialog box.

By default, the *Widow/Orphan control* option is active and Word tries to avoid creating a widow or orphan when inserting a soft page break. The other three options in the *Pagination* section of the dialog box are not active by default. Use the *Keep with next* option if you want to keep a line together with the next line. This is useful for keeping a heading together with the first line below the heading. If you want to keep a group of selected lines together, use the *Keep lines together* option. Use the *Page break before* option to tell Word to insert a page break before selected text.

Figure 1.7 Paragraph Dialog Box with Line and Page Breaks Tab Selected

Use options in this section to control the locations of page breaks in a document.

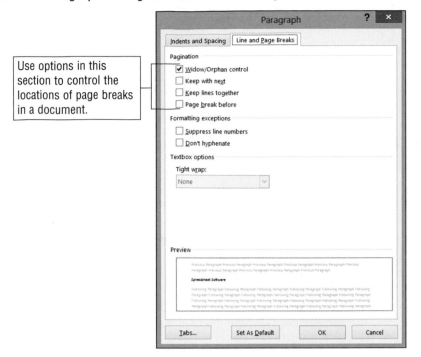

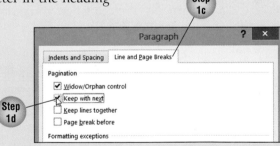

Project 5g **Keeping Text Together** Part 7 of 7

1. With **WL2-C1-P5-CompSoftware.docx** open, scroll through the document and notice that the *SPREADSHEET SOFTWARE* heading displays at the bottom of page 1 and the paragraph that follows it displays at the top of page 2. Keep the heading together with the paragraph of text by completing the following steps:
   a. Position the insertion point on any character in the heading *SPREADSHEET SOFTWARE*.
   b. Make sure the HOME tab is active and then click the Paragraph group dialog box launcher.
   c. At the Paragraph dialog box, click the Line and Page Breaks tab.
   d. Click the *Keep with next* check box to insert a check mark.
   e. Click OK to close the dialog box.
2. Scroll through the document and notice the heading *MULTIMEDIA SOFTWARE* that displays near the end of the document. Insert a soft page break at the beginning of the heading by completing the following steps:
   a. Move the insertion point to the beginning of the *MULTIMEDIA SOFTWARE* heading.
   b. Click the Paragraph group dialog box launcher.
   c. At the Paragraph dialog box with the Line and Page Breaks tab selected, click the *Page break before* check box to insert a check mark.
   d. Click OK to close the dialog box.
3. Save, print, and then close **WL2-C1-P5-CompSoftware.docx**.

Project **6** **Create and Format a Column Chart and Pie Chart**

5 Parts

You will use the Chart feature to create and format a column chart and then create and format a pie chart.

Creating Charts ■■■■■■■■■■■■■■■■■■■■■■■■■■■

A *chart* is a visual presentation of data. In Word, you can create a variety of charts, including bar and column charts, pie charts, area charts, and many more. To create a chart, click the INSERT tab and then click the Chart button in the Illustrations group. This displays the Insert Chart dialog box, as shown in Figure 1.8. At this dialog box, choose the desired chart type in the list at the left side, click the chart style, and then click OK.

When you click OK, a sample chart is inserted in the document and Excel opens with sample data, as shown in Figure 1.9. Type the desired data in the Excel worksheet cells over the existing data. As you type data, the chart in the Word document reflects the typed data. To type data in the Excel worksheet, click in the desired cell, type the data, and then press the Tab key to make the next cell active, press Shift + Tab to make the previous cell active, or press Enter to make the cell below active.

The sample worksheet contains a data range of four columns and five rows and the cells in the data range display with a light fill color. Excel uses the data in the range to create the chart in the document. You are not limited to four columns and five rows. Simply type data in cells outside the data range and Excel will expand the data range and incorporate the new data in the chart. This occurs because the table AutoExpansion feature is on by default. If you type data in a cell outside the data range, an AutoCorrect Options button displays in the lower right corner of the cell when you move away from the cell. Use this button if you want to turn off AutoExpansion.

Figure 1.8 Insert Chart Dialog Box

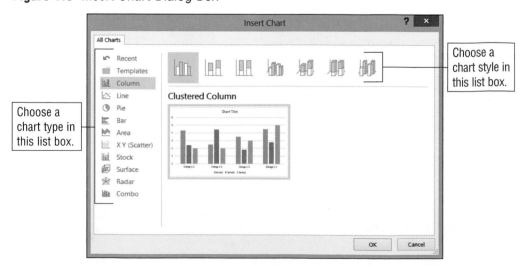

Figure 1.9 Sample Chart

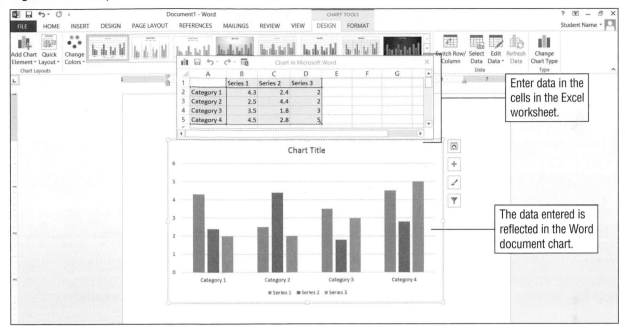

Enter data in the cells in the Excel worksheet.

The data entered is reflected in the Word document chart.

If you do not insert data in all four columns and five rows, decrease the size of the data range. To do this, position the mouse pointer on the small, square, blue icon that displays in the lower right corner of cell E5 until the pointer displays as a diagonally pointing two-headed arrow and then drag up to decrease the number of rows in the range and/or drag left to decrease the number of columns.

When you have entered all of the data in the worksheet, click the Close button that displays in the upper right corner of the screen. This closes the Excel window, expands the Word document window, and displays the chart in the document.

Project 6a   Creating a Column Chart   Part 1 of 5

1. At a blank document, click the INSERT tab and then click the Chart button in the Illustrations group.
2. At the Insert Chart dialog box, click OK.
3. Type **Sales 2013** in cell B1 in the Excel worksheet.
4. Press the Tab key and then type **Sales 2014** in cell C1.
5. Press the Tab key and then type **Sales 2015** in cell D1.
6. Press the Tab key. (This makes cell A2 active.)
7. Continue typing the remaining data in cells as indicated in Figure 1.10 on the next page. After typing the last entry, click in cell A1.
8. Click the Close button that displays in the upper right corner of the Excel window.
9. Save the document and name it **WL2-C1-P6-Charts**.

Figure 1.10 Project 6a

	A	B	C	D	E	F	G
1		Sales 2013	Sales 2014	Sales 2015			
2	Northeast	$729,300	$698,453	$798,340			
3	Southeast	$310,455	$278,250	$333,230			
4	Northwest	$610,340	$700,100	$525,425			
5	Southwest	$522,340	$500,278	$625,900			
6							
7							

Chart in Microsoft Word

Formatting with Chart Buttons

When you insert a chart in a document, four buttons display at the right side of the chart border, as shown in Figure 1.11. These buttons contain options for applying formatting to the entire chart.

Click the top button, Layout Options, and a side menu displays with text wrapping options. Click the next button, Chart Elements, and a side menu displays with chart elements, such as axis title, chart title, data labels, data table, gridlines, and a legend. Elements containing a check mark in the check box are included in the chart. Include other elements by inserting check marks in the check boxes for those elements you want in your chart.

Click the Chart Styles button that displays at the right side of the chart and a side menu gallery of styles displays. Scroll down the gallery and hover your mouse over an option and the style formatting is applied to your chart. Using this feature, you can scroll down the gallery and preview the style before you apply it to your chart. In addition to applying a chart style, you can use the Chart Styles button side menu gallery to change the chart colors. Click the Chart Styles button, click the COLOR tab that displays to the right of the STYLE tab, and then click the desired color option at the color palette that displays. Hover your mouse over a color option to view how the color change affects the elements in your chart.

Figure 1.11 Chart Buttons

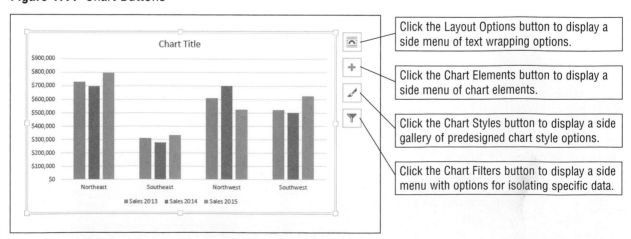

Click the Layout Options button to display a side menu of text wrapping options.

Click the Chart Elements button to display a side menu of chart elements.

Click the Chart Styles button to display a side gallery of predesigned chart style options.

Click the Chart Filters button to display a side menu with options for isolating specific data.

Use the bottom button, Chart Filters, to isolate specific data in your chart. When you click the button, a side menu displays. Specify the series or categories you want to display in your chart. To do this, remove check marks from those elements that you do not want to appear in your chart. After removing the desired check marks, click the Apply button that displays toward the bottom of the side menu. Click the NAMES tab at the Chart Filters button side menu and options display for turning on/off the display of column and row names.

HINT

Use a pie chart if the data series you want to plot has seven categories or less and the categories represent parts of a whole.

| **Project 6b** | **Formatting with Chart Buttons** | **Part 2 of 5** |

1. With **WL2-C1-P6-Charts.docx** open, make sure the chart is selected.
2. Click the Layout Options button that displays outside the upper right side of the chart and then click the *Square* option in the side menu (first option in the *With Text Wrapping* section).
3. Remove and add chart elements by completing the following steps:
   a. Click the Chart Elements button that displays below the Layout Options button outside the upper right side of the chart.
   b. At the side menu that displays, click the *Chart Title* check box to remove the check mark.
   c. Click the *Data Table* check box to insert a check mark.

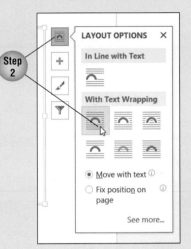

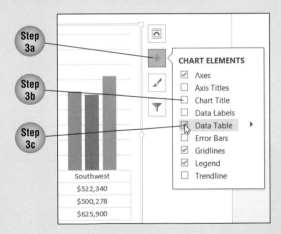

4. Apply a different chart style by completing the following steps:
   a. Click the Chart Styles button that displays below the Chart Elements button.
   b. At the side menu gallery, click the *Style 3* option (third option in the gallery).
   c. Click the COLOR tab at the top of the side menu and then click the *Color 4* option at the drop-down gallery (fourth row of color options in the *Colorful* section).
   d. Click the Chart Styles button to close the side menu.

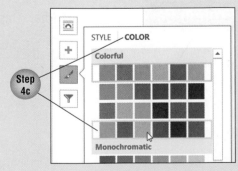

5. Display only Northeast and Southeast sales by completing the following steps:

a. Click the Chart Filters button that displays below the Chart Styles button.

b. Click the *Northwest* check box in the CATEGORIES section to remove the check mark.

c. Click the *Southwest* check box in the CATEGORIES section to remove the check mark.

d. Click the Apply button that displays near the bottom of the side menu.

e. Click the Chart Filters button to close the side menu.

f. After viewing only Northeast and Southeast sales, redisplay the other regions by clicking the Chart Filters button, clicking the *Northwest* and *Southwest* check boxes, and then clicking the Apply button.

g. Click the Chart Filters button to close the side menu.

6. Save **WL2-C1-P6-Charts.docx**.

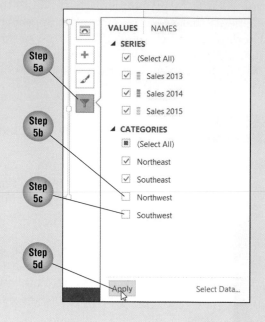

Changing the Chart Design

In addition to the buttons that display outside of the chart border, options on the CHART TOOLS DESIGN tab can be used to customize a chart, as shown in Figure 1.12. Use options on this tab to add a chart element, change the chart layout and colors, apply a chart style, select data and switch rows and columns, and change the chart type.

Figure 1.12 CHART TOOLS DESIGN Tab

Project 6c   **Changing the Chart Design**   **Part 3 of 5**

1. With **WL2-C1-P6-Charts.docx** open, make sure that the chart is selected and the CHART TOOLS DESIGN tab is active.

2. Change to a different layout by clicking the Quick Layout button in the Chart Layouts group and then clicking the *Layout 3* option (third column, first row in the drop-down gallery).

3. Click the *Style 7* thumbnail that displays in the Chart Styles group (seventh thumbnail option from the left).
4. Click the Add Chart Element button in the Chart Layouts group, point to *Chart Title* at the drop-down list, and then click *Centered Overlay* at the side menu.

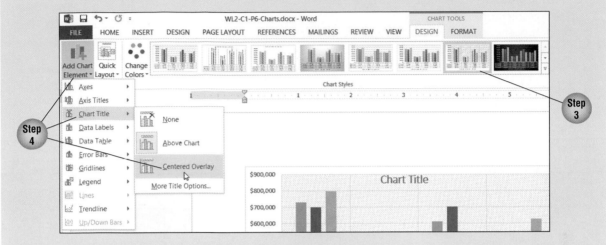

5. Select the words *Chart Title* and then type **Regional Sales**.
6. Click the chart border to deselect the chart title.
7. Edit the data by completing the following steps:
   a. Click the Edit Data button in the Data group.
   b. Click in cell C3.
   c. Type **375,250**. (The text you type replaces the original amount of $278,250.)
   d. Click in cell C5, type **550,300**, and then press the Tab key.
   e. Click the Close button that displays in the upper right corner of the Excel window.
8. Save **WL2-C1-P6-Charts.docx**.

Formatting and Customizing a Chart and Chart Elements

Use buttons on the CHART TOOLS FORMAT tab, shown in Figure 1.13, to format and customize a chart and chart elements. To format or modify a specific element in a chart, select the element. Do this by clicking the element or by clicking the Chart Elements button in the Current Selection group and then clicking the element at the drop-down list. With other options on the CHART TOOLS FORMAT tab, apply a shape style and Word Art style and arrange and size the chart or chart element.

Figure 1.13 CHART TOOLS FORMAT Tab

1. With **WL2-C1-P6-Charts.docx** open and the chart selected, click the CHART TOOLS FORMAT tab.
2. Apply a shape style to the chart title by completing the following steps:

   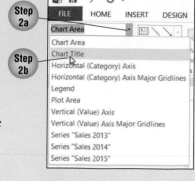

   a. Click the Chart Elements button arrow in the Current Selection group.
   b. Click *Chart Title* at the drop-down list.
   c. Click the *Colored Outline - Blue, Accent 1* style option (second option in the Shape Styles group).
3. Change the color of the Sales 2015 series by completing the followings steps:

   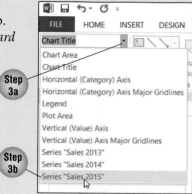

   a. Click the Chart Elements button arrow in the Current Selection group.
   b. Click *Series "Sales 2015"* at the drop-down list.
   c. Click the Shape Fill button arrow in the Shape Styles group.
   d. Click the *Dark Red* option (first color option in the *Standard Colors* section).

   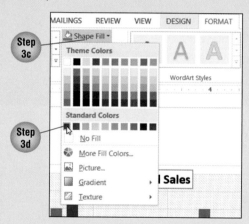

4. Apply a WordArt style to all of the text in the chart by completing the following steps:
   a. Click the Chart Elements button arrow.
   b. Click *Chart Area* at the drop-down list.
   c. Click the first WordArt style option in the WordArt Styles group (*Fill - Black, Text 1, Shadow*).
5. Change the size of the chart by completing the following steps:
   a. Click in the *Shape Height* measurement box and then type 3.
   b. Click in the *Shape Width* measurement box, type 5.5, and then press Enter.

6. With the chart selected (not a chart element), change the position of the chart by clicking the Position button in the Arrange group and then clicking the *Position in Top Center with Square Text Wrapping* option (second column, first row in the *With Text Wrapping* section).
7. Save and then print **WL2-C1-P6-Charts.docx**.

Formatting a Chart with Task Pane Options

Additional formatting options are available at various task panes. Display a task pane by clicking the Format Selection button in the Current Selection group on the CHART TOOLS FORMAT tab or a group task pane launcher. The Shape Styles and WordArt Styles groups on the CHART TOOLS FORMAT tab contain task pane launchers. The task pane that opens at the right side of the screen depends on the chart or chart element selected.

Project 6e   Creating and Formatting a Pie Chart   Part 5 of 5

1. With **WL2-C1-P6-Charts.docx** open, press Ctrl + End (which deselects the chart) and then press the Enter key 12 times to move the insertion point below the chart.
2. Click the INSERT tab and then click the Chart button in the Illustrations group.
3. At the Insert Chart dialog box, click *Pie* in the left panel and then click OK.
4. Type the data in the Excel worksheet cells as shown in Figure 1.14 on the next page. After typing the last entry, click in cell A1.
5. Click the Close button located in the upper right corner of the Excel window.
6. Click in the title *Percentage* and then type **Investments**.
7. Add data labels to the pie chart by completing the following steps:
   a. Click the Add Chart Element button in the Chart Layouts group on the CHART TOOLS DESIGN tab.
   b. Point to *Data Labels* at the drop-down list and then click *Inside End* at the side menu.

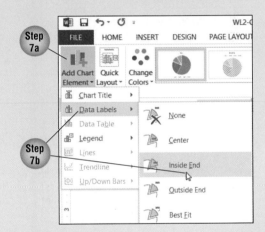

8. Click on the chart border to select the chart (and not a chart element).
9. Click the CHART TOOLS FORMAT tab.
10. Apply formatting to the chart with options at the Format Chart Area task pane by completing the following steps:
    a. With the chart selected, click the Shape Styles group task pane launcher.
    b. At the Format Chart Area task pane with the Fill & Line icon selected, click *FILL*. (This expands the options below *FILL*.)
    c. Click the *Gradient fill* option.
    d. Click the Effects icon located near the top of the task pane.
    e. Click *SHADOW* to expand the shadow options.
    f. Click the Presets button.
    g. Click the *Offset Bottom* option (second column, first row in the *Outer* section).

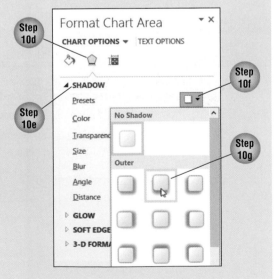

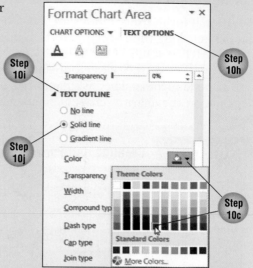

h. Click the TEXT OPTIONS tab that displays near the top of the task pane.

i. Click *TEXT OUTLINE* to expand the options.

j. Click the *Solid line* option.

k. Click the Color button and then click the *Blue, Accent 1, Darker 50%* option (fifth column, last row in the *Theme Colors* section).

11. Format the pie by completing the following steps:

a. Click in any piece of the pie. (This selects all of the pieces of the pie. Notice that the task pane name has changed to *Format Data Series*.)

b. Click the Effects icon that displays near the top of the task pane.

c. Click *3-D FORMAT* to expand the options.

d. Click the Top bevel button.

e. Click the *Soft Round* option at the drop-down gallery (second column, second row in the *Bevel* section).

f. Close the task pane by clicking the Close button that displays in the upper right corner of the task pane.

12. Click the chart border to select the chart (and not a chart element).

13. Change the size of the chart by completing the following steps:

a. Click in the *Shape Height* measurement box and then type 3.

b. Click in the *Shape Width* measurement box, type 5.5, and then press Enter.

14. Change the position of the chart by clicking the Position button in the Arrange group and then clicking the *Position in Bottom Center with Square Text Wrapping* option (second column, third row in the *With Text Wrapping* section).

15. Save, print, and then close **WL2-C1-P6-Charts.docx**.

Figure 1.14 Project 6e

	A	B
1	Assets	Percentage
2	Loans	34%
3	Bonds	22%
4	Mutuals	20%
5	Stocks	17%
6	Other	7%
7		

Chapter Summary

- Use the Bullets button to insert bullets before specific paragraphs of text and use the Numbering button to insert numbers.

- Insert custom numbers by clicking the Numbering button arrow and then clicking the desired option at the drop-down gallery.

- Define your own numbering formatting with options at the Define New Number Format dialog box. Display this dialog box by clicking the Numbering button arrow and then clicking *Define New Number Format* at the drop-down gallery.

- Insert custom bullets by clicking the Bullets button arrow and then clicking the desired option at the drop-down gallery.

- Define your own custom bullet with options at the Define New Bullet dialog box. Display this dialog box by clicking the Bullets button arrow and then clicking *Define New Bullet* at the drop-down gallery.

- Apply numbering to multilevel paragraphs of text by clicking the Multilevel List button in the Paragraph group on the HOME tab.

- Define your own multilevel list numbering with options at the Define New Multilevel List dialog box. Display this dialog box by clicking the Multilevel List button and then clicking *Define New Multilevel List* at the drop-down gallery.

- When typing a multilevel list, press the Tab key to move to the next level and press the Shift + Tab key to move to the previous level.

- Customize the layout of images with options at the Layout dialog box. Display this dialog box by clicking the Size group dialog box launcher on the PICTURE TOOLS FORMAT tab.

- The Layout dialog box contains three tabs. Click the Position tab to specify the position of the image in the document, click the Text Wrapping tab to specify a wrapping style for the image, and click the Size tab to display options for specifying the height and width of the image.

- Format an image with options in the Format Picture task pane. Display this task pane by clicking the Picture Styles group task pane launcher.

- Apply artistic effects to a picture or photograph with the Artistic Effects button in the Adjust group on the PICTURE TOOLS FORMAT tab or with options at the Format Picture task pane with the Effects icon selected.

- Text that appears at the top of every page is called a *header*; text that appears at the bottom of every page is called a *footer*.

- Insert predesigned headers and footers in a document or create your own.

- To create a header, click the Header button in the Header & Footer group on the INSERT tab, and then click *Edit Header*. At the Header pane, insert the desired elements or text. Complete similar steps to create a footer.

- Use buttons in the Insert group on the HEADER & FOOTER TOOLS DESIGN tab to insert elements such as the date and time, Quick Parts, pictures, and images into a header or footer.

- Word inserts headers and footers 0.5 inch from the edge of the page. Reposition a header or footer with buttons in the Position group on the HEADER & FOOTER TOOLS DESIGN tab.

- You can create a unique header or footer on the first page; omit a header or footer on the first page; create different headers or footers for odd and even pages; or create different headers or footers for sections in a document. Use options in the Options group on the HEADER & FOOTER TOOLS DESIGN tab to specify the type of header or footer you want to create.

- Insert page numbers in a document in a header or footer or with options from the Page Number button, which is located in the Header & Footer group on the INSERT tab.

- Remove page numbers with the *Remove Page Numbers* option from the Page Number button drop-down list.

- If you want to remove the page number from the first page, edit the page number as a header or footer.

- Format page numbers with options at the Page Number Format dialog box.

- To print sections or specific pages within a section, use the *Pages* text box at the Print backstage area. When specifying sections and pages, use the letter *s* before a section number and the letter *p* before a page number.

- Word attempts to avoid creating widows and orphans when inserting soft page breaks. Turn on or off the widow/orphan control feature at the Paragraph dialog box with the Line and Page Breaks tab selected. This dialog box also contains options for keeping a paragraph, group of paragraphs, or group of lines together.

- To present data visually, create a chart with the Chart button on the INSERT tab. Choose the desired chart type at the Insert Chart dialog box. Enter chart data in an Excel worksheet.

- Four buttons display at the right side of a selected chart. Use the Layout Options button to apply a text wrapping option, the Chart Elements button to add or remove chart elements, the Chart Styles button to apply a predesigned chart style, and the Chart Filters button to isolate specific data in the chart.

- Modify a chart design with options and buttons on the CHART TOOLS DESIGN tab.

- Cells in the Excel worksheet used to create a chart are linked to the chart in the slide. To edit chart data, click the Edit Data button on the CHART TOOLS DESIGN tab and then make changes to the text in the Excel worksheet.

- Customize the format of a chart and chart elements with options and buttons on the CHART TOOLS FORMAT tab. You can select the chart or a specific element, apply a style to a shape, apply a WordArt style to text, and arrange and size the chart.

- Apply formatting to a chart with options in task panes. Display a task pane by clicking the Format Selection button on the CHART TOOLS FORMAT tab or a group task pane launcher. The options in the task pane vary depending on the chart or chart element selected.

Commands Review

FEATURE	RIBBON TAB, GROUP	BUTTON, OPTION
bullets	HOME, Paragraph	
create footer	INSERT, Header & Footer	, Edit Footer
create header	INSERT, Header & Footer	, Edit Header
Define New Bullet dialog box	HOME, Paragraph	, Define New Bullet
Define New Multilevel List dialog box	HOME, Paragraph	, Define New Multilevel List
Define New Number Format dialog box	HOME, Paragraph	, Define New Number Format
footer	INSERT, Header & Footer	
header	INSERT, Header & Footer	
Insert Chart dialog box	INSERT, Illustrations	
multilevel list	HOME, Paragraph	
numbering	HOME, Paragraph	
Paragraph dialog box	HOME, Paragraph	
text box	INSERT, Text	

Concepts Check   Test Your Knowledge

Completion: In the space provided at the right, indicate the correct term, symbol, or command.

1. Define your own numbering format with options at this dialog box.   _____

2. A bullet that you create at the Define New Bullet dialog box is automatically included in this section in the Bullets button drop-down gallery.   _____

3. Click this button to number paragraphs of text at the left margin, first tab, second tab, and so on.   _____

4. When typing a multilevel list, press this combination of keys to move to the previous level.

_____

5. Specify the horizontal and vertical layout of an image in the Layout dialog box with this tab selected.

_____

6. Click this group task pane launcher on the PICTURE TOOLS FORMAT tab to display the Format Picture task pane.

_____

7. To create your own header, click the INSERT tab, click the Header button in the Header & Footer group, and then click this option at the drop-down list.

_____

8. By default, a header is positioned this distance from the top of the page.

_____

9. By default, headers and footers contain two tab settings: a center tab and this type of tab.

_____

10. When creating a header, clicking the *Different First Page* check box causes this pane to display.

_____

11. Type this in the *Pages* text box at the Print backstage area to print section 5.

_____

12. Type this in the *Pages* text box at the Print backstage area to print page 2 of section 4 and page 5 of section 8.

_____

13. The *Keep lines together* option is available at the Paragraph dialog box with this tab selected.

_____

14. When creating a chart, enter data in this.

_____

15. The Edit Data button is located on this tab.

_____

16. Use this button that displays at the right side of a selected chart to apply a text wrapping option.

_____

17. Use this button that displays at the right side of a selected chart to isolate specific data in a chart.

_____

Skills Check Assess Your Performance

Assessment

1 DEFINE AND APPLY CUSTOM BULLETS AND MULTILEVEL LISTS TO A TECHNOLOGY DOCUMENT

1. Open **TechTimeline.docx** and then save the document and name it **WL2-C1-A1-TechTimeline**.
2. Select the questions below the *TECHNOLOGY INFORMATION QUESTIONS* heading and then insert check mark (✓) bullets.
3. Define a cell phone symbol (📱)bullet in 14-point font size and then apply the symbol bullet to the seven paragraphs of text below the *TECHNOLOGY TIMELINE: PERSONAL COMMUNICATIONS TECHNOLOGY* heading. (You can find the cell phone symbol in the Webdings font [in approximately the ninth through eleventh rows].)
4. Select the paragraphs of text below the heading *INFORMATION SYSTEMS AND COMMERCE*, click the Multilevel List button, and then click the middle option in the top row of the *List Library* section.
5. Select the paragraphs of text below the heading *INTERNET* and then apply the same multilevel list numbering.
6. Save and then print page 3 of **WL2-C1-A1-TechTimeline.docx**.
7. Select the paragraphs of text below the heading *INFORMATION SYSTEMS AND COMMERCE* and then define a new multilevel list with the following specifications:
   a. Level 1 inserts arabic numbers (1, 2, 3), each followed by a period, and is aligned at 0 inch and indented at 0.25 inch.
   b. Level 2 inserts capital letters (A, B, C), each followed by a period, and is aligned at 0.25 inch and indented at 0.5 inch.
   c. Level 3 inserts arabic numbers (1, 2, 3), each followed by a right parenthesis, and is aligned at 0.5 inch and indented at 0.75 inch.
   d. Make sure the new multilevel list numbering is applied to the selected paragraphs.
8. Select the paragraphs of text below the heading *INTERNET* and then apply the new multilevel list numbering.
9. Insert a header that prints the page number at the right margin on all pages *except* the first page.
10. Insert the text *Cell phones* and *YouTube* in text boxes as shown in Figure 1.15 on the next page with the following specifications:
   a. Insert a text box below the arrow line located near the bottom of page 1 and then type **Cell phones** in the text box.
   b. Rotate the text in the text box 270 degrees.
   c. Remove the outline from the text box. **Hint: Do this with the Shape Outline button in the Shape Styles group**.
   d. Change the text wrapping to *Behind Text*.
   e. Drag the text box so it is positioned as shown in Figure 1.15.
   f. Complete similar steps to create the text box with the text *YouTube* and position the text box as shown in Figure 1.15.

11. Move the insertion point to the right of the text *Electronic Commerce* (item 2) located on page 2 and then insert a photograph image as shown in Figure 1.16 with the following specifications:

   a. Display the Insert Pictures window, search for *credit card for shopping*, and then insert the image shown in Figure 1.16. (If this photograph image is not available, choose another one that shows a credit card.)

   b. Change the height of the image to 2 inches.

   c. Apply shadow and glow effects of your choosing to the image.

   d. Apply the Paint Strokes artistic effect.

   e. Apply Tight text wrapping.

   f. Precisely position the photograph on the second page with an absolute horizontal measurement of 4.5 inches from the right edge of the page and an absolute vertical measurement of 4 inches below the top of the page.

   g. Compress the photograph. (Use the Compress Pictures button in the Adjust group on the PICTURE TOOLS FORMAT tab.)

12. Save, print, and then close **WL2-C1-A1-TechTimeline.docx**.

Figure 1.15 Assessment 1, Step 10

Figure 1.16 Assessment 1, Step 11

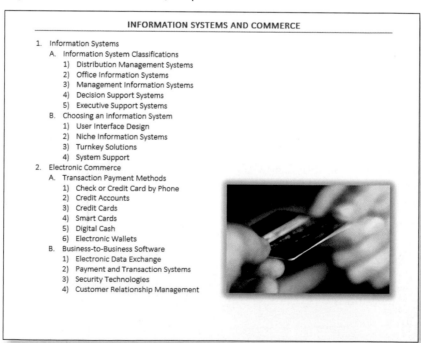

Assessment

2 INSERT SPECIALIZED HEADERS AND FOOTERS IN A REPORT

 Grade It

1. Open **Robots.docx** and then save the document and name it **WL2-C1-A2-Robots**.
2. Make the following changes to the document:
   a. Apply the Heading 2 style to the title *ROBOTS AS ANDROIDS*.
   b. Apply the Heading 3 style to the headings *Visual Perception*, *Audio Perception*, *Tactile Perception*, *Locomotion*, and *Navigation*.
   c. Change the style set to *Lines (Distinctive)*.
   d. Change the paragraph spacing to *Relaxed*. (Use the Paragraph Spacing button in the Document Formatting group on the DESIGN tab.)
   e. Center the title *ROBOTS AS ANDROIDS*.
   f. Keep the heading *Navigation* together with the paragraph of text that follows it.
3. Create an odd page footer that includes the following:
   a. Insert the current date at the left margin. (Choose the date option that displays the month spelled out, such as *January 1, 2015*.)
   b. Insert a clip art image related to *robot* in the middle of the footer. Change the height of the robot image to approximately 0.7 inches and the text wrapping to *Behind Text*. Drag the robot image down so it is positioned below the footer pane border.
   c. At the right margin, type **Page**, press the spacebar, and then insert a page number at the current position.
4. Create an even page footer that includes the following:
   a. At the left margin, type **Page**, press the spacebar, and then insert a page number at the current position.
   b. Insert in the middle of the footer the same clip art image you inserted in the odd page footer.
   c. Insert the current date at the right margin in the same format you chose for the odd page footer.
5. Save, print, and then close **WL2-C1-A2-Robots.docx**.

Assessment

3 FORMAT A REPORT INTO SECTIONS AND THEN FORMAT AND PRINT THE SECTIONS

 Grade It

1. Open **CompViruses.docx** and then save the document and name it **WL2-C1-A3-CompViruses**.
2. Insert at the beginning of the title *CHAPTER 2: SECURITY RISKS* a section break that begins a new page.
3. Create a footer for the first section in the document that prints *Chapter 1* at the left margin, the page number in the middle, and your first and last names at the right margin.
4. Edit the footer for the second section so it prints *Chapter 2* instead of *Chapter 1*. **Hint: Make sure you break the link.**
5. Print only section 2 pages.
6. Save and then close **WL2-C1-A3-CompViruses.docx**.

4 CREATE AND FORMAT A COLUMN CHART AND PIE CHART

1. At a blank document, use the data in Figure 1.17 to create a column chart (using the default chart style at the Insert Chart dialog box) with the following specifications:
   a. Use the Chart Elements button located outside the upper right border of the chart to add a data table and remove the legend.
   b. Apply the Style 4 chart style.
   c. Change the chart title to *Units Sold First Quarter*.
   d. Apply the Fill - Black, Text 1, Shadow WordArt style (first style) to the chart area.
   e. Change the chart height to 4 inches.
   f. Change the position of the chart to *Position in Top Center with Square Text Wrapping*.
2. Move the insertion point to the end of the document, press the Enter key twice, and then create a pie chart (using the default chart style at the Insert Chart dialog box) with the data shown in Figure 1.18 and with the following specifications:
   a. Apply the Style 3 chart style.
   b. Move the data labels to the inside end.
   c. Change the chart title to *Expense Distribution*.
   d. Apply the Colored Outline - Orange, Accent 2 shape style to the title (third shape style).
   e. Change the chart height to 3 inches and the width to 5.5 inches.
   f. Change the position of the chart to *Position in Bottom Center with Square Text Wrapping*.
3. Save the document and name it **WL2-C1-A4-Charts**.
4. Print and then close **WL2-C1-A4-Charts.docx**.

Figure 1.17 Assessment 4, Data for Column Chart

Salesperson	January	February	March
Barnett	55	60	42
Carson	20	24	31
Fanning	15	30	13
Han	52	62	58
Mahoney	49	52	39

Figure 1.18 Assessment 4, Data for Pie Chart

Category	Percentage
Salaries	67%
Travel	15%
Equipment	11%
Supplies	7%

5 INSERT A HORIZONTAL LINE IN A FOOTER

1. Word includes a horizontal line feature that you can use to insert a graphic line in a document or a header or footer. Look at the formatting options that are available at the Format Horizontal Line dialog box. At a blank document, display this dialog box by clicking the Borders button arrow in the Paragraph group on the HOME tab and then clicking *Horizontal Line* at the drop-down list. Click the horizontal line to select it, right-click the selected line, and then click *Format Horizontal Line* at the shortcut menu. When you are finished looking at the formatting options, click OK to close the dialog box.
2. Open **ShopOnline.docx** and then save the document and name it **WL2-C1-A5-ShopOnline**.
3. Keep the heading *ONLINE SHOPPING MALLS* together with the paragraph that follows it.
4. Create a footer and insert a 3-point horizontal line in Blue (eighth color option in the *Standard Colors* section).
5. Save, print, and then close **WL2-C1-A5-ShopOnline.docx**.

Visual Benchmark Demonstrate Your Proficiency

CREATE AND FORMAT AN INTERNATIONAL CORRESPONDENCE DOCUMENT

1. Open **IntlCorres.docx** and then save the document and name it **WL2-C1-VB-IntlCorres**.
2. Apply the following formatting so your document appears similar to the document shown in Figure 1.19 on the next page:
   • Change the top margin to 1.5 inches and the left and right margins to 1.25 inches.
   • Apply the Heading 1 style to the title and the Heading 2 style to the three headings. Change the style set to Shaded and change the theme colors to Green.
   • Use symbol bullets as shown in the figure. (Find the globe bullet in the Webdings font at the Symbol dialog box.)
   • Apply automatic numbering as shown in the figure and start numbering with 11 after the *CANADIAN CODES AND TERRITORIES* heading.
   • Apply any other formatting required to make your document look similar to the document in the figure.
3. Save, print, and then close **WL2-C1-VB-IntlCorres.docx**.

Figure 1.19 Visual Benchmark

INTERNATIONAL CORRESPONDENCE

With the increased number of firms conducting business worldwide, international written communication has assumed new importance. Follow these guidelines when corresponding internationally, especially with people for whom English is not the primary language:

- ✓ Use a direct writing style and clear, precise words.
- ✓ Avoid slang, jargon, and idioms.
- ✓ Develop an awareness of cultural differences that may interfere with the communication process.

INTERNATIONAL ADDRESSES

Use the company's letterhead or a business card as a guide for spelling and other information. Include the following when addressing international correspondence:

- Line 1: Addressee's Name, Title
- Line 2: Company Name
- Line 3: Street Address
- Line 4: City and Codes
- Line 5: COUNTRY NAME (capitalized)

CANADIAN CODES AND PROVINCES

1) ON – Ontario
2) QC – Quebec
3) NS – Nova Scotia
4) NB – New Brunswick
5) MB – Manitoba
6) BC – British Columbia
7) PE – Prince Edward Island
8) SK – Saskatchewan
9) AB – Alberta
10) NL – Newfoundland and Labrador

CANADIAN CODES AND TERRITORIES

11) NT – Northwest Territories
12) YT – Yukon
13) NU – Nunavut

Case Study   Apply Your Skills

Part 1

You work in the Human Resources department at Oceanside Medical Services. Your supervisor, Michael Jennison, has given you a Word document containing employee handbook information and asked you to format the book. Open the **OMSHandbook.docx** document, save it and name it **WL2-C1-CS-OMSHandbook**, and then apply the following formatting:

- Apply heading styles to the titles and headings.
- Apply a style set of your choosing.
- Apply a theme that makes the handbook easy to read.
- Define a new symbol bullet and then apply it to all of the currently bulleted paragraphs.
- Insert a section break that begins a new page at the beginning of each section heading (beginning with *Section 1: General Information*).
- Insert a footer that prints the section name at the left margin (except the first page) and page number at the right margin. Insert the correct section name for each section footer.

Part 2

After reviewing the formatted handbook, you decide to apply additional formatting to improve its readability and appearance. With **WL2-C1-CS-OMSHandbook.docx** open, apply the following formatting:

- Select the lines of text on the first page beginning with *Section 1: General Information* through *Compensation Procedures* and then define and apply a new multilevel list number format that applies capital letters followed by periods to the first level and arabic numbers (1, 2, 3) followed by periods to the second level. You determine the indents.
- Insert a cover page of your choosing and insert the appropriate information in the placeholders.

Save, print, and then close **WL2-C1-CS-OMSHandbook.docx**.

Part 3

Help

An orientation for new employees is scheduled for Friday, October 15, 2015, from 9:00 a.m. until 3:30 p.m. Michael Jennison will conduct the orientation and has asked you to prepare a flier about it that can be placed on all bulletin boards in the clinic. Include in the flier the date and times as well as the location, which is Conference Room 100. Include as bullets additional information about what will be covered during the orientation. Use the information in the multilevel list in the **WL2-C1-CS-OMSHandbook.docx** document to produce six to eight bulleted points. Using the Help feature, learn how to insert a picture watermark and then insert the **Ocean.jpg** file as a watermark. Make sure the text in the flier is readable. Include any other additional features to improve the appearance of the flier. Save the completed flier document and name it **WL2-C1-CS-Flier**. Print and then close **WL2-C1-CS-Flier.docx**.

Part 4

During the orientation, Mr. Jennison will discuss vacation allowances with the new employees and he wants to present the information in a readable format. He has asked you to look at the information in **OMSVacAllowances.docx** and then insert the information in tables. Apply formatting to make the tables attractive and the information easily readable. Save the completed document and name it **WL2-C1-CS-OMSVacAllowances**. Save, print, and then close **WL2-C1-CS-OMSVacAllowances.docx**.

WORD
MICROSOFT®

CHAPTER 2

Proofing Documents

PERFORMANCE OBJECTIVES

Upon successful completion of Chapter 2, you will be able to:

- Complete a spelling and grammar check on text in a document
- Display readability statistics
- Create a custom dictionary and change the default dictionary
- Display synonyms and antonyms for specific words using the thesaurus
- Display document word, paragraph, and character counts
- Use the translation features to translate words from English to other languages

Tutorials

2.1 Checking the Spelling and Grammar in a Document

2.2 Customizing Spelling and Grammar Checking

2.3 Creating a Custom Dictionary

2.4 Displaying Word Count

2.5 Using the Thesaurus

2.6 Translating Text to and from Different Languages

Microsoft Word includes proofing tools to help you create well-written, error-free documents. These tools include a spelling checker, grammar checker, and thesaurus. Word includes options for translating words from English to other languages, as well as a Mini Translator that will translate specific words in a document. In this chapter, you will learn how to use these proofing tools and how to create a custom dictionary. Model answers for this chapter's projects appear on the following page.

Note: Before beginning the projects, copy to your storage medium the WL2C2 subfolder from the WL2 folder on the CD that accompanies this textbook and then make WL2C2 the active folder.

Word
WL2C2

Project 1 Check Spelling and Grammar in an Investment Plan Document

EARLY DISTRIBUTIONS

If you want to withdraw funds or begin income from any PLAN20, PLAN30, or PLAN40 before you reach age 59, you may have to pay an extra 10 percent "early distributions" tax on the taxable amount. However, you will not have to pay an early distribution tax on any part of a withdrawal if:

- the distribution is because you are disabled
- you separated from your job at or after age 55 and take your withdrawal after that (not applicable for PLAN20)
- you begin annuity income withdrawal after you leave your job (termination is not required for PLAN40), as long as your annuity income consists of a series of regular substantially equal payments (at least annually) over your lifetime or life expectancy
- you have medical expenses in excess of 8 percent of your adjusted gross income and the withdrawal is less than or equal to your expenses (not applicable for PLAN20)
- you are required to make a payment to someone besides yourself under a MIRA plan

Prepared by
Logan Haverson

WL2-C2-P1-PlanDists.docx

Project 2 Check the Grammar in a Medical Database Document

Nationwide Medical Databases

The medical community looks forward to the day when medical records change from manila folders full of dusty documents to a nationwide registry off electronic medical records available to medical personnel anywhere. With these new medical database systems, doctors located anywhere in the world could pull up charts immediately, with a few clicks of the mouse. Full color 3-D X-rays could be included in electronic patient records. People receiving care away from home would no longer have to worry that their doctor did not have all of their medical records.

At this point, some obstacles may obstruct the widespread use of this new technology. Medical systems tend to cost much more than other systems due to legalities and the need for complicated approval processes. Everyone involved must have medical training, raising costs even further. Data validation is critical, as lives may be lost if data is faulty. Privacy issues are another roadblock. Medical records are as private and closely guarded as financial ones. Should any doctor be able to see a record? Can patients access their own records? How would incapacitated patients grant permission?

Some medical providers are embracing such databases with a more limited scope, only sharing information about patients in the same HBO, for example. So far, no nationwide system exists, but such systems may appear within the next few years.

Project 2b, WL2-C2-P2-MedData.docx

Project 3 Check the Spelling in an Online Banking Document

Online Banking in Brazil

Brazilian Rodrigo Abreu has not been inside a bank for several years, nor has he written a paper check for any regular expense. For about a decade, Mr. Abreu, a thirtyish technology executive, has made every kind of scheduled payment through the Internet arm of his Brazilian bank, Banco Itau. He pays his car insurance, buys stocks, and conducts e-commerce transactions through the bank's website. His mother, other family members, and all of his friends also do most of their business transactions online. Advanced Internet technology may not be generally associated with Brazil, where a vast majority of the population of 171.2 million has no online access. But when it comes to Internet banking, Brazil is the leader.

Brazil's economic problems in the early 1990s helped pressure major banks—Bradesco, Unibanco, and Banco Itau—to build advanced electronic payment systems that formed the backbone of the Internet services they offer today. At the time, the economy faced an almost daily inflationary rate of 3 percent. To battle the hyperinflation, banks built communications systems to clear checks and allow their customers to pay bills as soon as possible. That helped the customers avoid losing money during processing. "We were able to cash checks within 24 hours when the U.S. banks were still taking nearly a week," said Milton Monteiro, who is vice president and is in charge of Internet banking at Banco Itau. "We had to be very efficient."

By 1993, each major Brazilian bank had built a complex private network so that when a customer's paycheck came in it was cleared overnight and moved into an account that was hedged against inflation. Home banking was coming into fashion and people were already dialing directly into the banks' networks to move money and pay bills instantly. In the United States, meanwhile, manual check processing and human bank tellers were still the norm.

While many United States banks are catching up with the range of their online offerings, Bradesco, Banco Itau, and Unibanco still have a wider array of Internet services. Brazilians can complete nearly any type of financial transaction through the banks' websites. Banks offer e-commerce portals, advanced business-to-business services, brokerage services, direct deposit, and bill-paying, all integrated into their websites. In fact, under a bill-paying standard now used in Brazil, bank customers can simply type in the bar code number of any bill; the bank immediately knows its amount and pays it upon request.

Source: Lipschultz, David. The New York Times.

WL2-C2-P3-BankBrazil.docx

Project 4 Translate Text

Résumé Styles

The traditional chronological résumé lists your work experience in reverse-chronological order (starting with your current or most recent position). The functional style deemphasizes the "where" and "when" of your career and instead groups similar experience, talents, and qualifications, regardless of when they occurred. Today, however, most résumés follow neither a strictly chronological nor strictly functional format; rather, they are an effective mixture of the two styles usually known as a "combination" or "hybrid" format.

Estilos de currículum

El currículum cronológico tradicional muestra su experiencia de trabajo en orden cronológico inverso (comenzando con su posición actual o más reciente). El estilo funcional deemphasizes el "dónde" y "cuándo" de su carrera y en su lugar grupos similares experiencia, talentos y calificaciones, independientemente de cuando ocurrieron. Hoy, sin embargo, la mayoría currículos siguen ni un formato estrictamente cronológico ni estrictamente funcional; más bien, son una mezcla eficaz de los dos estilos generalmente conocido como una "combinación" o formato de "hibrido".

WL2-C2-P4-ResumeStyles.docx

TRANSLATION		
English to Spanish		
English to French		
Term	**Spanish**	**French**
Central	centrico	centre
Data	datos	donnees
Directory	directorio	repertoire
External	externo	exterieur

WL2-C2-P4-TranslateTerms.docx

Model Answers

Project **1** **Check Spelling and Grammar in an Investment Plan Document** **1 Part**

You will open an investment plan document and then complete a spelling and grammar check on the document.

Checking the Spelling and Grammar in a Document ■■■

Word provides proofing tools to help you create professional, polished documents. Two of these tools are the spelling checker and grammar checker.

The spelling checker works by finding misspelled words and offering replacement words. It also finds duplicate words and irregular capitalization. When you spell check a document, the spelling checker compares the words in your document with the words in its dictionary. If the spelling checker finds a match, it passes over the word. If the spelling checker does not find a match, it stops. The spelling checker stops when it discovers the following kinds of errors and unfamiliar words:

- a misspelled word (when the misspelling does not match another word in the dictionary)
- typographical errors (such as transposed letters)
- double word occurrences (such as *the the*)
- irregular capitalization
- some proper names
- jargon and some technical terms

The grammar checker searches a document for errors in grammar, punctuation, and word usage. Using the spelling checker and grammar checker can help you create well-written documents, but it does not replace the need for proofreading.

Begin a spelling and grammar check by clicking the REVIEW tab and then clicking the Spelling & Grammar button. (You can also press the keyboard shortcut F7.) If Word detects a possible spelling error, it selects the text containing the error and displays the Spelling task pane, similar to the one shown in Figure 2.1. Possible corrections for the word display in the Spelling task pane list box along with buttons you can click to change or ignore the spelling error, as described in Table 2.1. The Spelling task pane also displays a definition of the selected word in the task pane list box.

Quick Steps

Check Spelling and Grammar
1. Click REVIEW tab.
2. Click Spelling & Grammar button.
3. Change or ignore errors.
4. Click OK.

Spelling & Grammar

HINT

Complete a spelling and grammar check on a portion of a document by first selecting the text and then clicking the Spelling & Grammar button.

Figure 2.1 Spelling Task Pane with Error Selected

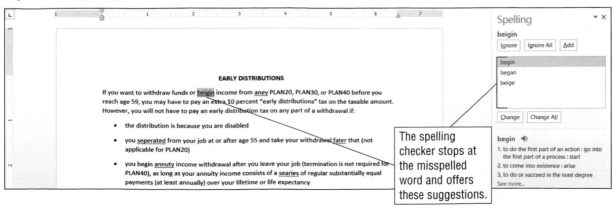

Table 2.1 Spelling Task Pane and Grammar Task Pane Buttons

Button	Function
Ignore	During spell checking, skips that occurrence of the word; in grammar checking, leaves currently selected text as written.
Ignore All	During spell checking, skips that occurrence of the word and all other occurrences of the word in the document.
Add	Adds the selected word to the main spelling check dictionary.
Delete	Deletes the currently selected word(s).
Change	Replaces the selected word with the selected word in the task pane list box.
Change All	Replaces the selected word and all other occurrences of it with the selected word in the task pane list box.

If Word detects a grammar error, it selects the word(s) or sentence containing the error and displays possible corrections in the Grammar task pane. Depending on the error selected, some of the buttons described in Table 2.1 may display in the Grammar task pane. A description of the grammar rule, with suggestions on how to correct an error, may display in the lower half of the Grammar task pane. Choose to ignore or change errors found by the grammar checker by clicking the Change, Change All, Ignore, or Ignore All buttons.

Editing During a Spelling and Grammar Check

When checking the spelling and grammar in a document, you can temporarily leave the Spelling or Grammar task pane, make corrections in the document, and then resume the spelling and grammar check. Click in the document oustide the task pane, make changes or edits, and then click the Resume button in the task pane.

Customizing Spell Checking

▼ **Quick Steps**

**Change Spell
Checking Options**
1. Click FILE tab.
2. Click *Options*.
3. Click *Proofing*.
4. Specify options.
5. Click OK.

Customize the spelling checker with options at the Word Options dialog box with the *Proofing* option selected, as shown in Figure 2.2. Display this dialog box by clicking the FILE tab and then clicking *Options*. At the Word Options dialog box, click *Proofing* in the left panel. Use options at this dialog box to customize spell checking by identifying what you want the spelling checker to review or ignore. You can also create or edit a custom dictionary for use in spell checking.

Figure 2.2 Word Options Dialog Box with *Proofing* Selected

Click *Proofing* to display spelling check and grammar check options.

Click this button to create a custom dictionary.

Insert a check mark in this check box to tell Word to display words that sound similar to other words.

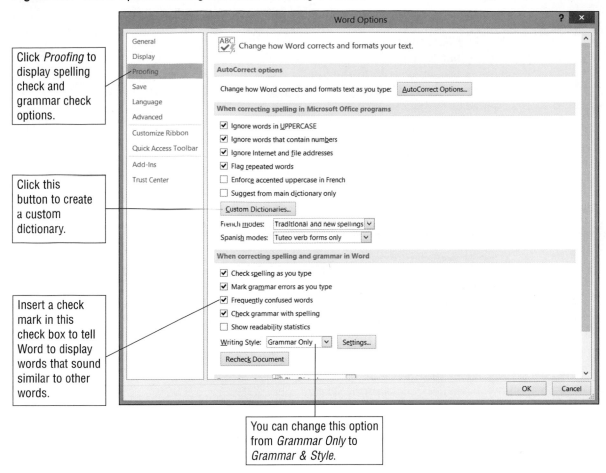

You can change this option from *Grammar Only* to *Grammar & Style*.

Project 1 **Spell Checking a Document with Words in Uppercase and with Numbers**   Part 1 of 1

1. Open **PlanDists.docx** and then save the document and name it **WL2-C2-P1-PlanDists**.
2. Review spell checking options by completing the following steps:
   a. Click the FILE tab.
   b. Click *Options*.
   c. At the Word Options dialog box, click the *Proofing* option in the left panel.
   d. Make sure that the *Ignore words in UPPERCASE* check box and the *Ignore words that contain numbers* check box each contain a check mark.
   e. Click OK to close the dialog box.

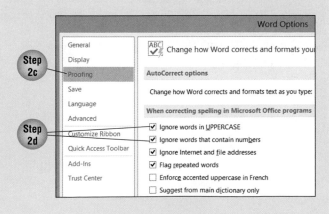

3. Complete a spelling check on the document by completing the following steps:
   a. Click the REVIEW tab.
   b. Click the Spelling & Grammar button in the Proofing group.
   c. The spelling checker selects the word *beigin* and displays the Spelling task pane. The proper spelling, *begin*, is selected in the Spelling task pane list box and a definition of *begin* displays below the list box. Click the Change button (or Change All button).

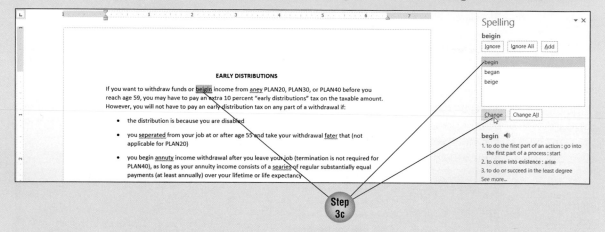

Step 3c

   d. The spelling checker selects the word *aney*. The proper spelling of the word is selected in the task pane list box, so click the Change button.
   e. The spelling checker selects *seperated*. The proper spelling is selected in the task pane list box, so click the Change button.
   f. The spelling checker selects *fater*. The proper spelling *after* is not selected in the task pane list box, but it is one of the words suggested. Click *after* in the task pane list box and then click the Change button.
   g. The spelling checker selects *annuty*. The proper spelling is selected in the task pane list box, so click the Change button.
   h. The spelling checker selects *searies*. The proper spelling is selected in the task pane list box, so click the Change button.
   i. The spelling checker selects *to* (this is a double word occurrence). Click the Delete button to delete the second occurrence of *to*.
   j. The spelling checker selects *Haverson*. This is a proper name, so click the Ignore button.
   k. When the message displays telling you that the spelling and grammar check is complete, click the OK button.

Step 3f

Step 3i

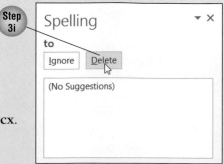

4. Save, print, and then close **WL2-C2-P1-PlanDists.docx**.

Check the Grammar in a Medical Database Document **3 Parts**

You will check the grammar in a document, change grammar settings, and then check the grammar again. You will also display a word count for the document.

Checking the Grammar in a Document

When performing a spelling and grammar check, Word stops and highlights text that may contain grammatical errors and displays the Grammar task pane, similar to what is shown in Figure 2.3. Like the spelling checker, the grammar checker does not find every error in a document and may stop at correct sentences. Using the grammar checker can help you create well-written documents, but using it does not satisfy the need for proofreading.

If the grammar checker detects a possible grammatical error in the document, Word selects the sentence containing the possible error and inserts a possible correction in the Grammar task pane list box. The Grammar task pane may also display information on the grammar rule that may have been broken and offer possible methods for correcting the error. Choose to ignore or change errors found by the grammar checker by clicking the Change, Change All, Ignore, or Ignore All buttons.

The Spelling task pane and the Grammar task pane include a pronunciation feature that will speak the word currently selected in the task pane list box. To hear the word pronounced, click the speaker icon located to the right of the word below the task pane list box. For this feature to work, you must turn on your computer speakers.

Read grammar suggestions carefully. Some suggestions may not be valid and a problem identified by the grammar checker may not actually be an issue.

Figure 2.3 Grammar Task Pane with Grammar Error Selected

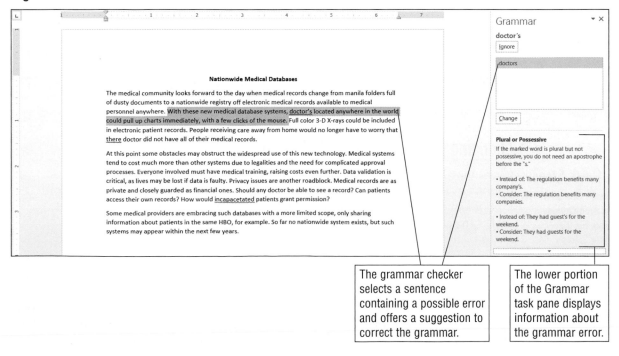

The grammar checker selects a sentence containing a possible error and offers a suggestion to correct the grammar.

The lower portion of the Grammar task pane displays information about the grammar error.

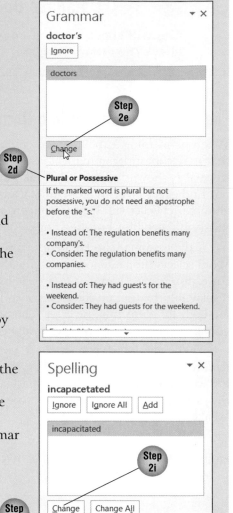

1. Open **MedData.docx** and then save it and name it **WL2-C2-P2-MedData**.
2. Check the grammar in the document by completing the following steps:
   a. Click the REVIEW tab.
   b. Click the Spelling & Grammar button in the Proofing group.
   c. The grammar checker selects the sentence that begins *With these new medical database systems* and displays *doctors* in the list box.
   d. Read the information on plural or possessive that displays below the list box in the task pane.
   e. Click the Change button to change *doctor's* to *doctors*.
   f. The grammar checker selects *there* in the document and displays *their* in the list box.
   g. Read the definitions of *there* and *their* that display in the task pane and then click the Change button.
   h. The spelling checker selects the word *incapacetated* and displays the proper spelling in the task pane list box. Listen to the pronunciation of the word *incapacitated* by clicking the speaker icon that displays at the right of the word *incapacitated* located below the list box. (You must have your computer speakers turned on to hear the pronunciation.)
   i. With the proper spelling of *incapacitated* selected in the task pane list box, click the Change button.
   j. At the message telling you that the spelling and grammar check is complete, click OK.
3. Save **WL2-C2-P2-MedData.docx**.

Changing Grammar Checking Options

Customize the type of grammar check that you perform on a document with options in the *When correcting spelling and grammar in Word* section of the Word Options dialog box with *Proofing* selected (see Figure 2.2). Remove the check marks from those options that you do not want active in a document.

By default, the grammar checker reviews only the grammar in a document. The *Writing Style* option at the Word Options dialog box with *Proofing* selected has a default setting of *Grammar Only*. You can change this default setting to *Grammar & Style*. To determine what style issues the grammar checker will select, click the Settings button to display the Grammar Settings dialog box with grammar and style options. Insert check marks for those options that you want active and remove the check marks from those options that you want inactive during a grammar check.

1. With **WL2-C2-P2-MedData.docx** open, change grammar checking settings by completing the following steps:
   a. Click the FILE tab.
   b. Click *Options*.
   c. At the Word Options dialog box, click the *Proofing* option in the left panel.
   d. Click the down-pointing arrow at the right side of the *Writing Style* option box and then click *Grammar & Style* at the drop-down list.
   e. Click the Recheck Document button.
   f. At the message that displays, click Yes.
   g. Click OK to close the Word Options dialog box.
2. Complete a grammar and style check on the document by completing the following steps:
   a. Press Ctrl + Home to move the insertion point to the beginning of the document.
   b. Make sure the REVIEW tab is selected.
   c. Click the Spelling & Grammar button in the Proofing group.
   d. When the grammar checker selects the sentence that begins *At this point some obstacles may* and displays *point,* in the list box, click the Change button.

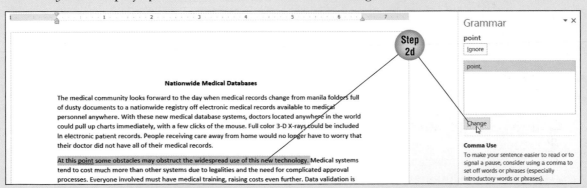

   e. When the grammar checker selects the sentence that begins *So far no nationwide system* and displays *far,* in the list box, click the Change button.
   f. At the message telling you that the spelling and grammar check is complete, click OK.
3. Save and then print **WL2-C2-P2-MedData.docx**.

Displaying Readability Statistics

When completing a spelling and grammar check, you can display readability statistics about the document. Figure 2.4 on the next page displays the readability statistics for **WL2-C2-P2-MedData.docx**. Statistics include word, character, paragraph, and sentence count; average number of sentences per paragraph, words per sentence, and characters per word; and readability information such as the percentage of passive sentences in the document, the Flesch Reading Ease score, and the Flesch-Kincaid grade-level rating. Control the display of readability statistics with the *Show readability statistics* check box in the Word Options dialog box with *Proofing* selected.

▼ **Quick Steps**

Show Readability Statistics
1. Click FILE tab.
2. Click *Options*.
3. Click *Proofing*.
4. Click *Show readability statistics* check box.
5. Click OK.
6. Complete spelling and grammar check.

Figure 2.4 Readability Statistics Dialog Box

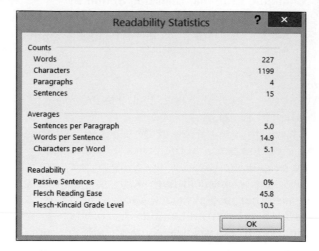

The Flesch Reading Ease score is based on the average number of syllables per word and the average number of words per sentence. The higher the score, the greater the number of people who will be able to understand the text in the document. Standard writing generally scores in the 60 to 70 range. The Flesch-Kincaid Grade Level score is based on the average number of syllables per word and the average number of words per sentence. The score indicates a grade level. Standard writing is generally scored at the seventh or eighth grade level.

Project 2c Displaying Readability Statistics   Part 3 of 3

1. With **WL2-C2-P2-MedData.docx** open, display readability statistics about the document by completing the following steps:
   a. Click the FILE tab and then click *Options*.
   b. At the Word Options dialog box, click *Proofing* in the left panel.
   c. Click the *Show readability statistics* check box to insert a check mark.
   d. Click OK to close the Word Options dialog box.
   e. At the document, make sure the REVIEW tab is selected and then click the Spelling & Grammar button.

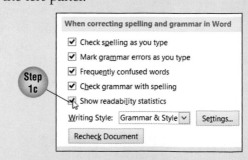

Step 1c

   f. Look at the readability statistics that display in the Readability Statistics dialog box and then click OK to close the dialog box.
2. Change the grammar checking options back to the default by completing the following steps:
   a. Click the FILE tab and then click *Options*.
   b. At the Word Options dialog box, click *Proofing* in the left panel.
   c. Click the *Show readability statistics* check box to remove the check mark.
   d. Click the down-pointing arrow at the right side of the *Writing Style* option box and then click *Grammar Only* at the drop-down list.
   e. Click OK to close the Word Options dialog box.
3. Save and then close **WL2-C2-P2-MedData.docx**.

> You will open a document, create a custom dictionary, add specific terms to the custom dictionary, and then complete a spelling check. You will also use a dictionary to define words in a document.

Creating a Custom Dictionary

When completing a spelling check on a document, Word uses the RoamingCustom.dic custom dictionary by default. You can add or remove words from this default dictionary. In a multiple-user environment, you might also consider adding your own custom dictionary and then selecting it as the default. This feature allows multiple users to create their own dictionaries to use when spell checking documents.

To create a custom dictionary, display the Word Options dialog box with *Proofing* selected and then click the Custom Dictionaries button. This displays the Custom Dictionaries dialog box, as shown in Figure 2.5. To create a new dictionary, click the New button. At the Create Custom Dictionary dialog box, type a name for the dictionary in the *File name* text box and then press Enter. The new dictionary name displays in the *Dictionary List* list box in the Custom Dictionaries dialog box. You can use more than one dictionary when spell checking a document. Insert a check mark in the check box next to any dictionary you want to use.

Changing the Default Dictionary

At the Custom Dictionaries dialog box, the default dictionary displays in the *Dictionary List* list box followed by *(Default)*. Change this default by clicking the desired dictionary name in the list box and then clicking the Change Default button.

Removing a Dictionary

Remove a custom dictionary with the Remove button at the Custom Dictionaries dialog box. To do this, display the Custom Dictionaries dialog box, click the dictionary name in the *Dictionary List* list box, and then click the Remove button. You are not prompted to confirm the removal, so make sure you select the correct dictionary name before clicking the Remove button.

Figure 2.5 Custom Dictionaries Dialog Box

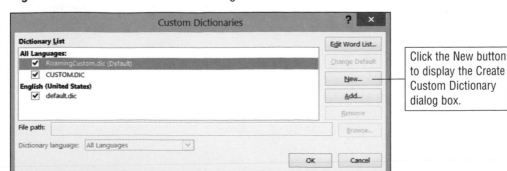

Click the New button to display the Create Custom Dictionary dialog box.

Quick Steps
Create a Custom Dictionary
1. Click FILE tab.
2. Click *Options*.
3. Click *Proofing*.
4. Click Custom Dictionaries button.
5. Click New button.
6. Type name for dictionary; press Enter.

HINT

When you change custom dictionary settings in one Microsoft Office program, the change affects all of the other programs in the suite.

Quick Steps
Remove a Custom Dictionary
1. Click FILE tab.
2. Click *Options*.
3. Click *Proofing*.
4. Click Custom Dictionaries button.
5. Click custom dictionary name.
6. Click Remove.
7. Click OK.

1. Open **BankBrazil.docx**, notice the wavy red lines indicating words not recognized by the spelling checker (words not in the custom dictionary), and then close the document.

2. Create a custom dictionary, add words to the dictionary, and then change the default dictionary by completing the following steps:

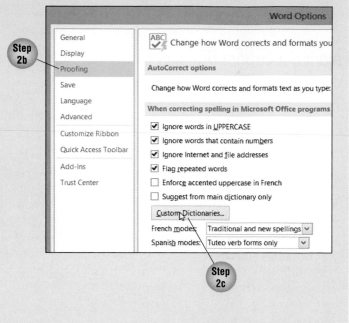

   a. Click the FILE tab and then click *Options*.
   b. At the Word Options dialog box, click *Proofing* in the left panel.
   c. Click the Custom Dictionaries button.
   d. At the Custom Dictionaries dialog box, click the New button.
   e. At the Create Custom Dictionary dialog box, type your first and last names (without a space between them) in the *File name* text box and then press Enter.
   f. At the Custom Dictionaries dialog box, add a word to your dictionary by completing the following steps:
      1) Click the name of your dictionary in the *Dictionary List* list box.
      2) Click the Edit Word List button.
      3) At the dialog box for your custom dictionary, type **Abreu** in the *Word(s)* text box.
      4) Click the Add button.

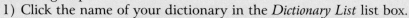

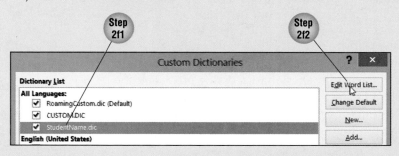

   g. Complete steps similar to those in Steps 2f3 and 2f4 to add the following words:
      Banco
      Itau
      Bradesco
      Unibanco
      Monteiro
      Lipschultz

h. When you have added all of the words, click the OK button to close the dialog box.
i. At the Custom Dictionaries dialog box with the name of your dictionary selected in the *Dictionary List* list box, click the Change Default button. (Notice that the word *(Default)* displays after your custom dictionary.)

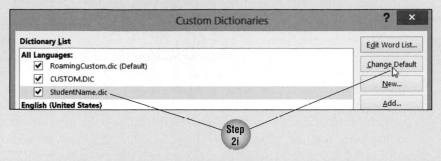

Step 2i

j. Click OK to close the Custom Dictionaries dialog box.
k. Click OK to close the Word Options dialog box.
3. Open **BankBrazil.docx** and then save the document and name it **WL2-C2-P3-BankBrazil**.
4. Complete a spelling and grammar check on your document and correct misspelled words. (The spelling checker will not stop at the words you added to your custom dictionary.)
5. Save and then print **WL2-C2-P3-BankBrazil.docx**.
6. Change the default dictionary and then remove your custom dictionary by completing the following steps:
    a. Click the FILE tab and then click *Options*.
    b. At the Word Options dialog box, click *Proofing* in the left panel.
    c. Click the Custom Dictionaries button.
    d. At the Custom Dictionaries dialog box, click *RoamingCustom.dic* in the *Dictionary List* list box.
    e. Click the Change Default button. (This changes the default back to the RoamingCustom.dic dictionary.)
    f. Click the name of your dictionary in the *Dictionary List* list box.
    g. Click the Remove button.
    h. Click OK to close the Custom Dictionaries dialog box.
    i. Click OK to close the Word Options dialog box.

Displaying Word Count ■■■■■■■■■■■■■■■■■■■■■■

Word counts your words as you type and the Status bar displays the total number of words in your document. If you want to display more information—such as the number of pages, paragraphs, and lines—display the Word Count dialog box. Display the Word Count dialog box by clicking the word count section of the Status bar or by clicking the REVIEW tab and then clicking the Word Count button in the Proofing group.

Count words in a portion of the document, rather than the entire document, by selecting the portion of text and then displaying the Word Count dialog box. If you want to determine the total word count of several sections throughout a document, select the first section, hold down the Ctrl key, and then select the other sections.

▼ Quick Steps

Display the Word Count Dialog Box
Click word count section of Status bar.
OR
1. Click REVIEW tab.
2. Click Word Count button.

Word Count

Using the Thesaurus ■■■■■■■■■■■■■■■■■■■■■

Word offers a Thesaurus feature for finding synonyms, antonyms, and related words for a particular word. *Synonyms* are words that have the same or nearly the same meaning. When you are using the thesaurus, Word may display *antonyms* for some words, which are words with opposite meanings. The thesaurus can help you to improve the clarity of business documents.

▼ Quick Steps

Use the Thesaurus
1. Click REVIEW tab.
2. Click Thesaurus button.
3. Type word in search text box.
4. Press Enter.

Thesaurus

To use the thesaurus, click the REVIEW tab and then click the Thesaurus button in the Proofing group. (You can also use the keyboard shortcut Shift + F7.) Doing this displays the Thesaurus task pane. Click in the search box located near the top of the Thesaurus task pane, type the word for which you want to find synonyms and/or antonyms, and then press Enter or click the Start searching button (which contains a magnifying glass icon). Searching causes a list of synonyms and antonyms to display in the task pane list box. You can also find synonyms and antonyms for a word in a document by selecting the word and then displaying the Thesaurus task pane. Figure 2.6 shows the Thesaurus task pane with synonyms and antonyms for the word *normally* displayed.

Depending on the word you are looking up, the words in the Thesaurus task pane list box may display followed by *(n.)* for *noun*, *(adj.)* for *adjective* or *(adv.)* for *adverb*. Antonyms may display at the end of the list of related synonyms and are followed by *(Antonym)*. If a dictionary is installed on your computer, a definition of the selected word will display below the task pane list box.

The thesaurus provides synonyms for the selected word as well as a list of related synonyms. For example, in the task pane list box shown in Figure 2.6, the

Figure 2.6 Thesaurus Task Pane

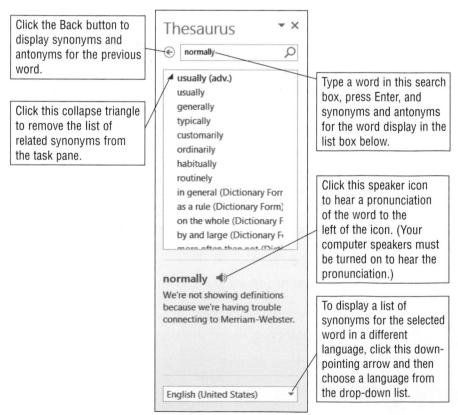

main synonym *usually* displays for *normally* and is preceded by a collapse triangle (a right-and-down-pointing triangle). The collapse triangle indicates that the list of related synonyms is displayed. When you click the collapse triangle, the list of related synonyms is removed from the task pane list box and the collapse triangle changes to an expand triangle (a right-pointing triangle). Click a word in the Thesaurus task pane list box to see synonyms for that word.

As you look up synonyms and antonyms for various words, you can display the list of synonyms and antonyms for the previous word by clicking the Back button (left-pointing arrow) located to the left of the search box. Click the down-pointing triangle located to the left of the Close button in the upper right corner of the task pane and a drop-down list displays with options for moving, sizing, and closing the task pane.

If you select a word in the document and then display the Thesaurus task pane, you can replace the selected word by hovering the mouse over the desired word in the task pane until a down-pointing arrow displays. Click the down-pointing arrow and then click *Insert* at the drop-down list.

The Thesaurus task pane, like the Spelling task pane and Grammar task pane, includes a pronunciation feature that will state the word currently selected in the Thesaurus task pane. To hear the word pronounced, click the speaker icon located to the right of the word below the task pane list box. (For this feature to work, your computer speakers must be turned on.)

The Thesaurus task pane also includes a language option for displaying synonyms of the selected word in a different language. To use this feature, click the down-pointing arrow at the right side of the option box located at the bottom of the task pane and then click the desired language at the drop-down list.

Project 3b Displaying the Word Count and Using the Thesaurus   Part 2 of 4

1. With **WL2-C2-P3-BankBrazil.docx** open, click the word count section of the Status bar.
2. After reading the statistics in the Word Count dialog box, click the Close button.
3. Display the Word Count dialog box by clicking the REVIEW tab and then clicking the Word Count button in the Proofing group.
4. Click the Close button to close the Word Count dialog box.
5. Use the thesaurus to change the word *normally* in the first paragraph to *generally* by completing the following steps:
   a. Select the word *normally* in the first paragraph (first word in the seventh line of text).
   b. Click the REVIEW tab, if necessary.
   c. Click the Thesaurus button in the Proofing group.
   d. At the Thesaurus task pane, hover the mouse pointer over the synonym *generally*, click the down-pointing arrow that displays at the right of the word, and then click *Insert* at the drop-down list.

Step 1

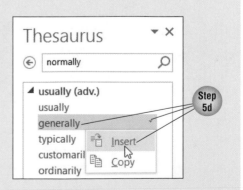

Step 5d

e. Click the word *generally* in the Thesaurus task pane.

f. If your computer speakers are turned on, listen to the pronunciation of the word *generally* by clicking the speaker icon next to the word located below the task pane list box.

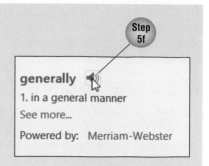

6. Follow similar steps to make the following changes using the thesaurus:

a. Change *acquaintances* in the first paragraph to *friends*.

b. Change *combat* in the second paragraph to *battle*.

7. Close the Thesaurus task pane by clicking the Close button located in the upper right corner of the task pane.

8. Save **WL2-C2-P3-BankBrazil.docx**.

Another method for displaying synonyms of a word is to use a shortcut menu. To do this, position the mouse pointer on the word and then click the right mouse button. At the shortcut menu that displays, point to *Synonyms* and then click the desired synonym at the side menu. Click the *Thesaurus* option at the bottom of the side menu to display synonyms and antonyms for the word in the Thesaurus task pane.

Project 3c　**Replacing Synonyms Using a Shortcut Menu**　　Part 3 of 4

1. With **WL2-C2-P3-BankBrazil.docx** open, position the mouse pointer on the word *vogue* located in the second sentence of the third paragraph.

2. Click the right mouse button.

3. At the shortcut menu that displays, point to *Synonyms* and then click *fashion* at the side menu.

4. Save **WL2-C2-P3-BankBrazil.docx**.

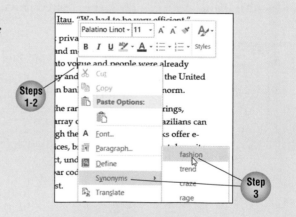

Defining Words ■■■■■■■■■■■■■■■■■■■■■■■■■■■

Define

If a dictionary is installed on your computer, the Thesaurus task pane displays a definition of the selected word. Another method for displaying the definition of a word is to click the Define button in the Proofing group on the REVIEW tab. A dictionary task pane opens at the right side of the screen with a definition of the word. If your computer does not have a dictionary installed, a list of dictionaries that you can download will display. Click the name of the dictionary that you want to use and then click *Download*.

Note: A dictionary must be installed on your computer to complete this project.

1. With **WL2-C2-P3-BankBrazil.docx** open, display definitions for words by completing the following steps:
   a. Select the word *e-commerce* that displays in the third sentence of the first paragraph.
   b. Make sure the REVIEW tab is active and then click the Define button in the Proofing group.
   c. Read the definition that displays in the dictionary task pane.

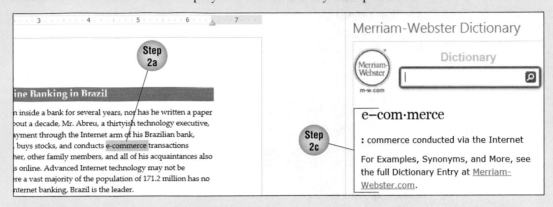

   d. Select the word *economy* that displays in the second sentence of the second paragraph.
   e. Read the definition that displays.
2. Close the dictionary task pane by clicking the Close button located in the upper right corner of the task pane.
3. Save, print, and then close **WL2-C2-P3-BankBrazil.com**.

Project 4 Translate Text   1 Part

You will use the translation feature to translate text from English to Spanish and English to French.

Translating Text to and from Different Languages ■■■■■

Word provides features for translating text from one language into another. The Thesaurus task pane provides one method for translating words. The Translate button in the Language group on the REVIEW tab provides additional translation methods. Click the Translate button and a drop-down list displays with options for translating the entire document or selected text and for turning on the Mini Translator.

Click the first option, *Translate Document*, and Word sends your document for translation by Microsoft Translator. When you click the option, a message displays telling you that Word is about to send your document for translation in unencrypted HTML format and asking if you want to continue. To continue to the translator, click the Send button.

Click the second option, *Translate Selected Text*, and Microsoft Translator will translate the selected text in a document and insert the translation in the Research task pane. The Research task pane displays at the right side of the screen and includes options for translating text to and from different languages.

▼ Quick Steps

Translate an Entire Document
1. Open document.
2. Click REVIEW tab.
3. Click Translate button.
4. Click *Translate Document* at drop-down list.
5. Click Send button.

Translate Selected Text
1. Select text.
2. Click REVIEW tab.
3. Click Translate button.
4. Click *Translate Selected Text*.

Translate

 **Quick Steps**

Turn on Mini Translator
1. Click REVIEW tab.
2. Click Translate button.
3. Click *Mini Translator*.

HINT

Hold down the Alt key and then click anywhere in the document to display the Research task pane.

Click the third option, *Mini Translator*, to turn on this feature. With the Mini Translator turned on, point to a word or select a phrase in your document and the translation of the text displays in a box above the text. To turn off the Mini Translator, click the *Mini Translator* option at the Translate button drop-down list. When the Mini Translator is turned on, the icon positioned to the left of the *Mini Translator* option displays with a light blue background.

Use the fourth option in the Translate button drop-down list, *Choose Translation Language*, to specify the language from which you want to translate and the language to which you want to translate. When you click the option, the Translation Language Options dialog box displays, as shown in Figure 2.7. At this dialog box, specify the translation language and whether you want to translate the entire document or turn on the Mini Translator. You may need to specify languages in the *Translate from* and *Translate to* option boxes before using the Mini Translator.

Figure 2.7 Translation Language Options Dialog Box

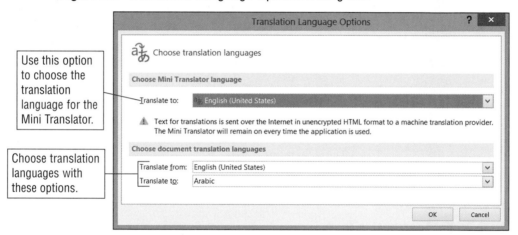

Use this option to choose the translation language for the Mini Translator.

Choose translation languages with these options.

Project 4 | **Using the Translate Button** | **Part 1 of 1**

Note: Check with your instructor before completing this exercise.

1. Open **ResumeStyles.docx** and then save the document and name it **WL2-C2-P4-ResumeStyles**.
2. Change the translation language to Spanish by completing the following steps:
   a. Click the REVIEW tab.
   b. Click the Translate button in the Language group and then click the *Choose Translation Language* option at the drop-down list.

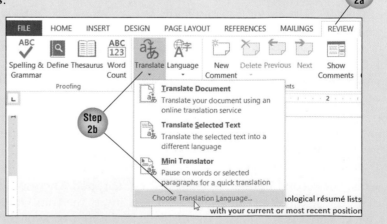

c. At the Translation Language Options dialog box, make sure that *English (United States)* displays in the *Translate from* option box.

d. Click the down-pointing arrow at the right of the *Translate to* option box in the *Choose document translation languages* section and then click *Spanish (Spain)* at the drop-down list. (Skip this step if *Spanish (Spain)* is already selected.)

e. Click OK to close the dialog box.

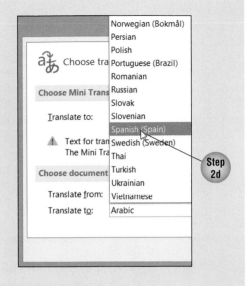

Step 2d

3. Translate the entire document to Spanish by completing the following steps:

a. Click the Translate button and then click the *Translate Document [English (United States) to Spanish (Spain)]* option.

b. At the message telling you that Word is about to send the document for translation over the Internet in unencrypted HTML format, click the Send button.

c. In a few moments, the Microsoft Translator window will open. (If the window does not display, click the button representing the translator on the Status bar.)

d. Select the translated text.

e. Press Ctrl + C to copy the text.

f. Close the Microsoft Translator window.

g. At the **WL2-C2-P4-ResumeStyles.docx** document, press Ctrl + End to move the insertion point to the end of the document and then press Ctrl + V to insert the copied text.

4. Save, print, and then close **WL2-C2-P4-ResumeStyles.docx**.

5. Open **TranslateTerms.docx** and then save the document and name it **WL2-C2-P4-TranslateTerms**.

6. Translate the word *Central* into Spanish by completing the following steps:

a. Click the REVIEW tab.

b. Click the Translate button and then click the *Choose Translation Language* option at the drop-down list.

c. At the Translation Language Options dialog box, click the down-pointing arrow at the right of the *Translate to* option box in the *Choose Mini Translator language* section and then click *Spanish (Spain)* at the drop-down list. (Skip this step if *Spanish (Spain)* is already selected.)

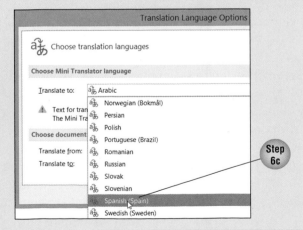

Step 6c

d. Click OK to close the dialog box.

e. Click the Translate button and then click *Mini Translator [Spanish (Spain)]* at the drop-down list. (This turns on the Mini Translator.)

f. Hover the mouse pointer over the word *Central* in the table. (The Mini Translator displays dimmed above the word.) Move the mouse pointer to the Mini Translator and then look at the translation that displays in the box above the word. Type one of the Spanish terms in the *Spanish* column.

g. Complete steps similar to those in Step 6f to display Spanish translations for the remaining terms. For each term, type the corresponding Spanish term in the appropriate location in the table. Type the terms without any accents or special symbols.

7. Use the Mini Translator to translate terms into French by completing the following steps:

a. Click the Translate button and then click the *Choose Translation Language* option at the drop-down list.

b. At the Translation Language Options dialog box, click the down-pointing arrow at the right of the *Translate to* option box in the *Choose Mini Translator Lanuguage* section, and then click *French (France)* at the drop-down list.

c. Click OK to close the dialog box.

d. With the Mini Translator turned on, hover the mouse pointer over the word *Central* in the table. (The Mini Translator displays dimmed above the word.)

e. Move the mouse pointer to the Mini Translator and then choose one of the French terms and type it in the *French* column.

f. Complete steps similar to those in Steps 7d and 7e to display French translations for the remaining terms. For each term, type the corresponding French term in the appropriate location in the table. Type the terms without any accents or special symbols.

8. Turn off the Mini Translator by clicking the Translate button and then clicking *Mini Translator [French (France)]* at the drop-down list.

9. Save, print, and then close **WL2-C2-P4-TranslateTerms.docx**.

Chapter Summary

- The spelling checker matches the words in your document with the words in its dictionary. If a match is not found, the word is selected and possible corrections are suggested.

- When checking the spelling and grammar in a document, you can temporarily leave the Spelling task pane or Grammar task pane, make corrections in the document, and then resume checking.

- Customize spell checking options at the Word Options dialog box with *Proofing* selected in the left panel.

- Use the grammar checker to search a document for correct grammar, style, punctuation, and word usage.

- Customize grammar checking with options in the *When correcting spelling and grammar in Word* section of the Word Options dialog box with *Proofing* selected.

- To display readability statistics for a document, insert a check mark in the *Show readability statistics* check box in the Word Options dialog box with *Proofing* selected and then complete a spelling and grammar check.

- Word uses the RoamingCustom.dic custom dictionary when spell checking a document. Add your own custom dictionary at the Custom Dictionaries dialog box. Display this dialog box by clicking the Custom Dictionaries button at the Word Options dialog box with *Proofing* selected.
- The Word Count dialog box displays the number of pages, words, characters, paragraphs, and lines in a document. Display this dialog box by clicking the word count section of the Status bar or clicking the Word Count button in the Proofing group on the REVIEW tab.
- Use the thesaurus to find synonyms and antonyms for words in your document. Display synonyms and antonyms at the Thesaurus task pane or by right-clicking a word and then pointing to *Synonyms* at the shortcut menu.
- Use the Translate button in the Language group on the REVIEW tab to translate a document, a selected section of text, or a word from one language to another.

Commands Review

FEATURE	RIBBON TAB, GROUP/OPTION	BUTTON, OPTION	KEYBOARD SHORTCUT
Mini Translator	REVIEW, Language	🔤, *Mini Translator*	
spelling and grammar checker	REVIEW, Proofing	✓	F7
Thesaurus task pane	REVIEW, Proofing	📖	Shift + F7
translate selected text	REVIEW, Language	🔤, *Translate Selected Text*	
translate text in document	REVIEW, Language	🔤, *Translate Document*	
Translation Language Options dialog box	REVIEW, Language	🔤, *Choose Translation Language*	
Word Count dialog box	REVIEW, Proofing	🔢	
Word Options dialog box	FILE, *Options*		

Concepts Check   Test Your Knowledge

Completion: In the space provided at the right, indicate the correct term, symbol, or command.

1. Click this tab to display the Proofing group.   _____

2. Use this keyboard shortcut to begin checking the spelling and grammar in a document.   _____

3. During a spelling check, click this button to skip the occurrence of the selected word and all other occurrences of the word in the document.

_____

4. Click this button in the Spelling task pane to replace the selected word with the selected word in the list box.

_____

5. To display the Word Options dialog box with spelling and grammar options, click the FILE tab, click *Options*, and then click this option in the left panel.

_____

6. This is the default setting for the *Writing Style* option at the Word Options dialog box with *Proofing* selected.

_____

7. When completing a spelling check on a document, Word uses this custom dictionary by default.

_____

8. This is the keyboard shortcut to display the Thesaurus task pane.

_____

9. When you click the Translate button and then click the *Translate Document* option, the text in the document is translated by this.

_____

10. Turn on this feature to point to a word or selected text and view a quick translation.

_____

Skills Check   Assess Your Performance

Assessment

1   CHECK SPELLING IN A PUNCTUATION DOCUMENT

1. Open **QuoteMarks.docx** and then save the document and name it **WL2-C2-A1-QuoteMarks**.
2. Complete a spelling and grammar check on the document. (Make all of the suggested changes *except* ignore the suggestion to change *Another's* to *another's*.)
3. Apply the Heading 1 style to the title of the document and the Heading 2 style to the headings in the document (which currently display in bold).
4. Apply the Parallax theme.
5. Center the document title.
6. Save, print, and then close **WL2-C2-A1-QuoteMarks.docx**.

Assessment

2 CHECK SPELLING AND GRAMMAR AND PROOFREAD A LETTER

1. Open **AirMiles.docx** and then save the document and name it **WL2-C2-A2-AirMiles**.
2. Complete a spelling and grammar check on the document. (Proper names are spelled correctly.)
3. After completing the spelling and grammar check, proofread the letter and make necessary changes. (The letter contains mistakes that the spelling and grammar checker will not select.) Replace the *XX* near the end of the document with your initials.
4. Select the entire document and then change the font to 12-point Candara.
5. Save, print, and then close **WL2-C2-A2-AirMiles.docx**.

Assessment

3 CUSTOMIZE OPTIONS AND CHECK SPELLING AND GRAMMAR IN A DOCUMENT

1. Open **CyberScenario.docx** and then save the document and name it **WL2-C2-A3-CyberScenario**.
2. Display the Word Options dialog box with *Proofing* selected, change the *Writing Style* option to *Grammar & Style*, and then close the dialog box.
3. Complete a spelling and grammar check on the document.
4. Apply formatting to enhance the appearance of the document.
5. Display the Word Options dialog box with *Proofing* selected, change the *Writing Style* option to *Grammar Only*, and then close the dialog box.
6. Save, print, and then close **WL2-C2-A3-CyberScenario.docx**.

Assessment

4 TRANSLATE AND INSERT WORDS IN A TABLE

1. At a blank document, create a table and use the translation feature to find the Spanish and French translations for the following terms:
   - abbreviation
   - adjective
   - adverb
   - punctuation
   - grammar
   - hyphen
   - paragraph
2. Type the English words in the first column of the table, the corresponding Spanish words in the second column, and the corresponding French words in the third column. (You do not need to include accents or special symbols.)
3. Apply formatting to enhance the appearance of the table.
4. Save the document and name it **WL2-C2-A4-Translations**.
5. Print and then close **WL2-C2-A4-Translations.docx**.

Visual Benchmark Demonstrate Your Proficiency

USE THE TRANSLATOR FEATURE

1. Open **CCDonations.docx** and then save it and name the document **WL2-C2-VB-CCDonations**.
2. Type the paragraph of text below the heading *English:* as shown in Figure 2.8 and then complete a spelling and grammar check of the text.
3. Select the paragraph of text below the heading *English:* and then translate the paragraph into Spanish and then into French. Copy the translated text into the document as shown in Figure 2.8. (Your translations may vary slightly from what is shown in Figure 2.8.)
4. Use the Curlz MT font for the headings at the beginning of each paragraph and for the quote that displays toward the bottom of the letter. Apply paragraph shading as shown in the figure.
5. Save, print, and then close **WL2-C2-VB-CCDonations.docx**.

Case Study Apply Your Skills

Part 1

You work in the executive offices at Nickell Industries and have been asked to develop a writing manual for employees. The company has not used a consistent theme when formatting documents, so you decide to choose a theme and use it when formatting all Nickell documents. Open **NIManual.docx** and then save the document and name it **WL2-C2-CS-NIManual**. Check the spelling and grammar in the document. Make the following changes to the document:

- Insert a section break at the beginning of the title *Editing and Proofreading*.
- Apply styles of your choosing to the titles and headings in the document.
- Apply the theme you have chosen for company documents.
- Insert headers and/or footers.
- Create a cover page.

Save the document.

Figure 2.8 Visual Benchmark

Cordova Children's Community Center

Support Your Local Community Center

English:

As you consider your donation contributions for the coming year, we ask that you consider supporting your community by supporting the Cordova Children's Community Center. The center is a nonprofit agency providing educational and recreational activities for children. Please stop by for a visit. Our dedicated staff will be available to discuss with you the services offered by the center, how your donation dollars are spent, and provide information on current and future activities and services.

Spanish:

Cuando usted considere sus contribuciones de donación para el próximo año, pedimos que usted considere apoyar su comunidad apoyando el Cordova comunidad centro infantil. El centro es una agencia sin fines de lucro actividades educativas y recreativas para los niños. Favor de pasar por una visita. Nuestro personal estará disponible para discutir con usted los servicios ofrecidos por el centro, cómo se gastan sus dólares de donación y proporcionar información sobre las actividades actuales y futuras y servicios.

French:

Lorsque vous envisagez vos contributions de don pour l'année prochaine, nous demandons que vous envisagez de soutenir votre communauté en soutenant le centre communautaire pour les enfants de Cordova. Le centre est un organisme à but non lucratif offrant des activités éducatives et récréatives pour les enfants. S'il vous plaît arrêter par pour une visite. Notre personnel dévoué sera disponible pour discuter avec vous des services offerts par le centre, comment vos dollars de dons sont dépensés et fournir des informations sur les services et les activités actuelles et futures.

"Children are our most valuable natural resources." ~ Herbert Hoover

770 Sunrise Terrace ◆ Santa Fe, NM 87509 ◆ 505-555-7700

Part 2

As you review the writing manual document, you decide to highlight the points for developing document sections. You decide that a vertical block list SmartArt graphic will present the ideas in an easy-to-read format and provide some visual interest to the manual. Insert a page break at the end of the **WL2-C2-CS-NIManual.docx** document, type the title *Developing a Document*, and insert the following in the appropriate shapes:

Beginning

- Introduce main idea.
- Get reader's attention.
- Establish positive tone.

Middle

- Provide detail for main idea.
- Lead reader to intended conclusion.

End

- State conclusion.
- State action you want reader to take.

Apply theme colors that follow the theme you chose for company documents. Save the document.

Part 3

You decide to purchase some reference books on grammar and punctuation. Using the Internet, search bookstores for books that provide information on grammar and punctuation and then choose three books. You know that the books will be purchased soon, so you decide to add the information in the writing manual document, telling readers what reference books are available. Include this information on a separate page at the end of the **WL2-C2-CS-NIManual.docx** document. Save, print, and then close the document.

Part 4

Nickell Industries does business in other countries, including Mexico. One of the executives in the Finance department has asked you to translate into Spanish some terms that will be used to develop an invoice. Create a document that translates the following terms from English to Spanish and also include in the document the steps for translating text. Your reason for doing this is that if the executive knows the steps, she can translate text at her own computer.

- city
- telephone
- invoice
- product
- description
- total

Format the document with the theme you chose for company documents and add any other enhancements to improve the appearance of the document. Save the completed document and name it **WL2-C2-CS-Translations**. Print and then close **WL2-C2-CS-Translations.docx**.

MICROSOFT
WORD

Automating and Customizing Formatting

PERFORMANCE OBJECTIVES

Upon successful completion of Chapter 3, you will be able to:

- Insert exceptions and add words to and delete words from the AutoCorrect dialog box
- Customize AutoFormat
- Use the AutoCorrect Options button
- Sort and insert building blocks
- Create, edit, modify, and delete building blocks
- Insert, update, and delete fields from Quick Parts
- Customize the Quick Access toolbar
- Customize the ribbon

Microsoft Word offers a number of features to help you customize documents and streamline the formatting of documents. In this chapter, you will learn how to customize the AutoCorrect feature and use the AutoCorrect Options button. You will also learn how to build a document using building blocks; create, save, and edit your own building blocks; and customize the Quick Access toolbar and the ribbon. Model answers for this chapter's projects appear on the following pages.

Note: Before beginning computer projects, copy to your storage medium the WL2C3 subfolder from the WL2 folder on the CD that accompanies this textbook and then make WL2C3 the active folder.

Terra Travel Services

Family Adventure Vacations

Namibia and Victoria Falls Adventure

Terra Travel Services is partnering with Family Adventure Vacations® to provide adventurous and thrilling family vacations. Our first joint adventure is a holiday trip to Namibia. Namibia is one of the most fascinating holiday destinations in Africa and offers comfortable facilities, great food, cultural interaction, abundant wildlife, and a wide variety of activities to interest people of all ages.

During the 12-day trip, you and your family will travel across Namibia through national parks, enjoying the beautiful and exotic scenery and watching wildlife in natural habitats. You will cruise along the Kwando and Chobe rivers and spend time at the Okapuka Lodge located near Windhoek, the capital of Namibia.

If you or your family member is a college student, contact one of our college travel adventure consultants to learn more about the newest Student Travel package titled "STudent STyle" that offers a variety of student discounts, rebates, and free travel accessories for qualifying participants.

Through the sponsorship of Ameria Resorts, we are able to offer you a 15 percent discount for groups of twelve or more people.

For additional information on the Namibia adventure, as well as other exciting vacation specials, please visit our website at www.emcp.net/terratravel or visit www.emcp.net/famadv.

1050 Marietta Street ❖ Atlanta, GA 30315 ❖ 1-888-555-2288 ❖ www.emcp.net/terratravel

Project 1 Create a Travel Document Using AutoCorrect

WL2-C3-P1-TTSAfrica.docx

JANUARY 2, 2015

NORTHLAND SECURITY SYSTEMS

COMPUTER VIRUSES AND SECURITY RISKS

STUDENT NAME

Cover Page

Project 2 Build a Document with Predesigned and Custom Building Blocks

WL2-C3-P2-CompViruses.docx

CONTENTS

CHAPTER 1: COMPUTER VIRUSES

One of the most familiar forms of risk to computer security is the computer virus. A computer virus is a program written by a hacker or cracker designed to perform some kind of trick upon an unsuspecting victim. The trick performed in some cases is mild, such as drawing an offensive image on the screen, or changing all of the characters in a document to another language. Sometimes the trick is much more severe, such as reformatting the hard drive and erasing all the data, or damaging the motherboard so that it cannot operate properly.

TYPES OF VIRUSES

Viruses can be categorized by their effect, which include nuisance, data-destructive, espionage, and hardware-destructive. A nuisance virus usually does no real damage, but is rather just an inconvenience. The most difficult part of a computer to replace is the data on the hard drive. The installed programs, the documents, databases, and saved emails form the heart of a personal computer. A data-destructive virus is designed to destroy this data. Some viruses are designed to create a backdoor into a system to bypass security. Called espionage viruses, they do no damage, but rather allow a hacker or cracker to enter the system later for the purpose of stealing data or spying on the work of the competitor. Very rarely, a virus is created that attempts to damage the hardware of the computer system itself. Called hardware-destructive viruses, these bits of programming can weaken or destroy chips, drives, and other components.

METHODS OF VIRUS OPERATION

Viruses can create effects that range from minor and annoying to highly destructive, and are operated and transmitted by a variety of methods. An email virus is normally transmitted as an attachment to a message sent over the Internet. Email viruses require the victim to click on the attachment and cause it to execute. Another common form of virus transmission is by a macro, a small subprogram that allows users to customize and automate certain functions. A macro virus is written specifically for one program, which then becomes infected when it opens a file with the virus stored in its macros. The boot sector of a compact disc or hard drive contains a variety of information, including how the disc is organized and whether it is capable of loading an operating system. When a disc is left in a drive and the computer reboots, the operating system automatically reads the boot sector to learn about that disc and to attempt to start any operating system on that disc. A boot sector virus is designed to alter the boot sector of a disc, so that whenever the operating system reads the boot sector, the computer will automatically become infected.

Other methods of virus infection include the Trojan horse virus, which hides inside another legitimate program or data file, and a stealth virus, which is designed to hide itself from detection software. Polymorphic viruses alter themselves to prevent antivirus software from detecting them by examining familiar patterns. Polymorphic viruses alter themselves randomly as they move from computer to computer, making detection more difficult. Multipartite viruses alter their form of attack. Their name derives from their ability to attack in several different ways. They may first infect the boot sector, and then later move on to become a Trojan horse type by infecting a disc file. These viruses are more sophisticated, and therefore more difficult to guard against. Another type of virus is the logic bomb, which generally sits quietly

---

dormant waiting for a specific event or set of conditions to occur. A famous logic bomb was the widely publicized Michelangelo virus.

which infected personal computers and caused them to display a message on the artist's birthday.

CHAPTER 2: SECURITY RISKS

Although hackers, crackers, and viruses garner the most attention as security risks, companies face a variety of other dangers to their hardware and software systems. Principally, these risks involve types of system failure, employee theft, and the cracking of software for copying.

SYSTEMS FAILURE

A fundamental element in making sure that computer systems operate properly is protecting the electrical power that runs them. Power interruptions such as blackouts and brownouts have very adverse effects on computers. An inexpensive type of power strip called a surge protector can guard against power fluctuations and can also serve as an extension cord and splitter. A much more vigorous power protection system is an uninterruptible power supply (UPS), which provides a battery backup. Similar in nature to a power strip but much more bulky and a bit more expensive, a UPS provides not only steady spike-free power, but also keeps computers running during a blackout.

EMPLOYEE THEFT

Although accurate estimates are difficult to pinpoint, businesses certainly lose millions of dollars a year in stolen computer hardware and software. Often, in large organizations,

such theft goes unnoticed or unreported. Someone takes a hard drive or a scanner home for legitimate use, then leaves the job some time later, and keeps the machine. Sometimes, employees take components to add to their home PC systems or a thief breaks into a business and hauls away computers. Such thefts cost far more than the price of the stolen computers because they also involve the cost of replacing the lost data, the cost of the time lost while the machines are gone, and the cost of installing new machines and training people to use them.

CRACKING SOFTWARE FOR COPYING

A common goal of hackers is to crack a software protection scheme. A crack is a method of circumventing a security scheme that prevents a user from copying a program. A common protection scheme for software is to require that the installation CD be resident in the drive whenever the program runs. Making copies of the CD with a burner, however, easily fools this protection scheme. Some game companies are taking the extra step of making duplication difficult by scrambling some of the data on the original CDs, which CD burners will automatically correct when copying. When the copied and corrected CD is used, the software checks for the scrambled track information. If the error is not found, the software will not run.

FAMILY ADVENTURE VACATIONS

6553 Copper Avenue ◆ Albuquerque, NM 87107 ◆ 505-555-4910

January 2, 2015

Mrs. Jody Lancaster
Pacific Sky Cruise Lines
120 Montgomery Boulevard
Los Angeles, CA 97032

Dear Jody:

Your colorful brochures have made quite an impression on our clients, and consequently, we have given away our entire stock. Please send us an additional box of brochures as well as information and fact sheets about the various specialized cruises coming up.

Are you planning to offer the "Northern Lights" cruise next year? The cruise has been very popular with our clients, and I have had three inquiries in the past three weeks regarding the cruise. As soon as you know the dates of the cruise and stateroom prices, please let me know.

Sincerely,

Student Name
Travel Consultant

WL2-C3-P3-PSLtr.docx

Visit our website at www.emcp.net/worldwide to learn about our weekly vacation specials!

"Making your vacation dreams a reality"

Project 3 Create a Letter Document Using Custom Building Blocks

WL2-C3-P3-PSLtr.docx

FAMILY ADVENTURE VACATIONS

6553 Copper Avenue ◆ Albuquerque, NM 87107 ◆ 505-555-4910

January 2, 2015

Mrs. Jody Lancaster
Pacific Sky Cruise Lines
120 Montgomery Boulevard
Los Angeles, CA 97032

Dear Jody:

I imagine you are extremely busy finalizing the preparations for the Pacific Sky Cruise Line's inaugural trip to the Alaska Inside Passage. The promotional literature you provided our company has been very effective in enticing our clients to sign up. This letter is a confirmation of the thirty staterooms that we have reserved for our clients for the inaugural cruise. We have reserved ten each of the following staterooms:

- Category H: Inside stateroom with two lower beds
- Category D: Deluxe ocean-view stateroom with window, sitting area, and two lower beds
- Category B: Superior deluxe ocean-view stateroom with window, sitting area, and two lower beds
- Category S: Superior deluxe suite with ocean view, private balcony, sitting area, and two lower beds

With only a few weeks to go before the cruise, I want to make sure our clients' bookings are finalized so they can enjoy the eight-day, seven-night cruise to the Alaska Inside Passage. Please confirm the stateroom reservations and send me a fax or email with the confirmation numbers.

Sincerely,

Student Name
Senior Travel Consultant

WL2-C3-P4-PSLtr.docx

"Making your vacation dreams a reality"

Project 4 Create a Letter Document with Modified Building Blocks

WL2-C3-P4-PSLtr.docx

Chapter 3 ■ Automating and Customizing Formatting

83

TESTING AGREEMENT

THIS AGREEMENT is made by and between Frontier Video Productions and _____ ("Licensee") having a principal place of business located at _____.

In consideration of the mutual covenants and premises herein contained, the parties hereto agree as follows:

Frontier Video Productions grants to Licensee a non-exclusive, non-transferable license to use the Software on a single computer at Licensee's business location solely for beta testing and internal use until _____, 20__, at which time the Software and all copies shall be returned to Frontier Video Productions.

In consideration for receiving a copy of the Software for testing, Licensee agrees to serve as a beta testing site for the Software and will notify Frontier Video Productions of all problems and ideas for enhancements which come to Licensee's attention during the period of this Agreement, and hereby assigns to Frontier Video Productions all rights, title and interest to such enhancements and all property rights therein including without limitation all patent, copyright, trade secret, mask work, trademark, moral right, or other intellectual property rights.

This Agreement shall be governed, construed, and enforced in accordance with the laws of the United States of America and of the State of California. Any notice required by this Agreement shall be given by prepaid, first class, certified mail, return receipt requested.

Frontier Video Productions: Licensee:

_____   _____
Name   Name

First Draft
WL2-C3-P5-TestAgrmnt.docx
1/2/2015 2:39:00 PM

TESTING AGREEMENT

THIS AGREEMENT is made by and between Frontier Video Productions and _____ ("Licensee") having a principal place of business located at _____.

In consideration of the mutual covenants and premises herein contained, the parties hereto agree as follows:

Frontier Video Productions grants to Licensee a non-exclusive, non-transferable license to use the Software on a single computer at Licensee's business location solely for beta testing and internal use until _____, 20__, at which time the Software and all copies shall be returned to Frontier Video Productions.

In consideration for receiving a copy of the Software for testing, Licensee agrees to serve as a beta testing site for the Software and will notify Frontier Video Productions of all problems and ideas for enhancements which come to Licensee's attention during the period of this Agreement, and hereby assigns to Frontier Video Productions all rights, title and interest to such enhancements and all property rights therein including without limitation all patent, copyright, trade secret, mask work, trademark, moral right, or other intellectual property rights.

This Agreement shall be governed, construed, and enforced in accordance with the laws of the United States of America and of the State of California. Any notice required by this Agreement shall be given by prepaid, first class, certified mail, return receipt requested.

Frontier Video Productions: Licensee:

_____   _____
Name   Name

First Draft
WL2-C3-P5-FVAgrmnt.docx
1/2/2015 3:17:00 PM

Project 5 Insert Document Properties and Fields in an Agreement Document   WL2-C3-P5-TestAgrmnt.docx

WL2-C3-P5-FVPAgrmnt.docx

NATURAL INTERFACE APPLICATIONS

A major area of artificial intelligence has the goal of creating a more natural interface between human and machine. Currently, computer users are restricted in most instances to using a mouse and keyboard for input. For output, they must gaze at a fairly static, two-dimensional screen. Speakers are used for sound, and a printer for hard copy. The user interface consists of typing, pointing, and clicking. New speech recognition and natural-language technologies promise to change that soon.

SPEECH RECOGNITION

One of the most immediately applicable improvements comes in the area of speech recognition. Rather than typing information into the computer, users can direct it with voice commands. A computer that can take dictation and perform requested actions is a real step forward in convenience and potential. Speech recognition has developed rather slowly, mainly because the typical PC did not have the necessary speed and capacity until very recently.

NATURAL-LANGUAGE INTERFACE

Computers that are able to communicate using spoken English, Japanese, or any of the hundreds of other languages currently in use around the world, would certainly be helpful. In the not-so-distant future, computers will most likely be able to read, write, speak, and understand many human languages. Language translators already exist, and they are getting better all the time.

Programmers can look forward to a human-language computer interface. With better interfaces, programmers may be able to describe what they want using natural (human) languages, rather than writing programs in the highly restrictive and rather alien programming languages in use today. Natural-language interfaces are an area of artificial intelligence that is broader in scope than simple speech recognition. The goal is to have a machine that can read a set of news articles on any topic and understand what it has read. Ideally, it could then write its own report summarizing what it has learned.

VIRTUAL REALITY

Virtual reality (VR) describes the concept of creating a realistic world within the computer. Online games with thousands of interacting players already exist. In these games people can take on a persona and move about a virtual landscape, adventuring and chatting with other players. The quality of a virtual reality system is typically characterized in terms of its immersiveness, which measures how real the simulated world feels and how well it can

STUDENT NAME   1

---

make users accept the simulated world as their own and forget about reality. With each passing year, systems are able to provide increasing levels of immersion. Called by some the "ultimate in escapism," VR is becoming increasingly common—and increasingly realistic.

MENTAL INTERFACE

Although still in the experimental phase, a number of interfaces take things a bit further than VR, and they don't require users to click a mouse, speak a word, or even lift a finger. Mental interfaces use sensors mounted around the skull to read the alpha waves given off by our brains. Thinking of the color blue could be used to move the mouse cursor to the right, or thinking of the number seven could move it to the left. The computer measures brain activity and interprets it as a command, eliminating the need to physically manipulate a mouse to move the screen cursor. While this technology has obvious applications for assisting people with disabilities, military researchers are also using it to produce a superior form of interface for pilots.

STUDENT NAME   2

Project 6 Minimize the Ribbon and Customize the Quick Access Toolbar and Ribbon   WL2-C3-P6-InterfaceApps.docx

You will create several AutoCorrect entries, open a letterhead document, and then use the AutoCorrect entries to type text in the document.

Customizing AutoCorrect ■■■■■■■■■■■■■■■■■■■■■■■■

The AutoCorrect feature in Word corrects certain text automatically as you type. Control what types of corrections are made with options at the AutoCorrect dialog box with the AutoCorrect tab selected, as shown in Figure 3.1.

Display this dialog box by clicking the FILE tab, clicking *Options*, clicking *Proofing*, clicking the AutoCorrect Options button, and then clicking the AutoCorrect tab. At the dialog box, turn AutoCorrect features on or off by inserting or removing check marks from the check boxes, specify AutoCorrect exceptions, replace frequently misspelled words with the correct spellings, add frequently used words, and specify keys to quickly insert the words in a document.

Specifying AutoCorrect Exceptions

The check box options at the AutoCorrect dialog box with the AutoCorrect tab selected identify the types of corrections made by AutoCorrect. Make exceptions to the corrections with options at the AutoCorrect Exceptions dialog box, shown in Figure 3.2 on the next page. Display this dialog box by clicking the Exceptions button at the AutoCorrect dialog box with the AutoCorrect tab selected.

▼ **Quick Steps**

Display the AutoCorrect Exceptions Dialog Box
1. Click FILE tab.
2. Click *Options*.
3. Click *Proofing*.
4. Click AutoCorrect Options button.
5. Click AutoCorrect tab.
6. Click Exceptions button.

Figure 3.1 AutoCorrect Dialog Box with AutoCorrect Tab Selected

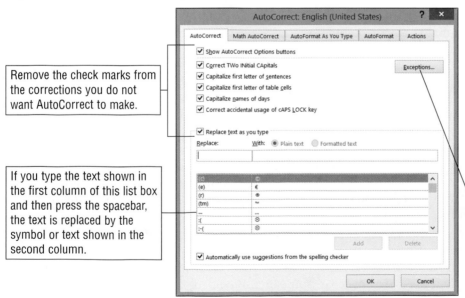

Remove the check marks from the corrections you do not want AutoCorrect to make.

If you type the text shown in the first column of this list box and then press the spacebar, the text is replaced by the symbol or text shown in the second column.

Click this button to display the AutoCorrect Exceptions dialog box.

Figure 3.2 AutoCorrect Exceptions Dialog Box

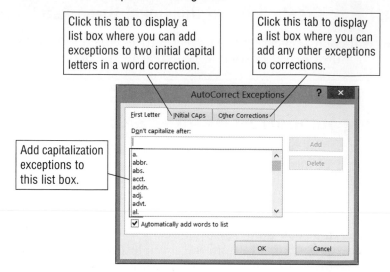

Click this tab to display a list box where you can add exceptions to two initial capital letters in a word correction.

Click this tab to display a list box where you can add any other exceptions to corrections.

Add capitalization exceptions to this list box.

AutoCorrect usually capitalizes a word that comes after an abbreviation ending in a period, since a period usually ends a sentence. Exceptions to this general practice display in the AutoCorrect Exceptions dialog box with the First Letter tab selected. Many exceptions already display in the dialog box but you can add additional exceptions by typing each desired exception in the *Don't capitalize after* text box and then clicking the Add button.

By default, AutoCorrect corrects the use of two initial capital letters in a word. If you do not want AutoCorrect to correct the capitalizing of two initial capitals in a word, display the AutoCorrect Exceptions dialog box with the INitial CAps tab selected and then type the exception text in the *Don't correct* text box. At the AutoCorrect Exceptions dialog box with the Other Corrections tab selected, type text that you do not want corrected in the *Don't correct* text box. Delete exceptions from the dialog box with any of the tabs selected by clicking the desired text in the list box and then clicking the Delete button.

Adding Words to AutoCorrect

▼ Quick Steps

Add a Word to AutoCorrect
1. Click FILE tab.
2. Click *Options*.
3. Click *Proofing*.
4. Click AutoCorrect Options button.
5. Click AutoCorrect tab.
6. Type misspelled or abbreviated word.
7. Press Tab.
8. Type correctly spelled or complete word.
9. Click Add button.
10. Click OK.

You can add words you commonly misspell and/or typographical errors you often make to AutoCorrect. For example, if you consistently type *relavent* instead of *relevant*, you can add *relavent* to AutoCorrect and tell it to correct it as *relevant*. The AutoCorrect dialog box also contains a few symbols you can insert in a document. For example, type *(c)* and AutoCorrect changes the text to ©. Type *(r)* and AutoCorrect changes the text to ®. The symbols display at the beginning of the AutoCorrect dialog box list box.

You can also add an abbreviation to AutoCorrect that, when typed, will insert an entire word (or words) in the document. For example, in Project 1a, you will add *fav* to AutoCorrect, which will insert *Family Adventure Vacations* when you type *fav* and then press the spacebar. You can also control the capitalization of the word (or words) inserted by controlling the capitalization of the abbreviation. For example, in Project 1a, you will add *Na* to AutoCorrect, which will insert *Namibia* when you type *Na* and *NAMIBIA* when you type *NA*.

Note that the AutoCorrect feature does not automatically correct text in hyperlinks. AutoCorrect is available only in Word, Outlook, and Visio.

1. At a blank document, click the FILE tab and then click *Options*.
2. At the Word Options dialog box, click *Proofing* in the left panel.
3. Click the AutoCorrect Options button in the *AutoCorrect options* section.
4. At the AutoCorrect dialog box with the AutoCorrect tab selected, add an exception to AutoCorrect by completing the following steps:

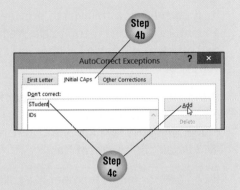

   a. Click the Exceptions button.
   b. At the AutoCorrect Exceptions dialog box, click the INitial CAps tab.
   c. Click in the *Don't correct* text box, type **STudent**, and then click the Add button.
   d. Click in the *Don't correct* text box, type **STyle**, and then click the Add button.
   e. Click the OK button.
5. At the AutoCorrect dialog box with the AutoCorrect tab selected, click in the *Replace* text box and then type **fav**.
6. Press the Tab key (which moves the insertion point to the *With* text box) and then type **Family Adventure Vacations**.
7. Click the Add button. (This adds *fav* and *Family Adventure Vacations* to AutoCorrect and also selects *fav* in the *Replace* text box.)

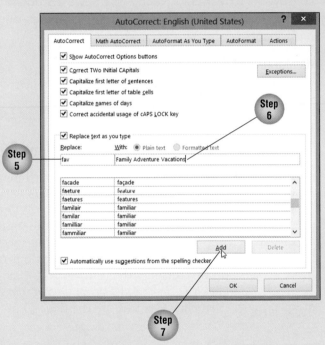

8. Type **Na** in the *Replace* text box. (The text *fav* is automatically removed when you begin typing *Na*.)
9. Press the Tab key and then type **Namibia**.
10. Click the Add button.
11. With the insertion point positioned in the *Replace* text box, type **vf**.
12. Press the Tab key and then type **Victoria Falls**.
13. Click the Add button.
14. With the insertion point positioned in the *Replace* text box, type **tts**.
15. Press the Tab key and then type **Terra Travel Services**.
16. Click the Add button.
17. Click OK to close the AutoCorrect dialog box and then click OK to close the Word Options dialog box.
18. Open **TTSLtrhd.docx** and then save the document and name it **WL2-C3-P1-TTSAfrica**.
19. Type the text shown in Figure 3.3 on the next page. Type the text exactly as shown (including bolding and centering *fav* at the beginning of the document). AutoCorrect will correct words as you type.
20. Save **WL2-C3-P1-TTSAfrica.docx**.

Figure 3.3 Project 1a

fav

Na and vf Adventure

tts is partnering with fav(r) to provide adventurous and thrilling family vacations. Our first joint adventure is a holiday trip to Na. Na is one of the most fascinating holiday destinations in Africa and offers comfortable facilities, great food, cultural interaction, abundant wildlife, and a wide variety of activities to interest people of all ages.

During the 12-day trip, you and your family will travel across Na through national parks, enjoying the beautiful and exotic scenery and watching wildlife in natural habitats. You will cruise along the Kwando and Chobe rivers and spend time at the Okapuka Lodge located near Windhoek, the capital of Na.

If you or your family member is a college student, contact one of our college travel adventure consultants to learn more about the newest Student Travel package titled "STudent STyle" that offers a variety of student discounts, rebates, and free travel accessories for qualifying participants.

tts and fav are offering a 15 percent discount if you sign up for this once-in-a-lifetime trip to Na. This exciting adventure is limited to twenty people, so don't wait to sign up.

Using the AutoCorrect Options Button

AutoCorrect
Options

After AutoCorrect corrects a portion of text, hover the mouse pointer near the text and a small blue box displays below the corrected text. Move the mouse pointer to this blue box and the AutoCorrect Options button displays. Click this button to display a drop-down list with the options to change back to the original version, stop automatically correcting the specific text, and display the AutoCorrect dialog box. If the AutoCorrect Options button does not display, turn on the feature. To do this, display the AutoCorrect dialog box with the AutoCorrect tab selected, click the *Show AutoCorrect Options buttons* check box to insert a check mark, and then click OK to close the dialog box.

Project 1b **Using the AutoCorrect Options Button** Part 2 of 3

1. With **WL2-C3-P1-TTSAfrica.docx** open, select and then delete the last paragraph.
2. With the insertion point positioned on the blank line below the last paragraph of text (you may need to press the Enter key), type the following text.(AutoCorrect will automatically change *Ameria* to *America*, which you will change in the next step.) **Through the sponsorship of Ameria Resorts, we are able to offer you a 15 percent discount for groups of twelve or more people.**
3. Change the spelling of *America* back to *Ameria* by completing the following steps:
   a. Position the mouse pointer over *America* until a blue box displays below the word.
   b. Position the mouse pointer on the blue box until the AutoCorrect Options button displays.

c. Click the AutoCorrect Options button and then click the *Change back to "Ameria"* option.

4. Save and then print **WL2-C3-P1-TTSAfrica.docx**.

Step 3c

Through the sponsorship of America Resorts, we are able to offer you a 15 of twelve or more people.

↶ Change back to "Ameria"
Stop Automatically Correcting "Ameria"
⌐ Control AutoCorrect Options...

Customizing AutoFormatting

When you type text, Word provides options to automatically apply some formatting, such as changing a fraction to a fraction character (1/2 to ½), changing numbers to ordinals (1st to 1st), changing an Internet or network path to a hyperlink (www.emcp.net to www.emcp.net), and applying bullets or numbers to text. The AutoFormatting options display in the AutoCorrect dialog box with the AutoFormat As You Type tab selected, as shown in Figure 3.4. Display this dialog box by clicking the FILE tab and then clicking *Options*. At the Word Options dialog box, click *Proofing* in the left panel and then click the AutoCorrect Options button. At the AutoCorrect dialog box, click the AutoFormat As You Type tab. At the dialog box, remove the check marks from those options you want to turn off and insert check marks for those options you want Word to format automatically.

Deleting AutoCorrect Text

You can delete AutoCorrect text from the AutoCorrect dialog box. To do this, display the AutoCorrect dialog box with the AutoCorrect tab selected, click the desired word or words in the list box, and then click the Delete button.

Figure 3.4 AutoCorrect Dialog Box with the AutoFormat As You Type Tab Selected

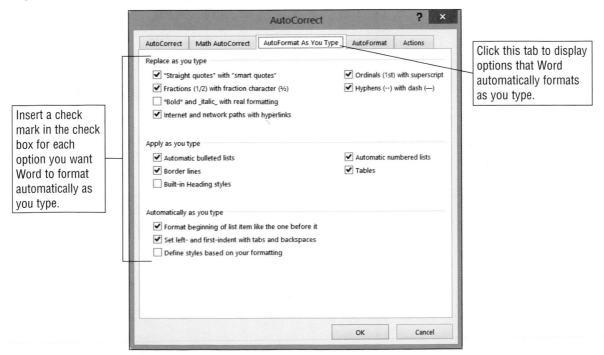

1. Make sure **WL2-C3-P1-TTSAfrica.docx** is open.
2. Suppose that you need to add a couple of web addresses to a document and you do not want the addresses automatically formatted as hyperlinks (since you are sending the document as hard copy rather than electronically). Turn off the AutoFormatting of web addresses by completing the following steps:
   a. Click the FILE tab and then click *Options*.
   b. At the Word Options dialog box, click *Proofing* in the left panel.
   c. Click the AutoCorrect Options button.
   d. At the AutoCorrect dialog box, click the AutoFormat As You Type tab.
   e. Click the *Internet and network paths with hyperlinks* check box to remove the check mark.
   f. Click OK to close the AutoCorrect dialog box.
   g. Click OK to close the Word Options dialog box.
3. Press Ctrl + End to move the insertion point to the end of the document, press the Enter key, and then type the text shown in Figure 3.5.
4. Turn on the AutoFormatting feature you turned off in Step 2 by completing Steps 2a through 2g (except in Step 2e, insert the check mark rather than remove it).
5. Delete *fav* from AutoCorrect by completing the following steps:
   a. Click the FILE tab and then click *Options*.
   b. At the Word Options dialog box, click *Proofing* in the left panel.
   c. Click the AutoCorrect Options button.
   d. At the AutoCorrect dialog box, click the AutoCorrect tab.
   e. Click in the *Replace* text box and then type **fav**. (This selects the entry in the list box.)
   f. Click the Delete button.
6. Complete steps similar to those in Step 5 to delete the *Na*, *tts*, and *vf* AutoCorrect entries.

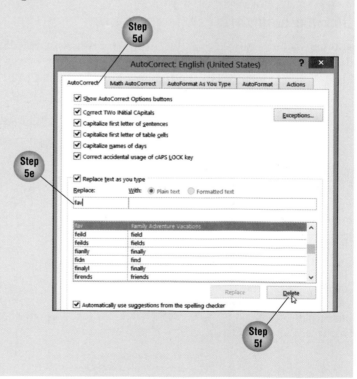

7. Delete the exceptions you added to the AutoCorrect Exceptions dialog box by completing the following steps:
  a. At the AutoCorrect dialog box with the AutoCorrect tab selected, click the Exceptions button.
  b. At the AutoCorrect Exceptions dialog box, if necessary, click the INitial CAps tab.
  c. Click *STudent* in the list box and then click the Delete button.
  d. Click *STyle* in the list box and then click the Delete button.
  e. Click OK to close the AutoCorrect Exceptions dialog box.
8. Click OK to close the AutoCorrect dialog box.
9. Click OK to close the Word Options dialog box.
10. Save, print, and then close **WL2-C3-P1-TTSAfrica.docx**.

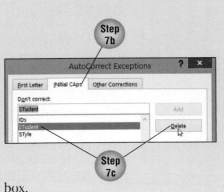

Figure 3.5 Project 1c

For additional information on the Na adventure, as well as other exciting vacation specials, please visit our website at www.emcp.net/terratravel or visit www.emcp.net/famadv.

Project 2 | **Build a Document with Predesigned and Custom Building Blocks** | **1 Part**

You will open a report document and then add elements to the document by inserting predesigned building blocks.

Inserting Quick Parts

Word includes a variety of tools for inserting data such as text, fields, objects, and other items to help build a document. To view some of the tools available, click the Quick Parts button in the Text group on the INSERT tab. Doing this displays a drop-down list of choices for inserting document properties, fields, and building blocks, as well as options for saving selected data to the AutoText gallery and Quick Part gallery.

Quick Parts

Inserting Building Blocks

Building blocks are tools for developing a document. Word provides a number of building blocks that you can insert into a document, or you can create your own.

▼ Quick Steps

Insert a Building Block
1. Click INSERT tab.
2. Click Quick Parts button.
3. Click *Building Blocks Organizer* at drop-down list.
4. Click desired building block.
5. Click Insert button.
6. Click Close.

To insert a building block into a document, click the INSERT tab, click the Quick Parts button in the Text group, and then click *Building Blocks Organizer* at the drop-down list. This displays the Building Blocks Organizer dialog box, shown in Figure 3.6. The dialog box displays columns of information about the building blocks. The columns in the dialog box display the building block name, the gallery that contains the building block, the template in which the building block is stored, the behavior of the building block, and a brief description.

The Building Blocks Organizer dialog box is a central location for viewing all of the predesigned building blocks available in Word. You used some of the building blocks in previous chapters when you inserted a predesigned header or footer, cover page, page number, and watermark. Other galleries in the Building Blocks Organizer dialog box containing predesigned building blocks include bibliographies, equations, tables of contents, tables, and text boxes. The Building Blocks Organizer dialog box provides a convenient location for viewing and inserting building blocks.

Sorting Building Blocks

▼ Quick Steps

Sort Building Blocks
1. Click INSERT tab.
2. Click Quick Parts button.
3. Click *Building Blocks Organizer* at drop-down list.
4. Click desired column heading.

When you open the Building Blocks Organizer dialog box, the building blocks display in the list box sorted by the *Gallery* column. Sort the building blocks by other columns by clicking the column headings. For example, to sort building blocks alphabetically by name, click the *Name* column heading.

Figure 3.6 Building Blocks Organizer Dialog Box

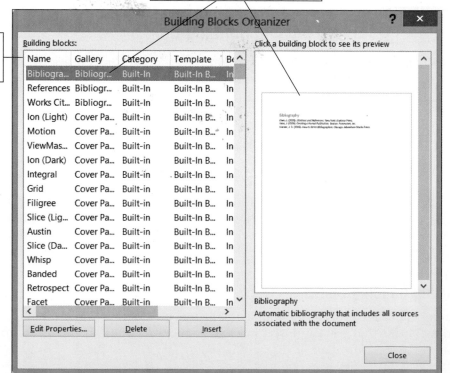

1. Open **CompViruses.docx** and then save the document and name it **WL2-C3-P2-CompViruses**.
2. Make the following changes to the document:
   a. Insert a continuous section break at the beginning of the first paragraph below the title *CHAPTER 1: COMPUTER VIRUSES*.
   b. Insert a section break that begins a new page at the beginning of the title *CHAPTER 2: SECURITY RISKS* located in the middle of the second page.
   c. Insert a continuous section break at the beginning of the first paragraph below the title *CHAPTER 2: SECURITY RISKS*.
   d. Change the line spacing to 1.0 for the entire document.
   e. Format the paragraphs in the section below the title *CHAPTER 1: COMPUTER VIRUSES* into two columns of equal width.
   f. Balance the columns where the text ends on the second page. ***Hint: Balance columns by inserting a continuous section break.***
   g. Format the paragraphs in the section below the second title *CHAPTER 2: SECURITY RISKS* into two columns of equal width.
   h. Balance the columns where the text ends on the page.
3. Sort the building blocks and then insert a table of contents building block by completing the following steps:
   a. Press Ctrl + Home, press Ctrl + Enter to insert a page break, and then press Ctrl + Home to move the insertion point back to the beginning of the document.
   b. Click the INSERT tab, click the Quick Parts button in the Text group, and then click *Building Blocks Organizer* at the drop-down list.
   c. At the Building Blocks Organizer dialog box, notice the arrangement of building blocks in the list box. (The building blocks are most likely organized alphabetically by the *Gallery* column.)
   d. Click the *Name* column heading. (This sorts the building blocks alphabetically by name. However, some blank building blocks may display at the beginning of the list box.)

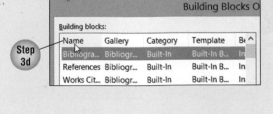

   e. Scroll down the list box and then click *Automatic Table 1*. (You may see only a portion of the name. Click the name and the full name as well as a description display in the dialog box below the preview of the table of contents building block.)
   f. Click the Insert button that displays near the bottom of the dialog box. (This inserts a Contents page at the beginning of the document and uses the heading styles applied to the titles and headings in the document to create the table of contents.)
4. Insert a footer building block by completing the following steps:
   a. Click the Quick Parts button on the INSERT tab and then click *Building Blocks Organizer*.
   b. Scroll down the Building Blocks Organizer list box, click the *Sempahore* footer, and then click the Insert button.

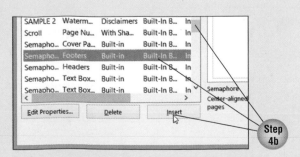

c. Decrease the *Footer from Bottom* measurement to 0.3 inch (located in the Position group on the HEADER & FOOTER TOOLS DESIGN tab).

d. Click the DESIGN tab, click the Theme Colors button, and then click *Red* at the drop-down list. (This changes the color of the footer text to Red.)

e. Double-click in the document.

5. Insert a cover page building block by completing the following steps:

a. Press Ctrl + Home to move the insertion point to the beginning of the document.

b. Click the INSERT tab, click the Quick Parts button, and then click *Building Blocks Organizer*.

c. Scroll down the Building Blocks Organizer list box, click the *Semaphore* cover page, and then click the Insert button.

d. Click the *[DATE]* placeholder and then type today's date.

e. Click the *[DOCUMENT TITLE]* placeholder and then type **Northland Security Systems**. (The text you type will be converted to all uppercase letters.)

f. Click the *[DOCUMENT SUBTITLE]* placeholder and then type **Computer Viruses and Security Risks**.

g. Select the name that displays above the [COMPANY NAME] placeholder and then type your first and last names.

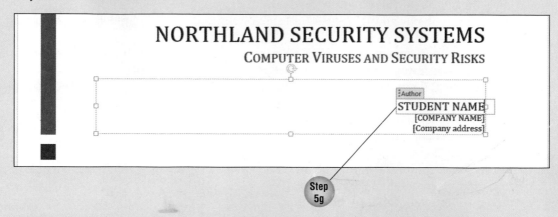

Step
5g

h. Select and then delete the [COMPANY NAME] placeholder.

i. Select and then delete the [Company address] placeholder.

6. Scroll through the document and look at each page in the document. The semaphore footer and cover page building blocks you inserted have similar formatting and are part of the *Semaphore* group. Using building blocks from the same group provides consistency in the document and gives it a polished and professional appearance.

7. Save, print, and then close **WL2-C3-P2-CompViruses.docx**.

Project ▌3▐ Create a Letter Document Using Custom Building Blocks

3 Parts

You will create custom building blocks and then use those building blocks to prepare a business letter.

Saving Content as Building Blocks

If you find yourself typing and formatting the same data on a regular basis, consider saving the data as a ***building block***. Saving commonly created data as a building block saves you time and reduces errors that might occur each time you type data or apply formatting. You can save content as a building block in a specific gallery. For example, you can save a text box in the Text Box gallery, save content in the Header gallery, save content in the Footer gallery, and so on. To save content in a specific gallery, use the button for the desired gallery.

For example, to save a text box in the Text Box gallery, use the Text Box button. To do this, select the text box, click the INSERT tab, click the Text Box button, and then click the *Save Selection to Text Box Gallery* option at the drop-down gallery. At the Create New Building Block dialog box that displays, as shown in Figure 3.7, type a name for the text box building block, type a description if desired, and then click OK.

To save content in the Header gallery, select the content, click the INSERT tab, click the Header button, and then click the *Save Selection to Header Gallery* option at the drop-down gallery. This displays the Create New Building Block dialog box, as shown in Figure 3.7 (except *Headers* displays with the *Gallery* option box). Complete similar steps to save content to the Footer gallery and Cover Page gallery.

When you save data as a building block, it becomes available in the Building Blocks Organizer dialog box. If you save content as a building block in a specific gallery, the building block is available at both the Building Blocks Organizer dialog box and the gallery. For example, if you save a building block in the Footer gallery, the building block is available when you click the Footer button on the INSERT tab.

Content you save as a building block is saved in the Building Blocks.dotx template or Normal.dotm template. Saving a building block in either template makes it available each time you open Word. In a public environment such as a school, you may not be able to save data to a template. Before completing Project 3, check with your instructor to determine if you can save your building blocks. In Project 4b, you will be instructed to delete the building blocks you create.

▼ Quick Steps

Save Content to a Text Box Gallery
1. Select content.
2. Click INSERT tab.
3. Click Text Box button.
4. Click *Save Selection to Text Box Gallery.*

Save Content to a Header Gallery
1. Select content.
2. Click INSERT tab.
3. Click Header button.
4. Click *Save Selection to Header Gallery.*

Save Content to a Footer Gallery
1. Select content.
2. Click INSERT tab.
3. Click Footer button.
4. Click *Save Selection to Footer Gallery.*

When selecting content to save as a building block, turn on the display of nonprinting characters by clicking the Show/Hide ¶ button in the Paragraph group on the HOME tab.

Figure 3.7 Create New Building Block Dialog Box

At this dialog box, type the building block name, specify the gallery and category, and enter a description of the building block.

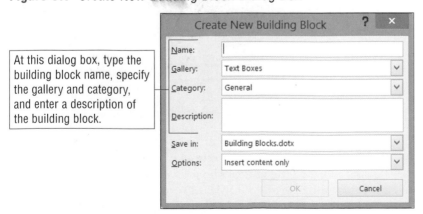

▼ Quick Steps

Save Content to the
AutoText Gallery
1. Select content.
2. Click INSERT tab.
3. Click Quick Parts
   button.
4. Point to AutoText.
5. Click *Save Selection to
   AutoText Gallery*.

Saving Content to the AutoText Gallery

You can save content as a building block in the AutoText gallery. The building block can easily be inserted into a document by clicking the INSERT tab, clicking the Quick Parts button, pointing to *AutoText*, and then clicking the desired AutoText building block at the side menu. To save content in the AutoText gallery, type and format the desired content and then select the content. Click the INSERT tab, click the Quick Parts button, point to *AutoText*, and then click the *Save Selection to AutoText Gallery* option at the side menu. You can also press Alt + F3 to display the dialog box. At the Create New Building Block dialog box, type a name for the building block, type a description if desired, and then click OK.

▼ Quick Steps

Save Content to the
Quick Part Gallery
1. Select content.
2. Click INSERT tab.
3. Click Quick Parts
   button.
4. Click *Save Selection to
   Quick Part Gallery*.

Saving Content to the Quick Part Gallery

Not only can you save content in the AutoText gallery, but you can also save selected content in the Quick Part gallery. To do this, select the desired content, click the INSERT tab, click the Quick Parts button, and then click the *Save Selection to Quick Part Gallery* option at the drop-down gallery. This displays the Create New Building Block dialog box with *Quick Parts* specified in the *Gallery* option box and *Building Blocks.dotx* specified in the *Save in* option box. Type a name for the building block, type a description if desired, and then click OK.

| **Project 3a** | **Saving Content to the Text Box, Footer, AutoText, and Quick Part Galleries** | **Part 1 of 3** |

1. Open **FAVContent.docx**.
2. Save the text box as a building block in the Text Box gallery by completing the following steps:
   a. Select the text box by clicking in the text box and then clicking the text box border.
   b. Click the INSERT tab, click the Text Box button, and then click *Save Selection to Text Box Gallery* at the drop-down list.
   c. At the Create New Building Block dialog box, type your last name followed by **FAVTextBox** and then click OK.

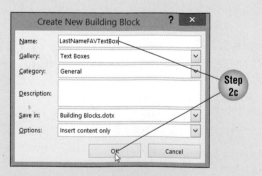

3. Save content as a building block in the Footer gallery by completing the following steps:
   a. Select the text *"Making your vacation dreams a reality"* located below the text box. (Make sure you select the paragraph mark at the end of the text. If necessary, click the Show/Hide ¶ button in the Paragraph group on the HOME tab to display the paragraph mark.)
   b. Click the Footer button in the Header & Footer group on the INSERT tab and then click *Save Selection to Footer Gallery* at the drop-down list.

c. At the Create New Building Block dialog box, type your last name followed by **FAVFooter** and then click OK.

4. Save the company name *Pacific Sky Cruise Lines* and the address below it as a building block in the AutoText gallery by completing the following steps:

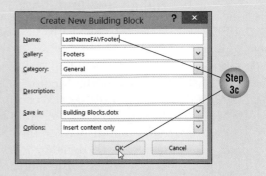

a. Select the company name and address (the two lines below the company name). Make sure you include the paragraph mark at the end of the last line of the address.

b. Click the Quick Parts button in the Text group on the INSERT tab, point to *AutoText,* and then click *Save Selection to AutoText Gallery* at the side menu.

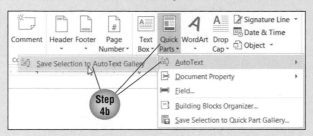

c. At the Create New Building Block dialog box, type your last name and then type **PacificSky**.

d. Click OK to close the dialog box.

5. Type your name and company title and then save the text as a building block in the AutoText gallery by completing the following steps:

a. Move the insertion point to a blank line a double space below the Pacific Sky Cruise Lines address.

b. Type your first and last names and then press the spacebar.

c. Press the Down Arrow key to move the insertion point to the next line and then type **Travel Consultant**. (Do not press the Enter key.)

d. Select your first and last names and the title *Travel Consultant*. (Include the paragraph mark at the end of the title.)

e. Press Alt + F3.

f. At the Create New Building Block dialog box, type your last name and then type **Title**.

g. Click OK to close the dialog box.

6. Save the letterhead as a building block in the Quick Part gallery by completing the following steps:

a. Select the letterhead text (the company name *FAMILY ADVENTURE VACATIONS*, the address below the name, and the paragraph mark at the end of the address and telephone number).

b. Click the Quick Parts button in the Text group on the INSERT tab and then click *Save Selection to Quick Part Gallery* at the drop-down list.

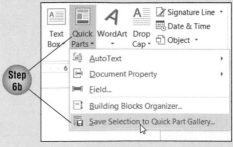

c. At the Create New Building Block dialog box, type your last name and then type **FAV**.

d. Click OK to close the dialog box.

7. Close **FAVContent.docx** without saving it.

Editing Building Block Properties

▼ **Quick Steps**

Edit a Building Block
1. Click INSERT tab.
2. Click Quick Parts button.
3. Click *Building Blocks Organizer*.
4. Click desired building block.
5. Click Edit Properties button.
6. Make desired changes.
7. Click OK.
OR
1. Click desired button.
2. Right-click custom building block.
3. Click *Edit Properties*.
4. Make desired changes.
5. Click OK.

You can make changes to the properties of a building block with options at the Modify Building Block dialog box. This dialog box contains the same options as the Create New Building Block dialog box.

Display the Modify Building Block dialog box by opening the Building Blocks Organizer dialog box, clicking the desired building block in the list box, and then clicking the Edit Properties button. You can also display this dialog box for a building block that displays in the drop-down gallery. To do this, click the Quick Parts button, right-click the building block that displays in the drop-down gallery, and then click *Edit Properties* at the shortcut menu. Make desired changes to the Modify Building Block dialog box and then click OK. At the message asking if you want to redefine the building block entry, click Yes.

You can also display this dialog box for a custom building block in a button drop-down gallery by clicking the button, right-clicking the custom building block, and then clicking the *Edit Properties* option at the shortcut menu. For example, to modify a custom text box building block, click the INSERT tab, click the Text Box button, and then scroll down the drop-down list to display the custom text box building block. Right-click the custom text box and then click *Edit Properties* at the shortcut menu.

Project 3b Editing Building Block Properties   Part 2 of 3

1. At a blank document, click the INSERT tab, click the Quick Parts button in the Text group, and then click *Building Blocks Organizer* at the drop-down list.
2. At the Building Blocks Organizer dialog box, click the *Gallery* column heading to sort the building blocks by gallery. (This displays the AutoText galleries at the beginning of the list.)
3. Scroll to the right in the list box and notice that the building block that displays with your last name followed by *PacificSky* does not contain a description. Edit the building block properties by completing the following steps:
   a. Click the building block in the AutoText gallery that begins with your last name followed by *PacificSky*. (The entire building block name does not display in the list box. To view the entire name, click the building block name in the *Building Blocks* list box and then look at the name that displays below the preview page at the right side of the dialog box.)
   b. Click the Edit Properties button located at the bottom of the dialog box.
   c. At the Modify Building Block dialog box, click in the *Name* text box and then type **Address** at the end of the name.
   d. Click in the *Description* text box and then type **Inserts the Pacific Sky name and address.**
   e. Click OK to close the dialog box.
   f. At the message asking if you want to redefine the building block entry, click Yes.
   g. Close the Building Blocks Organizer dialog box.

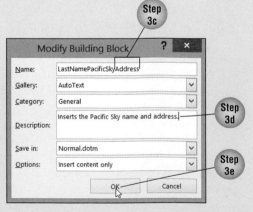

4. Edit the letterhead building block by completing the following steps:

a. Click the Quick Parts button in the Text group on the INSERT tab, right-click the Family Adventure Vacations letterhead building block that begins with your last name, and then click *Edit Properties* at the shortcut menu.

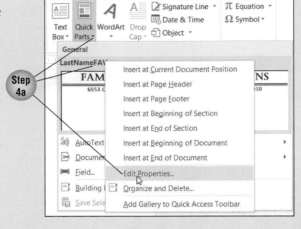

b. At the Modify Building Block dialog box, click in the *Name* text box and then type **Letterhead** at the end of the name.

c. Click in the *Description* text box and then type **Inserts the Family Adventure Vacations letterhead including the company name and address.**

d. Click OK to close the dialog box.

e. At the message asking if you want to redefine the building block entry, click Yes.

Inserting Custom Building Blocks

Any content that you save as a building block can be inserted in a document using the Building Blocks Organizer dialog box. Some content can also be inserted using specific drop-down galleries. For example, insert a custom text box building block by clicking the Text Box button on the INSERT tab and then clicking the desired text box at the drop-down gallery. Insert a custom header at the Header button drop-down gallery, a custom footer at the Footer button drop-down gallery, a custom cover page at the Cover Page button drop-down gallery, and so on.

You can use the button drop-down gallery to specify where you want custom building block content inserted in a document. To do this, display the button drop-down gallery, right-click the custom building block, and then click the desired location at the shortcut menu. For example, if you click the INSERT tab, click the Quick Parts button, and then right-click the *FAVLetterhead* building block (preceded by your last name), a shortcut menu displays, as shown in Figure 3.8.

Figure 3.8 Quick Parts Button Drop-down List Shortcut Menu

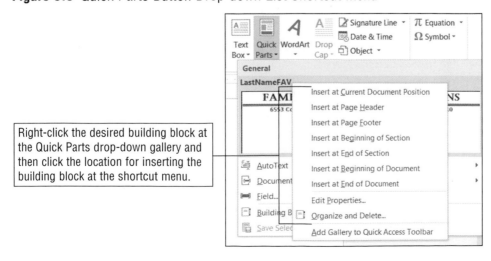

Right-click the desired building block at the Quick Parts drop-down gallery and then click the location for inserting the building block at the shortcut menu.

1. At the blank document, click the *No Spacing* style thumbnail in the Styles group on the HOME tab and then change the font to Candara.
2. Insert the letterhead building block as a header by completing the following steps:
   a. Click the INSERT tab.
   b. Click the Quick Parts button, right-click the Family Adventure Vacations letterhead (preceded by your last name), and then click the *Insert at Page Header* option at the shortcut menu.
3. Press the Enter key twice, type the current date, and then press the Enter key five times.
4. Type **Mrs. Jody Lancaster** and then press the Enter key.
5. Insert the Pacific Sky Cruise Lines name and address building block by clicking the Quick Parts button, pointing to *AutoText*, and then clicking the Pacific Sky Address building block (preceded by your last name) at the side menu.

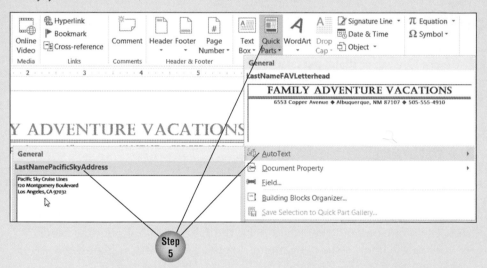

6. Press the Enter key once and then insert a letter document by completing the following steps:
   a. Click the Object button arrow in the Text group on the INSERT tab and then click *Text from File* at the drop-down list.
   b. At the Insert File dialog box, navigate to the WL2C3 folder on your storage medium and then double-click *PacificSkyLetter01.docx*.
7. With the insertion point positioned a double space below the last paragraph of text in the body of the letter, type **Sincerely,** and then press the Enter key four times.
8. Insert your name and title building block by clicking the Quick Parts button, pointing to *AutoText*, and then clicking your name and title at the side menu.
9. Press the Enter key and then type **WL2-C3-P3-PSLtr.docx**.

10. Press the Enter key five times and then insert the custom text box you saved as a building block by completing the following steps:
   a. Click the Text Box button in the Text group on the INSERT tab.
   b. Scroll to the end of the drop-down gallery and then click your custom text box. (Your custom text box will display in the *General* section of the drop-down gallery.)
   c. Click in the document to deselect the text box.

11. Insert the custom footer you created by completing the following steps:
   a. Click the INSERT tab.
   b. Click the Footer button in the Header & Footer group.
   c. Scroll to the end of the drop-down gallery and then click your custom footer. (Your custom footer will display in the *General* section of the drop-down gallery.)
   d. Close the footer pane by double-clicking in the document.

12. Save the completed letter and name it **WL2-C3-P3-PSLtr**.

13. Print and then close **WL2-C3-P3-PSLtr.docx**.

Project 4   Create a Letter Document with Modified Building Blocks   2 Parts

> You will modify your custom building blocks and use them to prepare a business letter. You will then delete your custom building blocks.

Modifying Custom Building Blocks

You can insert a building block in a document, make corrections or changes, and then save the building block with the same name or a different name. Save a building block with the same name when you want to update the building block to reflect any changes. Save the building block with a new name when you want to use an existing building block as the foundation for creating a new building block.

To save a modified building block with the same name, insert the building block into the document and then make the desired modifications. Select the building block data and then specify the gallery. At the Create New Building Block dialog box, type the original name and description and then click OK. At the message asking if you want to redefine the building block entry, click Yes.

1. As a travel consultant at Family Adventure Vacations, you have been given a promotion and are now a senior travel consultant. You decide to modify your name and title building block by completing the following steps:

   a. At a blank document, click the INSERT tab, click the Quick Parts button in the Text group, point to *AutoText*, and then click your name and title building block at the side menu.

   b. Edit your title so it displays as *Senior Travel Consultant*.

   c. Select your name and title, click the Quick Parts button, point to *AutoText*, and then click the *Save Selection to AutoText Gallery* option.

   d. At the Create New Building Block dialog box, type the original name (your last name followed by *Title*).

   e. Click OK.

   f. At the message asking if you want to redefine the building block entry, click Yes.

   g. With your name and title selected, press the Delete key to remove them from the document.

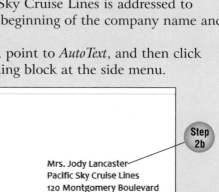

2. Since most of the correspondence you send to Pacific Sky Cruise Lines is addressed to Jody Lancaster, you decide to include her name at the beginning of the company name and address by completing the following steps:

   a. Click the INSERT tab, click the Quick Parts button, point to *AutoText*, and then click the Pacific Sky Cruise Lines name and address building block at the side menu.

   b. Type the name **Mrs. Jody Lancaster** above the name of the cruise line.

   c. Select the name, company name, and address.

   d. Click the Quick Parts button, point to *AutoText*, and then click the *Save Selection to AutoText Gallery* option.

   e. At the Create New Building Block dialog box, type the original name (your last name followed by *PacificSkyAddress*).

   f. Click OK.

   g. At the message asking if you want to redefine the building block entry, click Yes.

3. Close the document without saving it.

4. Create a business letter by completing the following steps:

   a. Press Ctrl + N to display a blank document, click the *No Spacing* style in the Styles group on the HOME tab, and then change the font to Candara.

   b. At the blank document, insert the Family Adventure Vacations letterhead building block as a page header.

   c. Press the Enter key twice, type today's date, and then press the Enter key four times.

   d. Insert the building block that includes Jody Lancaster's name as well as the cruise line name and address.

   e. Press the Enter key and then insert the file named **PacificSkyLetter02.docx** located in the WL2C3 folder on your storage medium. ***Hint: Do this with the Object button in the Text group on the INSERT tab.***

   f. Type **Sincerely,** and then press the Enter key four times.

g. Insert the building block that contains your name and title.

h. Press the Enter key and then type **WL2-C3-P4-PSLtr.docx**.

i. Insert the footer building block you created.

j. Double-click in the document to make the document active.

5. Save the completed letter and name it **WL2-C3-P4-PSLtr**.

6. Print and then close **WL2-C3-P4-PSLtr.docx**.

Deleting Building Blocks

If you no longer use a building block you created, consider deleting it. To do this, display the Building Blocks Organizer dialog box, click the building block you want to delete, and then click the Delete button. At the message asking if you are sure you want to delete the selected building block, click Yes.

Another method for deleting a custom building block is to right-click the building block at the drop-down gallery and then click the *Organize and Delete* option at the shortcut menu. This displays the Building Blocks Organizer dialog box with the building block selected. Click the Delete button that displays at the bottom of the dialog box and then click Yes at the confirmation message box.

▼ Quick Steps

Delete a Building Block
1. Display Building Blocks Organizer dialog box.
2. Click building block.
3. Click Delete button.
4. Click Yes.
5. Close dialog box.
OR
1. Display desired button drop-down gallery.
2. Right-click building block.
3. Click *Organize and Delete* option.
4. Click Delete button.
5. Click Yes.
6. Close dialog box.

Project 4b   **Deleting Building Blocks**   **Part 2 of 2**

1. At a blank document, delete the FAVLetterhead building block (preceded by your last name) by completing the following steps:

a. Click the INSERT tab and then click the Quick Parts button in the Text group.

b. Right-click the FAVLetterhead building block (preceded by your last name) and then click *Organize and Delete* at the shortcut menu.

c. At the Building Blocks Organizer dialog box with the building block selected, click the Delete button.

d. At the message that displays asking if you are sure you want to delete the selected building block, click Yes.

e. Close the Building Blocks Organizer dialog box.

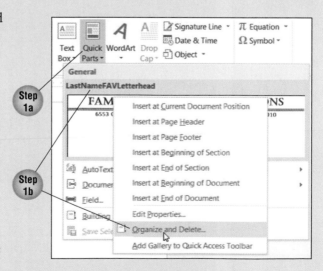

2. Delete the PacificSkyAddress building block (preceded by your last name) by completing the following steps:
   a. Click the Quick Parts button, point to *AutoText*, and then right-click the PacificSkyAddress building block (preceded by your last name).
   b. Click *Organize and Delete* at the shortcut menu.
   c. At the Building Blocks Organizer dialog box with the building block selected, click the Delete button.
   d. At the message asking if you are sure you want to delete the selected building block, click Yes.
   e. Close the Building Blocks Organizer dialog box.
3. Complete steps similar to those in Step 2 to delete the Title building block (preceded by your last name).
4. Delete the custom footer (located in the Footer gallery) by completing the following steps:
   a. Click the Footer button on the INSERT tab.
   b. Scroll down the drop-down gallery to display your custom footer.
   c. Right-click your footer and then click *Organize and Delete* at the shortcut menu.
   d. At the Building Blocks Organizer dialog box with the building block selected, click the Delete button.
   e. At the message asking if you are sure you want to delete the selected building block, click Yes.
   f. Close the Building Blocks Organizer dialog box.
5. Delete the custom text box (located in the Text Box gallery) by completing the following steps:
   a. Click the Text Box button in the Text group on the INSERT tab.
   b. Scroll down the drop-down gallery to display your custom text box.
   c. Right-click your text box and then click *Organize and Delete* at the shortcut menu.
   d. At the Building Blocks Organizer dialog box with the building block selected, click the Delete button.
   e. At the message asking if you are sure you want to delete the selected building block, click Yes.
   f. Close the Building Blocks Organizer dialog box.
6. Close the document without saving it.

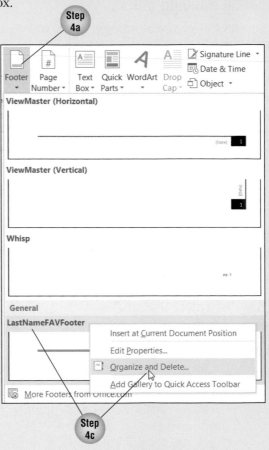

<table>
<tr><td>**Project 5**</td><td>**Insert Document Properties and Fields in an Agreement Document**</td><td>**3 Parts**</td></tr>
</table>

You will open a testing agreement document and then insert and update document properties and fields.

Inserting Document Properties

If you click the Quick Parts button on the INSERT tab and then point to *Document Property* at the drop-down list, a side menu displays with document property options. Click an option at this side menu and a document property placeholder is inserted in the document. Type the desired text in the placeholder.

If you insert a document property placeholder in multiple locations in a document, updating one of the placeholders will automatically update all occurrences of that placeholder in the document. For example, in Project 5a, you will insert a Company document property placeholder in six locations in a document. You will then change the content in the first occurrence of the placeholder and the remaining placeholders will update to reflect the change.

When you click the FILE tab, the Info backstage area displays containing information about the document. Document properties display at the right side of the Info backstage area and include information such as the document size, number of pages, title, and comments. Some of the document properties that you insert with the Quick Parts button will display at the Info backstage area.

<table>
<tr><td>**Project 5a**</td><td>**Inserting Document Property Placeholders**</td><td>**Part 1 of 3**</td></tr>
</table>

1. Open **TestAgrmnt.docx** and then save the document and name it **WL2-C3-P5-TestAgrmnt**.
2. Select the first occurrence of *FP* in the document (located in the first line of text after the title) and then insert a document property placeholder by completing the following steps:
   a. Click the INSERT tab, click the Quick Parts button in the Text group, point to *Document Property*, and then click *Company* at the side menu.
   b. Type **Frontier Productions** in the Company placeholder.
   c. Press the Right Arrow key to move the insertion point outside the Company placeholder.
3. Select each remaining occurrence of *FP* in the document (it appears five more times) and insert the Company document property placeholder. (The company name, *Frontier Productions*, will automatically be inserted in the Company placeholder.)

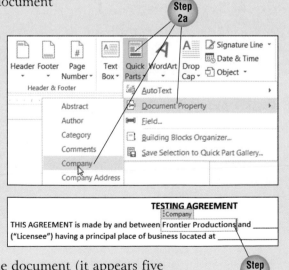

4. Press Ctrl + End to move the insertion point to the end of the document and then insert a Comments document property placeholder by completing the following steps:
   a. Click the Quick Parts button, point to *Document Property*, and then click *Comments* at the side menu.
   b. Type **First Draft** in the Comments placeholder.
   c. Press the Right Arrow key.
   d. Press Shift + Enter.
5. Click the FILE tab, make sure the *Info* option is selected, and then notice that the comment you typed in the Comments document property placeholder displays at the right side of the backstage area. Click the Back button to display the document.
6. Save and then print **WL2-C3-P5-TestAgrmnt.docx**.
7. Click in the first occurrence of the company name *Frontier Productions* and then click the Company placeholder tab. (This selects the Company placeholder.)
8. Type **Frontier Video Productions**.
9. Press the Right Arrow key. (Notice that the other occurrences of the Company document property placeholder are automatically updated to reflect the new name.)
10. Save **WL2-C3-P5-TestAgrmnt.docx**.

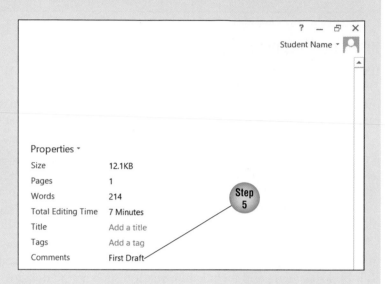

Step 5

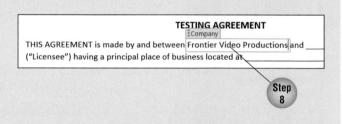

Step 8

Inserting Fields

Quick Steps

Insert a Field
1. Click INSERT tab.
2. Click Quick Parts button.
3. Click *Field* at drop-down list.
4. Click desired field.
5. Click OK.

Fields are placeholders for data that varies and main documents that are merged with data source files. You have inserted fields in a main document, inserted the date and time field, inserted page numbering in a document, and so on. Word provides buttons for many of the types of fields that you may want to insert into a document as well as options at the Field dialog box, shown in Figure 3.9. This dialog box contains a list of all available fields. Just as the Building Blocks Organizer dialog box is a central location for building blocks, the Field dialog box is a central location for fields. To display the Field dialog box, click the INSERT tab, click the Quick Parts button in the Text group, and then click *Field* at the drop-down list. At the Field dialog box, click the desired field in the *Field names* list box and then click OK.

Figure 3.9 Field Dialog Box

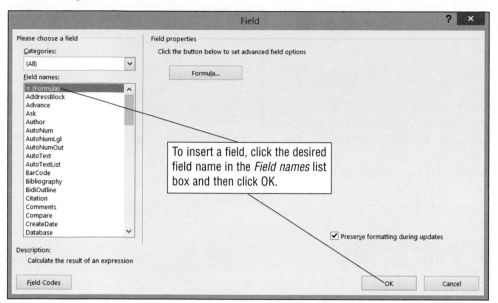

To insert a field, click the desired field name in the *Field names* list box and then click OK.

Project 5b **Inserting Fields**   **Part 2 of 3**

1. With **WL2-C3-P5-TestAgrmnt.docx** open, press Ctrl + End and then insert a field that inserts the current file name by completing the following steps:
   a. Click the INSERT tab, click the Quick Parts button in the Text group, and then click *Field* at the drop-down list.
   b. At the Field dialog box, scroll down the *Field names* list box and then double-click *FileName*. (This inserts the current file name in the document and closes the Field dialog box.)
2. Insert a field that provides the date the file is printed by completing the following steps:
   a. Press Shift + Enter.
   b. Click the Quick Parts button and then click *Field* at the drop-down list.
   c. At the Field dialog box, scroll down the *Field names* list box and then double-click *PrintDate*. (The date and time will display with zeros. The correct date and time will be filled in when you send the document to the printer.)
3. Insert a header and then insert a field in the header by completing the following steps:
   a. Click the Header button in the Header & Footer group and then click *Edit Header* at the drop-down list.
   b. In the header pane, press the Tab key twice. (This moves the insertion point to the right tab at the right margin.)
   c. Click the INSERT tab, click the Quick Parts button in the Text group, and then click *Field* at the drop-down list.

Step 1b

d. At the Field dialog box, scroll down the *Field names* list box and then click once on *Date*.
e. In the *Date formats* list box, click the format that will insert the date in figures followed by the time (hours and minutes).
f. Click OK to close the dialog box.
g. Double-click in the document.
4. Save and then print **WL2-C3-P5-TestAgrmnt.docx**.

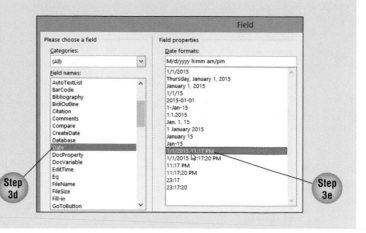

Step 3d

Step 3e

Updating Fields

▼ **Quick Steps**

Update a Field
1. Click field.
2. Click Update tab.
OR
1. Click field.
2. Press F9.
OR
1. Right-click field.
2. Click *Update Field*.

Some fields, such as the date and time, will update automatically when you open the document. For example, open **WL2-C3-P5-TestAgrmnt.docx** and the time in the header is automatically updated. You can manually update a field by clicking the field and then clicking the Update tab (if possible; some fields do not have an Update tab), by clicking the field and then pressing F9, or by right-clicking the field and then clicking *Update Field* at the shortcut menu. You can also update all of the fields in a document (except headers, footers, and text boxes) by pressing Ctrl + A to select the document and then pressing F9.

Project 5c **Updating Fields** Part 3 of 3

1. With **WL2-C3-P5-TestAgrmnt.docx** open, update the time in the header by completing the following steps:
   a. Double-click the header.
   b. Click the date and time and then click the Update tab.
   c. Double-click in the document.
2. Save the document and name it **WL2-C3-P5-FVPAgrmnt**.
3. Press Ctrl + A to select the entire document and then press F9.
4. Save, print, and then close **WL2-C3-P5-FVPAgrmnt.docx**.

Project 6 **Minimize the Ribbon and Customize the Quick Access Toolbar and Ribbon** **3 Parts**

You will open a document and then minimize the ribbon, customize the Quick Access toolbar by adding and removing buttons, and customize the ribbon by inserting a new tab.

Displaying Ribbon Options ■■■■■■■■■■■■■■■■■

Control how much of the ribbon displays on the screen with the Ribbon Display Options button located in the upper right corner of the screen. Click this button and a drop-down list displays with options for hiding the ribbon, showing only the tabs, or showing tabs and commands. You can also turn off the display of the ribbon by clicking the Collapse the Ribbon button located above the vertical scroll bar or by pressing the keyboard shortcut Ctrl + F1. Redisplay the ribbon by double-clicking any tab or by pressing Ctrl + F1.

Ribbon Display Options

Collapse the Ribbon

Customizing the Quick Access Toolbar ■■■■■■■■■■■■■

The Quick Access toolbar contains buttons for some of the most commonly performed tasks. By default, the toolbar contains the Save, Undo, and Redo buttons. You can easily add or remove basic buttons to or from the Quick Access toolbar with options at the Customize Quick Access Toolbar drop-down list. Display this list by clicking the Customize Quick Access Toolbar button that displays at the right side of the toolbar. Insert a check mark before each button that you want displayed on the toolbar and remove the check mark from each button that you do not want to appear.

The Customize Quick Access Toolbar button drop-down list includes an option for moving the location of the Quick Access toolbar. By default, the Quick Access toolbar is positioned above the ribbon. To move the toolbar below the ribbon, click the *Show Below the Ribbon* option at the drop-down list.

You can add buttons or commands from a tab to the Quick Access toolbar. To do this, click the tab, right-click the desired button or command, and then click *Add to Quick Access Toolbar* at the shortcut menu.

▼ **Quick Steps**

Customize the Quick Access Toolbar
1. Click Customize Quick Access Toolbar button.
2. Insert check mark before each desired button.
3. Remove check mark before each undesired button.

Customize Quick Access Toolbar

Project 6a **Changing Ribbon Options and Customizing the Quick Access Toolbar**   Part 1 of 3

1. Open **InterfaceApps.docx** and then save the document and name it **WL2-C3-P6-InterfaceApps**.
2. Collapse the ribbon by clicking the Collapse the Ribbon button that displays above the vertical scroll bar.
3. Double-click a tab to redisplay the ribbon.
4. Hide the ribbon by clicking the Ribbon Display Options button in the upper right corner of the screen and then clicking *Auto-hide Ribbon* at the drop-down list.
5. Redisplay the ribbon by clicking the Ribbon Display Options button and then clicking *Show Tabs and Commands* at the drop-down list.
6. Add the New button to the Quick Access toolbar by clicking the Customize Quick Access Toolbar button that displays at the right of the toolbar and then clicking *New* at the drop-down list.
7. Add the Open button to the Quick Access toolbar by clicking the Customize Quick Access Toolbar button that displays at the right of the toolbar and then clicking *Open* at the drop-down list.
8. Click the New button on the Quick Access toolbar. (This displays a new blank document.)

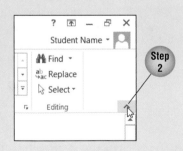

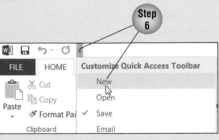

9. Close the document.
10. Click the Open button on the Quick Access toolbar to display the Open backstage area.
11. Press the Esc key to return to the document.
12. Move the Quick Access toolbar by clicking the Customize Quick Access Toolbar button and then clicking *Show Below the Ribbon* at the drop-down list.
13. Move the Quick Access toolbar back to the default position by clicking the Customize Quick Access Toolbar button and then clicking *Show Above the Ribbon* at the drop-down list.
14. Add the Margins and Themes buttons to the Quick Access toolbar by completing the following steps:
    a. Click the PAGE LAYOUT tab.
    b. Right-click the Margins button in the Page Setup group and then click *Add to Quick Access Toolbar* at the shortcut menu.
    c. Click the DESIGN tab.
    d. Right-click the Themes button in the Themes group and then click *Add to Quick Access Toolbar* at the shortcut menu.

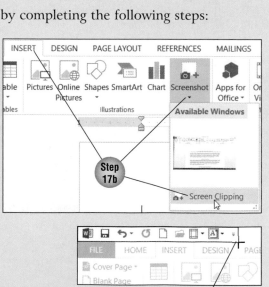

15. Change the top margin by completing the following steps:
    a. Click the Margins button on the Quick Access toolbar and then click *Custom Margins* at the drop-down list.
    b. At the Page Setup dialog box, change the top margin to 1.5 inches and then click OK.
16. Change the theme by clicking the Themes button on the Quick Access toolbar and then clicking *View* at the drop-down list.
17. Create a screenshot of the Quick Access toolbar by completing the following steps:
    a. Click the New button on the Quick Access toolbar. (This displays a new blank document.)
    b. Click the INSERT tab, click the Screenshot button in the Illustrations group, and then click *Screen Clipping* at the drop-down list.
    c. In a few moments, the **WL2-C3-P6-InterfaceApps** document displays in a dimmed manner. Using the mouse, drag down and to the right from the upper left corner of the screen to capture the Quick Access toolbar and then release the mouse button.
    d. With the screenshot image inserted in the document, print the document and then close the document without saving it.
18. Save **WL2-C3-P6-InterfaceApps.docx**.

The Customize Quick Access Toolbar button drop-down list contains 11 of the most commonly used buttons. You can, however, insert many other buttons on the toolbar. To display the buttons available, click the Customize Quick Access Toolbar button and then click *More Commands* at the drop-down list. This displays the Word Options dialog box with *Quick Access Toolbar* selected in the left panel, as shown in Figure 3.10. Another method for displaying this dialog box is to click the FILE tab, click *Options*, and then click *Quick Access Toolbar* in the left panel of the Word Options dialog box.

To reset the Quick Access toolbar to the default (Save, Undo, and Redo buttons), click the Reset button that displays near the bottom of the dialog box. At the message asking if you are sure you want to restore the Quick Access toolbar shared between all documents to its default contents, click Yes.

You can customize the Quick Access toolbar for all documents or for a specific document. To customize the toolbar for the currently open document, display the Word Options dialog box with *Quick Access Toolbar* selected, click the down-pointing arrow at the right side of the *Customize Quick Access Toolbar* option, and then click the *For (document name)* option where the name of the currently open document displays.

▼ **Quick Steps**

Add Buttons to the Quick Access Toolbar from the Word Options Dialog Box
1. Click Customize Quick Access Toolbar button.
2. Click *More Commands* at drop-down list.
3. Click desired command at left list box.
4. Click Add button.
5. Click OK.

Figure 3.10 Word Options Dialog Box with Quick Access Toolbar Selected

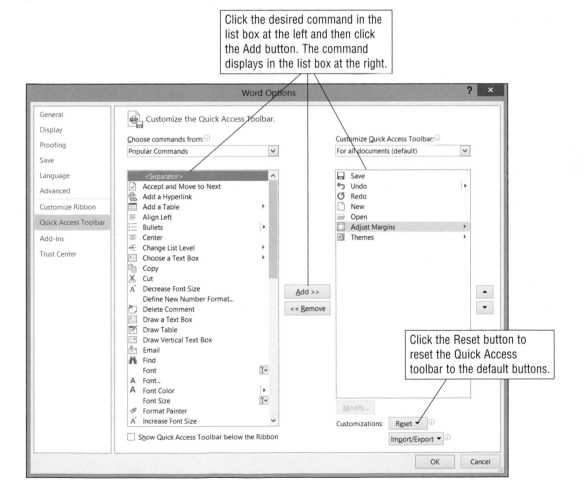

Click the desired command in the list box at the left and then click the Add button. The command displays in the list box at the right.

Click the Reset button to reset the Quick Access toolbar to the default buttons.

The *Choose commands from* option has a default setting of *Popular Commands*. At this setting, the list box below the option displays only a portion of all of the commands available to insert as a button on the Quick Access toolbar. To display all of the commands available, click the down-pointing arrow at the right side of the *Choose commands from* option box and then click *All Commands*. The drop-down list also contains options for specifying commands that are not currently available on the ribbon, as well as commands on the FILE tab and various other tabs.

To add a button, click the desired command in the list box at the left side of the commands list box and then click the Add button that displays between the two list boxes. Continue adding all of the desired buttons and then click OK to close the dialog box.

Project 6b   **Inserting and Removing Buttons from the Quick Access Toolbar**   **Part 2 of 3**

1. With **WL2-C3-P6-InterfaceApps.docx** open, reset the Quick Access toolbar by completing the following steps:
   a. Click the Customize Quick Access Toolbar button that displays at the right of the Quick Access toolbar and then click *More Commands* at the drop-down list.
   b. At the Word Options dialog box, click the Reset button that displays near the bottom of the dialog box and then click *Reset only Quick Access Toolbar* at the drop-down list.

   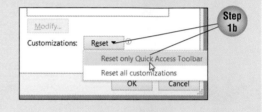

   c. At the message asking if you are sure you want to restore the Quick Access toolbar shared between all documents to its default contents, click Yes.
   d. Click OK to close the dialog box.
2. Insert buttons on the Quick Access toolbar for the currently open document by completing the following steps:
   a. Click the Customize Quick Access Toolbar button and then click *More Commands*.
   b. At the Word Options dialog box, click the down-pointing arrow at the right of the *Customize Quick Access Toolbar* option and then click *For WL2-C3-P6-InterfaceApps.docx* at the drop-down list.

   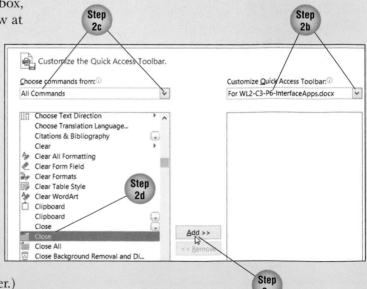

   c. Click the down-pointing arrow at the right of the *Choose commands from* option box and then click *All Commands*.
   d. Scroll down the list box and then click the second *Close* command (the option preceded by a Close icon). (Commands are listed in alphabetical order.)
   e. Click the Add button that displays between the two list boxes.
   f. Scroll up the list box and then click *Add a Footer*.

g. Click the Add button.

h. Click OK to close the dialog box.

i. Check the Quick Access toolbar and notice that the two buttons now display along with the default buttons.

3. Insert a footer by completing the following steps:

   a. Click the Footer button on the Quick Access toolbar.

   b. Click *Integral* at the drop-down list.

   c. Select the name that displays in the footer and then type your first and last names.

   d. Double-click in the document.

4. Save and then print **WL2-C3-P6-InterfaceApps.docx**.

5. Close the document by clicking the Close button on the Quick Access toolbar.

Customizing the Ribbon ■■■■■■■■■■■■■■■■■■■■■■■■■

In addition to customizing the Quick Access toolbar, you can customize the ribbon by creating a new tab and inserting groups with buttons on the new tab. To customize the ribbon, click the FILE tab and then click *Options*. At the Word Options dialog box, click *Customize Ribbon* in the left panel and the dialog box displays as shown in Figure 3.11.

Figure 3.11 Word Options Dialog Box with Customize Ribbon Selected

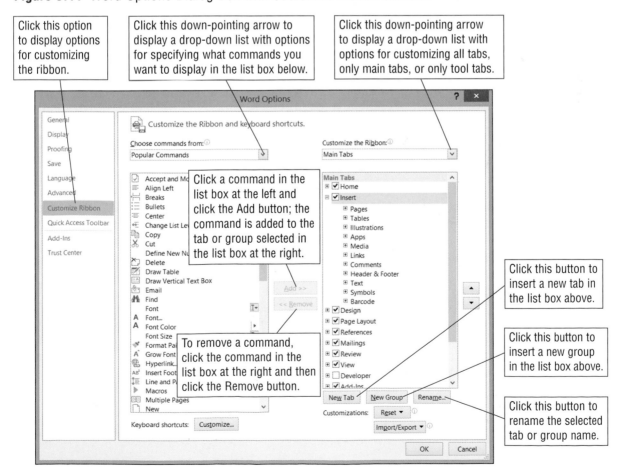

Click this option to display options for customizing the ribbon.

Click this down-pointing arrow to display a drop-down list with options for specifying what commands you want to display in the list box below.

Click this down-pointing arrow to display a drop-down list with options for customizing all tabs, only main tabs, or only tool tabs.

Click a command in the list box at the left and click the Add button; the command is added to the tab or group selected in the list box at the right.

To remove a command, click the command in the list box at the right and then click the Remove button.

Click this button to insert a new tab in the list box above.

Click this button to insert a new group in the list box above.

Click this button to rename the selected tab or group name.

At the *Choose commands from* drop-down list, you can choose to display only popular commands, which is the default, or you can choose to display all commands, commands not on the ribbon, and all tabs or commands on the FILE tab, main tabs, tool tabs, and custom tabs and groups. The commands in the list box vary depending on the option you select at the *Choose commands from* option drop-down list. Click the down-pointing arrow at the right of the Customize the Ribbon option and a drop-down list displays with options for customizing all of the tabs, only the main tabs, or only tool tabs. By default, *Main Tabs* is selected.

Creating a New Tab

Add a command to an existing tab or create a new tab and then add commands in groups on the new tab. To create a new tab, click the tab name in the list box at the right side of the dialog box that you want to precede the new tab and then click the New Tab button that displays at the bottom of the list box. This inserts a new tab in the list box along with a new group below the new tab (see Figure 3.11). Move the new tab up or down in the list box by clicking the new tab and then clicking the Move Up or Move Down button. Both buttons display at the right of the list box.

Renaming a Tab and Group

Rename a tab by clicking the tab in the list box and then clicking the Rename button that displays below the list box at the right. At the Rename dialog box, type the desired name for the tab and then click OK. You can also display the Rename dialog box by right-clicking the tab name and then clicking *Rename* at the shortcut menu.

Complete similar steps to rename the group. When you click the group name and then click the Rename button (or right-click the group name and then click *Rename* at the shortcut menu), a Rename dialog box displays, containing a variety of symbols. Use the symbols to identify new buttons in the group, rather than the group name.

Adding Commands to a Tab Group

Add commands to a tab by clicking the group name on the tab, clicking the desired command in the list box at the left, and then clicking the Add button that displays between the two list boxes. Remove commands in a similar manner. Click the command you want to remove from the tab group and then click the Remove button that displays between the two list boxes.

Resetting the Ribbon

If you have customized the ribbon by adding tabs and groups, you can remove all of the customizations and return to the original ribbon by clicking the Reset button that displays below the list box at the right side of the dialog box. When you click the Reset button, a drop-down list displays with two options: *Reset only selected Ribbon tab* and *Reset all customizations*. If you click the *Reset all customizations* option, a message displays asking if you want to delete all ribbon and Quick Access toolbar customizations for this program. At this message, click Yes to reset all of the customizations to the ribbon.

1. Open **WL2-C3-P6-InterfaceApps.docx** and then add a new tab and group by completing the following steps:
   a. Click the FILE tab and then click *Options*.
   b. At the Word Options dialog box, click *Customize Ribbon* in the left panel.
   c. Click *View* that displays in the list box at the right side of the dialog box. (Do not click the check box before *View*.)
   d. Click the New Tab button located below the list box. (This inserts a new tab below *View*.)

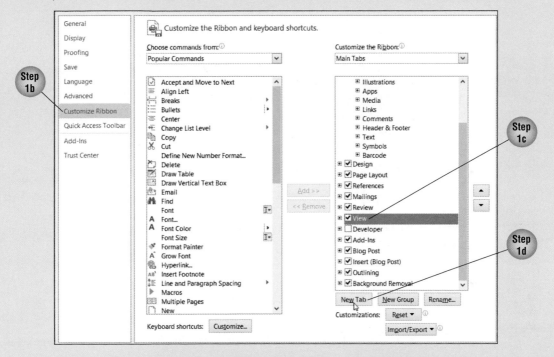

2. Rename the tab and group by completing the following steps:
   a. Click *New Tab (Custom)*. (Do not click the check box.)
   b. Click the Rename button that displays below the list box.
   c. At the Rename dialog box, type your initials and then click OK.
   d. Click *New Group (Custom)* that displays below your initials tab.
   e. Click the Rename button.
   f. At the Rename dialog box, type **IP Movement** and then click OK. (Use *IP* to stand for *insertion point*.)

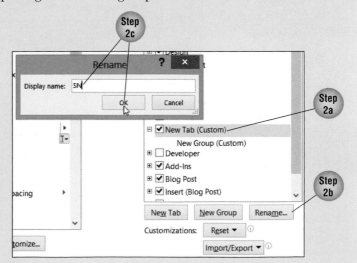

3. Add buttons to the IP Movement (Custom) group by completing the following steps:

   a. Click *IP Movement (Custom)* in the list box at the right side.

   b. Click the down-pointing arrow at the right of the *Choose commands from* option box and then click *Commands Not in the Ribbon* at the drop-down list.

   c. Scroll down the list box at the left side of the dialog box (the list displays alphabetically), click the *End of Document* command, and then click the Add button that displays between the two list boxes. (This inserts the command below the *IP Movement (Custom)* group name.)

   d. With the *End of Line* command selected in the list box at the left side of the dialog box, click the Add button.

   e. Scroll down the list box at the left side of the dialog box, click the *Page Down* command, and then click the Add button.

   f. Click the *Page Up* command in the list box and then click the Add button.

   g. Scroll down the list box, click the *Start of Document* command, and then click the Add button.

   h. With the *Start of Line* command selected in the list box, click the Add button.

4. Click OK to close the Word Options dialog box.

5. Move the insertion point in the document by completing the following steps:

   a. Click the tab containing your initials.

   b. Click the End of Document button in the IP Movement group on the tab.

   c. Click the Start of Document button in the IP Movement group.

   d. Click the End of Line button.

   e. Click the Start of Line button.

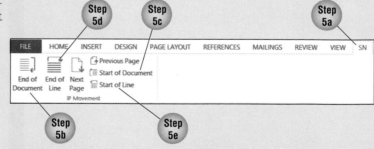

6. Create a screenshot of the ribbon with the tab containing your initials the active tab by completing the following steps:

   a. Make sure your tab is active and then press Ctrl + N to display a new blank document.

   b. Click the INSERT tab, click the Screenshot button in the Illustrations group, and then click *Screen Clipping* at the drop-down list.

   c. In a few moments, the **WL2-C3-P6-InterfaceApps.docx** document displays in a dimmed manner. Using the mouse, drag from the upper left corner of the screen down and to the right to capture the Quick Access toolbar and the buttons on the tab containing your initials, and then release the mouse button.

   d. With the screenshot image inserted in the document, print the document and then close the document without saving it.

7. Reset the Quick Access toolbar and ribbon by completing the following steps:
   a. Click the FILE tab and then click *Options*.
   b. At the Word Options dialog box, click *Customize Ribbon* in the left panel.
   c. Click the Reset button that displays below the list box at the right side of the dialog box and then click *Reset all customizations* at the drop-down list.

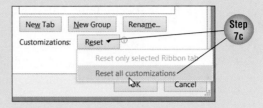

   d. At the message asking if you want to delete all ribbon and Quick Access toolbar customizations, click Yes.
   e. Click OK to close the Word Options dialog box. (The buttons you added to the Quick Access toolbar will display while this document is open.)
8. Save and then close **WL2-C3-P6-InterfaceApps.docx**.

Chapter Summary

- You can add words to AutoCorrect during a spelling check and at the AutoCorrect dialog box. Display the AutoCorrect dialog box by clicking the FILE tab, clicking *Options*, clicking *Proofing*, and then clicking the AutoCorrect Options button.

- Display the AutoCorrect Exceptions dialog box by clicking the Exceptions button at the AutoCorrect dialog box with the AutoCorrect tab selected. Specify AutoCorrect exceptions at this dialog box.

- Use the AutoCorrect Options button that displays when you hover the mouse over corrected text to change corrected text back to the original spelling, stop automatically correcting specific text, or display the AutoCorrect dialog box.

- When typing text, control what Word formats automatically with options at the AutoCorrect dialog box with the AutoFormat As You Type tab selected.

- Word provides a number of predesigned building blocks that you can use to help build a document.

- Insert building blocks at the Building Blocks Organizer dialog box. Display the dialog box by clicking the Quick Parts button on the INSERT tab and then clicking *Building Blocks Organizer* at the drop-down list. Sort building blocks in the dialog box by clicking the desired column heading.

- You can save content as building blocks to specific galleries, such as the Text Box, Header, Footer, and Cover Page galleries.

- Save content to the AutoText gallery by selecting the content, clicking the INSERT tab, clicking the Quick Parts button, pointing to *AutoText*, and then clicking the *Save Selection to AutoText Gallery* option.

- Save content to the Quick Part gallery by selecting the content, clicking the INSERT tab, clicking the Quick Parts button, and then clicking *Save Selection to Quick Part Gallery* at the drop-down gallery.

- Insert a building block at the Building Blocks Organizer dialog box by displaying the dialog box, clicking the desired building block in the *Building blocks* list box, and then clicking the Insert button.

- Insert a custom building block from a gallery using a button by clicking the specific button (such as the Text Box, Header, Footer, or Cover Page button), scrolling down the drop-down gallery, and then clicking the custom building block that displays near the end of the gallery.

- Insert a custom building block saved to the AutoText gallery by clicking the INSERT tab, clicking the Quick Parts button, pointing to *AutoText*, and then clicking the desired building block at the side menu.

- Insert a custom building block saved to the Quick Part gallery by clicking the INSERT tab, clicking the Quick Parts button, and then clicking the desired building block at the drop-down list.

- Edit a building block with options at the Modify Building Block dialog box. Display this dialog box by displaying the Building Blocks Organizer dialog box, clicking the desired building block, and then clicking the Edit Properties button.

- Delete a building block at the Building Blocks Organizer dialog box by clicking the building block, clicking the Delete button, and then clicking Yes at the confirmation question.

- Insert a document property placeholder by clicking the INSERT tab, clicking the Quick Parts button, pointing to *Document Property*, and then clicking the desired option at the side menu.

- Fields are placeholders for data and can be inserted with options at the Field dialog box, which is a central location for all of the fields provided by Word. Display the Field dialog box by clicking the Quick Parts button and then clicking *Field*.

- Some fields in a document update automatically when you open the document or you can manually update a field by clicking the field and then clicking the Update tab, pressing F9, or right-clicking the field and then clicking *Update Field*.

- Control how much of the ribbon displays with options from the Ribbon Display Options button drop-down list. Click the Collapse the Ribbon button or press Ctrl + F1 to collapse/display the ribbon.

- Customize the Quick Access toolbar with options from the Customize Quick Access Toolbar button drop-down list and options at the Word Options dialog box with the *Quick Access Toolbar* selected.

- Add a button or command to the Quick Access toolbar by right-clicking the desired button or command and then clicking *Add to Quick Access Toolbar* at the shortcut menu.

- With options at the Word Options dialog box with *Quick Access Toolbar* selected, you can reset the Quick Access toolbar and display all of the options and buttons available for adding to the Quick Access toolbar. You can customize the Quick Access toolbar for all documents or for a specific document.

- With options at the Word Options dialog box with *Customize Ribbon* selected, you can rename a tab or group, add a command tab to a new group, remove a command from a tab group, and reset the ribbon.

Commands Review

FEATURE	RIBBON TAB, GROUP/OPTION	BUTTON, OPTION	KEYBOARD SHORTCUT
AutoCorrect dialog box	FILE, *Options*	*Proofing*, AutoCorrect Options	
Building Blocks Organizer dialog box	INSERT, Text	, *Building Blocks Organizer*	
Create New Building Block dialog box	INSERT, Text	, *Save Selection to Quick Part Gallery*	Alt + F3
collapse/display ribbon		^	Ctrl + F1
Document Property side menu	INSERT, Text	, *Document Property*	
Field dialog box	INSERT, Text	, *Field*	
Ribbon Display Options button			
Word Options dialog box	FILE, *Options*		

Concepts Check   Test Your Knowledge

Completion: In the space provided at the right, indicate the correct term, symbol, or command.

1. This feature corrects certain words automatically as you type them. _____

2. Use this button, which displays when you hover the mouse pointer over corrected text, to change corrected text back to the original spelling. _____

3. The Quick Parts button is located on this tab. _____

4. This dialog box is a central location where you can view all of the predesigned building blocks. _____

5. To save a text box as a building block, select the text box, click the INSERT tab, click the Text Box button, and then click this option at the drop-down gallery. _____

6. With the Quick Parts button, you can save a custom building block in the Quick Part gallery or this gallery. _____

7. Delete a building block at this dialog box. _____

8. Complete these steps to display the Field dialog box. _____

9. Manually update a field by pressing this key on the keyboard.

_____

10. Collapse the ribbon by clicking the Collapse the Ribbon button or using this keyboard shortcut.

_____

11. Add or remove basic buttons to or from the Quick Access toolbar with options at this drop-down list.

_____

12. This is the default setting for the *Choose commands from* option at the Word Options dialog box with *Quick Access Toolbar* selected in the left panel.

_____

13. Add a new tab at the Word Options dialog box with this option selected in the left panel.

_____

Skills Check   Assess Your Performance

Assessment

1   **FORMAT A HEALTH PLAN DOCUMENT WITH AUTOCORRECT AND BUILDING BLOCKS**

1. Open **KLHPlan.docx** and then save the document and name it **WL2-C3-A1-KLHPlan**.
2. Add the following text to AutoCorrect:
   a. Insert *kl* in the *Replace* text box and insert *Key Life Health Plan* in the *With* text box.
   b. Insert *m* in the *Replace* text box and insert *medical* in the *With* text box.
3. With the insertion point positioned at the beginning of the document, type the text shown in Figure 3.12.
4. Make the following changes to the document:
   a. Apply the Heading 1 style to the title *Key Life Health Plan*.
   b. Apply the Heading 2 style to the four headings in the document.
   c. Apply the Lines (Simple) style set.
   d. Apply the Frame theme.
5. Insert the Ion (Dark) header building block.
6. Insert the Ion (Dark) footer building block. Click the *[DOCUMENT TITLE]* placeholder and then type **key life health plan**. Select the name that displays at the right side of the footer and then type your first and last names.
7. Decrease the value in the *Footer from Bottom* measurement box to *0.3"*.
8. Double-click in the document.
9. Press Ctrl + End to move the insertion point to the end of the document, press the Enter key, and then insert the *FileName* field.
10. Press Shift + Enter and then insert the *PrintDate* field.
11. Save and then print **WL2-C3-A1-KLHPlan.docx**.
12. Delete the two entries you made at the AutoCorrect dialog box.
13. Close **WL2-C3-A1-KLHPlan.docx**.

Figure 3.12 Assessment 1

kl

How the Plan Works

When you enroll in the kl, you and each eligible family member select a plan option. A kl
option includes a main m clinic, any affiliated satellite clinics, and designated hospitals.
Family members may choose different m plan options and can easily change options.

Some m plan options do not require you to choose a primary care physician. This means
a member may self-refer for specialty care within that m plan option. However, members
are encouraged to establish an ongoing relationship with a primary care physician and
develop a valuable partnership in the management of their m care.

kl provides coverage for emergency m services outside the service area. If the m
emergency is not life threatening, call your primary care physician to arrange for care
before going to an emergency facility. If you have a life-threatening emergency, go directly
to the nearest appropriate facility. Any follow-up care to emergency m services must be
coordinated within your plan option.

Assessment

2 FORMAT A PROPERTY PROTECTION ISSUES REPORT

 Grade It

1. Open **PropProIssues.docx** and then save the document
   and name it **WL2-C3-A2-PropProIssues**.
2. Make the following changes to the document:
   a. Select the entire document and then change the spacing after paragraphs to
      6 points.
   b. Press Ctrl + Home and then press Ctrl + Enter to insert a hard page break.
   c. Apply the Heading 1 style to the two titles (*PROPERTY PROTECTION
      ISSUES* and *REFERENCES*).
   d. Apply the Heading 2 style to the three headings in the document.
   e. Apply the Banded theme.
   f. Apply the Paper theme colors.
   g. Format the paragraphs of text below the title *REFERENCES* using a
      hanging indent.
   h. Indent the second paragraph in the *Fair Use* section 0.5 inch from the left
      and right margins.
3. Press Ctrl + Home to move the insertion point to the beginning of the document
   and then insert the Automatic Table 2 table of contents building block.
4. Make sure the Heading 1 style is applied to the title *TABLE OF CONTENTS*.
5. Insert the Banded header building block, click the [DOCUMENT TITLE]
   placeholder, and then type **property protection issues**.
6. Insert the Banded footer building block.
7. Double-click in the document.

8. Press Ctrl + Home and then insert the Banded cover page building block with the following specifications:
   a. Select the title *PROPERTY PROTECTION ISSUES* and then change the font size to 28 points.
   b. Select the name that displays near the bottom of the cover page above the [COMPANY NAME] placeholder and then type your first and last names.
   c. Click the *[COMPANY NAME]* placeholder and then type **woodland legal services**.
   d. Select and then delete the [Company address] placeholder.
9. Press Ctrl + End to move the insertion point to the end of the document, press the Enter key, and then insert a field that will insert the file name.
10. Press Shift + Enter and then insert a field that will insert the current date and time.
11. Save, print, and then close **WL2-C3-A2-PropProIssues.docx**.

Assessment

3 CREATE BUILDING BLOCKS AND PREPARE AN AGREEMENT

1. Open **WLSCSFooter.docx**.
2. Select the entire document, save the selected text in a custom building block in the Footer gallery, and name the building block with your initials followed by *WLSCSFooter*. **Hint: Use the Footer button to save the content to the Footer gallery.**
3. Close **WLSCSFooter.docx**.
4. Open **WLSCSHeading.docx**.
5. Select the entire document, save the selected text in a custom building block in the Quick Part gallery, and name the building block with your initials followed by *WLSCSHeading*.
6. Close **WLSCSHeading.docx**.
7. At a blank document, type the text shown in Figure 3.13. (Make sure you apply bold formatting to *Fees*).
8. Select the entire document, save the selected text in a custom building block in the AutoText gallery, and name the building block with your initials followed by *WLSCSFeesPara*.
9. Close the document without saving it.
10. At a blank document, create an agreement with the following specifications:
    a. Insert the custom building block in the Quick Part gallery that is named with your initials followed by *WLSCSHeading*.

Figure 3.13 Assessment 3

Fees: My hourly rate is $350, billed in one-sixth (1/6th) of an hour increments. All time spent on work performed, including meetings, telephone calls, correspondences, and emails, will be billed at the hourly rate set forth in this paragraph. Additional expenses such as out-of-pocket expenses for postage, courier fees, photocopying charges, long distance telephone charges, and search fees, will be charged at the hourly rate set forth in this paragraph.

b. Insert the custom building block in the AutoText gallery that is named with your initials followed by *WLSCSFeesPara*.

c. Insert the file named **WLSRepAgrmnt.docx** located in the WL2C3 folder on your storage medium. ***Hint: Use the* Text from File *option from the Object button arrow drop-down list.***

d. Insert the footer custom building block that is named with your initials followed by *WLSCSFooter*. ***Hint: Do this with the Footer button.***

11. Save the completed agreement and name it **WL2-C3-A3-WLSRepAgrmnt**.

12. Print and then close **WL2-C3-A3-WLSRepAgrmnt.docx**.

13. Press Ctrl + N to open a blank document.

14. Click the INSERT tab, click the Quick Parts button, and then point to *AutoText*.

15. Press the Print Screen button on your keyboard and then click in the document.

16. At the blank document, click the Paste button.

17. Print the document and then close it without saving it.

Assessment

4 CREATE A CUSTOM TAB AND GROUP

1. At a blank screen, create a new tab with the following specifications:
   a. Insert the new tab after the *View* tab option in the list box at the Word Options dialog box with *Customize Ribbon* selected.
   b. Rename the tab *C3* followed by your initials.
   c. Rename the custom group below your new tab as *File Management*.
   d. Change the *Choose commands from* option to *File Tab*.
   e. From the list box at the left side of the dialog box, add the following commands to the File Management group on the new tab: *Close, Open, Quick Print, Save As*, and *Save As Other Format*.
   f. Change the *Choose commands from* option to *Popular Commands*.
   g. From the list box at the left side of the dialog box, add the *New* command.
   h. Click OK to close the Word Options dialog box.

2. At the blank screen, click your new tab (the one that begins with *C3* and is followed by your initials).

3. Click the Open button in the File Management group on your new tab.

4. At the Open backstage area, click **WL2-C3-A3-WLSRepAgrmnt.docx** that displays at the beginning of the Recent Documents list.

5. Use the Save As button in the File Management group on the new tab to save the document and name it **WL2-C3-A4-WLSRepAgrmnt**.

6. Save the document in the Word 97-2003 format by completing the following steps:
   a. Make sure the new tab is active.
   b. Click the Save As button arrow. (This is the second Save As button in the File Management group on your new tab.)
   c. Click *Word 97-2003 Document* at the drop-down list.
   d. At the Save As dialog box with *Word 97-2003 Document (*.doc)* selected in the *Save as type* option box, type **WL2-C3-A4-WLSRA-Word97-2003Format** and then press the Enter key.
   e. Close the document by clicking the Close button in the File Management group on the new tab.

7. Click the Open button on the new tab and then click *WL2-C3-A4-WLSRepAgrmnt.docx* in the Recent Documents list.
8. Send the document to the printer by clicking the Quick Print button on the new tab.
9. Close the document by clicking the Close button on the new tab.
10. Click the New Blank Document button on the new tab.
11. At the blank document, click the New Blank Document button on the new tab. (You now have two blank documents open.)
12. Click the INSERT tab, click the Screenshot button, and then click *Screen Clipping* at the drop-down list.
13. When the first blank document displays in a dimmed manner, use the mouse to select the Quick Access toolbar and ribbon, including the new tab with the File Management group buttons you created.
14. Print the document containing the screen clipping and then close the document without saving it.
15. Display the Word Options dialog box with *Customize Ribbon* selected and then reset the ribbon back to the default.

Assessment

5 INSERT AN EQUATION BUILDING BLOCK

1. The Building Blocks Organizer dialog box contains a number of predesigned equations that you can insert in a document. At a blank document, display the Building Blocks Organizer dialog box and then insert one of the predesigned equations.
2. Select the equation and then click the EQUATION TOOLS DESIGN tab. Notice the groups of commands available for editing an equation.
3. Type the steps you followed to insert the equation and type a list of the groups available on the EQUATION TOOLS DESIGN tab and then delete the equation.
4. Save the document and name it **WL2-C3-A5-Equations**. Print and then close the document.

Visual Benchmark   Demonstrate Your Proficiency

CREATE AN AGREEMENT WITH BUILDING BLOCKS AND AUTOCORRECT TEXT

1. At a blank document, create the document shown in Figure 3.14 with the following specifications:
   a. Create AutoCorrect entries for *Woodland Legal Services* (use wls) and *Till-Harris Management* (use thm). Use these AutoCorrect entries when typing the text in Figure 3.14.
   b. Insert the WLSCSHeading building block (the one preceded by your initials) at the beginning of the document and insert the WLSCSFooter as a footer (the one preceded by your initials).
   c. Justify the six paragraphs of text in the document and then center-align the signature lines.
2. Save the completed document and name it **WL2-C3-VB-THMAgrmnt**.
3. Print and then close **WL2-C3-VB-THMAgrmnt.docx**.
4. Open a blank document, display the AutoCorrect dialog box, and then display the *thm* entry. Press the Alt + Print Screen button, close the dialog box, close the Word Options dialog box, and then click the Paste button at the blank document. (This inserts an image of the AutoCorrect dialog box. Alt + Print Screen makes a capture of the active dialog box.)
5. Press Ctrl + End and then press the Enter key.
6. Complete steps similar to those in Step 4 to make a screen capture of the AutoCorrect dialog box with the *wls* entry displayed and insert the screen capture image in the document (below the first screen capture image).
7. Make sure both images display on one page. Print and then close the document without saving it.
8. At a blank document, delete the *wls* and *thm* AutoCorrect entries and custom building blocks you created in Assessment 3.

Figure 3.14 Visual Benchmark

REPRESENTATION AGREEMENT

Carlos Sawyer, Attorney at Law

This agreement is made between Carlos Sawyer of Woodland Legal Services, hereafter referred to as "Woodland Legal Services" and Till-Harris Management for legal services to be provided by Woodland Legal Services.

Legal Representation: Woodland Legal Services will perform the legal services required by Till-Harris Management, keep Till-Harris Management informed of progress and developments, and respond promptly to Till-Harris Management's inquiries and communications.

Attorney's Fees and Costs: Till-Harris Management will pay Woodland Legal Services for attorney's fees for legal services provided under this agreement at the hourly rate of the individuals providing the services. Under this agreement, Till-Harris Management will pay all costs incurred by Woodland Legal Services for representation of Till-Harris Management. Costs will be advanced by Woodland Legal Services and then billed to Till-Harris Management unless the costs can be met from deposits.

Deposit for Fees: Till-Harris Management will pay to Woodland Legal Services an initial deposit of $5,000, to be received by Woodland Legal Services on or before November 1, 2015. Twenty percent of the deposit is nonrefundable and will be applied against attorney's fees. The refundable portion will be deposited by Woodland Legal Services in an interest-bearing trust account. Till-Harris Management authorizes Woodland Legal Services to withdraw the principal from the trust account to pay attorney's fees in excess of the nonrefundable portion.

Statement and Payments: Woodland Legal Services will send Till-Harris Management monthly statements indicating attorney's fees and costs incurred, amounts applied from deposits, and current balance owed. If no attorney's fees or costs are incurred for a particular month, the statement may be held and combined with that for the following month. Any balance will be paid in full within 30 days after the statement is mailed.

Effective Date of Agreement: The effective date of this agreement will be the date when it is executed by both parties.

Client: _____ Date: _____

Attorney: _____ Date: _____

7110 FIFTH STREET ◆ SUITE 200 ◆ OMAHA NE 68207 ◆ 402-555-7110

Case Study   Apply Your Skills

You have been hired as the office manager for Highland Construction Company. The address of the company is 9025 Palmer Park Boulevard, Colorado Springs, CO 80904, and the telephone number is (719) 555-4575. You are responsible for designing business documents that have a consistent visual style and formatting. You decide that your first task is to create a letterhead document. Create a letterhead for Highland Construction Company. Consider including the company name, address, and telephone number, along with a clip art image and/or any other elements to add visual interest to the letterhead. Save the completed letterhead document and name it **WL2-C3-CS-HCCLetterhead**. Using the text and elements in the letterhead document, create a building block and name it with your initials followed by *HCCLetterhead*. Save, print, and then close **WL2-C3-CS-HCCLetterhead.docx**. Create the following additional building blocks for your company. (Use your initials in the names of the building blocks; you decide on the names.)

- Create a building block footer that contains a border line (in a color matching the colors in the letterhead) and the company slogan:
  Building Dreams Since 1985
- Create the following complimentary close building block:
  Sincerely,

  Your Name
  Office Manager
- Create the following company name and address building block:
  Mr. Eric Rashad
  Roswell Industries
  1020 Wasatch Street
  Colorado Springs, CO 80902
- Create the following company name and address building block:
  Ms. Claudia Sanborn
  S & S Supplies
  537 Constitution Avenue
  Colorado Springs, CO 80911

At a blank document, create a letter to Eric Rashad by inserting the company letterhead (the building block that begins with your initials followed by *HCCLetterhead*). Type today's date, press the Enter key twice, and then insert the Eric Rashad building block. Type an appropriate salutation (such as *Dear Mr. Rashad:*), insert the file named **HCCLetter.docx**, and then insert your complimentary close building block. Finally, insert the footer building block you created for the company. Check the letter and make modifcations to spacing as needed. Save the letter and name it **WL2-C3-CS-RashadLtr**. Print and then close the letter. Complete similar steps to create a letter to Claudia Sanborn. Save the completed letter and name it **WL2-C3-CS-SanbornLtr**. Print and then close the letter.

Part 3

At a blank document, insert the company letterhead building block you created in Part 1, type the title *Company Services*, and then insert a SmartArt graphic of your choosing that contains the following text:

> Residential Construction
> Commercial Construction
> Design Consultation
> Site Preparation

Apply a heading style to the *Company Services* title, insert the company footer building block, and then save the document and name it **WL2-C3-CS-CoServices**. Print and then close the document.

Part 4

Create an AutoCorrect entry that will replace *hcc* with *Highland Construction Company* and *bca* with *Building Construction Agreement*. Open **HCCAgrmnt.docx** and then type the text shown in Figure 3.15 at the beginning of the document. Apply or insert the following to the document:

- Insert at the end of the document a date printed field and a file name field.
- Insert your footer building block as a footer.
- Insert a cover page of your choosing.

Add or apply any other enhancements to improve the appearance of the document and then save the document and name it **WL2-C3-CS-HCCAgrmnt**. Print and then close the document.

Part 5

Make sure you are connected to the Internet and then display the New backstage area. Choose a business card template, download the template, and then create business cards for Highland Construction Company. Include your name and title (Office Manager) on the cards. Save the completed business cards document and name it **WL2-C3-CS-HCCBusCards**. Print and then close the document. Delete the building blocks you created and then delete the AutoCorrect entries *hcc* and *bca*.

Figure 3.15 Case Study, Part 4

bca

THIS bca made this _____day of _____, 2015 by and between hcc and _____, hereinafter referred to as "owner," for the considerations hereinafter named, hcc and owner agree as follows:

Financing Arrangements: The owner will obtain a construction loan to finance construction under this bca. If adequate financing has not been arranged within 30 days of the date of this bca, or the owner cannot provide evidence to hcc of other financial ability to pay the full amount, then hcc may treat this bca as null and void, and retain the down payment made on the execution of this bca.

WORD
MICROSOFT®

CHAPTER 4

Customizing Themes, Creating Macros, and Navigating in a Document

PERFORMANCE OBJECTIVES

Upon successful completion of Chapter 4, you will be able to:

- Create custom theme colors, theme fonts, and theme effects
- Save a custom theme
- Apply, edit, and delete custom themes
- Reset to the template theme
- Apply styles and modify existing styles
- Record, run, and delete macros
- Assign a macro to a keyboard command
- Manage macro security
- Navigate in a document using the Navigation pane, thumbnails, bookmarks, hyperlinks, and cross-references
- Insert hyperlinks to a location in the same document, a different document, a file in another program, and an email address

Tutorials

4.1 Creating Custom Theme Colors and Theme Fonts

4.2 Saving a Document Theme

4.3 Applying, Editing, and Deleting a Custom Theme

4.4 Applying and Modifying Styles

4.5 Recording and Running Macros

4.6 Inserting and Navigating with Bookmarks

4.7 Creating and Editing Hyperlinks

4.8 Inserting Hyperlinks to Other Locations

4.9 Creating a Cross-Reference

The Microsoft Office suite offers themes to provide you with consistent formatting and help you create documents with a professional and polished look. You can use the themes provided by Office or create your own custom themes. Word provides a number of predesigned styles, grouped into style sets, for applying consistent formatting to text in documents. Word also includes a time-saving feature called *macros* that automates the formatting of a document.

In this chapter, you will learn about customizing themes; how to modify an existing style; how to record and run macros; and how to insert hyperlinks, bookmarks, and cross-references to provide additional information for readers and to allow for more efficient navigation within a document. Model answers for this chapter's projects appear on the following pages.

Note: Before beginning the projects, copy to your storage medium the WL2C4 subfolder from the WL2 folder on the CD that accompanies this textbook and then make WL2C4 the active folder.

Northland Security Systems

Northland Security Systems Mission
We are a full-service computer information security management and consulting firm offering a comprehensive range of services to help businesses protect electronic data.

Security Services
Northland Security Systems is dedicated to helping businesses, private and public, protect vital company data through on-site consultation, product installation and training, and 24-hour telephone support services. We show you how computer systems can be compromised, and we walk you through the steps you can take to protect your company's computer system.

Security Software
We offer a range of security management software to protect your business against viruses, spyware, adware, intrusion, spam, and policy abuse.

- Security Management Software
- Security Software Training
- On-Site Consultation
- 24-Hour Telephone Support

Northland Security Systems

Security and Privacy
We partner with you to assess, plan, design, implement, and manage a security-rich environment to protect you, your systems, and your customers.

Specialized Services

- Firewall Implementation
- Internal Security Assessment
- Secured Remote Access
- Two-Factor Authentication
- Antivirus Solutions

Project 1 Apply Custom Themes to Documents

WL2-C4-P1-NSSServices.docx

WL2-C4-P1-NSSSecurity.docx

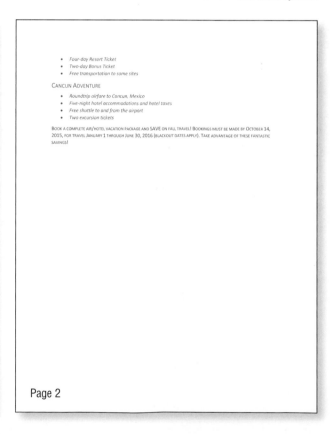

Project 2 Format a Travel Document with Styles

WL2-C4-P2-BTAdventures.docx

Page 1

Page 2

Model Answers

Document 1 (left, top): WL2-C4-P3-WriteResumes.docx

Resume Strategies

Following are core strategies for writing an effective and successful resume:

1. Who are you and how do you want to be perceived?
2. Sell it to me ... don't tell it to me.
3. Use keywords.
4. Use the "big" and save the "little."
5. Make your resume "interviewable."
6. Eliminate confusion with structure and content.
7. Use function to demonstrate achievement.
8. Remain in the realm of reality.
9. Be confident.

Writing Style

Always write in the first person, dropping the word "I" from the front of each sentence. This style gives your resume a more aggressive and more professional tone than the passive, third-person voice. Here are some examples:

First Person:

Manage 22-person team responsible for design and marketing of a new portfolio of PC-based applications for Landmark's consumer-sales division.

Third Person:

Ms. Sanderson manages a 22-person team responsible for design and marketing of a new portfolio of PC-based application for Landmark's consumer-sales division.

Phrases to Avoid

Try not to use phrases such as "responsible for" and "duties included." These words create a passive tone and style. Instead, use active verbs to describe what you did. Compare these two ways of conveying the same information:

Responsible for all marketing and special events for the store, including direct mailing, in-store fashion shows, and new-product introductions and promotions.

Orchestrated a series of marketing and special-event programs for McGregor's, one of the company's largest and most profitable operating locations. Managed direct-mail campaigns, in-store fashion shows, and new-product introductions and promotions.

Document 2 (right, top): WL2-C4-P3-GSHLtr.docx

ST. FRANCIS HOSPITAL

May 12, 2015

Mr. Victor Durham
Good Samaritan Hospital
1201 James Street
St. Louis, MO 62033

Dear Victor:

Congratulations on obtaining eight new registered nurse positions at your hospital. The attached registered nurse job description is generic. Depending on the specialty, you may want to include additional responsibilities:

Procedural
Uses the nursing process to prescribe, coordinate, and delegate patient care from admission through discharge.
Analyzes the patient's condition and reports changes to the appropriate health care provider.
Observes patient for signs and symptoms, collects data on patient, and reports and documents results.

Teaching
Teaches patient, family, staff, and students.
Assumes responsibility for patient and family teaching and discharge planning.
Participates in orientation of new staff and/or acts as preceptor.

I am interested in hearing about your recruitment plan. We are hiring additional medical personnel in the fall at St. Francis, and I need to begin formulating a recruitment plan.

Sincerely,

Marcus Knowles

XX
WL2-C4-P3-GSHLtr.docx

3500 MEEKER BOULEVARD ◊ REDFIELD, NE 68304 ◊ 308-555-5000

Project 3 Record and Run Macros

WL2-C4-P3-WriteResumes.docx

WL2-C4-P3-GSHLtr.docx

Document 3 (bottom): Computer Viruses Report

Page 1

CHAPTER 1: UNAUTHO...

Like uncharted wilderness, the Internet lacks borders. This... so valuable and yet so vulnerable. Over its short life, the In... system has not been able to keep pace. The security risks... grouped into three categories: unauthorized access, inform...

Hackers, individuals who gain access to computers and net... of unauthorized access. Hackers tend to exploit sites and p... place. However, they also gain access to more challenging... strategies. Many hackers claim they hack merely because... security measures. They rarely have a more malicious mot... damage the sites that they invade. In fact, hackers dislike... damage. They refer to hackers with malicious or criminal i...

USER IDS AND PAS...

To gain entry over the Internet to a secure computer syste... user ID and password combination. User IDs are easy to c... information. Sending an email, for example, displays the s... very public. The only missing element is the password. Had... are common; they have programs that generate thousand... systematically over a period of hours or days. Password Su...

SYSTEM BACKD...

Programmers can sometimes inadvertently aid hackers by... and information systems. One such unintentional entrance... password that provides the highest level of authorization... the early days of system development to allow other prog... system to fix problems. Through negligence or by design, t... behind in the final version of the system. People who know... bypassing the security, perhaps years later, when the back...

SPOOFING

A sophisticated way to break into a network via the Intern... fooling another computer by pretending to send informati... altering the address that the system automatically puts on... one that the receiving computer is programmed to accept...

Page 2

SPYWARE...

Spyware is a type of software that allows an intruder to sp... technology takes advantage of loopholes in the computer'... witness and record another person's every mouse click or... can record activities and gain access to passwords and cre... requires the user to install it on the machine that is being s... strangers on the Internet could simply begin watching you... someone might be able to install the software without the... greeting, for example, the program can operate like a virus... spyware unknowingly.

CHAPTER 2: INFORM...

Information can be a company's most valuable possession... included in the category of industrial espionage, is unfortu... This is due in part to the invisible nature of software and d... and manages to download the company database from the... the company that anything is amiss. The original database... has.

WIRELESS DEVICE...

The growing number of wireless devices has created a new... such as cameras, Web phones, networked computers, PDA... inherently less secure than wired devices. Security is quite... wireless technologies for handheld computers and cell pho... manufacturers have tended to sacrifice security to move a... viruses are appearing in emails for cell phones and PDAs. V... systems, hackers and spies are enjoying a free hand with th... security protocols for wireless networks is Wired Equivale... the standard for wireless local area networks. Newer versi... make it more difficult for hackers to intercept and modify... infrared signals.

DATA BROWS...

Data browsing is a less damaging form of information theft... in many organizations have access to networked database... people. Accessing this information without an official reaso...

Page 3

large problem with data browsing in the late 1990s. Some employees were fired and the rest were given specialized training in appropriate conduct.

CHAPTER 3: COMPUTER VIRUSES

One of the most familiar forms of risk to computer security is the computer virus. A computer virus is a program written by a hacker or cracker designed to perform some kind of trick upon an unsuspecting victim. The trick performed in some cases is mild, such as drawing an offensive image on the screen, or changing all of the characters in a document to another language. Sometimes the trick is much more severe, such as reformatting the hard drive and erasing all the data, or damaging the motherboard so that it cannot operate properly. Computer Virus Presentation

TYPES OF VIRUSES

Viruses can be categorized by their effect, which include nuisance, data-destructive, espionage, and hardware-destructive. A nuisance virus usually does no real damage, but is rather just an inconvenience. The most difficult part of a computer to replace is the data on the hard drive. The installed programs, the documents, databases, and saved emails form the heart of a personal computer. A data-destructive virus is designed to destroy this data. Some viruses are designed to create a backdoor into a system to bypass security. Called espionage viruses, they do no damage, but rather allow a hacker or cracker to enter the system later for the purpose of stealing data or spying on the work of the competitor. Very rarely, a virus is created that attempts to damage the hardware of the computer system itself. Called hardware-destructive viruses, these bits of programming can weaken or destroy chips, drives, and other components. (For more information, refer to Spyware.)

METHODS OF VIRUS OPERATION

Viruses can create effects that range from minor and annoying to highly destructive, and are operated and transmitted by a variety of methods. An email virus is normally transmitted as an attachment to a message sent over the Internet. Email viruses require the victim to click on the attachment and cause it to execute. Another common form of virus transmission is by a macro, a small subprogram that allows users to customize and automate certain functions. A macro virus is written specifically for one program, which then becomes infected when it opens a file with the virus stored in its macros. The boot sector of a floppy disk or hard disk contains a variety of information, including how the disk is organized and whether it is capable of loading an operating system. When a disk is left in a drive and the computer reboots, the operating system automatically reads the boot sector to learn about that disk and to attempt to start any operating system on that disk. A boot sector virus is designed to alter the boot sector of a disk, so that whenever the operating system reads the boot sector, the computer will automatically become infected.

Other methods of virus infection include the Trojan horse virus, which hides inside another legitimate program or data file, and the stealth virus, which is designed to hide itself from detection software.

Project 4 Navigate and Insert Hyperlinks in a Computer Viruses Report

WL2-C4-P4-VirusesSecurity.docx

Polymorphic viruses alter themselves to prevent antivirus software from detecting them by examining familiar patterns. Polymorphic viruses alter themselves randomly as they move from computer to computer, making detection more difficult. Multipartite viruses alter their form of attack. Their name derives from their ability to attack in several different ways. They may first infect the boot sector and then later move on to become a Trojan horse type by infecting a disk file. These viruses are more sophisticated, and therefore more difficult to guard against. Another type of virus is the logic bomb, which generally sits quietly dormant waiting for a specific event or set of conditions to occur. A famous logic bomb was the widely publicized Michelangelo virus, which infected personal computers and caused them to display a message on the artist's birthday.

CHAPTER 4: SECURITY RISKS

Although hackers, crackers, and viruses garner the most attention as security risks, a company faces a variety of other dangers to its hardware and software systems. Principally, these risks involve types of system failure, employee theft, and the cracking of software for copying. Click to view types of viruses

SYSTEMS FAILURE

A fundamental element in making sure that computer systems operate properly is protecting the electrical power that runs them. Power interruptions such as blackouts and brownouts have very adverse effects on computers. An inexpensive type of power strip called a surge protector can guard against power fluctuations and can also serve as an extension cord and splitter. A much more vigorous power protection system is an uninterruptible power supply (UPS), which provides a battery backup. Similar in nature to a power strip, but much more bulky and a bit more expensive, a UPS provides not only steady spike-free power, but also keeps computers running during a blackout.

EMPLOYEE THEFT

Although accurate estimates are difficult to pinpoint, businesses certainly lose millions of dollars a year in stolen computer hardware and software. Often, in large organizations, such theft goes unnoticed or unreported. Someone takes a hard drive or a scanner home for legitimate use, then leaves the job sometime later, and keeps the machine. Sometimes, employees take components to add to their home PC systems or a thief breaks into a business and hauls away computers. Such thefts cost far more than the price of the stolen computers because they also involve the cost of replacing the lost data, the cost of the time lost while the machines are gone, and the cost of installing new machines and training people to use them.

CRACKING SOFTWARE FOR COPYING

A common goal of hackers is to crack a software protection scheme. A crack is a method of circumventing a security scheme that prevents a user from copying a program. A common protection scheme for

Page 4

---

software is to require that the installation CD be resident in the drive whenever the program runs. Making copies of the CD with a burner, however, easily fools this protection scheme. Some game companies are taking the extra step of making duplication difficult by scrambling some of the data on the original CDs, which CD burners will automatically correct when copying. When the copied and corrected CD is used, the software checks for the scrambled track information. If the error is not found, the software will not run.

Hold down the Ctrl key and then click the logo shown below to display a list of training courses offered by Northland Security Systems

Click to send an email

Page 5

Project [1] Apply Custom Themes to Documents   5 Parts

You will create custom theme colors and theme fonts and then apply theme effects. You will save the changes as a custom theme, which you will apply to a company services document and a company security document.

Customizing Themes ■■■■■■■■■■■■■■■■■■■■■■■■■■■■

A document you create in Word is based on the Normal.dotm template. This template provides your document with default layout, formatting, styles, and theme formatting. The default template provides a number of built-in or predesigned themes. You have used some of these built-in themes to apply colors, fonts, and effects to content in documents. The same built-in themes are available in Microsoft Word, Excel, Access, PowerPoint, and Outlook. Because the same themes are available across these applications, you can brand your business files—such as documents, workbooks, databases, and presentations—with a consistent and professional appearance.

A *theme* is a combination of theme colors, theme fonts, and theme effects. Within a theme, you can change any of these three elements with the additional buttons in the Document Formatting group on the DESIGN tab. You can switch from the default theme (called *Office*) to one of the built-in themes or create your own custom theme. A theme you create will display in the *Custom* section of the Themes drop-down gallery. To create a custom theme, change the theme colors, theme fonts, and/or theme effects.

The Themes, Theme Colors, and Theme Fonts buttons in the Document Formatting group on the DESIGN tab display visual representations of the current theme. For example, the Themes button displays an uppercase and lowercase A with colored squares below it. If you change the theme colors, the changes are reflected in the small, colored squares on the Themes button and the four squares on the Theme Colors button. If you change the theme fonts, the letters on the Themes button and the Theme Fonts button reflect the change.

Themes

Theme Colors

Theme Fonts

Creating Custom Theme Colors

To create custom theme colors, click the DESIGN tab, click the Theme Colors button, and then click *Customize Colors* at the drop-down gallery. This displays the Create New Theme Colors dialog box, similar to the one shown in Figure 4.1. Theme colors contain four text and background colors, six accent colors, and two hyperlink colors, as shown in the *Themes colors* section of the dialog box. Change a color in the list box by clicking the color button at the right side of the color option and then clicking the desired color at the color palette.

After you have made all desired changes to colors, click in the *Name* text box, type a name for the custom theme colors, and then click the Save button. This saves the custom theme colors and also applies the color changes to the active document. Display the custom theme by clicking the Theme Colors button. Your custom theme will display toward the top of the drop-down gallery in the *Custom* section.

▼ **Quick Steps**

Create Custom Theme Colors
1. Click DESIGN tab.
2. Click Theme Colors button.
3. Click *Customize Colors*.
4. Change to desired background, accent, and hyperlink colors.
5. Type name for custom theme colors.
6. Click Save button.

Figure 4.1 Create New Theme Colors Dialog Box

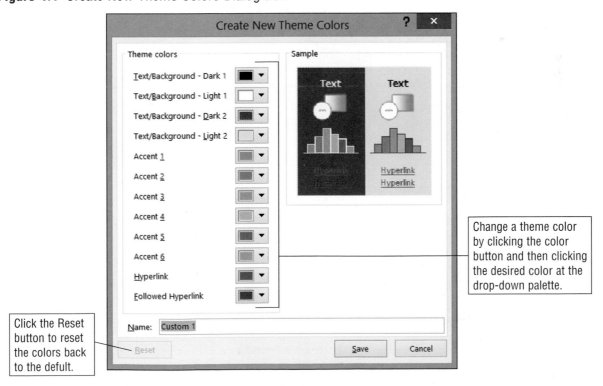

Change a theme color by clicking the color button and then clicking the desired color at the drop-down palette.

Click the Reset button to reset the colors back to the defult.

Resetting Custom Theme Colors

If you make changes to colors at the Create New Theme Colors dialog box and then decide you do not like the changes, click the Reset button in the lower left corner of the dialog box. Clicking this button resets the colors back to the default Office theme colors.

Project 1a **Creating Custom Theme Colors** Part 1 of 5

Note: If you are running Word 2013 on a computer connected to a network in a public environment, such as a school, you may need to complete all parts of Project 1 during the same session. Network system software may delete your custom themes when you exit Word. Check with your instructor.

1. At a blank document, click the DESIGN tab.
2. Click the Theme Colors button in the Document Formatting group and then click *Customize Colors* at the drop-down gallery.
3. At the Create New Theme Colors dialog box, click the color button that displays to the right of the *Text/Background - Light 1* option and then click the *Dark Red* color in the color palette (first color in the *Standard Colors* section).
4. Click the color button that displays to the right of the *Accent 1* option and then click the *Yellow* color in the color palette (fourth color in the *Standard Colors* section).

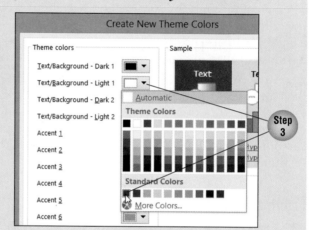

5. You decide that you do not like the colors you have chosen, so you decide to start over. To do this, click the Reset button located in the lower left corner of the dialog box.
6. Click the color button that displays to the right of the *Text/Background - Dark 2* option and then click the *Blue* color in the color palette (eighth color in the *Standard Colors* section).
7. Change the color for the *Accent 1* option by completing the following steps:
   a. Click the color button that displays to the right of the *Accent 1* option.
   b. Click the *More Colors* option in the color palette.
   c. At the Colors dialog box, click the Standard tab.
   d. Click the *Dark Green* color, as shown at the right.
   e. Click OK to close the dialog box.
8. Save the custom colors by completing the following steps:
   a. Select the current text in the *Name* text box.
   b. Type your first and last names.
   c. Click the Save button.
9. Close the document without saving it.

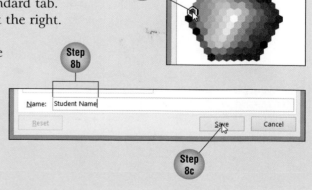

Creating Custom Fonts

To create a custom theme font, click the DESIGN tab, click the Theme Fonts button, and then click *Customize Fonts* at the drop-down gallery. This displays the Create New Theme Fonts dialog box. At this dialog box, choose a font for headings and a font for body text. Type a name for the custom fonts in the *Name* text box and then click the Save button.

▼ Quick Steps

Create Custom Fonts
1. Click DESIGN tab.
2. Click Theme Fonts button.
3. Click *Customize Fonts*.
4. Choose fonts.
5. Type name for custom theme fonts.
6. Click Save button.

Project 1b | **Creating Custom Theme Fonts** | **Part 2 of 5**

1. At a blank document, click the DESIGN tab.
2. Click the Theme Fonts button in the Document Formatting group and then click the *Customize Fonts* option at the drop-down gallery.
3. At the Create New Theme Fonts dialog box, click the down-pointing arrow at the right side of the *Heading font* option box, scroll up the drop-down list, and then click *Arial*.
4. Click the down-pointing arrow at the right side of the *Body font* option box, scroll down the drop-down list, and then click *Cambria*.
5. Save the custom fonts by completing the following steps:
   a. Select the current text in the *Name* text box.
   b. Type your first and last names.
   c. Click the Save button.
6. Close the document without saving it.

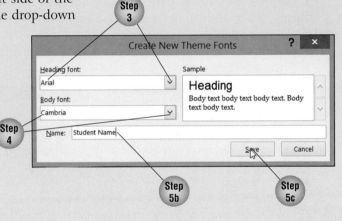

Applying Custom Theme Colors and Fonts

Apply to your document the custom theme colors you created by clicking the Theme Colors button in the Document Formatting group on the DESIGN tab and then clicking the custom theme colors option that displays near the top of the drop-down gallery in the *Custom* section. Complete similar steps to apply custom theme fonts.

Applying Theme Effects

The options in the Theme Effects button drop-down gallery apply sets of line and fill effects to graphics in a document. You cannot create your own theme effects but you can apply a theme effect and then save the formatting as your own document theme.

♦ **Quick Steps**

Save a Document Theme
1. Click DESIGN tab.
2. Click Themes button.
3. Click *Save Current Theme*.
4. Type name for theme.
5. Click Save button.

Saving a Document Theme

Once you have customized theme colors and fonts and applied theme effects to a document, you can save them in a custom document theme. To do this, click the Themes button in the Document Formatting group on the DESIGN tab and then click *Save Current Theme* at the drop-down gallery. This displays the Save Current Theme dialog box, which has many of the same options as the Save As dialog box. Type a name for your custom document theme in the *File name* text box and then click the Save button.

Project 1c   Applying Theme Effects and Saving a Document Theme   Part 3 of 5

1. Open **NSSServices.docx** and then save the document and name it **WL2-C4-P1-NSSServices**.
2. Make the following changes to the document:
   a. Apply the Title style to the company name *Northland Security Systems*.
   b. Apply the Heading 1 style to the heading *Northland Security Systems Mission*.
   c. Apply the Heading 2 style to the remaining headings, *Security Services* and *Security Software*.
3. Apply the custom theme colors you saved by completing the following steps:
   a. Click the DESIGN tab.
   b. Click the Theme Colors button in the Document Formatting group.
   c. Click the theme colors option with your name that displays near the top of the drop-down gallery in the *Custom* group.

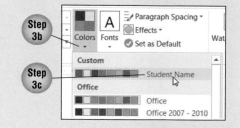

4. Apply the custom theme fonts you saved by clicking the Theme Fonts button in the Document Formatting group and then clicking the custom theme font with your name.
5. Apply a theme effect by clicking the Theme Effects button in the Document Formatting group and then clicking *Glossy* at the drop-down gallery.
6. Make the following changes to the SmartArt graphic:
   a. Click near the graphic to select it. (When the graphic is selected, a light gray border displays around it.)
   b. Click the SMARTART TOOLS DESIGN tab.
   c. Click the Change Colors button and then click *Colorful Range - Accent Colors 5 to 6* (the last color option in the *Colorful* section).
   d. Click the More button at the right side of the SmartArt Styles group and then click *Cartoon* in the *3-D* section (third column, first row in the *3-D* section).
   e. Click outside the SmartArt graphic to deselect it.

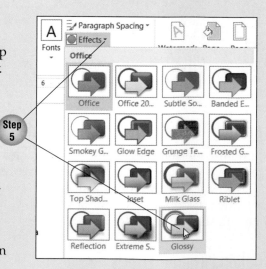

7. Save the custom theme colors and font, as well as the Glossy theme effect, as a custom document theme by completing the following steps:
   a. Click the DESIGN tab.
   b. Click the Themes button in the Document Formatting group.

c. Click the *Save Current Theme* option that displays at the bottom of the drop-down gallery.

d. At the Save Current Theme dialog box, type your first and last names in the *File name* text box and then click the Save button.

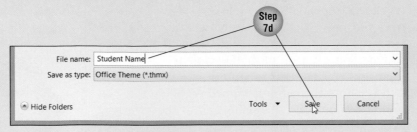

Step
7d

| File name: | Student Name | ⌄ |
| Save as type: | Office Theme (*.thmx) | ⌄ |

⊕ Hide Folders   Tools ▾   Save   Cancel

8. Save and then print **WL2-C4-P1-NSSServices.docx**.

Editing Custom Themes

Custom theme colors and theme fonts can be edited. To edit custom theme colors, click the DESIGN tab and then click the Theme Colors button in the Document Formatting group. At the drop-down gallery of custom and built-in theme colors, right-click your custom theme colors and then click *Edit* at the shortcut menu. This displays the Edit Theme Colors dialog box, which contains the same options as the Create New Theme Colors dialog box. Make the desired changes to the theme colors and then click the Save button.

To edit custom theme fonts, click the Theme Fonts button in the Document Formatting group on the DESIGN tab, right-click your custom theme fonts, and then click *Edit* at the shortcut menu. This displays the Edit Theme Fonts dialog box, which contains the same options as the Create New Theme Fonts dialog box. Make the desired changes to the theme fonts and then click the Save button.

▼ **Quick Steps**

Edit Custom Theme Colors or Fonts
1. Click DESIGN tab.
2. Click Theme Colors button or Theme Fonts button.
3. Right-click desired custom theme colors or fonts.
4. Click *Edit*.
5. Make desired changes.
6. Click Save button.

Project 1d   **Editing Custom Themes**   **Part 4 of 5**

1. With **WL2-C4-P1-NSSServices.docx** open, edit the theme colors by completing the following steps:
   a. If necessary, click the DESIGN tab.
   b. Click the Theme Colors button.
   c. Right-click the custom theme colors named with your first and last names.
   d. Click *Edit* at the shortcut menu.
   e. At the Edit Theme Colors dialog box, click the color button that displays to the right of the *Text/Background - Dark 2* option.
   f. Click the *More Colors* option in the color palette.

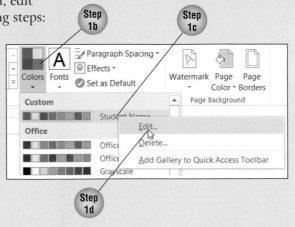

Step 1b   Step 1c

Step 1d

g. At the Colors dialog box, click the Standard tab.

h. Click the *Dark Green* color. (This is the same color you chose for *Accent 1* in Project 1a.)

i. Click OK to close the dialog box.

j. Click the Save button.

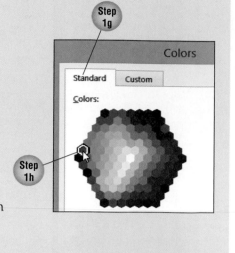

2. Edit the theme fonts by completing the following steps:

a. Click the Theme Fonts button in the Document Formatting group.

b. Right-click the custom theme fonts named with your first and last names and then click *Edit* at the shortcut menu.

c. At the Edit Theme Fonts dialog box, click the down-pointing arrow at the right side of the *Body font* option box, scroll down the drop-down list, and then click *Constantia*.

d. Click the Save button.

3. Apply a different theme effect by clicking the Theme Effects button in the Document Formatting group and then clicking *Extreme Shadow* at the drop-down gallery. (This applies a shadow behind each shape.)

4. Save the changes to the custom theme by completing the following steps:

a. Click the Themes button and then click *Save Current Theme* at the drop-down gallery.

b. At the Save Current Theme dialog box, click the theme named with your first and last names in the content pane.

c. Click the Save button.

d. At the message telling you that the theme already exists and asking if you want to replace it, click Yes.

5. Save, print, and then close **WL2-C4-P1-NSSServices.docx**.

Resetting a Template Theme

▼ **Quick Steps**

Reset a Template Theme
1. Click DESIGN tab.
2. Click Themes button.
3. Click *Reset to Theme from Template*.

Delete Custom Theme Colors or Fonts
1. Click DESIGN tab.
2. Click Theme Colors or Theme Fonts button.
3. Right-click desired custom theme.
4. Click *Delete*.
5. Click Yes.

If you apply a built-in theme other than the Office default theme or if you apply a custom theme, you can reset the theme back to the template default. To do this, click the Themes button and then click the *Reset to Theme from Template* at the drop-down gallery. If you are working in the default template provided by Word, clicking this option resets the theme to the Office default theme.

Deleting Custom Themes

Delete custom theme colors from the Theme Colors button drop-down gallery, delete custom theme fonts from the Theme Fonts drop-down gallery, and delete custom themes from the Save Current Theme dialog box.

To delete custom theme colors, click the Theme Colors button, right-click the theme you want to delete, and then click *Delete* at the shortcut menu. At the message asking if you want to delete the theme colors, click Yes. To delete custom theme fonts, click the Theme Fonts button, right-click the theme you want to delete, and then click *Delete* at the shortcut menu. At the message asking if you want to delete the theme fonts, click Yes.

Delete a custom theme (including custom colors, fonts, and effects) at the Themes button drop-down gallery or at the Save Current Theme dialog box. To delete a custom theme from the drop-down gallery, click the Themes button, right-click the custom theme, click *Delete* at the shortcut menu, and then click Yes at the message that displays. To delete a custom theme from the Save Current Theme dialog box, click the Themes button and then click *Save Current Theme* at the drop-down gallery. At the dialog box, click the custom theme document name, click the Organize button on the dialog box toolbar, and then click *Delete* at the drop-down list. If a message displays asking if you are sure you want to send the theme to the Recycle Bin, click Yes.

▼ **Quick Steps**

Delete a Custom Theme
1. Click DESIGN tab.
2. Click Themes button.
3. Right-click custom theme.
4. Click *Delete.*
5. Click Yes.

Changing Default Settings

If you apply formatting to a document—such as a specific style set, theme, and paragraph spacing—and then decide that you want the formatting available for future documents, you can save the formatting as the default. To do this, click the Set as Default button in the Document Formatting group on the DESIGN tab. At the message box that displays asking if you want the current style set and theme as the default and telling you that the settings will be applied to new documents, click the Yes button.

Project 1e   **Applying and Deleting Custom Themes**   Part 5 of 5

1. Open **NSSSecurity.docx** and then save the document and name it **WL2-C4-P1-NSSSecurity**.
2. Apply the Title style to the company name and apply the Heading 1 style to the two headings in the document.
3. Apply your custom theme by completing the following steps:
   a. Click the DESIGN tab.
   b. Click the Themes button.
   c. Click the custom theme named with your first and last names that displays at the top of the drop-down gallery in the *Custom* section.
4. Save and then print **WL2-C4-P1-NSSSecurity.docx**.
5. Reset the theme to the Office default theme by clicking the Themes button and then clicking *Reset to Theme from Template* at the drop-down gallery.
6. Save and then close **WL2-C4-P1-NSSSecurity.docx**.
7. Press Ctrl + N to display a new blank document.
8. Delete the custom theme colors by completing the following steps:
   a. Click the DESIGN tab.
   b. Click the Theme Colors button in the Document Formatting group.
   c. Right-click the custom theme colors named with your first and last names.
   d. Click *Delete* at the shortcut menu.
   e. At the question asking if you want to delete the theme colors, click Yes.
9. Complete steps similar to those in Step 8 to delete the custom theme fonts named with your first and last names.
10. Delete the custom theme by completing the following steps:
    a. Click the Themes button.
    b. Right-click the custom theme named with your first and last names.

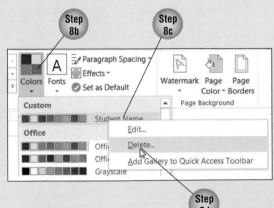

Project 2 Format a Travel Document with Styles   1 Part

You will open a First Choice Travel document, change the style set, and apply styles.

Formatting with Styles ■■■■■■■■■■■■■■■■■■■■

A *style* is a set of formatting instructions that you can apply to text. Word provides a number of predesigned styles and groups those that apply similar formatting into style sets. While a theme changes the overall colors, fonts, and effects used in a document, a style set changes font and paragraph formatting for the entire document. Using the styles within a style set, you can apply formatting that gives your document a uniform and professional appearance.

Displaying Styles in a Style Set

The default style set is named *Word 2013,* and the styles in it are available in the Styles group on the HOME tab. Several styles display as *thumbnails*, or miniature representations, in the Styles group. Generally, the visible style thumbnails include the Normal, No Spacing, Heading 1, Heading 2, Title, Subtitle, and Subtitle Emphasis styles. (Depending on your monitor and screen resolution, you may see more or fewer style thumbnails in the Styles group.) The styles change to reflect the style set that has been applied to the active document. Click the More button to the right of the style thumbnails in the Styles group and a drop-down gallery displays containing all of the styles available in the default style set. Hover your mouse pointer over a style in the drop-down gallery to see how the style will format text in your document.

You can also display the styles available in the style set by clicking either the down-pointing arrow or up-pointing arrow to the right of the style thumbnails. Clicking the down-pointing arrow scrolls down the style set, displaying the next styles. Clicking the up-pointing arrow scrolls up the set of styles.

Applying Styles

HINT

You can also display the Styles task pane by pressing Alt + Ctrl + Shift + S.

A variety of methods are available for applying styles to text in a document. Apply a style by clicking the style thumbnail in the Styles group on the HOME tab or by clicking the More button and then clicking the style at the drop-down gallery. The Styles task pane provides another method for applying a style. Display the Styles task pane, shown in Figure 4.2, by clicking the Styles group task pane launcher.

Figure 4.2 Styles Task Pane

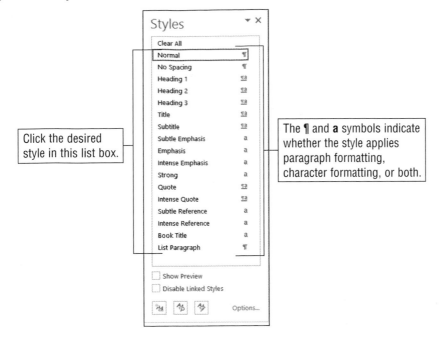

Click the desired style in this list box.

The ¶ and **a** symbols indicate whether the style applies paragraph formatting, character formatting, or both.

The styles in the currently selected style set display in the task pane followed by the paragraph symbol (¶), indicating that the style applies paragraph formatting, or the character symbol (**a**), indicating that the style applics character formatting. If both characters display to the right of a style, the style applies both paragraph and character formatting. In addition to displaying styles that apply formatting, the Styles task pane also displays a *Clear All* style that clears all formatting from the selected text.

If you hover the mouse pointer over a style in the Styles task pane, a ScreenTip displays with information about the formatting applied by the style. Apply a style in the Styles task pane by clicking the style. Close the Styles task pane by clicking the Close button located in the upper right corner of the task pane.

Modifying a Style

If a predesigned style contains most, but not all, of the formatting you want applied to text in your document, consider modifying the style. For example, the Heading 1 style might apply most of the formatting you want for headings in your document, but you want to apply a different font or alignment. To edit a predesigned style, right-click the style in the Styles group or in the Styles task pane and then click *Modify* at the shortcut menu. This displays the Modify Styles dialog box, shown in Figure 4.3. Use options at this dialog box to make changes such as renaming the style, applying or changing formatting, and specifying whether you want the modified style available only in the current document or all new documents.

The *Formatting* section of the dialog box contains a number of buttons and options for applying formatting. Additional options are available by clicking the Format button in the lower left corner of the dialog box and then clicking an option at the drop-down list. For example, display the Font dialog box by clicking the Format button and then clicking Font at the drop-down list.

▼ **Quick Steps**

Apply a Style
Click desired style in Styles group.
OR
1. Click More button in Styles group on HOME tab.
2. Click desired style.
OR
1. Display Styles task pane.
2. Click desired style in task pane.

H I N T

You can also apply styles at the Apply Styles window. Display this window with the keyboard shortcut Ctrl + Shift + S or by clicking the More button at the right side of the style thumbnails in the Styles group on the HOME tab and then clicking *Apply Styles* at the drop-down gallery.

Figure 4.3 Modify Styles Dialog Box

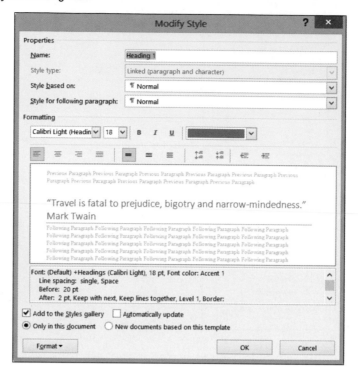

Project 2 Applying and Modifying Styles   Part 1 of 1

1. Open **BTAdventures.docx** and then save the document and name it **WL2-C4-P2-BTAdventures**.
2. Apply styles using the Styles task pane by completing the following steps:
   a. Move the insertion point to the end of the document and then select the last paragraph.
   b. With the HOME tab active, click the Styles group task pane launcher. (This displays the Styles task pane.)
   c. Click the *Subtle Reference* style in the Styles task pane. (Notice that the style is followed by the character symbol *a*, indicating that the style applies character formatting.)
   d. Select the bulleted text below the heading *Disneyland Adventure* and then click the *Subtle Emphasis* style in the Styles task pane.
   e. Apply the *Subtle Emphasis* style to the bulleted text below the *Florida Adventure* heading and the *Cancun Adventure* heading.
   f. Select the quote by Mark Twain that displays at the beginning of the document and then click *Quote* in the Styles task pane.
   g. After noticing the formatting of the quote, remove the formatting by making sure the text is selected and then clicking *Clear All* near the top of the Styles task pane.
   h. With the Mark Twain quote still selected, click the *Intense Quote* style in the Styles task pane.

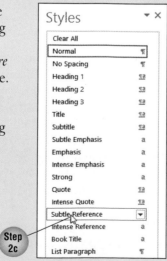

Step 2c

3. Modify the Heading 1 style by completing the following steps:
   a. Right-click the Heading 1 style in the Styles group.
   b. Click *Modify* at the shortcut menu.

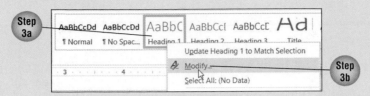

   c. At the Modify Styles dialog box, click the Bold button in the *Formatting* section.
   d. Click the Center button in the *Formatting* section.

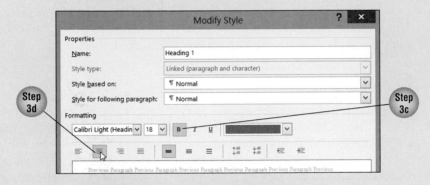

   e. Click OK to close the Modify Styles dialog box.
4. Modify the Heading 2 style by completing the following steps:
   a. Right-click the *Heading 2* style in the Styles task pane and then click *Modify* at the shortcut menu.
   b. At the Modify Styles dialog box, click the Format button in the lower left corner of the dialog box and then click *Font* at the drop-down list.
   c. At the Font dialog box, click the down-pointing arrow at the right side of the *Font color* option box and then click *Dark Red* (first option in the *Standard Colors* section).
   d. Click the *Small caps* check box to insert a check mark.
   e. Click OK to close the Font dialog box.
   f. Click the Format button in the dialog box and then click *Paragraph* at the drop-down list.
   g. At the Paragraph dialog box, click the up arrow in the *After* measurement box (this displays *6 pt* in the measurement box).
   h. Click OK to close the Paragraph dialog box and then click OK to close the Modify Styles dialog box.
5. Close the Styles task pane.
6. Save, print, and then close **WL2-C4-P2-BTAdventures.docx**.

Project **3** Record and Run Macros   **5 Parts**

You will record several macros, run the macros in a document, assign a macro to a keyboard command, delete a macro, and specify macro security settings.

Creating Macros ▪■■■■■■■■■■■■■■■■■■■■

Macros are time-saving tools that automate the formatting of Word documents. The word *macro* was coined by computer programmers for a collection of commands used to make a large programming job easier and save time. Two basic steps are involved in working with macros: recording a macro and running a macro. When you record a macro, all of the keys pressed and dialog boxes displayed are recorded and become part of the macro. After a macro is recorded, you can run it to carry out the actions you recorded.

Recording a Macro

▼ Quick Steps

Record a Macro
1. Click DEVELOPER tab.
2. Click Record Macro button.
OR
1. Click VIEW tab.
2. Click Macros button arrow.
3. Click *Record Macro.*
4. Make changes at Record Macro dialog box.
5. Click OK.
6. Complete macro steps.
7. Click Stop Recording button.
OR
7. Click macro icon on Status bar.

Record Macro

Macros

Recording a macro involves turning on the macro recorder, performing the steps to be recorded, and then turning off the recorder. Both the VIEW tab and DEVELOPER tab contain buttons for recording a macro. If the DEVELOPER tab does not appear on the ribbon, turn on the display of this tab by opening the Word Options dialog box with *Customize Ribbon* selected in the left panel, inserting a check mark in the *Developer* check box in the list box at the right, and then clicking OK to close the dialog box.

To record a macro, click the Record Macro button in the Code group on the DEVELOPER tab. You can also click the VIEW tab, click the Macros button arrow in the Macros group, and then click *Record Macro* at the drop-down list. This displays the Record Macro dialog box, shown in Figure 4.4. At the Record Macro dialog box, type a name for the macro in the *Macro name* text box. A macro name must begin with a letter and can contain only letters and numbers. Type a description for the macro in the *Description* text box located at the bottom of the dialog box. A macro description can contain a maximum of 255 characters and may include spaces.

Figure 4.4 Record Macro Dialog Box

By default, Word stores macros in the Normal template. Macros stored in this template are available for any document based on the template. In a company or school setting, where computers may be networked, consider storing macros in personalized documents or templates. Specify the location for macros with the *Store macro in* option box at the Record Macro dialog box (refer to Figure 4.4).

After typing the macro name, specifying where the macro is to be stored, and typing a description of the macro, click OK to close the Record Macro dialog box. At the open document, a macro icon displays near the left side of the Status bar and the mouse displays with a cassette icon attached. In the document, perform the actions to be recorded. If you are selecting text as part of the macro, use the keyboard to select text because a macro cannot record selections made by the mouse. When all of the steps have been completed, click the Stop Recording button (previously the Record Macro button) located in the Code group on the DEVELOPER tab or click the macro icon that displays near the left side of the Status bar.

Stop Recording

When you record macros in Project 3a, you will be instructed to name the macros beginning with your initials. Recorded macros are stored in the Normal template document by default and display at the Macros dialog box. If the computer you are using is networked, macros recorded by other students will also display at the Macros dialog box. Naming macros with your initials will enable you to distinguish your macros from the macros of other users.

Project 3a **Recording Macros**   **Part 1 of 5**

1. Turn on the display of the DEVELOPER tab by completing the following steps. (Skip to Step 2 if the DEVELOPER tab is already visible.)
   a. Click the FILE tab and then click *Options*.
   b. At the Word Options dialog box, click *Customize Ribbon* in the left panel.
   c. In the list box at the right, click the *Developer* check box to insert a check mark.

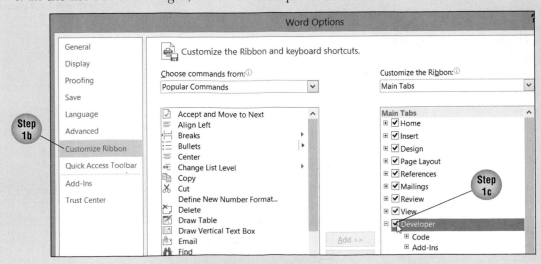

   d. Click OK to close the dialog box.

2. Record a macro that selects text, indents a paragraph of text, and then applies italic formatting by completing the following steps:
   a. Open **MacroText.docx** and then position the insertion point at the left margin of the paragraph that begins with *This is text to use for creating macros.*
   b. Click the DEVELOPER tab.
   c. Click the Record Macro button in the Code group on the DEVELOPER tab.

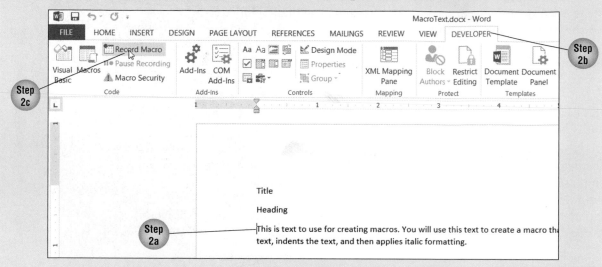

   d. At the Record Macro dialog box, type **XXXIndentItalics** in the *Macro name* text box. (Type your initials in place of the *XXX*.)
   e. Click inside the *Description* text box and then type **Select text, indent text, and apply italic formatting.** (If text displays in the *Description* text box, select the text first and then type the description.)
   f. Click OK.
   g. At the document, press F8 to turn on the Extend mode.
   h. Hold down the Shift key and the Ctrl key and then press the Down Arrow key. (Shift + Ctrl + Down Arrow is the keyboard shortcut to select a paragraph.)
   i. Click the HOME tab.
   j. Click the Paragraph group dialog box launcher.
   k. At the Paragraph dialog box, click the up-pointing arrow in the *Left* measurement box until *0.5"* displays.
   l. Click the up-pointing arrow in the *Right* measurement until *0.5"* displays.
   m. Click OK.
   n. Press Ctrl + I to apply italic formatting.

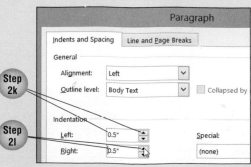

o. Press the Esc key and then press the Left Arrow key. (This deselects the text.)

p. Click the macro icon on the Status bar to turn off the macro recording.

Step 2p

3. Record a macro that applies formatting to a heading by completing the following steps:

a. Move the insertion point to the beginning of the text *Heading*.

b. Click the DEVELOPER tab and then click the Record Macro button in the Code group.

c. At the Record Macro dialog box, type **XXXHeading** in the *Macro name* text box. (Type your initials in place of the *XXX*.)

d. Click inside the *Description* text box and then type **Select text, change font size, turn on bold and italic, and insert bottom border line.** (If text displays in the *Description* text box, select the text first and then type the description.)

e. Click OK.

f. At the document, press F8 and then press the End key.

g. Click the HOME tab.

h. Click the Bold button in the Font group.

i. Click the Italic button in the Font group.

j. Click the Font Size button arrow in the Font group and then click *12* at the drop-down gallery.

k. Click the Borders button arrow in the Paragraph group and then click *Bottom Border* at the drop-down list.

l. Press the Home key. (This moves the insertion point back to the beginning of the heading and deselects the text.)

m. Click the macro icon on the Status bar to turn off the macro recording.

4. Close the document without saving it.

Running a Macro

To run a recorded macro, click the Macros button in the Code group on the DEVELOPER tab or click the Macros button on the VIEW tab. This displays the Macros dialog box, shown in Figure 4.5. At this dialog box, double-click the desired macro in the list box or click the macro and then click the Run button.

Quick Steps

Run a Macro
1. Click DEVELOPER tab.
2. Click Macros button.
3. At Macros dialog box, double-click macro in list box.
OR
1. Click VIEW tab.
2. Click Macros button.
3. At Macros dialog box, double-click macro in list box.

Figure 4.5 Macros Dialog Box

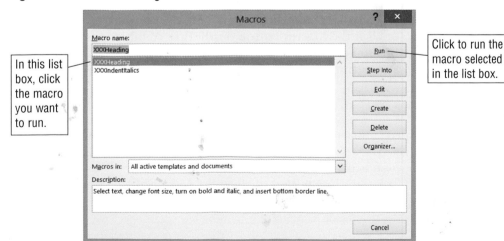

In this list box, click the macro you want to run.

Click to run the macro selected in the list box.

1. Open **WriteResumes.docx** and save the document with the name **WL2-C4-P3-WriteResumes**.
2. With the insertion point positioned at the beginning of the heading *Resume Strategies*, run the XXXHeading macro by completing the following steps:
   a. Click the VIEW tab.
   b. Click the Macros button in the Macros group.
   c. At the Macros dialog box, click *XXXHeading* in the list box.
   d. Click the Run button.

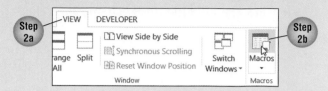

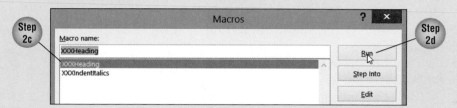

3. Complete steps similar to those in Steps 2a–2d to run the macro for the two other headings in the document: *Writing Style* and *Phrases to Avoid*.
4. Move the insertion point to the beginning of the paragraph below *First Person* and then complete the following steps to run the XXXIndentItalics macro:
   a. Click the DEVELOPER tab.
   b. Click the Macros button in the Code group.
   c. At the Macros dialog box, double-click *XXXIndentItalics* in the list box.
5. Complete steps similar to those in Step 4a–4c to run the XXXIndentItalics macro for the paragraph below *Third Person*, the paragraph that begins *Responsible for all marketing and special events*, and the paragraph that begins *Orchestrated a series of marketing and special-event programs*.
6. Save, print, and then close **WL2-C4-P3-WriteResumes.docx**.

Pausing and Resuming a Macro

When recording a macro, you can temporarily suspend the recording, perform actions that are not recorded, and then resume recording the macro. To pause the recording of a macro, click the Pause Recording button in the Code group on the DEVELOPER tab or click the Macros button on the VIEW tab and then click *Pause Recording* at the drop-down list. To resume recording the macro, click the Resume Recorder button (previously the Pause Recording button).

Pause

Deleting a Macro

If you no longer need a macro that you have recorded, you can delete it. To delete a macro, display the Macros dialog box, click the macro name in the list box, and then click the Delete button. At the message asking if you want to delete the macro, click Yes. Click the Close button to close the Macros dialog box.

1. At a blank document, delete the XXXIndentItalics macro by completing the following steps:
   a. Click the DEVELOPER tab and then click the Macros button in the Code group.
   b. At the Macros dialog box, click *XXXIndentItalics* in the list box.
   c. Click the Delete button.

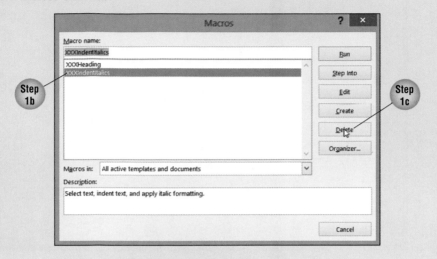

   d. At the message asking if you want to delete the macro, click Yes.
   e. Click the Close button to close the Macros dialog box.
2. Close the document without saving it.

Assigning a Macro to a Keyboard Command

Consider assigning macros that you use regularly to keyboard commands. To run a macro that has been assigned to a keyboard command, simply press the assigned keys. A macro can be assigned to a keyboard command with the following combinations:

    Alt + letter
    Ctrl + letter
    Alt + Ctrl + letter
    Alt + Shift + letter
    Ctrl + Shift + letter
    Alt + Ctrl + Shift + letter

Word already uses many combinations for Word functions. For example, pressing Alt + Ctrl + C inserts the copyright symbol.

Assign a macro to a keyboard command at the Customize Keyboard dialog box, as shown in Figure 4.6. Specify the keyboard command by pressing the desired keys, such as Alt + D. The keyboard command you enter displays in the *Press new shortcut key* text box. Word inserts the message *Currently assigned to:* below the *Current keys* list box. If the keyboard command is already assigned to a command, the command is listed after the *Currently assigned to:* message. If Word has not used the keyboard command, *[unassigned]* displays after the *Currently assigned to:* message. When assigning a keyboard command to a macro, make sure you use an unassigned keyboard command.

Figure 4.6 Customize Keyboard Dialog Box

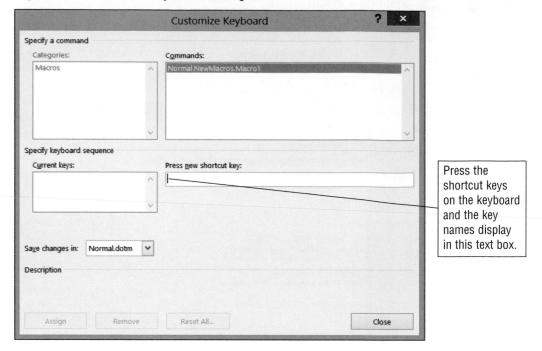

Press the shortcut keys on the keyboard and the key names display in this text box.

In Project 3d, you will record a macro and then assign it to a keyboard command. When you delete a macro, the keyboard command is no longer assigned to that action. This allows you to use the key combination again.

Project 3d | **Assigning a Macro to a Keyboard Command** | **Part 4 of 5**

1. Record a macro named *XXXFont* that selects text and applies font formatting and assign it to the keyboard command Alt + Ctrl + A by completing the following steps:
   a. At a blank document, click the DEVELOPER tab and then click the Record Macro button in the Code group.
   b. At the Record Macro dialog box, type **XXXFont** in the *Macro name* text box. (Type your initials in place of *XXX*.).
   c. Click inside the *Description* text box and then type **Select text and change the font and font color.**
   d. Click the Keyboard button.

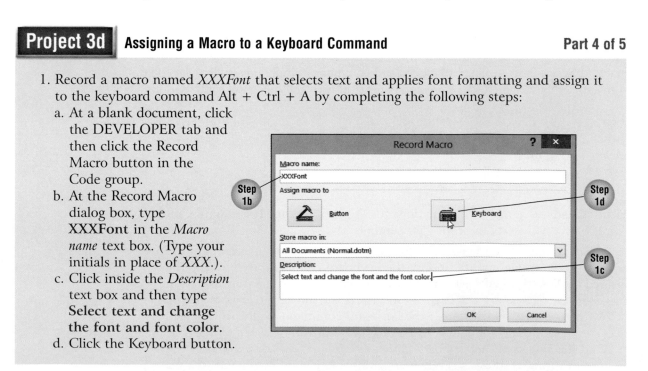

Step 1b

Step 1d

Step 1c

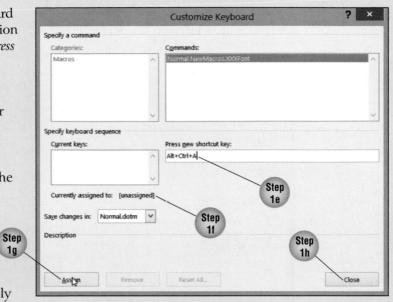

e. At the Customize Keyboard dialog box with the insertion point positioned in the *Press new shortcut key* text box, press Alt + Ctrl + A.

f. Check to make sure *[unassigned]* displays after *Currently assigned to:*.

g. Click the Assign button.

h. Click the Close button.

i. At the document, click the HOME tab.

j. Press Ctrl + A.

k. Click the Font group dialog box launcher.

l. At the Font dialog box, click *Cambria* in the *Font* list box and apply the Dark Blue font color (ninth color from left in the *Standard Colors* section).

m. Click OK to close the Font dialog box.

n. At the document, press the Down Arrow on the keyboard.

o. Click the macro icon on the Status bar to turn off the macro recording.

2. Close the document without saving it.

3. Open **GSHLtr.docx** and save the document with the name **WL2-C4-P3-GSHLtr**.

4. Run the XXXFont macro by pressing Alt + Ctrl + A.

5. Run the XXXHeading macro for the heading *Procedural* and the heading *Teaching*.

6. Save, print, and then close **WL2-C4-P3-GSHLtr.docx**.

Specifying Macro Security Settings

Some macros can create a potential security risk by introducing or spreading a virus to your computer or network. For this reason, Microsoft Word provides macro security settings for specifying what actions you want to perform with macros in a document. To display the macro security settings, click the DEVELOPER tab and then click the Macro Security button in the Code group. This displays the Trust Center with *Macro Settings* selected in the left panel, as shown in Figure 4.7.

Choose the first option, *Disable all macros without notification*, and all of the macros and security alerts are disabled. The second option, *Disable all macros with notification*, is the default setting. At this setting, a security alert appears if a macro is present and you can choose to enable the macro. If you choose the third option, *Disable all macros except digitally signed macros*, a digitally signed macro by a trusted publisher will automatically run, but you will still need to enable a digitally signed macro by a publisher that is not trusted. The last option, *Enable all macros (not recommended; potentially dangerous code can run)*, will allow all macros to run but, as the option implies, this is not recommended.

The changes that you make to the macro security settings in Word apply only to Word. The macro security settings are not changed in the other applications in the Office suite.

HINT

The Trust Center can also be opened by displaying the Word Options dialog box, clicking Trust Center in the left panel, and then clicking the Trust Center Settings button.

Figure 4.7 Trust Center

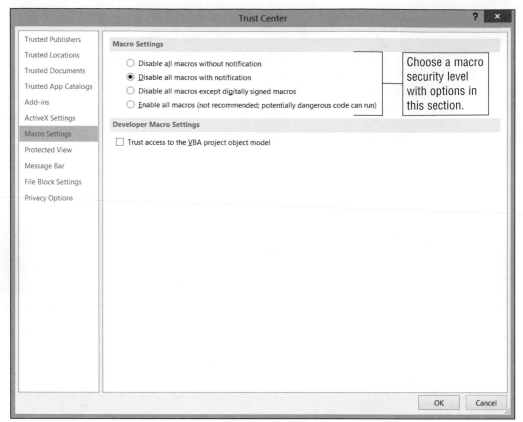

Saving a Macro-Enabled Document or Template

By default, the macros you create are saved in the Normal.dotm template. The .dotm extension identifies the template as *macro-enabled*. A template or document must be macro-enabled for a macro to be saved in it. You can also save macros in a specific document or template to make them available when you open that document or template. To specify a location for saving a macro, display the Record Macro dialog box, click the down-pointing arrow at the right side of the *Store macro in* option box, and then click the desired document or template.

Save a document containing macros as a macro-enabled document. To do this, display the Save As dialog box and then change the *Save as type* option to *Word Macro-Enabled Document (*.docm)*. Save a template containing macros as a macro-enabled template by changing the *Save as type* option at the Save As dialog box to *Word Macro-Enabled Template (*.dotm)*.

If you are using Microsoft Word in a public setting, such as a school, you may not be able to change macro security settings. If that is the case, skip to Step 4.

1. Open **Affidavit.docx**.
2. Change the macro security setting by completing the following steps:
   a. Click the DEVELOPER tab and then click the Macro Security button in the Code group.
   b. At the Trust Center, click *Disable all macros without notification*.
   c. Click OK.

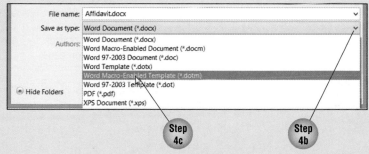

3. Change the macro security setting again by completing the following steps:
   a. Click the Macro Security button in the Code group.
   b. At the Trust Center, click *Disable all macros with notification*.
   c. Click OK.
4. Save the document as a macro-enabled template by completing the following steps:
   a. Press F12 to display the Save As dialog box.
   b. At the Save As dialog box, click the down-pointing arrow at the right side of the *Save as type* option box.
   c. Click *Word Macro-Enabled Template (*.dotm)* at the drop-down list.
   d. Select the text in the *File name* text box and then type **WL2-C4-P3-AffidavitTemplate**.
   e. Make sure the WL2C4 folder on your storage medium is the active folder.
   f. Click the Save button.
5. Close **WL2-C4-P3-AffidavitTemplate.dotm**.

Project 4 Navigate and Insert Hyperlinks in a Computer Viruses Report   5 Parts

You will open a report on computer viruses and computer security and insert and then navigate in the report with the Navigation pane, bookmarks, hyperlinks, and cross-references.

Navigating in a Document ■■■■■■■■■■■■■■■■■■■■■

Word includes a number of features for navigating in a document. In addition to the navigating features you have already learned, you can navigate using the Navigation pane and by inserting bookmarks, hyperlinks, and cross references.

Navigating Using the Navigation Pane

▼ **Quick Steps**

Display the Navigation Pane
1. Click VIEW tab.
2. Click *Navigation Pane* check box.

To use the Navigation pane to navigate in a document, click the VIEW tab and then click the *Navigation Pane* check box in the Show group to insert a check mark. The Navigation pane displays at the left side of the screen, as shown in Figure 4.8, and includes a search text box and a pane with three tabs.

Click the first Navigation pane tab, HEADINGS, and titles and headings with certain styles applied display in the Navigation pane. Click a title or heading in the pane and the insertion point moves to that title or heading. Click the PAGES tab and a thumbnail of each page displays in the pane. Click a thumbnail to move the insertion point to that specific page. Click the RESULTS tab to browse the current search results in the document.

Close the Navigation pane by clicking the *Navigation Pane* check box in the Show group on the VIEW tab to remove the check mark. Another option is to click the Close button located in the upper right corner of the pane.

Figure 4.8 Navigation Pane

Click the HEADINGS tab and titles and headings with certain styles applied display in the Navigation pane.

Click the PAGES tab to display a thumbnail of each page in the Navigation pane.

Click the RESULTS tab to browse the current search results in the document.

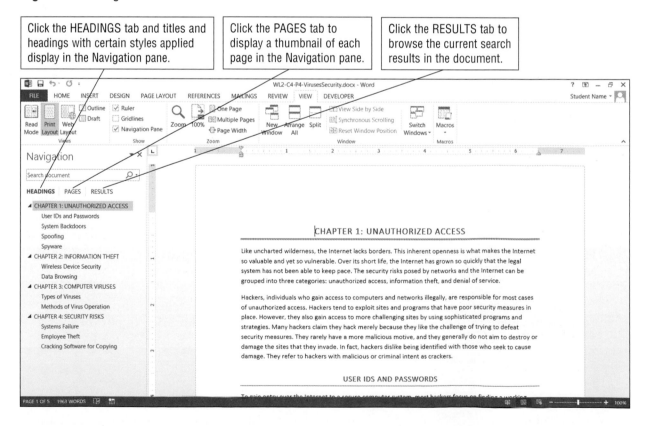

1. Open **VirusesSecurity.docx** and then save the document and name it **WL2-C4-P4-VirusesSecurity**.

2. Since this document has heading styles applied, you can easily navigate in the document with the Navigation pane by completing the following steps:
   a. Click the VIEW tab.
   b. Click the *Navigation Pane* check box in the Show group to insert a check mark. (This displays the Navigation pane at the left side of the screen.)
   c. With the HEADINGS tab active, click the *CHAPTER 2: INFORMATION THEFT* heading in the Navigation pane.
   d. Click *CHAPTER 3: COMPUTER VIRUSES* in the Navigation pane.
   e. Click *Systems Failure* in the Navigation pane.

3. Navigate in the document using thumbnails by completing the following steps:
   a. Click the PAGES tab in the Navigation pane. (This displays page thumbnails in the pane.)
   b. Click the page 1 thumbnail in the Navigation pane. (You may need to scroll up the Navigation pane to display this thumbnail.)
   c. Click the page 3 thumbnail in the Navigation pane.

4. Close the Navigation pane by clicking the Close button in the upper right corner of the Navigation pane.

5. Save **WL2-C4-P4-VirusesSecurity.docx**.

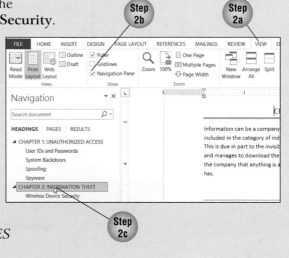

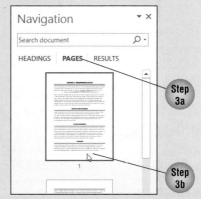

Inserting and Navigating with Bookmarks

When working in a long document, you may find it useful to mark a place in the document with a bookmark so you can quickly move the insertion point to the location. Create bookmarks for locations in a document at the Bookmark dialog box.

To create a bookmark, position the insertion point at the desired location, click the INSERT tab, and then click the Bookmark button in the Links group. This displays the Bookmark dialog box, as shown in Figure 4.9. Type a name for the bookmark in the *Bookmark name* text box and then click the Add button. Repeat these steps as many times as needed to insert the desired bookmarks. Give each bookmark a unique name. A bookmark name must begin with a letter and can contain numbers, but not spaces. Use the underscore character if you want to separate words in a bookmark name.

By default, the bookmarks you insert are not visible in the document. Turn on the display of bookmarks at the Word Options dialog box with *Advanced* selected. Display this dialog box by clicking the FILE tab and then clicking *Options*. At the Word Options dialog box, click the *Advanced* option in the left panel. Click the

▼ Quick Steps

Insert a Bookmark
1. Position insertion point at desired location.
2. Click INSERT tab.
3. Click Bookmark button.
4. Type name for bookmark.
5. Click Add button.

Bookmark

Figure 4.9 Bookmark Dialog Box

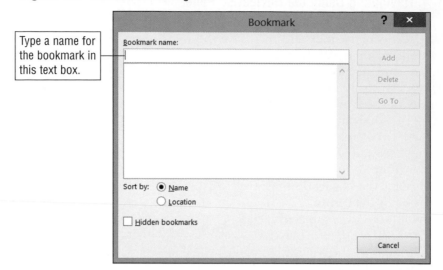

Type a name for the bookmark in this text box.

Show bookmarks check box in the *Show document content* section to insert a check mark. Complete similar steps to turn off the display of bookmarks. A bookmark displays in the document as an I-beam marker.

HINT

Bookmark brackets do not print.

You can also create a bookmark for selected text. To do this, first select the text and then complete the steps to create a bookmark. When you create a bookmark for selected text, a left bracket ([) indicates the beginning of the selected text and a right bracket (]) indicates the end of the selected text.

▼ Quick Steps

Navigate with Bookmarks
1. Click INSERT tab.
2. Click Bookmark button.
3. Double-click desired bookmark name.

After you insert bookmarks in a document, you can move the insertion point to a specific bookmark. To do this, display the Bookmark dialog box and then double-click the bookmark name or click the bookmark name and then click the Go To button. When Word stops at the location of the bookmark, click the Close button to close the dialog box. If you move the insertion point to a bookmark created with selected text, Word moves the insertion point to the bookmark and selects the text. Delete bookmarks in the Bookmark dialog box by clicking the bookmark name in the list box and then clicking the Delete button.

Project 4b | **Inserting and Navigating with Bookmarks** | **Part 2 of 5**

1. With **WL2-C4-P4-VirusesSecurity.docx** open, turn on the display of bookmarks by completing the following steps:
   a. Click the FILE tab and then click *Options*.
   b. At the Word Options dialog box, click *Advanced* in the left panel.
   c. Scroll down the dialog box and then click the *Show bookmarks* check box in the *Show document content* section to insert a check mark.
   d. Click OK to close the dialog box.
2. Insert a bookmark by completing the following steps:
   a. Move the insertion point to the beginning of the paragraph in the *TYPES OF VIRUSES* section (the paragraph that begins *Viruses can be categorized*).
   b. Click the INSERT tab.
   c. Click the Bookmark button in the Links group.

d. At the Bookmark dialog box, type **Viruses** in the *Bookmark name* text box.

e. Click the Add button.

3. Using steps similar to those in Steps 2a–2e, insert a bookmark named *Electrical* at the beginning of the paragraph in the *SYSTEMS FAILURE* section.

4. Navigate to the Viruses bookmark by completing the following steps:

a. If necessary, click the INSERT tab.

b. Click the Bookmark button in the Links group.

c. At the Bookmark dialog box, click *Viruses* in the list box.

d. Click the Go To button.

5. With the Bookmark dialog box open, delete the Electrical bookmark by clicking *Electrical* in the list box and then clicking the Delete button.

6. Click the Close button to close the Bookmark dialog box.

7. Save **WL2-C4-P4-VirusesSecurity.docx**.

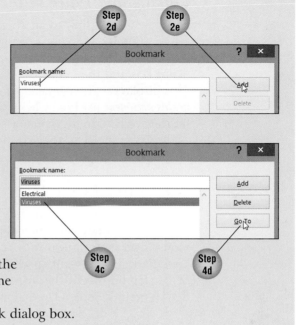

Inserting Hyperlinks

Hyperlinks can serve a number of purposes in a document. They can be used to navigate to a specific location in the document, to display a different document, to open a file in a different program, to create a new document, and to link to an email address.

Insert a hyperlink by clicking the Hyperlink button located in the Links group on the INSERT tab. This displays the Insert Hyperlink dialog box, as shown in Figure 4.10. You can also display the Insert Hyperlink dialog box by pressing Ctrl + K. At this dialog box, identify what you want to link to and the location of the link. Click the ScreenTip button to customize the hyperlink's ScreenTip.

▼ **Quick Steps**

Insert a Hyperlink
1. Click INSERT tab.
2. Click Hyperlink button.
3. Make desired changes at Insert Hyperlink dialog box.
4. Click OK.

Hyperlink

Figure 4.10 Insert Hyperlink Dialog Box

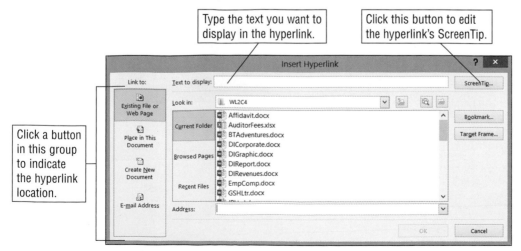

Linking to a Place in the Document

To create a hyperlink to another location in the document, you first need to mark the location by applying a heading style to the text or inserting a bookmark. To hyperlink to a heading or bookmark in a document, display the Insert Hyperlink dialog box and then click the Place in This Document button in the *Link to* section. This displays text with heading styles applied and bookmarks in the *Select a place in this document* list box. Click the desired heading style or bookmark name and the heading or bookmark name displays in the *Text to display* text box. Leave the text as displayed or select the text and then type the text you want to appear in the document.

Navigating Using Hyperlinks

Navigate to a hyperlink by hovering the mouse over the hyperlink text, holding down the Ctrl key, and then clicking the left mouse button. When you hover the mouse over hyperlink text, a ScreenTip displays with the name of the heading or bookmark. If you want specific information to display in the ScreenTip, click the ScreenTip button in the Insert Hyperlink dialog box, type the desired text in the Set Hyperlink ScreenTip dialog box, and then click OK.

Project 4c **Inserting Hyperlinks** **Part 3 of 5**

1. With **WL2-C4-P4-VirusesSecurity.docx** open, insert a hyperlink to a bookmark in the document by completing the following steps:

a. Position the insertion point at the immediate right of the period that ends the first paragraph of text in the *CHAPTER 4: SECURITY RISKS* section (located on page 4).

b. Press the spacebar once.

c. If necessary, click the INSERT tab.

d. Click the Hyperlink button in the Links group.

e. At the Insert Hyperlink dialog box, click the Place in This Document button in the *Link to* section.

f. Scroll down the *Select a place in this document* list box and then click *Viruses,* which displays below *Bookmarks* in the list box.

g. Select the text that displays in the *Text to display* text box and then type **Click to view types of viruses**.

h. Click the ScreenTip button located in the upper right corner of the dialog box.

i. At the Set Hyperlink ScreenTip dialog box, type **View types of viruses** and then click OK.

j. Click OK to close the Insert Hyperlink dialog box.

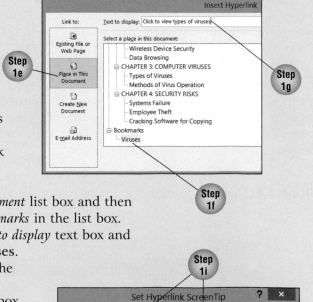

2. Navigate to the hyperlinked location by hovering the mouse over the <u>Click to view types of viruses</u> hyperlink, holding down the Ctrl key, and then clicking the left mouse button.
3. Insert a hyperlink to a heading in the document by completing the following steps:
   a. Press Ctrl + Home to move the insertion point to the beginning of the document.
   b. Move the insertion point to the immediate right of the period that ends the second paragraph in the document and then press the spacebar.
   c. Click the Hyperlink button on the INSERT tab.
   d. At the Insert Hyperlink dialog box with the Place in This Document button selected in the *Link to* section, click the *Methods of Virus Operation* heading in the *Select a place in this document* list box.
   e. Click OK to close the Insert Hyperlink dialog box.
4. Navigate to the hyperlinked heading by hovering the mouse over the <u>Methods of Virus Operation</u> hyperlink, holding down the Ctrl key, and then clicking the left mouse button.
5. Save **WL2-C4-P4-VirusesSecurity.docx**.

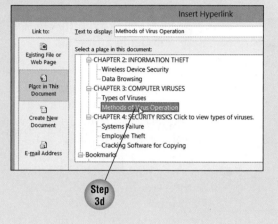

Step 3d

Linking to a File in Another Program

In some situations, you may want to provide information to your readers from a variety of sources, such as a Word document, Excel worksheet, or PowerPoint presentation. To link a Word document to a file in another application, display the Insert Hyperlink dialog box and then click the Existing File or Web Page button in the *Link to* section. Use the *Look in* option to navigate to the folder containing the desired file and then click the file name. Make other changes in the Insert Hyperlink dialog box as needed and then click OK.

Linking to a New Document

In addition to linking to an existing document, you can create a hyperlink to a new document. To do this, display the Insert Hyperlink dialog box and then click the Create New Document button in the *Link to* section. Type a name for the new document in the *Name of new document* text box and then specify if you want to edit the document now or later.

Linking Using a Graphic

You can insert a hyperlink to a file or website in a graphic such as a clip art image, picture, or text box. To hyperlink with a graphic, select the graphic, click the INSERT tab, and then click the Hyperlink button or right-click the graphic and then click *Hyperlink* at the shortcut menu. At the Insert Hyperlink dialog box, specify where you want to link to and the text you want to display in the hyperlink.

Linking to an Email Address

Insert a hyperlink to an email address at the Insert Hyperlink dialog box. To do this, click the E-Mail Address button in the *Link to* group, type the desired address in the *E-mail address* text box, and then type a subject for the email in the *Subject* text box. Click in the *Text to display* text box and then type the text you want to display in the document. To use this feature, the email address you use must be set up in Outlook.

| **Project 4d** | **Inserting a Hyperlink to Another Program, a New Document, and Using a Graphic** | **Part 4 of 5** |

1. The file **WL2-C4-P4-VirusesSecurity.docx** contains information used by Northland Security Systems. The company also has a PowerPoint presentation that contains similar information. Link the document with the presentation by completing the following steps:
   a. Move the insertion point to the immediate right of the period that ends the first paragraph in the *CHAPTER 3: COMPUTER VIRUSES* section and then press the spacebar.
   b. If necessary, click the INSERT tab.
   c. Click the Hyperlink button in the Links group.
   d. At the Insert Hyperlink dialog box, click the Existing File or Web Page button in the *Link to* section.
   e. Click the down-pointing arrow at the right side of the *Look in* list box and then navigate to the WL2C4 folder on your storage medium.
   f. Click *NSSPres.pptx* in the list box.
   g. Select the text in the *Text to display* text box and then type **Computer Virus Presentation**.
   h. Click OK to close the Insert Hyperlink dialog box.

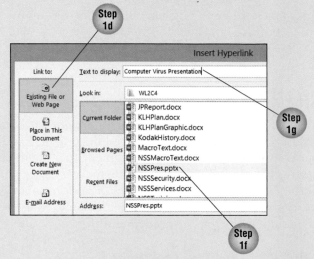

2. View the PowerPoint presentation by completing the following steps:
   a. Position the mouse pointer over the <u>Computer Virus Presentation</u> hyperlink, hold down the Ctrl key, and then click the left mouse button.
   b. At the PowerPoint presentation, click the Slide Show button in the view area on the Status bar.
   c. Click the left mouse button to advance each slide.
   d. Click the left mouse button at the black screen that displays the message *End of slide show, click to exit*.
   e. Close the presentation and PowerPoint by clicking the Close button (which contains an X) in the upper right corner of the screen.
3. Insert a hyperlink with a graphic by completing the following steps:
   a. Press Ctrl + End to move the insertion point to the end of the document.
   b. Click the compass image to select it.
   c. Click the Hyperlink button on the INSERT tab.

d. At the Insert Hyperlink dialog box, make sure the Existing File or Web Page button is selected in the *Link to* group.

e. Navigate to the WL2C4 folder on your storage medium and then double-click **NSSTraining.docx**. (This selects the document name and closes the dialog box.)

f. Click outside the clip art image to deselect it.

4. Navigate to **NSSTraining.docx** by hovering the mouse pointer over the compass image, holding down the Ctrl key, and then clicking the left mouse button.

5. Close the document by clicking the File tab and then clicking the *Close* option.

6. Insert a hyperlink to a new document by completing the following steps:

a. Move the insertion point to the immediate right of the period that ends the paragraph in the *USER IDS AND PASSWORDS* section and then press the spacebar.

b. Click the Hyperlink button on the INSERT tab.

c. Click the Create New Document button in the *Link to* section.

d. In the *Name of new document* text box, type **PasswordSuggestions**.

e. Edit the text in the *Text to display* text box so it displays as *Password Suggestions*.

f. Make sure the *Edit the new document now* option is selected.

g. Click OK.

h. At the blank document, turn on bold formatting, type **Please type any suggestions you have for creating secure passwords:**, turn off bold formatting, and then press the Enter key.

i. Save and then close the document.

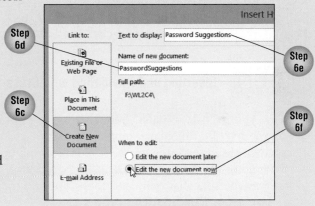

7. Press Ctrl + End to move the insertion point to the end of the document and then press the Enter key four times.

8. Insert a hyperlink to your email address or your instructor's email address by completing the following steps:

a. Click the Hyperlink button.

b. At the Insert Hyperlink dialog box, click the E-mail Address button in the *Link to* group.

c. Type your email address or your instructor's email address in the *E-mail address* text box.

d. Select the current text in the *Text to display* text box and then type **Click to send an email**.

e. Click OK to close the dialog box.

Optional: If you have Outlook set up, hold down the Ctrl key, click the Click to send an email hyperlink, and then send a message indicating that you have completed inserting hyperlinks in the WL2-C4-P4-VirusesSecurity.docx document.

9. Save **WL2-C4-P4-VirusesSecurity.docx**.

Creating a Cross-Reference

▼ **Quick Steps**

Insert a Cross-Reference
1. Type introductory text.
2. Click INSERT tab.
3. Click Cross-reference button.
4. Identify reference type, where to refer, and specific text.
5. Click Insert.
6. Click Close.

Cross-reference

A *cross-reference* in a Word document refers the reader to another location within the document. This feature is useful in a long document or a document containing related information. References to items such as headings, figures, and tables are also helpful to readers. For example, you can insert a cross-reference that refers readers to another location with more information about the topic, to a specific table, or to a specific page. Cross-references are inserted in a document as hyperlinks.

To insert a cross-reference, type introductory text, click the INSERT tab, and then click the Cross-reference button in the Links group. This displays the Cross-reference dialog box. At the Cross-reference dialog box, identify the reference type, where to refer, and the specific text.

The reference identified in the Cross-reference dialog box displays immediately after the introductory text. To move to the specified reference, hold down the Ctrl key, position the mouse pointer over the introductory text (the pointer turns into a hand), and then click the left mouse button.

Project 4e	**Inserting and Navigating with Cross-References**	**Part 5 of 5**

1. With **WL2-C4-P4-VirusesSecurity.docx** open, insert a cross-reference in the document by completing the following steps:
   a. Move the insertion point so it is positioned immediately right of the period that ends the paragraph in the *TYPES OF VIRUSES* section.
   b. Press the spacebar once and then type **(For more information, refer to.**
   c. Press the spacebar once.
   d. If necessary, click the INSERT tab.
   e. Click the Cross-reference button in the Links group.
   f. At the Cross-reference dialog box, click the down-pointing arrow at the right side of the *Reference type* option box and then click *Heading* at the drop-down list.
   g. Click *Spyware* in the *For which heading* list box.
   h. Click the Insert button.
   i. Click the Close button to close the dialog box.
   j. At the document, type a period followed by a right parenthesis.
2. Move to the reference text by holding down the Ctrl key, positioning the mouse pointer over *Spyware* until the pointer turns into a hand, and then clicking the left mouse button.

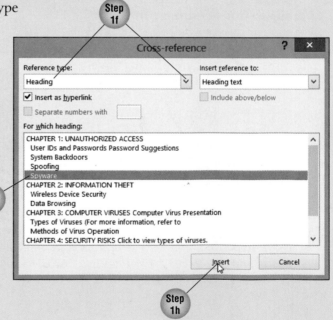

3. Save **WL2-C4-P4-VirusesSecurity.docx**.
4. Print the document.
5. Turn off the display of bookmarks by completing the following steps:
   a. Click the FILE tab and then click *Options*.
   b. At the Word Options dialog box, click *Advanced* in the left panel.
   c. Click the *Show bookmarks* check box in the *Show document content* section to remove the check mark.
   d. Click OK to close the dialog box.
6. Close **WL2-C4-P4-VirusesSecurity.docx**.

Chapter Summary

- Create custom theme colors with options at the Create New Theme Colors dialog box and create custom theme fonts with options at the Create New Theme Fonts dialog box.

- Click the Reset button in the Create New Theme Colors dialog box to reset colors back to the default Office theme colors.

- Create custom theme colors and custom theme fonts, apply a theme effect, and then save the changes in a custom theme. Save a custom theme at the Save Current Theme dialog box. Display this dialog box by clicking the Themes button in the Document Formatting group on the DESIGN tab and then clicking *Save Current Theme* at the drop-down gallery.

- Apply custom theme colors by clicking the Theme Colors button and then clicking the custom theme that displays near the top of the drop-down gallery. Complete similar steps to apply custom theme fonts and a custom theme.

- You can edit and delete custom themes. Delete a custom theme at the Themes button drop-down gallery or at the Save Current Theme dialog box.

- Click the *Reset to Theme from Template* option at the Themes button drop-down gallery to reset the theme to the template default.

- A *style* is a set of formatting instructions you can apply to text in a document. Word provides a number of predesigned styles grouped into style sets.

- Styles within a style set are available in the Styles group on the HOME tab.

- Apply a style by clicking the style thumbnail in the Styles group on the HOME tab, or clicking a style in the Styles task pane. Display the Styles task pane by clicking the Styles group task pane launcher.

- Modify a predesigned style with options at the Modify Styles dialog box. Display this dialog box by right-clicking the style in the Styles group or in the Styles task pane and then clicking *Modify* at the shortcut menu.

- Recording a macro involves turning on the macro recorder, performing the steps to be recorded, and then turning off the recorder.

- Run a macro by displaying the Macros dialog box and then double-clicking the desired macro name.

- Temporarily suspend the recording of a macro by clicking the Pause Recording button in the Code group on the DEVELOPER tab.

- Delete a macro by displaying the Macros dialog box, clicking the macro name to be deleted, and then clicking the Delete button.
- Assign a macro to a keyboard command at the Record Macro dialog box. To run a macro that has been assigned a keyboard command, press the keys assigned to the macro.
- Specify macro security settings at the Trust Center with *Macro Settings* selected in the left panel. Display the Trust Center by clicking the Macro Security button in the Code group on the DEVELOPER tab.
- Save a document as a macro-enabled document or a template as a macro-enabled template with the *Save as type* option at the Save As dialog box.
- Navigate in a document with the Navigation pane or by inserting bookmarks, hyperlinks, and cross-references.
- Insert bookmarks with options at the Bookmark dialog box.
- Insert hyperlinks in a document with options at the Insert Hyperlink dialog box. Insert a hyperlink to an existing file or web page, a location in the current document, a new document, or an email. You can also use a graphic to link to a file or website.
- Create a cross-reference with options at the Cross-reference dialog box.

Commands Review

FEATURE	RIBBON TAB, GROUP	BUTTON, OPTION	KEYBOARD SHORTCUT
Bookmark dialog box	INSERT, Links		
Create New Theme Colors dialog box	DESIGN, Document Formatting	, *Customize Colors*	
Create New Theme Fonts dialog box	DESIGN, Document Formatting	, *Customize Fonts*	
Cross-reference dialog box	INSERT, Links		
Insert Hyperlink dialog box	INSERT, Links		Ctrl + K
Macros dialog box	DEVELOPER, Code OR VIEW, Macros		Alt + F8
Record Macro dialog box	DEVELOPER, Code OR VIEW, Macros		
Save Current Theme dialog box	DESIGN, Document Formatting	, *Save Current Theme*	
Styles task pane	HOME, Styles		Alt + Ctrl + Shift + S
theme effects	DESIGN, Document Formatting		
Trust Center	DEVELOPER, Code		

Concepts Check   Test Your Knowledge

Completion: In the space provided at the right, indicate the correct term, symbol, or command.

1. The Themes button is located on this tab. _____

2. Create custom theme colors at this dialog box. _____

3. A theme that you save displays in this section in the Themes button drop-down gallery. _____

4. If you hover the mouse pointer over a style in the Styles task pane, this displays with information about the formatting applied. _____

5. This tab contains the Record Macro button in the Code group. _____

6. A macro name must begin with a letter and can contain only letters and these. _____

7. When macro recording is turned on, a macro icon displays on this. _____

8. Delete a macro at this dialog box. _____

9. Assign a macro to a keyboard command at this dialog box. _____

10. The *Navigation Pane* check box is located in the Show group on this tab. _____

11. The Bookmark button is located in this group on the INSERT tab. _____

12. Turn on the display of bookmarks in a document with the *Show bookmarks* check box in this dialog box with *Advanced* selected. _____

13. Navigate to a hyperlink by hovering the mouse over the hyperlink text, holding down this key, and then clicking the left mouse button. _____

14. To link a Word document to a file in another application, click this button in the *Link to* group in the Insert Hyperlink dialog box. _____

15. By default, cross-references are inserted in a document as this. _____

Skills Check   Assess Your Performance

Assessment

1 CREATE AND APPLY CUSTOM THEMES TO A MEDICAL PLANS DOCUMENT

1. At a blank document, create custom theme colors named with your initials that make the following color changes:
   a. Change the Accent 1 color to *Dark Red* (the first option in the *Standard Colors* section).
   b. Change the Accent 5 color to *Gold, Accent 4, Darker 50%* (eighth column, bottom row in the *Theme Colors* section).
2. Create custom theme fonts named with your initials that change the heading font to Corbel and the body font to Garamond.
3. Click the Theme Effects button and then click *Top Shadow* at the drop-down gallery (first column, third row).
4. Save the custom theme and name it with your initials. **Hint: Do this with the Save Current Theme *option at the* Themes *drop-down gallery.***
5. Close the document without saving the changes.
6. Open **KLHPlan.docx** and then save the document and name it **WL2-C4-A1-KLHPlan**.
7. Make the following changes to the document:
   a. Apply the Lines (Simple) style set.
   b. With the insertion point positioned at the beginning of the document, type the title **Key Life Health Plan**.
   c. Apply the Heading 1 style to the title.
   d. Apply the Heading 2 style to the three headings in the document.
8. Move the insertion point to the end of the document, press Ctrl + Enter to insert a page break, and then insert the document **KLHPlanGraphic.docx**. **Hint: Do this with the Object button arrow on the INSERT tab.**
9. Apply the custom theme you created by clicking the DESIGN tab, clicking the Themes button, and then clicking the custom theme named with your initials.
10. Save, print, and then close **WL2-C4-A1-KLHPlan.docx**.
11. At a blank document, delete the custom theme colors named with your initials, the custom theme fonts named with your initials, and the custom theme named with your initials.

Assessment

2 RECORD AND RUN FORMATTING MACROS

1. Open **MacroText.docx** and then create a macro named *XXXTitle* (where *XXX* is your initials) with the following specifications:
   a. Position the insertion point at the beginning of the word *Title* and then turn on the macro recorder.
   b. Press the F8 key and then press the End key.
   c. Click the Center button and then click the Bold button.
   d. Change the font size to 14 points.

e. Click the Shading button arrow and then click *Blue, Accent 1, Lighter 40%* (fifth column, fourth row in the *Theme Colors* section).

f. Use the Borders button and insert a bottom border.

g. Turn off the macro recorder.

2. Create a macro named *XXXHd* (where *XXX* is your initials) with the following specifications:

a. Position the insertion point at the beginning of the word *Heading* and then turn on the macro recorder.

b. Press the F8 key and then press the End key.

c. Click the Bold button and then click the Italic button.

d. Change the font size to 12 points.

e. Click the Shading button arrow and then click *Blue, Accent 1, Lighter 80%* (fifth column, second row in the *Theme Colors* section).

f. Turn off the macro recorder.

3. Create a macro named *XXXDocFont* (where *XXX* is your initials) that selects the entire document and then changes the font to Cambria. Assign the macro the keyboard shortcut Alt + D.

4. Close **MacroText.docx** without saving it.

5. Open **WebReport.docx** and save the document with the name **WL2-C4-A2-WebReport**.

6. Press Alt + D to run the XXXDocFont macro.

7. Run the XXXTitle macro for the two titles in the document: *Navigating the Web* and *Searching the Web*.

8. Run the XXXHd macro for the four headings in the document: *IPs and URLs, Browsing Web Pages, Search Engines*, and *How Search Engines Work*.

9. Save, print, and then close **WL2-C4-A2-WebReport.docx**.

10. Delete the macros you created in this assessment: XXXDocFont, XXXTitle, and XXXHd.

Assessment

3   FORMAT AND NAVIGATE IN A CORPORATE REPORT DOCUMENT

1. Open **DIReport.docx** and then save the document and name it **WL2-C4-A3-DIReport**.

2. Move the insertion point to any character in the second paragraph in the document (the paragraph that begins *Assist the company's board of directors in fulfilling*), turn on the display of the Styles task pane, apply the *Intense Quote* style to the paragraph, and then turn off the display of the Styles task pane.

3. Apply the Lines (Distinctive) style set.

4. Turn on the display of bookmarks.

5. Move the insertion point to the end of the third paragraph in the document (the paragraph that begins *The audit committee selects*) and then insert a bookmark named *Audit*.

6. Move the insertion point to the end of the first paragraph in the *FEES TO INDEPENDENT AUDITOR* section, following the *(Excel worksheet)* text, and then insert a bookmark named *Audit_Fees*.

7. Move the insertion point to the end of the last paragraph of text in the document and then insert a bookmark named *Compensation*.

8. Navigate in the document using the bookmarks.

9. Move the insertion point to the end of the first paragraph in the *COMMITTEE RESPONSIBILITIES* section, press the spacebar, and then insert a hyperlink to the Audit_Fees bookmark.

10. Select the text *(Excel worksheet)* that displays at the end of the first paragraph in the *FEES TO INDEPENDENT AUDITOR* section and then insert a hyperlink to **AuditorFees.xlsx**, which is located in the WL2C4 folder on your storage medium.

11. Move the insertion point to the end of the document, click the clip art image, and then insert a hyperlink to the Word document named **DIGraphic.docx** located in the WL2C4 folder on your storage medium. At the Insert Hyperlink dialog box, create a ScreenTip with the text *Click to view a long-term incentives graphic.*

12. Hold down the Ctrl key and then click the *(Excel worksheet)* hyperlink and then print the Excel worksheet that displays by clicking the FILE tab, clicking the *Print* option, and then clicking the Print button in the Print backstage area.

13. Close the Excel program without saving the workbook.

14. Hold down the Ctrl key and then click the clip art to display the Word document containing the graphic. Print the graphic document and then close the document.

15. Save, print, and then close **WL2-C4-A3-DIReport.docx**.

Assessment

4 ASSIGN MACROS TO THE QUICK ACCESS TOOLBAR

1. In this chapter, you have learned how to record a macro and assign a keyboard shortcut to a macro. A macro can also be assigned to a button on the Quick Access toolbar. Using the Help feature, search for and then read the article *Create or run a macro.* Learn specifically how to assign a macro to a button.

2. Open **NSSMacroText.docx** and then use the document to create the following macros:

   a. Create a macro named *XXXNSSDocFormat* (where *XXX* is your initials) and assign it to a button (you determine the button icon) that selects the entire document (use Ctrl + A), applies the No Spacing style (click the *No Spacing* style in the Styles group), changes the line spacing to double (press Ctrl + 2), and changes the font to Constantia.

   b. Create a macro named *XXXNSSHeading* (where *XXX* is your initials) and assign it to a button (you determine the button icon) that selects a line of text (at the beginning of the line, press F8 and then press the End key), changes the font size to 12 points, turns on bold formatting, centers text, and then deselects the text.

3. Close **NSSMacroText.docx** without saving changes.

4. Open **EmpComp.docx** and save the document with the name **WL2-C4-A4-EmpComp**.

5. Click the button on the Quick Access toolbar to run the XXXNSSDocFormat macro.

6. Run the XXXNSSHeading macro (using the button on the Quick Access toolbar) for the title *COMPENSATION* and the five headings in the document.

7. Keep the heading, *Overtime*, with the paragraph of text that follows it.

8. Save, print, and then close **WL2-C4-A4-EmpComp.docx**.

9. Open a blank document and then open another blank document. Make a screenshot of the Quick Access toolbar. (Use the *Screen Clippings* option from the ScreenShot button drop-down list.) Print the document containing the screenshot and then close the document without saving it.

10. At the blank document, delete the macro buttons from the Quick Access toolbar and then delete the macros from the Macros dialog box.
11. Remove the DEVELOPER tab from the ribbon. (Do this by displaying the Word Options dialog box with *Customize Ribbon* selected in the left panel. Remove the check mark from the *Developer* check box, and then click OK to close the dialog box.)

Visual Benchmark   Demonstrate Your Proficiency

INSERT SMARTART GRAPHICS IN A BUSINESS DOCUMENT

1. Open **DIRevenues.docx** and then save the document and name it **WL2-C4-VB-DIRevenues**.
2. Create the following custom theme colors named with your first and last names with the following changes:
   a. Change the Text/Background - Dark 2 color to *Orange, Accent 2, Darker 50%* (sixth column, last row in the *Theme Colors* section).
   b. Change the Accent 1 color to *Green, Accent 6, Darker 50%* (tenth column, last row in the *Theme Colors* section).
   c. Change the Accent 4 color to *Orange, Accent 2, Darker 50%*.
   d. Change the Accent 6 color to *Green, Accent 6, Darker 25%*.
3. Create the following custom theme fonts named with your first and last names with the following changes:
   a. Change the heading font to *Copperplate Gothic Bold*.
   b. Change the body font to *Constantia*.
4. Apply the Riblet theme effect.
5. Save the custom theme and name it *WL2C4* followed by your initials. ***Hint: Do this with the* Save Current Theme *option at the* Themes *drop-down gallery.***
6. Center the title and reposition the SmartArt graphic as shown in Figure 4.7.
7. Save, print, and then close **WL2-C4-VB-DIRevenues.docx**.
8. Open **DICorporate.docx** and then save the document and name it **WL2-C4-VB-DICorporate**.
9. Apply the WL2C4 (followed by your initials) custom theme to the document.
10. Center the title and reposition the SmartArt graphic as shown in Figure 4.8 on page 171.
11. Save, print, and then close **WL2-C4-VB-DICorporate.docx**.
12. At a blank document, use the Print Screen button to make a screen capture of the Theme Colors drop-down gallery (make sure your custom theme colors display), a screen capture of the Theme Fonts drop-down gallery (make sure your custom theme fonts display), and a screen capture of the Save Current Theme dialog box (make sure your custom themes are visible). Insert all three screen capture images on the same page. (You will need to size the images.)
13. Save the document and name it **WL2-C4-VB-ScreenImages**.
14. Print and then close **WL2-C4-VB-ScreenImages.docx**.
15. At a blank document, delete the custom color theme you created, as well as the custom font theme and the custom theme.

Figure 4.7 Visual Benchmark 1

DEARBORN INDUSTRIES

REVENUES

We are evaluating markets for our current and future products. Prior to the fourth quarter of 2015, we recorded revenues as a result of development contracts with government entities focused on the design of flywheel technologies. We have produced and placed several development prototypes with potential customers and shipped preproduction units.

RESEARCH AND DEVELOPMENT

Our cost of research and development consists primarily of the cost of compensation and benefits for research and support staff, as well as materials and supplies used in the engineering design and development process. These costs decreased significantly during 2015 as we focused on reducing our expenditure rate by reducing product design and development activities.

PREFERRED STOCK DIVIDENDS

Prior to our initial public offering of our common stock, we had various classes of preferred stock outstanding, each of which was entitled to receive dividends. We accrued dividend expenses monthly according to the requirements of each class of preferred stock.

Figure 4.8 Visual Benchmark 2

DEARBORN INDUSTRIES

CORPORATE VISION

Dearborn Industries will be the leading developer of clean and environmentally friendly products. Building on strong leadership, development, and resources, we will provide superior-quality products and services to our customers and consumers around the world.

CORPORATE VALUES

We value the environment in which we live, and we will work to produce and maintain energy-efficient and environmentally safe products and strive to reduce our carbon footprint on the environment.

CORPORATE LEADERSHIP

Dearborn Industries employees conduct business under the leadership of the chief executive officer, who is subject to the oversight and direction of the board of directors. Four vice presidents work with the chief executive officer to manage and direct business.

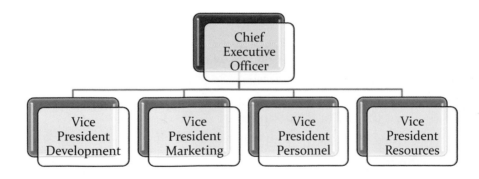

Case Study   Apply Your Skills

Part 1

You work for Jackson Photography and want to create a new letterhead for the company. Open **JPLtrd.docx** and then customize the text and clip art to create an attractive and professional-looking letterhead. Save the completed letterhead with the same name (**JPLtrd.docx**). Create a building block with the letterhead.

Part 2

At a blank document, create and then save custom theme colors that match the letterhead you created in Part 1. Create and then save custom theme fonts that apply the Arial font to headings and the Constantia font to body text. Apply a custom theme effect of your choosing. Save the custom theme in the Save Current Theme dialog box and name it with your initials followed by *JP*.

Part 3

At a blank document, insert the company letterhead building block you created in Part 1, type the title **Photography Services**, and then insert a SmartArt graphic of your choosing that contains the following text:

- Wedding Photography
- Sports Portraits
- Senior Portraits
- Family Portraits
- Processing

Apply a heading style to the *Photography Services* title, apply the custom theme to the document, and then save the document and name it **WL2-C4-CS-JPServices**.

Part 4

Open **JPReport.docx** and then save the document and name it **WL2-C4-CS-JPReport**. Apply or insert the following in the document:

- Apply your custom theme.
- Apply the Intense Quote style to the quote at the beginning and the quote at the end of the document.
- Insert a footer of your choosing in the document.

Apply any other enhancements to improve the appearance of the document. Save **WL2-C4-CS-JPReport.docx**.

Part 5

With **WL2-C4-CS-JPReport.docx** open, insert at the end of the third paragraph in the *Photography* section a hyperlink that links to the document **KodakHistory.docx** located in the WL2C4 folder on your storage medium. Using the Internet, research and locate at least one company that sells digital cameras. At the end of the document, insert text that tells the reader to click the hyperlink text to link to that particular site on the Internet and then insert the hyperlink to the website you found. Save, print, and then close **WL2-C4-CS-JPReport.docx**.

WORD
MICROSOFT®

Performance Assessment

Note: Before beginning unit assessments, copy to your storage medium the WL2U1 subfolder from the WL2 folder on the CD that accompanies this textbook and then make WL2U1 the active folder.

Word
WL2U1

Assessing Proficiency ■■■■■■■■■■■■■■■■

In this unit, you have learned how to customize the spelling, grammar, and AutoCorrect features in a document; format documents with special features, such as customized bullets, numbering, headers, footers, and page numbering; automate formatting with macros; and apply and customize building blocks, themes, style sets, and styles.

Assessment 1 Format Stock Awards Document

1. Open **CMStocks.docx** and then save the document and name it **WL2-U1-A1-CMStocks**.
2. Apply the Title style to the title *Clearline Manufacturing*.
3. Apply the Heading 1 style to the headings *Stock Awards* and *Employee Stock Plan*.
4. Apply the Centered style set.
5. Select the bulleted paragraphs of text and then define a new picture bullet. At the Insert Pictures window, search for *blue globe with grid lines* and download the globe with blue grid lines and a black background.
6. Select the lines of text below the *Employee Stock Plan* heading and then apply a multilevel list (middle option in top row of the *List Library* section of the Multilevel List button drop-down gallery).
7. With the text still selected, define a new multilevel list that inserts capital letters followed by periods (A., B., C.) for level 2 and inserts arabic numbers followed by periods (1., 2., 3.) for level 3. (Make sure the new multilevel list applies to the selected text.)
8. Save, print, and then close **WL2-U1-A1-CMStocks.docx**.

Assessment 2 Format a Future of Computer Ethics Report

1. Open **FutureEthics.docx** and then save the document and name it **WL2-U1-A2-FutureEthics**.
2. Keep the heading *Self-Replicating Robots* (located at the bottom of the first page) together with the paragraph of text that follows it.
3. Keep the title *REFERENCES* (located at the bottom of the second page) together with the paragraph of text that follows it.
4. Insert the *FileName* and *PrintDate* fields at the end of the document (on separate lines).

5. Create an odd page footer that prints the document title *Future of Computer Ethics* at the left margin and the page number at the right margin. Also create an even page footer that prints the page number at the left margin and document title at the right margin.
6. Save, print, and then close **WL2-U1-A2-FutureEthics.docx**.

Assessment 3 Create and Format a Column Chart

1. At a blank document, use the data in Figure U1.1 to create a column chart with the following specifications:
   a. Choose the 3-D Clustered Column chart type.
   b. Apply the Layout 3 chart layout.
   c. Apply the Style 5 chart style.
   d. Change the chart title to *2015 Sales*.
   e. Insert a data table with legend keys.
   f. Select the chart area, apply the Subtle Effect - Green, Accent 6 shape style (last column, fourth row), and apply the Offset Bottom shadow shape effect (second column, first row in Outer section).
   g. Select the Second Half series and then apply the Dark Red shape fill.
   h. Change the chart height to 4 inches and chart width to 6.25 inches.
   i. Use the Position button in the Arrange group to position the chart in the middle of the page with square text wrapping.
2. Save the document with the name **WL2-U1-A3-SalesChart**.
3. Print **WL2-U1-A3-SalesChart.docx**.
4. With the chart selected, display the Excel worksheet and edit the data in the worksheet by changing the following:
   a. Change the amount in cell C2 from *$285,450* to *$302,500*.
   b. Change the amount in cell C4 from *$180,210* to *$190,150*.
5. Save, print, and then close **WL2-U1-A3-SalesChart.docx**.

Figure U1.1 Assessment 3

Salesperson	First Half	Second Half
Bratton	$235,500	$285,450
Daniels	$300,570	$250,700
Hughes	$170,200	$180,210
Marez	$358,520	$376,400

Assessment 4 Create and Format a Pie Chart

1. At a blank document, use the data in Figure U1.2 to create a pie chart with the following specifications:
   a. Apply the Layout 6 chart layout.
   b. Apply the Style 3 chart style.
   c. Change the chart title to *District Expenditures*.
   d. Move the legend to the left side of the chart.

e. Select the chart area, apply Gold, Accent 4, Lighter 80% shape fill (eighth column, second row in the *Theme Colors* section), and apply the Gray-50%, 11 pt glow, Accent color 3 glow shape effect (third column, third row in the *Glow Variations* section).

f. Select the legend and apply a Blue shape outline (eighth option in the *Standard Colors* section).

g. Apply the WordArt style Fill - Blue, Accent 1, Outline - Background 1, Hard Shadow - Accent 1 (third column, third row) to the chart title text.

h. Move the data labels to the inside ends of the pie pieces.

i. Select the legend and move it so it is centered between the left edge of the chart border and the pie.

j. Use the Position button in the Arrange group to center the chart at the top of the page.

2. Save the document with the name **WL2-U1-A4-ExpendChart**.

3. Print and then close **WL2-U1-A4-ExpendChart.docx**.

Figure U1.2 Assessment 4

	Percentage
Basic Education	42%
Special Needs	20%
Support Services	19%
Vocational	11%
Compensatory	8%

Assessment 5 Navigate in a Smoke Detector Report

1. Open **SmokeDetectors.docx** and then save the document and name it **WL2-U1-A5-SmokeDetectors**.

2. If necessary, turn on the display of bookmarks. (Do this at the Word Options dialog box with *Advanced* selected in the left panel.)

3. Move the insertion point to the end of the paragraph in the *Types of Smoke Detectors* section and then insert a bookmark named *Types*.

4. Move the insertion point to the end of the last paragraph in the *Safety Tips* section and then insert a bookmark named *Resources*.

5. Move the insertion point to the end of the first paragraph in the *Taking Care of Smoke Detectors* section (located at the bottom of the second page) and then insert a bookmark named *Maintenance*.

6. Navigate in the document using the bookmarks.

7. Select the text *(NFPA website)* that displays at the end of the first paragraph in the document and then insert a hyperlink to the website www.nfpa.org.

8. Hold down the Ctrl key and then click the *(NFPA website)* hyperlink. At the NFPA home page, navigate to web pages that interest you and then close your browser.

9. Move the insertion point to the end of the document and then create a hyperlink with the clip art image to the Word document named **SmokeDetectorFacts.docx**.

10. Click outside the clip art image to deselect it.
11. Hold down the Ctrl key and then click the clip art image. At the **SmokeDetectorFacts.docx** document, read the information, print the document, and then close the document.
12. Save, print, and then close **WL2-U1-A5-SmokeDetectors.docx**.

Assessment 6 Format a Computer Devices Report

1. Open **CompDevices.docx** and then save the document and name it **WL2-U1-A6-CompDevices**.
2. With the insertion point positioned at the beginning of the document, press Ctrl + Enter to insert a page break.
3. Apply the Heading 1 style to the two titles in the document: *COMPUTER INPUT DEVICES* and *COMPUTER OUTPUT DEVICES*.
4. Apply the Heading 2 style to the six headings in the document.
5. Apply the Minimalist style set.
6. Apply the Yellow Orange theme colors.
7. Apply the Corbel theme fonts.
8. Insert a section break that begins a new page at the beginning of the title *COMPUTER OUTPUT DEVICES* (located on the third page).
9. Create a footer for the first section in the document that prints *Computer Input Devices* at the left margin, the page number in the middle, and your first and last names at the right margin.
10. Edit the footer for the second section so it prints *Computer Output Devices* instead of *Computer Input Devices*. (Make sure you deactivate the *Link to Previous* feature.)
11. Move the insertion point to the beginning of the document and then insert the Slice (Dark) cover page. Type **COMPUTER DEVICES** as the document title and type **Computer Input and Output Devices** as the document subtitle.
12. Move the insertion point to the beginning of the second page (blank page) and then insert the Automatic Table 1 table of contents building block.
13. Save, print, and then close **WL2-U1-A6-CompDevices.docx**.

Assessment 7 Format a Building a Website Document

1. Open **BuildWebsite.docx** and then save the document and name it **WL2-U1-A7-BuildWebsite**.
2. Display the Word Options dialog box with *Proofing* selected in the left panel, insert a check mark in the *Show readability statistics* check box, change the *Writing Style* option to *Grammar & Style*, and then close the dialog box.
3. Complete a spelling and grammar checker on the document. Click the Ignore button when the grammar checker selects a sentence and displays the message *Passive Voice (consider revising)* in the Grammar task pane. After completing the spelling and grammar check, proofread the document and make any necessary changes not selected during the spelling and grammar check.
4. Format the document with the following:
   a. Apply the Title style to the title *Building a Website*; apply the Heading 1 style to the headings *Planning a Website*, *Choosing a Host*, and *Organizing the Site*; and apply the Heading 3 style to the subheadings *Free Web-Hosting Services*, *Free Hosting from ISPs*, and *Fee-Based Hosting Services*.
   b. Format the text (except the title) into two evenly spaced columns. Balance the end of the text on the second page.
   c. Apply the Shaded style set and then center the title.

    d. Apply the Blue Warm theme colors and the Garamond theme fonts.

    e. Insert the Ion (Dark) header building block.

    f. Insert the Ion (Dark) footer building block. Type **BUILDING A WEBSITE** as the document title and type your first and last names at the right side of the footer.

5. Display the Word Options dialog box with *Proofing* selected in the left panel, remove the check mark from the *Show readability statistics* check box, change the *Writing Style* option to *Grammar Only*, and then close the dialog box.

6. Save, print, and then close **WL2-U1-A7-BuildWebsite.docx**.

Assessment 8 Format an Equipment Rental Agreement

1. At a blank document, create custom theme colors named with your initials that make the following color changes:

    a. Change the Text/Background - Dark 2 color to *Orange, Accent 2, Darker 50%* (sixth column, last row in the Theme Colors section).

    b. Change the Accent 1 color to *Green, Accent 6, Darker 25%* (tenth column, last row in the Theme Colors section).

2. Create custom theme fonts named with your initials that apply the Verdana font to headings and Cambria font to body text.

3. Save the custom theme and name it with your initials. (Do this with the *Save Current Theme* option at the Themes button drop-down gallery.)

4. Close the document without saving the changes.

5. Open **MRCForm.docx** and then save the document and name it **WL2-U1-A8-MRCForm**.

6. Search for all occurrences of *mrc* and replace them with *Meridian Rental Company*.

7. Add the following text to AutoCorrect:

    a. Insert *mrc* in the *Replace* text box and insert *Meridian Rental Company* in the *With* text box.

    b. Insert *erag* in the *Replace* text box and insert *Equipment Rental Agreement* in the *With* text box.

8. Move the insertion point to the blank line below the *Default* heading (located on the third page) and then type the text shown in Figure U1.3 on the next page. Use the Numbering feature to number the paragraphs with a lowercase letter followed by a right parenthesis. (If the AutoCorrect feature capitalizes the first word after the letter and right parenthesis, use the AutoCorrect options button to return the letter to lowercase.)

9. Apply the Title style to the title *Equipment Rental Agreement* and apply the Heading 1 style to the headings in the document: *Lease, Rent, Use and Operation of Equipment, Insurance, Risk of Loss, Maintenance, Return of Equipment, Warranties of Lessee, Default,* and *Further Assurances*.

10. Apply the Centered style set.

11. Apply your custom theme to the document.

12. Insert the Sample 1 watermark building block.

13. Insert the Banded footer building block.

14. Delete the two entries you made at the AutoCorrect dialog box.

15. Save, print, and then close **WL2-U1-A8-MRCForm.docx**.

16. At a blank document, delete the custom theme colors, custom theme fonts, and custom theme named with your initials.

Figure U1.3 Assessment 8

Upon the occurrence of default, mrc may, without any further notice, exercise any one or more of the following remedies:

   a) terminate this erag as to any or all items of Equipment;

   b) cause Lessee at its expense to promptly return the Equipment to mrc in the condition set forth in this erag;

   c) use, hold, sell, lease, or otherwise dispose of the Equipment or any item of it on the premises of Lessee or any other location without affecting the obligations of Lessee as provided in this erag;

   d) proceed by appropriate action either at law or in equity to enforce performance by Lessee of the applicable covenants of this erag or to recover damages for the breach of them; or

   e) exercise any other rights accruing to mrc under any applicable law upon a default by Lessee.

Assessment 9 Create and Run Macros

1. Open a blank document and then create the following macros:
   a. Create a macro named *XXXAPMFormat* (use your initials in place of the *XXX*) that changes the top margin to 1.5 inches and then selects the entire document and changes the font to Candara.
   b. Create a macro named *XXXAPMSubtitle* with the keyboard command Alt + S that selects the line (press F8 and then press the End key), changes the font size to 12 points, turns on bold formatting, centers the text, and applies Blue, Accent 1, Lighter 80% paragraph shading (fifth column, second row in the Theme Colors section).
2. After recording the macros, close the document without saving it.
3. Open **Lease.docx** and then save the document and name it **WL2-U1-A9-Lease**.
4. Run the XXXAPMFormat macro.
5. Move the insertion point to the beginning of the heading *RENT* and then press Alt + S to run the XXXAPMSubtitle macro.
6. Run the XXXAPMSubtitle macro (using Alt + S) for the remaining headings: *DAMAGE DEPOSIT, USE OF PREMISES, CONDITION OF PREMISES, ALTERATIONS AND IMPROVEMENTS, NON-DELIVERY OF POSSESSION*, and *UTILITIES*.
7. Save, print, and then close **WL2-U1-A9-Lease.docx**.
8. Open **REAgrmnt.docx** and then save the document and name it **WL2-U1-A9-REAgrmnt**.
9. Run the XXXAPMFormat macro.
10. Run the XXXAPMSubtitle macro (using Alt + S) for each heading in the document: *Financing, New Financing, Closing Costs, Survey*, and *Attorney Fees*.
11. Save, print, and then close **WL2-U1-A9-REAgrmnt.docx**.
12. Delete the macros you created in this assessment: XXXAPMFormat and XXXAPMSubtitle.

Writing Activities ▪▪▪■▪■▪■▪■■▪■■▪

Activity 1 Create Building Blocks and Compose a Letter

You are the executive assistant to the director of the Human Resources department at Clearline Manufacturing. You are responsible for preparing employee documents, notices, reports, and forms. You decide to create building blocks to increase the efficiency of, and consistency in, department documents. Create the following:

- Create a letterhead for the company that includes the company name and any other enhancements to improve the appearance of the letterhead. Save the letterhead text as a building block.

- Create a building block footer that inserts the company address and telephone number. (You determine the address and telephone number.) Include a visual element to the footer, such as a border line.

- You send documents to the board of directors and so you decide to include the following names and addresses as building blocks:

  Mrs. Nancy Logan   Mr. Dion Jarvis
  12301 132nd Avenue East   567 Federal Street
  Warminster, PA 18974   Philadelphia, PA 19093

  Dr. Austin Svoboda
  9823 South 112th Street
  Norristown, PA 18974

- Create a complimentary close building block that includes *Sincerely yours,* your name, and the title *Executive Assistant.*

Write the body of a letter to a member of the board of directors and include at least the following information:

- Explain that the Human Resources department director has created a new employee handbook and that it will be made available to all new employees. Also mention that the attorney for Clearline Manufacturing has reviewed the handbook document and approved its content.

- Open the **CMHandbook.docx** document and then use the headings to summarize the contents of the document in a paragraph in the letter. Explain in the letter that a draft of the handbook is enclosed with the letter.

- Include any additional information you feel the directors may want to know.

Save the body of the letter as a separate document. Using the building blocks you created, along with the letter document, create letters to Nancy Logan, Dion Jarvis, and Austin Svoboda. Save the letters individually and then print them.

Activity 2 Create a Custom Theme

Create a custom theme for formatting documents that includes the colors and/or fonts you chose for the Clearline Manufacturing letterhead. Open the document named **CMHandbook.docx** and then save the document and name it **WL2-U1-Act2-CMHandbook**. Apply at least the following formatting to the document:

- The footer building block you created as a footer in the document
- Table of contents building block
- Cover page building block
- Draft watermark building block
- Formatting to the title, headings, and subheadings
- Any additional formatting that improve the appearance and readability of the document

Select the text *(Click to display Longevity Schedule.)* that displays at the end of the first paragraph in the *Longevity Pay* section and insert a hyperlink to the Excel file named **CMPaySchedule.xlsx** located in the WL2U1 folder on your storage medium. After inserting the hyperlink, click the hyperlink and make sure the Clearline worksheet displays and then close Excel.

Save, print, and then close **WL2-U1-Act2-CMHandbook.docx**. Delete the custom themes you created and the building blocks you created in Activity 1.

Internet Research ■■■■■■■■■■ ■■■■■■■■ ■■■■

Prepare Information on Printer Specifications

You are responsible for purchasing new color laser printers for the Human Resources department at Clearline Manufacturing. You need to research printers and then prepare a report about them to the director of the department. Using the Internet, search for at least two companies that produce color laser printers. Determine information such as printer make and model, printer performance, printer cost, and prices for printer cartridges. Using the information you find, prepare a report to the director, Deana Terril. Type at least one list in the report and then create and apply a customized bullet to the list. Insert a predesigned header or footer and create and apply a custom theme to the report document. Save the report document and name it **WL2-U1-Act3-Printers**. Print and then close **WL2-U1-Act3-Printers.docx**.

WORD
MICROSOFT®

Level 2

Unit 2 ■ Editing and Formatting Documents

WORD
MICROSOFT®

Inserting Special Features and References

PERFORMANCE OBJECTIVES

Upon successful completion of Chapter 5, you will be able to:

- Sort text in paragraphs, columns, and tables
- Sort records in a data source file
- Select specific records in a data source file for merging
- Insert nonbreaking spaces
- Find and replace special characters
- Create and use specialized templates
- Create footnotes and endnotes
- Insert and modify sources and citations
- Insert, modify, and format source lists

Tutorials

5.1 Sorting Text in Paragraphs, Columns, and Tables

5.2 Sorting Records in a Data Source File

5.3 Selecting Specific Records for Merging

5.4 Inserting Hyphens and Nonbreaking Characters

5.5 Finding and Replacing Special Characters

5.6 Creating and Using Templates

5.7 Creating Footnotes and Endnotes

5.8 Formatting the First Page of a Research Paper

5.9 Inserting and Modifying Sources and Citations

5.10 Inserting a Works Cited Page

In Word, you can sort text in paragraphs, columns, and tables, as well as sort records in a data source file. You can also select specific records in a data source file and merge them with a main document. Control the line breaks within text by inserting nonbreaking spaces and use the Find and Replace feature to search for special characters, such as nonprinting characters, in a document. Use the default template provided by Word to create a document or to create and use your own specialized template. When you prepare research papers and reports, citing information sources properly is important. In this chapter, you will learn to reference documents and acknowledge sources using footnotes, endnotes, citations, and bibliographies. Model answers for this chapter's projects appear on the following pages.

WL2C5

Note: Before beginning the projects, copy to your storage medium the WL2C5 subfolder from the WL2 folder on the CD that accompanies this textbook and then make WL2C5 the active folder.

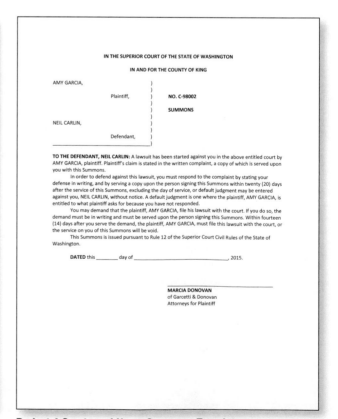

Project 1 Sort Company Information

Kelly Millerton, Chief Executive Officer

Chris Moreau, President

Danielle Roemer, President

Alexander Rohlman, President

Calvin Van Camp, Vice President

Amber Wahlstrom, Vice President

Eugene Whitman, Vice President

Employee	Department	Ext.
Millerton, Kelly	Administrative Services	102
Whitman, Eugene	Administrative Services	105
Langstrom, Jodie	Financial Services	421
Robertson, Jake	Financial Services	409
Holland, Bethany	Marketing	318
Iwami, Julia	Marketing	322

Salesperson	Sales, First Half	Sales, Second Half
Williams, Sylvia	$543,241	$651,438
Monroe, Nina	$623,598	$630,583
Gresham, Esther	$610,312	$593,412
Kaiser, Michael	$453,483	$510,382
Torres, Edward	$431,568	$486,340

Project 1 Sort Company Information

WL2-C5-P1-Sorting.docx

Mr. Martin Saunders
231 South 41st Street
P.O. Box 3321
Baltimore, MD 20156

Mrs. Darlene Fernandez
12115 South 42nd
#20-G
Baltimore, MD 20376

Mrs. Kaycee Stahl
450 Washington Ave.
Baltimore, MD 20376

Ms. Anita Grenwald
580 Capital Lane
#1002-B
Baltimore, MD 20384

Ms. Victoria Benoit
989 Graham Road
Rosedale, MD 20389

Mr. Steve Dutton
3490 East 145th
Apt. B
Baltimore, MD 20468

Ms. Amanda Perkins
9033 North Ridge Drive
Apt. #401
Baltimore, MD 20487

Mrs. Rebecca Bellamy
10291 East 212th Street
Towson, MD 21204

Mr. Brian Kaszycki
7613 33rd Street
Towson, MD 21204

Dr. Jillian Childers
5840 North 132nd
P.O. Box 9045
Rosedale, MD 21237

Mrs. Antonia Delaney
11220 East Madison
Rosedale, MD 21237

Mr. Gregory Hogan
622 First Street
Towson, MD 21252

WL2-C5-P2-Lbls01.docx

Mrs. Antonia Delaney
11220 East Madison
Rosedale, MD 21237

Mr. Gregory Hogan
622 First Street
Towson, MD 21252

Dr. Jillian Childers
5840 North 132nd
P.O. Box 9045
Rosedale, MD 21237

Mrs. Rebecca Bellamy
10291 East 212th Street
Towson, MD 21204

Mr. Brian Kaszycki
7613 33rd Street
Towson, MD 21204

WL2-C5-P2-Lbls02.docx

Mrs. Antonia Delaney
11220 East Madison
Rosedale, MD 21237

Mr. Gregory Hogan
622 First Street
Towson, MD 21252

Dr. Jillian Childers
5840 North 132nd
P.O. Box 9045
Rosedale, MD 21237

Mrs. Rebecca Bellamy
10291 East 212th Street
Towson, MD 21204

Ms. Victoria Benoit
989 Graham Road
Rosedale, MD 20389

Mr. Brian Kaszycki
7613 33rd Street
Towson, MD 21204

Project 2 Sort and Select Records in a Data Source File

WL2-C5-P2-Lbls03.docx

KEYBOARD SHORTCUTS

Microsoft Word includes a number of keyboard shortcuts you can use to access features and commands. The ScreenTip for some buttons displays the keyboard shortcut you can use to access the commands. For example, hover the mouse over the Font button and the ScreenTip displays Ctrl + Shift + F as the keyboard shortcut. Additional HOME tab Font group keyboard shortcut include Ctrl + B to bold text, Ctrl + I to italicize text, and Ctrl + U to underline text. You can also press Ctrl + Shift + + to turn on superscript and press Ctrl + = to turn on subscript.

Buttons in the Clipboard group include keyboard shortcuts. For example, to cut selected text press Ctrl + X, press Ctrl + C to copy selected text, and use the keyboard shortcut Ctrl + V to insert text. Ctrl + Shift + C is the keyboard command to turn on and off the Format Painter feature.

Project 3 Type a Keyboard Shortcut Document

WL2-C5-P3-Shortcuts.docx

IN THE SUPERIOR COURT OF THE STATE OF WASHINGTON

IN AND FOR THE COUNTY OF KING

AMY GARCIA,	)	
	)	
Plaintiff,	)	NO. C-98002
	)	
	)	SUMMONS
NEIL CARLIN,	)	
	)	
Defendant,	)	

TO THE DEFENDANT, NEIL CARLIN: A lawsuit has been started against you in the above entitled court by AMY GARCIA, plaintiff. Plaintiff's claim is stated in the written complaint, a copy of which is served upon you with this Summons.

In order to defend against this lawsuit, you must respond to the complaint by stating your defense in writing, and by serving a copy upon the person signing this Summons within twenty (20) days after the service of this Summons, excluding the day of service, or default judgment may be entered against you, NEIL CARLIN, without notice. A default judgment is one where the plaintiff, AMY GARCIA, is entitled to what plaintiff asks for because you have not responded.

You may demand that the plaintiff, AMY GARCIA, file his lawsuit with the court. If you do so, the demand must be in writing and must be served upon the person signing this Summons. Within fourteen (14) days after you serve the demand, the plaintiff, AMY GARCIA, must file this lawsuit with the court, or the service on you of this Summons will be void.

This Summons is issued pursuant to Rule 12 of the Superior Court Civil Rules of the State of Washington.

DATED this _____ day of _____, 2015.

_____
MARCIA DONOVAN
of Garcetti & Donovan
Attorneys for Plaintiff

Project 4 Create and Use a Summons Template

WL2-C5-P4-Summons.docx

Model Answers

NATURAL INTERFACE APPLICATIONS

A major area of artificial intelligence has the goal of creating a more natural interface between human and machine. Currently, computer users are restricted in most instances to using a mouse and keyboard for input. For output, they must gaze at a fairly static, two-dimensional screen. Speakers are used for sound, and a printer for hard copy. The user interface consists of typing, pointing, and clicking. New speech recognition and natural-language technologies promise to change that soon.[1]

Speech Recognition

One of the most immediately applicable improvements comes in the area of speech recognition. Rather than typing information into the computer, users can direct it with voice commands. A computer that can take dictation and perform requested actions is a real step forward in convenience and potential. Speech recognition has developed rather slowly, mainly because the typical PC did not have the necessary speed and capacity until very recently.[2]

Natural-Language Interface

Computers that are able to communicate using spoken English, Japanese, or any of the hundreds of other languages currently in use around the world, would certainly be helpful. In the not-so-distant future, computers will most likely be able to read, write, speak, and understand many human languages. Language translators already exist, and they are getting better all the time.

---

[1] Kevin Novak, *Artificial Intelligence* (Chicago: Home Town Publishing, 2015), 45-51.
[2] Heather Everson and Nicolas Reyes, "Integrating Speech Recognition," *Design Technologies* (2014): 24-26.

Page 1

Project 5 Insert Footnotes and Endnotes in Reports

WL2-C5-P5-InterfaceApps.docx

Programmers can look forward to a human-language computer interface. With better interfaces, programmers may be able to describe what they want using natural (human) languages, rather than writing programs in the highly restrictive and rather alien programming languages in use today. Natural-language interfaces are an area of artificial intelligence that is broader in scope than simple speech recognition. The goal is to have a machine that can read a set of news articles on any topic and understand what it has read. Ideally, it could then write its own report summarizing what it has learned.[3]

Virtual Reality

Virtual reality (VR) describes the concept of creating a realistic world within the computer. Online games with thousands of interacting players already exist. In these games people can take on a persona and move about a virtual landscape, adventuring and chatting with other players. The quality of a virtual reality system is typically characterized in terms of its immersiveness, which measures how real the simulated world feels and how well it can make users accept the simulated world as their own and forget about reality. With each passing year, systems are able to provide increasing levels of immersion. Called by some the "ultimate in escapism," VR is becoming increasingly common—and increasingly realistic.[4]

Mental Interface

Although still in the experimental phase, a number of interfaces take things a bit further than VR, and they don't require users to click a mouse, speak a word, or even lift a finger. Mental interfaces use sensors mounted around the skull to read the alpha waves

---

[3] James Glenovich, "Language Interfaces," *Corporate Computing* (2015): 8-12.
[4] William Curtis, *Virtual Reality Worlds* (San Francisco: Lilly Harris Publishers, 2013), 53-68.

Page 2

---

given off by our brains. Thinking of the color blue could be used to move the mouse cursor to the right, or thinking of the number seven could move it to the left. The computer measures brain activity and interprets it as a command, eliminating the need to physically manipulate a mouse to move the screen cursor. While this technology has obvious applications for assisting people with disabilities, military researchers are also using it to produce a superior form of interface for pilots.[5]

---

[5] Marilyn Beal, "Challenges of Artificial Intelligence," *Interface Design* (2015): 10-18.

Page 3

FUTURE OF THE INTERNET

The Internet is having trouble keeping up with the rapid increase in users and the increased workload created by the popularity of bandwidth-intensive applications such as music and video files. The broadband connections needed to enjoy these new applications are not evenly distributed. Several ongoing projects promise to provide solutions for these problems in the future. Once these connectivity problems are dealt with, people around the world will be able to enjoy the new web services that are only a few short years away.[1]

Satellite Internet Connections

Many people living in remote or sparsely populated areas are not served by broadband Internet connections. Cable or optical fiber networks are very expensive to install and maintain, and ISPs are not interested in providing service to areas or individuals unless they think it will be profitable. One hope for people without broadband connections is provided by satellite TV networks. Remote ISPs connect to the satellite network using antennae attached to their servers. Data is relayed to and from ISP servers to satellites, which are in turn connected to an Internet backbone access point. While the connection speeds might not be as fast as those offered by regular land-based broadband access, they are faster than the service twisted-pair cable can offer and much better than no access at all.[2]

Second Internet

A remedy for the traffic clogging the information highway is **Internet2**, a revolutionary new type of Internet currently under development. When fully operational, Internet2 will enable large research universities in the United States to collaborate and share huge amounts of complex scientific information at amazing speeds. Led by over 170 universities working in partnership with industry and government, the Internet2 consortium is developing and deploying advanced network technologies and applications.

Internet2 is a testing ground for universities to work together and develop advanced Internet technologies such as telemedicine, digital libraries, and virtual laboratories. Internet2 universities will be connected to an ultrahigh-speed network called the Abilene backbone. Each university will use state-of-the-art equipment to take advantage of transfer speeds provided by the network.

Internet Services for a Fee

Industry observers predict that large portals such as AOL, MSN, and Yahoo! will soon determine effective structures and marketing strategies to get consumers to pay for Internet services. This new market, called bring-your-own-access (BYOA), will combine essential *content*, for example, news and weather, with *services*, such as search, directory, email, IM, and online shopping, into a new product with monthly access charges. But to entice current and potential customers into the BYOA market, ISP and telecom companies must offer improvements in the areas of security,

---

[1] Joshua Abrahamson, *Future Trends in Computing* (Los Angeles: Gleason Rutherford Publishing, 2014), 5-9.
[2] Aileen Clements, *Satellite Systems* (Boston: Robison Publishing House, 2015), 23-51.

Page 1

WL2-C5-P5-InternetFuture.docx

Page 2 (top left)

privacy, and ease of use. Additionally, they are expected to develop new ways to personalize content and add value to the current range of Internet services.[3]

Internet in 2030

Ray Kurzweil, a computer futurist, has looked ahead to the year 2030 and visualized a Web that offers no clear distinctions between real and simulated environments and people. Among the applications he sees as very possible are computerized displays in eyeglasses that could offer simultaneous translations of foreign language conversations, nanobots (microscopic robots) that would work with our brains to extend our mental capabilities, and sophisticated avatars (simulated on-screen persons) that people will interact with online. Technologies that allow people to project their feelings as well as their images and voices may usher in a period when people could "be" with another person even though they are physically hundreds or even thousands of miles apart.

---

[3] Jolene Campbell, "Fee-Based Internet Services," *Connections* (2014): 5-8.

Page 2

Page 1 (top right)

Last Name 1

Student Name

Instructor Name

Course Title

Current Date

Mobile Security

Computing is no longer just a sit-at-your-desk type of activity—it is mobile. Mobile is convenient, but it also brings its own security risks. Various settings and tools can help you keep your portable devices and the information stored on it safer (Suong).

When you bring your computer with you, you are carrying a big investment in both dollars and data, so protecting it from theft and damage is important. Corporations are struggling with protecting information technology assets as their workforces begin to carry smaller devices, which are prone to being left behind by mistake or stolen. Protecting mobile devices is important and several devices and procedures exist to physically secure a laptop computer.

Laptops have a cable device you can use to tie them to an airport chair or desk in a field office to deter potential thieves from stealing them. The determined thief with enough time can cut the cable and get away with the laptop, so it is only a slight deterrent. If you want stronger protection, consider a service that allows you to remotely delete data if your computer is stolen and uses GPS to track your laptop (Jackson).

Many newer laptops include fingerprint readers. Because fingerprints are unique to each individual, being able to authenticate yourself with your own set of prints to gain access to your computer is a popular security feature. If somebody without a fingerprint

Page 1

Project 6 Cite Sources in a Mobile Security Report

WL2-C5-P6-MobileSecurity.docx

Page 2 (bottom left)

Last Name 2

match tries to get into the computer data, the system locks up. If you travel with a laptop, activating password protection and creating a secure password is a good idea.

Stopping thieves is one concern when you are on the road, but stopping employees from making costly mistakes regarding company data is another area where companies must take precautions. Making sure that employees who take company laptops outside of the office are responsible for safe and secure storage offsite is vital to company security (Nakamura). Policies might require them to keep backups of data on physical storage media or to back up data to a company network.

If you travel and access the Internet using a public location, you have to be very careful not to expose private information (Jackson). Anything you send over a public network can be accessed by malicious hackers and cybercriminals. Limit your use of online accounts to times when it is essential. "Be especially on guard when accessing your bank accounts, investment accounts, and retail accounts that store your credit card for purchases, and avoid entering your social security number" (Miraldi 19).

Page 2

Page 3 (bottom right)

Last Name 3

Works Cited

Jackson, Gabriel. "Securing Laptops and Mobile Devices." *Future Computing Technologies* (2015): 8-10.

Miraldi, Georgia. *Evolving Technology*. Houston: Rio Grande Publishing, 2015.

Nakamura, Janet. "Computer Security." *Current Technology Times* VI (2015): 20-28.

Suong, Chay. *Securing and Managing Mobile Devices*. 20 April 2014. 5 January 2015.
<www.emcp.net/publishing>.

Page 3

You will open a document containing information on company employees and
then sort data in paragraphs, columns, and tables.

Sorting Text in Paragraphs ■■■■■■■■■■■■■■■■■

Paragraphs of text in a document can be sorted alphanumerically, numerically, or
chronologically. For example, you might want to sort a list of company employees
to create an internal telephone directory or a list for a company-wide mailing.
Sorting items in a Word document is also an effective way to organize a list of
customers by zip code or by product purchased.

In an alphanumeric sort, punctuation marks or special symbols are sorted
first, followed by numbers and then text. If you sort paragraphs alphanumerically
or numerically, dates are treated as regular text. Also be aware that during a
paragraph sort, blank lines in a document are moved to the beginning.

To sort text, select the text and then click the Sort button in the Paragraph
group on the HOME tab. This displays the Sort Text dialog box containing
sorting options. The *Sort by* option box has a default setting of *Paragraphs*. This
default setting changes depending on the text in the document. For example, if
you are sorting items within a table, the *Sort by* option box has a default setting
of *Column 1*. The *Sort by* options will also vary depending on selections at the
Sort Options dialog box, shown in Figure 5.1. To display this dialog box, click
the Options button in the Sort Text dialog box. At the Sort Options dialog box,
specify how fields are separated.

▼ Quick Steps

Sort Text in Paragraphs
1. Click Sort button.
2. Make changes at Sort Text dialog box.
3. Click OK.

Display the Sort Options Dialog Box
1. Click Sort button.
2. Click Options button.

[Sort button icon]
Sort

Figure 5.1 Sort Options Dialog Box

In this section, specify how fields are separated.

Sort Options

Separate fields at
- ⦿ Tabs
- ○ Commas
- ○ Other: -

Sort options
- ■ Sort column only
- ☐ Case sensitive

Sorting language
English (United States)

OK   Cancel

▼ **Quick Steps**

Sort Text in Columns
1. Select specific text.
2. Click Sort button.
3. Click Options button.
4. Specify *Tabs* as separator.
5. Click OK.
6. Make changes at Sort Text dialog box.
7. Click OK.

When sorting on two fields, Word sorts the first field and then sorts the second field within the first.

Sorting Text in Columns

To sort text set in columns, the text must be separated with tabs. When sorting text in columns, Word considers the left margin *Field 1*, text typed at the first tab *Field 2*, and so on. When sorting text in columns, make sure the columns are separated from each other with only one tab, because Word recognizes each tab as a separate column. Thus, using more than one tab to separate columns may result in field numbers that correspond to empty columns.

Sorting on More Than One Field

When sorting text, you can sort on more than one field. For example, in Project 1a, Step 6, you will sort the department entries alphabetically and then sort the employee names alphabetically within the departments. To do this, specify the *Department* column in the *Sort by* option box and then specify the *Employee* column in the *Then by* option box. If a document contains columns with heading text, click the *Header row* option in the *My list has* section.

Project 1a **Sorting Text**   **Part 1 of 2**

1. Open **Sorting.docx** and then save the document and name it **WL2-C5-P1-Sorting**.
2. Sort the text alphabetically by first name by completing the following steps:
   a. Select the seven lines of text at the beginning of the document.
   b. Click the Sort button in the Paragraph group on the HOME tab.
   c. At the Sort Text dialog box, click OK.
3. Sort the text by last name by completing the following steps:
   a. With the seven lines of text still selected, click the Sort button.
   b. At the Sort Text dialog box, click the Options button.
   c. At the Sort Options dialog box, click *Other* and then press the spacebar. (This indicates that the first and last names are separated by a space.)
   d. Click OK.
   e. At the Sort Text dialog box, click the down-pointing arrow at the right side of the *Sort by* option box and then click *Word 2* at the drop-down list.
   f. Click OK.

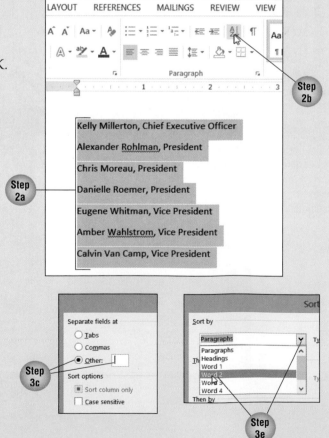

4. Sort text in columns by completing the following steps:
   a. Select the six lines of text set in columns below the headings *Employee, Department,* and *Ext.*
   b. Click the Sort button in the Paragraph group on the HOME tab.
   c. At the Sort Text dialog box, click the Options button.
   d. At the Sort Options dialog box, make sure the *Separate fields at* option is set to *Tabs* and then click OK to close the dialog box.
   e. At the Sort Text dialog box, click the down-pointing arrow at the right side of the *Sort by* option box and then click *Field 2* at the drop-down list. (The left margin is *Field 1* and the first tab is *Field 2*.)
   f. Click OK.
5. With the six lines of text still selected, sort the third column of text numerically by completing the following steps:
   a. Click the Sort button.
   b. Click the down-pointing arrow at the right side of the *Sort by* option box and then click *Field 4* at the drop-down list.
   c. Click OK.
6. Sort on two columns by completing the following steps:
   a. Select the seven lines of text set in columns, including the headings.
   b. Click the Sort button.
   c. At the Sort Text dialog box, click the *Header row* option in the *My list has* section of the dialog box.
   d. Click the down-pointing arrow at the right side of the *Sort by* option box and then click *Department*.
   e. Click the down-pointing arrow at the right side of the *Then by* option box and then click *Employee* at the drop-down list.
   f. Click OK.
7. Save **WL2-C5-P1-Sorting.docx**.

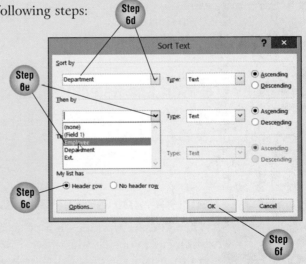

Sorting Text in Tables

Sorting text in columns within tables is similar to sorting columns of text separated by tabs. If a table contains a header, you can tell Word not to include the header row when sorting by clicking the *Header row* option in the *My list has* section of the Sort dialog box. The Sort Text dialog box becomes the Sort dialog box when sorting a table. If you want to sort only specific cells in a table, select the cells and then complete the sort.

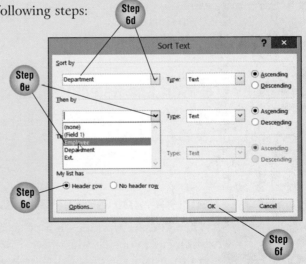

▼ **Quick Steps**

Sort Text in a Table
1. Position insertion point in table.
2. Click Sort button.
3. Make changes at Sort dialog box.
4. Click OK.

1. With **WL2-C5-P1-Sorting.docx** open, sort text in the first column in the table by completing the following steps:
   a. Position the insertion point in any cell in the table.
   b. Click the Sort button.
   c. At the Sort dialog box, make sure the *Header row* option is selected in the *My list has* section.
   d. Click the down-pointing arrow at the right side of the *Sort by* option box and then click *Sales, First Half* at the drop-down list.
   e. Click OK.
2. Sort the numbers in the third column in descending order by completing the following steps:
   a. Select all of the cells in the table except the cells in the first row.
   b. Click the Sort button.
   c. Click the down-pointing arrow at the right side of the *Sort by* option and then click *Column 3* at the drop-down list.
   d. Click *Descending*.
   e. Click OK.
3. Save, print, and then close **WL2-C5-P1-Sorting.docx**.

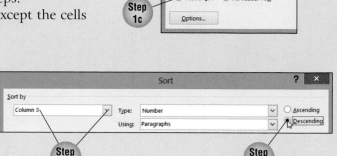

Project 2 Sort and Select Records in a Data Source File   3 Parts

You will sort data in a data source file, create labels and select specific records in a data source file, and then create labels.

▼ Quick Steps

Sort Records in a Data Source
1. Click MAILINGS tab.
2. Click Select Recipients button.
3. Click *Use an Existing List*.
4. Double-click desired file.
5. Click Edit Recipient List button.
6. At Mail Merge Recipients dialog box, sort by specific field by clicking field column heading.
7. Click OK.

Sorting and Selecting Records in a Data Source ■■■■■■

When you are working on a project that requires sorting data and merging documents, consider the order in which you want the merged documents printed and then sort the data before merging. To sort records in a data source, click the MAILINGS tab, click the Select Recipients button, and then click *Use an Existing List*. At the Select Data Source dialog box, navigate to the folder containing the data source file and then double-click the file. Click the Edit Recipient List button in the Start Mail Merge group on the MAILINGS tab and the Mail Merge Recipients dialog box displays, similar to the one shown in Figure 5.2.

Click the column heading to sort data in a specific column in ascending order. To perform additional sorts, click the down-pointing arrow at the right side of the column heading and then click the desired sort order. You can also click the <u>Sort</u> hyperlink located in the *Refine recipient list* section of the Mail Merge Recipients dialog box. Clicking this hyperlink displays the Filter and Sort dialog box with the Sort Records tab selected, as shown in Figure 5.3. The options at the dialog box are similar to the options available at the Sort Text (and Sort) dialog box.

Figure 5.2 Mail Merge Recipients Dialog Box

To sort on a specific field, click the column heading.

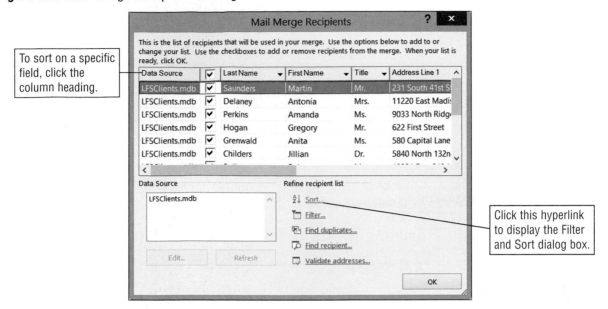

Click this hyperlink to display the Filter and Sort dialog box.

Figure 5.3 Filter and Sort Dialog Box with Sort Records Tab Selected

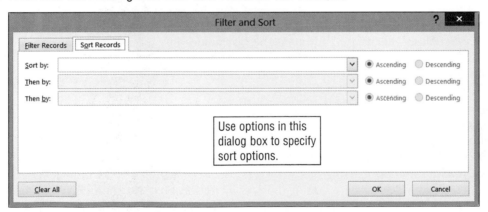

Use options in this dialog box to specify sort options.

Project 2a **Sorting Data in a Data Source**   **Part 1 of 3**

1. At a blank document, click the MAILINGS tab, click the Start Mail Merge button in the Start Mail Merge group, and then click *Labels* at the drop-down list.

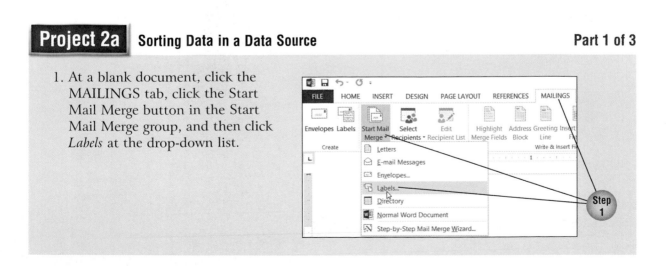

2. At the Label Options dialog box, click the down-pointing arrow at the right side of the *Label vendors* option box and then click *Avery US Letter* at the drop-down list. Scroll down the *Product number* list box, click *5160 Easy Peel Address Labels*, and then click OK.

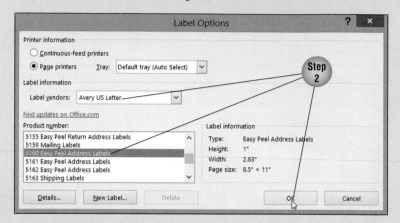

3. Click the Select Recipients button in the Start Mail Merge group and then click *Use an Existing List* at the drop-down list.
4. At the Select Data Source dialog box, navigate to the WL2C5 folder on your storage medium and then double-click the data source file named **LFSClients.mdb**.
5. Click the Edit Recipient List button in the Start Mail Merge group on the MAILINGS tab.
6. At the Mail Merge Recipients dialog box, click the *Last Name* column heading. (This sorts the last names in ascending alphabetical order.)
7. Scroll to the right to display the *City* field and then click the *City* column heading.
8. Sort records by zip code and then by last name by completing the following steps:
   a. Click the <u>Sort</u> hyperlink located in the *Refine recipient list* section of the Mail Merge Recipients dialog box.
   b. At the Filter and Sort dialog box with the Sort Records tab selected, click the down-pointing arrow at the right side of the *Sort by* option box and then click *ZIP Code* at the drop-down list. (You will need to scroll down the list to display the *ZIP Code* field.)
   c. Make sure *Last Name* displays in the *Then by* option box.
   d. Click OK to close the Filter and Sort dialog box.
   e. Click OK to close the Mail Merge Recipients dialog box.

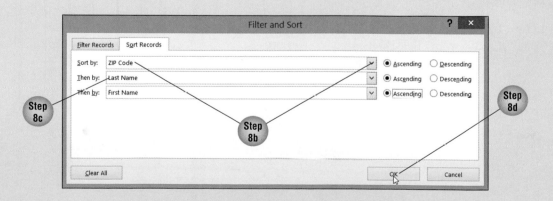

9. At the labels document, click the Address Block button in the Write & Insert Fields group.
10. At the Insert Address Block dialog box, click the OK button.
11. Click the Update Labels button in the Write & Insert Fields group.
12. Click the Finish & Merge button in the Finish group and then click *Edit Individual Documents* at the drop-down list.

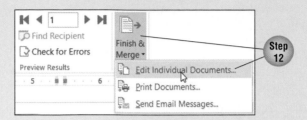

Step 12

13. At the Merge to New Document dialog box, make sure *All* is selected and then click OK.
14. Press Ctrl + A to select the entire document and then click the *No Spacing* style thumbnail in the Styles group on the HOME tab.
15. Save the merged labels and name the document **WL2-C5-P2-Lbls01**.
16. Print and then close **WL2-C5-P2-Lbls01.docx**.
17. Close the labels main document without saving it.

If you have a data source file with numerous records, you may sometimes want to merge the main document with only specific records in the data source. For example, you may want to send a letter to customers who have a specific zip code or live in a particular city. One method for selecting specific records is to display the Mail Merge Recipients dialog box and then insert or remove check marks from specific records.

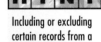

Including or excluding certain records from a merge is referred to as *filtering*.

Using check boxes to select specific records is useful in a data source containing a limited number of records, but it may not be practical in a data source containing many records. In a large data source, use options at the Filter and Sort dialog box with the Filter Records tab selected, as shown in Figure 5.4 on the next page. To display this dialog box, click the <u>Filter</u> hyperlink that displays in the *Refine recipient list* section of the Mail Merge Recipients dialog box.

When you select a field from the *Field* drop-down list, Word automatically inserts *Equal to* in the *Comparison* option box, but you can make other comparisons. Clicking the down-pointing arrow at the right of the *Comparison* option box causes a drop-down list to display with these additional options: *Not equal to, Less than, Greater than, Less than or equal, Greater than or equal, Is blank,* and *Is not blank.* Use one of these options to create a select equation.

Figure 5.4 Filter and Sort Dialog Box with Filter Records Tab Selected

Click this down-pointing arrow to specify the field on which you want to select.

Use the *Comparison* and *Compare to* options to specify records matching certain criteria.

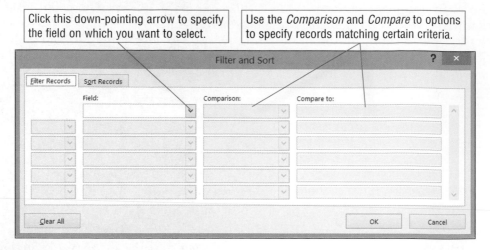

Project 2b   Selecting Records

Part 2 of 3

1. At a blank document, click the MAILINGS tab, click the Start Mail Merge button in the Start Mail Merge group, and then click *Labels* at the drop-down list.
2. At the Label Options dialog box, make sure *Avery US Letter* displays in the *Label vendors* option box and *5160 Easy Peel Address Labels* displays in the *Product number* list box and then click OK.
3. Click the Select Recipients button in the Start Mail Merge group and then click *Use an Existing List* at the drop-down list.
4. At the Select Data Source dialog box, navigate to the WL2C5 folder on your storage medium and then double-click the data source file named *LFSClients.mdb*.
5. Click the Edit Recipient List button.
6. At the Mail Merge Recipients dialog box, click the <u>Filter</u> hyperlink in the *Refine recipient list* section of the dialog box.
7. At the Filter and Sort dialog box with the Filter Records tab selected, click the down-pointing arrow at the right side of the *Field* option box and then click *ZIP Code* at the drop-down list. (You will need to scroll down the list to display *ZIP Code*. When *ZIP Code* is inserted in the *Field* option box, *Equal to* is inserted in the *Comparison* option box and the insertion point is positioned in the *Compare to* text box.)
8. Type **21000** in the *Compare to* text box.
9. Click the down-pointing arrow at the right side of the *Comparison* option box and then click *Greater than* at the drop-down list.

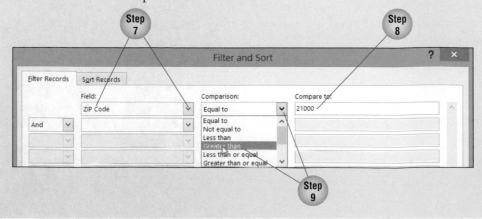

194   **Word Level 2** ▪ Unit 2

10. Click OK to close the Filter and Sort dialog box.
11. Click OK to close the Mail Merge Recipients dialog box.
12. At the labels document, click the Address Block button in the Write & Insert Fields group and then click OK at the Insert Address Block dialog box.
13. Click the Update Labels button in the Write & Insert Fields group.
14. Click the Finish & Merge button in the Finish group and then click *Edit Individual Documents* at the drop-down list.
15. At the Merge to New Document dialog box, make sure *All* is selected and then click OK.
16. Press Ctrl + A to select the entire document and then click the *No Spacing* style thumbnail in the Styles group on the HOME tab.
17. Save the merged labels and name the document **WL2-C5-P2-Lbls02**.
18. Print and then close **WL2-C5-P2-Lbls02.docx**.
19. Close the labels main document without saving it.

When a field is selected from the *Field* option box, Word automatically inserts *And* in the first box at the left side of the dialog box, but you can change this to *Or*, if necessary. With the *And* and *Or* options, you can specify more than one condition for selecting records. For example, in Project 2c, you will select all of the records of clients living in the cities of Rosedale or Towson. If the data source file contained another field, such as a specific financial plan for each customer, you could select all of the customers in a specific city that subscribe to a specific financial plan. In this situation, you would use the *And* option.

To clear the current options at the Filter and Sort dialog box with the Filter Records tab selected, click the Clear All button. This clears any text from text boxes and leaves the dialog box on the screen. Click the Cancel button if you want to close the Filter and Sort dialog box without specifying any records.

Project 2c   Selecting Records with Specific Cities   Part 3 of 3

1. At a blank document, click the MAILINGS tab, click the Start Mail Merge button in the Start Mail Merge group, and then click *Labels* at the drop-down list.
2. At the Label Options dialog box, make sure *Avery US Letter* displays in the *Label vendors* option box and *5160 Easy Peel Address Labels* displays in the *Product number* list box and then click OK.
3. Click the Select Recipients button in the Start Mail Merge group and then click *Use an Existing List* at the drop-down list.
4. At the Select Data Source dialog box, navigate to the WL2C5 folder on your storage medium and then double-click the data source file named **LFSClients.mdb**.
5. Click the Edit Recipient List button.
6. At the Mail Merge Recipients dialog box, click the Filter hyperlink in the *Refine recipient list* section of the dialog box.

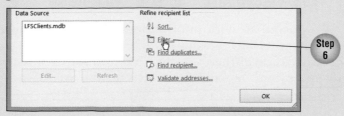

7. At the Filter and Sort dialog box with the Filter Records tab selected, click the down-pointing arrow at the right side of the *Field* option box and then click *City* at the drop-down list. (You will need to scroll down the list to display this field.)
8. Type **Rosedale** in the *Compare to* text box.
9. Click the down-pointing arrow to the right of the option box containing the word *And* (at the left side of the dialog box) and then click *Or* at the drop-down list.
10. Click the down-pointing arrow at the right side of the second *Field* option box and then click *City* at the drop-down list. (You will need to scroll down the list to display this field.)
11. With the insertion point positioned in the second *Compare to* text box (the one below the box containing *Rosedale*), type **Towson**.
12. Click OK to close the Filter and Sort dialog box.

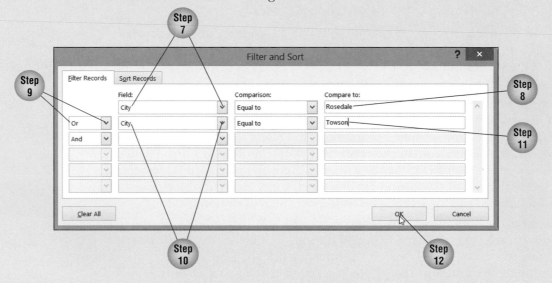

13. Click OK to close the Mail Merge Recipients dialog box.
14. At the labels document, click the Address Block button in the Write & Insert Fields group and then click OK at the Insert Address Block dialog box.
15. Click the Update Labels button in the Write & Insert Fields group.
16. Click the Finish & Merge button in the Finish group and then click *Edit Individual Documents* at the drop-down list.
17. At the Merge to New Document dialog box, make sure *All* is selected and then click OK.
18. Press Ctrl + A to select the entire document and then click the *No Spacing* style thumbnail in the Styles group on the HOME tab.
19. Save the merged labels and name the document **WL2-C5-P2-Lbls03**.
20. Print and then close **WL2-C5-P2-Lbls03.docx**.
21. Close the labels main document without saving it.

Project 3 Type a Keyboard Shortcut Document 2 Parts

You will type a document with information on keyboard shortcuts and use nonbreaking spaces within the shortcuts to keep them from splitting between two lines of text. You will then use the Find and Replace feature to search for all nonbreaking spaces and replace them with regular spaces.

Inserting Nonbreaking Spaces

As you type text in a document, Word makes line-end decisions and automatically wraps text to each successive line. In some situations, words and phrases that should remain together are broken across two lines. To control where text is broken and wrapped to the next line, consider inserting *nonbreaking spaces* between words. Press Ctrl + Shift + spacebar to insert a nonbreaking space. With the display of nonprinting characters turned on, a normal space displays as a dot and a nonbreaking space displays as a degree (°) symbol.

Project 3a	Inserting Nonbreaking Spaces	Part 1 of 2

1. At a blank document, turn on the display of nonprinting characters by clicking the Show/Hide ¶ button in the Paragraph group on the HOME tab.
2. Type the text shown in Figure 5.5 and insert nonbreaking spaces in the keyboard shortcuts by pressing Ctrl + Shift + spacebar before and after each plus symbol.
3. Turn off the display of nonprinting characters. Bold and center the title as shown in the figure.
4. Save the document and name it **WL2-C5-P3-Shortcuts**.

Figure 5.5 Project 3a

KEYBOARD SHORTCUTS

Microsoft Word includes a number of keyboard shortcuts you can use to access features and commands. The ScreenTip for some buttons displays the keyboard shortcut you can use to access the command. For example, hover the mouse over the Font button and the ScreenTip displays Ctrl + Shift + F as the keyboard shortcut. Additional HOME tab Font group keyboard shortcuts include Ctrl + B to bold text, Ctrl + I to italicize text, and Ctrl + U to underline text. You can also press Ctrl + Shift + + to turn on superscript and press Ctrl + = to turn on subscript.

Buttons in the Clipboard group include keyboard shortcuts. For example, to cut selected text press Ctrl + X, press Ctrl + C to copy selected text, and use the keyboard shortcut Ctrl + V to insert text. Ctrl + Shift + C is the keyboard command to turn on and off the Format Painter feature.

Finding and Replacing Special Characters

You can use the Find feature to find special text and the Find and Replace feature to find specific text and replace it with other text. You can also use these features to find special formatting, characters, and nonprinting elements in a document. To display a list of special characters and nonprinting elements, display the Find and Replace dialog box with either the Find or Replace tab selected, expand the dialog box, and then click the Special button. This displays a pop-up list similar to the one shown in Figure 5.6 on the next page.

▼ Quick Steps

Find and Replace a Special Character
1. Click Replace button.
2. Click More button.
3. Click Special button.
4. Click desired character.
5. Click in *Replace with* text box.
6. Click Special button.
7. Click desired character.
8. Click Replace All button.

Figure 5.6 Special Button Pop-up List

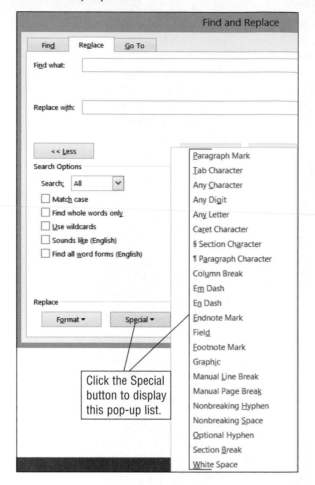

Paragraph Mark
Tab Character
Any Character
Any Digit
Any Letter
Caret Character
§ Section Character
¶ Paragraph Character
Column Break
Em Dash
En Dash
Endnote Mark
Field
Footnote Mark
Graphic
Manual Line Break
Manual Page Break
Nonbreaking Hyphen
Nonbreaking Space
Optional Hyphen
Section Break
White Space

Click the Special button to display this pop-up list.

Press Ctrl + H to display the Find and Replace dialog box with the Replace tab selected.

If you are not sure about the name of the special character you want to find or are unclear about the names of the special characters in the Special button pop-up list, access Word's list of special characters to see the characters and their names. Click the Symbol button in the Symbols group on the INSERT tab and a short list of symbols displays. Click the *More Symbols* option at the drop-down list and the Symbol dialog box displays. Click the Special Characters tab to see a list of characters and their names. For example, some users may not know the difference between an em dash (—) and an en dash (–). The *Character* list box at the Symbol dialog box shows both types of dashes.

Project 3b | **Finding and Replacing Nonbreaking Spaces** | **Part 2 of 2**

1. With **WL2-C5-P3-Shortcuts.docx** open, find all of the occurrences of nonbreaking spaces and replace them with regular spaces by completing the following steps:
   a. Click the Replace button in the Editing group on the HOME tab.
   b. At the Find and Replace dialog box with the Replace tab selected, click the More button.

c. With the insertion point positioned in the *Find what* text box, click the Special button that displays near the bottom of the dialog box.

d. At the pop-up list that displays, click *Nonbreaking Space*. (This inserts ^s in the *Find what* text box.)

e. Click in the *Replace with* text box (making sure it does not contain any text) and then press the spacebar once. (This tells the Find and Replace feature to find a nonbreaking space and replace it with a regular space.)

f. Click the Replace All button.

g. At the message telling you that Word completed the search and made the replacements, click OK.

h. Click the Less button in the Find and Replace dialog box.

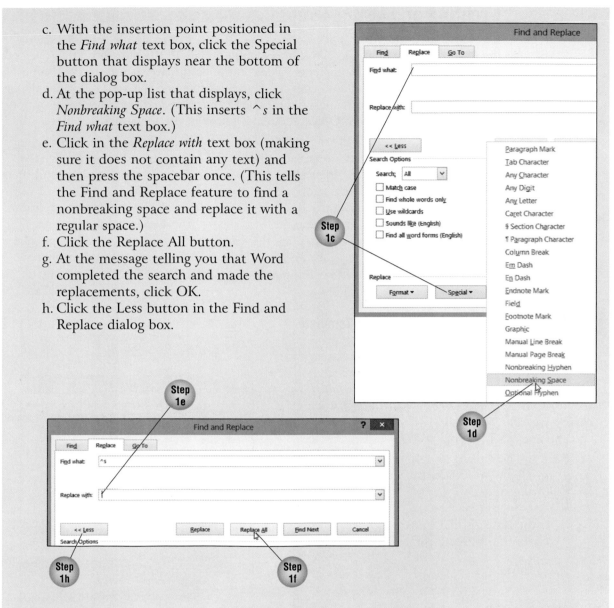

i. Click the Close button to close the Find and Replace dialog box.

2. Save, print, and then close **WL2-C5-P3-Shortcuts.docx**.

Project 4 Create and Use a Summons Template 2 Parts

You will open a summons legal document, save it as a template, and then use it to create other summons documents.

Creating and Using Templates ■■■■■■■■■■■■■■■■■■

If you use the contents of a document to create other documents, consider saving the document as a template. Save a personal template in the Custom Office Templates folder in the Documents folder on the hard drive. Check to determine the default personal template folder location by displaying the Word Options dialog box with *Save* selected in the left panel. The *Default personal templates location* option should display the Custom Office Templates folder in the Documents folder as the default location. If this is not the default location, check with your instructor.

To save a document as a template, display the Save As dialog box, change the *Save as type* option to *Word Template (*.dotx)*, type a name for the template, and then press Enter. Word template documents are saved with the .dotx file extension. You can also save a template as a macro-enabled template with the .dotm file extension. Another method for saving a template is to display the Export backstage area, click the *Change File Type* option, click the *Template (*.dotx)* option, and then click the Save As button. At the Save As dialog box, type a name for your template, navigate to the Custom Office Templates folder, and then click the Save button.

▼ **Quick Steps**

Create a Template
1. Display Save As dialog box.
2. Change *Save as type* to *Word Template (*.dotx).*
3. Type template name in *File name* text box.
4. Click Save.

Project 4a   **Saving a Document as a Template**   **Part 1 of 2**

Before completing this project, check to make sure the default location for personal templates is the Custom Office Templates folder in the Documents folder on the hard drive. If this is not the default location, check with your instructor.

1. Open **Summons.docx**.
2. Save the document as a template in the Custom Office Templates folder by completing the following steps:
   a. Press the F12 key.
   b. At the Save As dialog box, click the *Save as type* option box and then click *Word Template (*.dotx)*.
   c. Select the name in the *File name* text box and then type your last name followed by *Summons*.
   d. Press Enter or click the Save button.
3. Close the summons template.

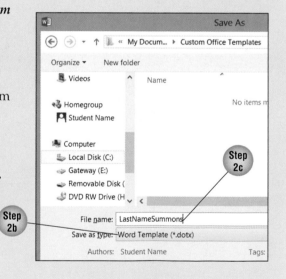

▼ **Quick Steps**

Creating a Document with a Template
1. Click FILE tab.
2. Click *New* option.
3. Click *PERSONAL.*
4. Click template.

To create a document with a template you saved to the *Custom Office Templates* folder, click the FILE tab and then click the *New* option. At the New backstage area, click the *PERSONAL* option. This displays the templates available in the Custom Office Templates folder. Click the template you want to open and a document opens based on that template.

1. Open the summons template as a document by completing the following steps:
   a. Click the FILE tab.
   b. Click the *New* option.
   c. At the New backstage area, click the *PERSONAL* option.
   d. Click the summons template that is preceded by your last name.

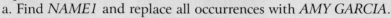
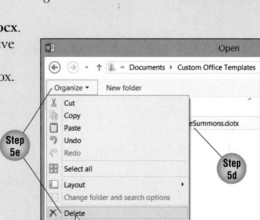

2. With the summons document open, find and replace text as follows:
   a. Find *NAME1* and replace all occurrences with *AMY GARCIA*.
   b. Find *NAME2* and replace all occurrences with *NEIL CARLIN*.
   c. Find *NUMBER* and replace with *C-98002*.
3. Save the document in the WL2C5 folder on your storage medium and name it **WL2-C5-P4-Summons**.
4. Print and then close **WL2-C5-P4-Summons.docx**.
5. Delete the summons template from the hard drive by completing the following steps:
   a. Press Ctrl + F12 to display the Open dialog box.
   b. At the Open dialog box, click *Documents* in the Navigation pane.
   c. Double-click the *Custom Office Templates* folder in the Content pane.
   d. Click the summons template that begins with your last name.
   e. Click the Organize button and then click *Delete* at the drop-down list.
6. Close the Open dialog box.

Project 5   **Insert Footnotes and Endnotes in Reports**   **3 Parts**

You will open a report on artificial intelligence and then insert, format, and modify footnotes. You will also open a report on the future of the Internet and then insert endnotes.

Quick Steps

Insert a Footnote
1. Click REFERENCES tab.
2. Click Insert Footnote button.
3. Type footnote text.

Insert an Endnote
1. Click REFERENCES tab.
2. Click Insert Endnote button.
3. Type endnote text.

Insert Footnote

Insert Endnote

H I N T

Ctrl + Alt + F is the keyboard shortcut to insert a footnote and Ctrl + Alt + D is the keyboard shortcut to insert an endnote.

Creating Footnotes and Endnotes ■■■■■■■■■■■■■■■■■

A research paper or report contains information from a variety of sources. To give credit to those sources, you can insert footnotes or endnotes in a document formatted in a specific reference style, such as Chicago style. (You will learn more about different reference styles in the next project.) A *footnote* is an explanatory note or source reference that is printed at the bottom of the page on which the corresponding information appears. An *endnote* is also an explanatory note or reference but it is printed at the end of the document.

Two steps are involved in creating a footnote or endnote. First, the note reference number is inserted in the document at the location where the corresponding information appears. The second step is to type the note entry text. Footnotes and endnotes are created in a similar manner.

To create a footnote, position the insertion point at the location the reference number is to appear, click the REFERENCES tab, and then click the Insert Footnote button in the Footnotes group. This inserts a number in the document along with a separator line at the bottom of the page and a superscript number below it. With the insertion point positioned immediately to the right of the superscript number, type the note entry text. Word automatically numbers footnotes with superscript arabic numbers and endnotes with superscript lowercase roman numerals.

Project 5a Creating Footnotes

Part 1 of 3

1. Open **InterfaceApps.docx** and then save the document and name it **WL2-C5-P5-InterfaceApps**.
2. Create the first footnote shown in Figure 5.7 by completing the following steps:
   a. Position the insertion point at the end of the first paragraph of text in the document.
   b. Click the REFERENCES tab.
   c. Click the Insert Footnote button in the Footnotes group.
   d. With the insertion point positioned at the bottom of the page immediately following the superscript number, type the first footnote shown in Figure 5.7.

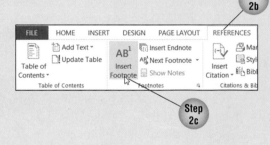

3. Move the insertion point to the end of the paragraph in the *Speech Recognition* section, and using steps similar to those in Steps 2c and 2d, create the second footnote shown in Figure 5.7.
4. Move the insertion point to the end of the second paragraph in the *Natural-Language Interface* section and then create the third footnote shown in Figure 5.7.
5. Move the insertion point to the end of the paragraph in the *Virtual Reality* section and then create the fourth footnote shown in Figure 5.7.
6. Move the insertion point to the end of the last paragraph in the document and then create the fifth footnote shown in Figure 5.7.
7. Save, print, and then close **WL2-C5-P5-InterfaceApps.docx**.

Figure 5.7 Project 5a

Kevin Novak, *Artificial Intelligence* (Chicago: Home Town Publishing, 2015), 45-51.

Heather Everson and Nicolas Reyes, "Integrating Speech Recognition," *Design Technologies* (2014): 24-26.

James Glenovich, "Language Interfaces," *Corporate Computing* (2015): 8-12.

William Curtis, *Virtual Reality Worlds* (San Francisco: Lilly Harris Publishers, 2013), 53-68.

Marilyn Beal, "Challenges of Artificial Intelligence," *Interface Design* (2015): 10-18.

Printing Footnotes and Endnotes

When you print a document containing footnotes, Word automatically reduces the number of text lines on a page to create space for the number of lines in the footnotes and the separator line. If the page does not contain enough space, the footnote number and entry text are moved to the next page. Word separates the footnotes from the text with a 2-inch separator line that begins at the left margin. When endnotes are created in a document, Word prints all of the endnote references at the end of the document, separated from the text by a 2-inch line.

Project 5b **Creating Endnotes**   **Part 2 of 3**

1. Open **InternetFuture.docx** and then save the document and name it **WL2-C5-P5-InternetFuture**.
2. Create the first endnote shown in Figure 5.8 by completing the following steps:
   a. Position the insertion point at the end of the first paragraph of text in the document.
   b. Click the REFERENCES tab.
   c. Click the Insert Endnote button in the Footnotes group.
   d. Type the first endnote shown in Figure 5.8.
3. Move the insertion point to the end of the paragraph in the *Satellite Internet Connections* section and then complete steps similar to those in Steps 2c and 2d to create the second endnote shown in Figure 5.8.
4. Move the insertion point to the end of the second paragraph in the *Second Internet* section and then create the third endnote shown in Figure 5.8.
5. Move the insertion point to the end of the paragraph in the *Internet Services for a Fee* section and then create the fourth endnote shown in Figure 5.8.
6. Save **WL2-C5-P5-InternetFuture.docx**.

Figure 5.8 Project 5b

Joshua Abrahamson, *Future Trends in Computing* (Los Angeles: Gleason Rutherford Publishing, 2014), 8-12.

Aileen Clements, *Satellite Systems* (Boston: Robison Publishing House, 2015), 23-51.

Terry Ventrella, "Future of the Internet," *Computing Today* (2015): 29-33.

Jolene Campbell, "Fee-Based Internet Services," *Connections* (2014): 5-8.

Viewing and Editing Footnotes and Endnotes

To view the entry text for a footnote or endnote where the note occurs within the document, position the mouse pointer on the note reference number. The footnote or endnote text displays in a box above the mark.

To view the footnotes in a document, click the Next Footnote button in the Footnotes group on the REFERENCES tab. This moves the insertion point to the location of the first footnote reference number following the location of the insertion point. To view the endnotes in a document, click the Next Footnote button arrow and then click *Next Endnote* at the drop-down list. With other options at the Next Footnote button drop-down list, you can view the previous footnote, next endnote, or previous endnote. You can move the insertion point to specific footnote text with the Show Notes button.

When you move, copy, or delete footnote or endnote reference numbers, all of the remaining footnotes or endnotes automatically renumber. To move a footnote or endnote, select the reference number and then click the Cut button in the Clipboard group on the HOME tab. Position the insertion point at the location you want the footnote or endnote inserted and then click the Paste button. To delete a footnote or endnote, select the reference number and then press the Delete key. This deletes the reference number as well as the footnote or endnote text.

Click the Footnotes group dialog box launcher and the Footnote and Endnote dialog box displays, as shown in Figure 5.9. At this dialog box, you can convert footnotes to endnotes and endnotes to footnotes; change the location of footnotes or endnotes; change the number formatting; start footnote or endnote numbering with a specific number, letter, and symbol; or change numbering within sections in a document.

Figure 5.9 Footnote and Endnote Dialog Box

Click this button to display the Convert Notes dialog box with options for converting footnotes to endnotes or endnotes to footnotes

Use these option boxes to specify a location for footnotes or endnotes.

Specify the formatting of the footnote or endnote number with options in this section of the dialog box.

Footnote and Endnote ? ✕

Location
- ○ Footnotes: Bottom of page
- ● Endnotes: End of document

Convert...

Footnote layout

Columns: Match section layout

Format

Number format: i, ii, iii, ...

Custom mark: ___ Symbol...

Start at: i

Numbering: Continuous

Apply changes

Apply changes to: Whole document

Insert   Cancel   Apply

1. With **WL2-C5-P5-InternetFuture.docx** open, edit the endnotes by completing the following steps:
   a. If necessary, click the REFERENCES tab.
   b. Click the Next Footnote button arrow and then click *Next Endnote* at the drop-down list.
   c. Click the Show Notes button to display the endnote text.
   d. Change the page numbers for the Joshua Abrahamson entry from *8-12* to *5-9*.
   e. Click the Show Notes button again to return to the reference number in the document.

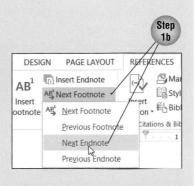

2. Press Ctrl + A to select the document (but not the endnote entry text) and then change the font to Constantia.
3. Change the fonts for the endnotes by completing the following steps:
   a. Press Ctrl + End to move the insertion point to the end of the document.
   b. Click on any endnote entry and then press Ctrl + A to select all of the endnote entries.
   c. Change the font to Constantia.
   d. Press Ctrl + Home.
4. Convert the endnotes to footnotes by completing the following steps:
   a. Click the REFERENCES tab and then click the Footnotes group dialog box launcher.
   b. At the Footnote and Endnote dialog box, click the Convert button.
   c. At the Convert Notes dialog box with the *Convert all endnotes to footnotes* option selected, click the OK button.
   d. Click the Close button to close the dialog box.
5. Change the footnote number format by completing the following steps:
   a. Click the Footnotes group dialog box launcher.
   b. Click the *Footnotes* option in the *Location* section of the dialog box.
   c. Click the down-pointing arrow at the right side of the *Footnotes* option and then click *Below text* at the drop-down list.
   d. Click the down-pointing arrow at the right side of the *Number format* option box and then click *a, b, c, …* at the drop-down list.
   e. Change the starting number by clicking the up-pointing arrow at the right side of the *Start at* option until *d* displays in the option box.
   f. Click the Apply button and then scroll through the document and notice the renumbering of the footnotes.
6. Change the footnote number format back to arabic numbers by completing the following steps:
   a. With the REFERENCES tab active, click the Footnotes group dialog box launcher.
   b. At the Footnote and Endnote dialog box, click the *Footnotes* option in the *Location* section.
   c. Click the down-pointing arrow at the right side of the *Number format* option box and then click *1, 2, 3, …* at the drop-down list.
   d. Change the starting number back to 1 by clicking the down-pointing arrow at the right side of the *Start at* option until *1* displays in the option box.
   e. Click the Apply button.

Step 5b — Footnote and Endnote dialog box

Footnote and Endnote

Location
- ○ Footnotes: Below text
- ○ Endnotes: End of document

Convert…

Footnote layout
- Columns: Match section layout

Format
- Number format: 1, 2, 3, …
- Custom mark:
- Start at:
- Numbering:

(drop-down list: 1, 2, 3, …; a, b, c, …; A, B, C, …; i, ii, iii, …; I, II, III, …; *, †, ‡, §, …)

Apply changes
- Apply changes to: Whole document

Insert   Cancel   Apply

7. Delete the third footnote by completing the following steps:
    a. Press Ctrl + Home.
    b. Make sure the REFERENCES tab is active and then click three times on the Next Footnote button in the Footnotes group.
    c. Select the third footnote reference number (superscript number) and then press the Delete key.
8. Save, print, and then close **WL2-C5-P5-InternetFuture.docx**.

Project 6 — Cite Sources in a Mobile Security Report   8 Parts

You will open a report on securing mobile devices, add information and insert source citations and a bibliography, and then modify and customize citation styles.

Creating Citations and Bibliographies ■■■■■■■■■■■■■■

In addition to using footnotes and endnotes to credit sources in a research paper or manuscript, consider inserting in-text citations and a works cited page to identify sources of quotations, facts, theories, and other borrowed or summarized material. An in-text citation acknowledges that you are borrowing information from a source rather than plagiarizing (stealing) someone else's words or ideas.

Word provides three commonly used editorial styles for citing references in research papers and reports: the American Psychological Association (APA) reference style, which is generally used in the social sciences and research fields; the Modern Language Association (MLA) style, which is generally used in the humanities and English composition; and the *Chicago Manual of Style* (Chicago), which is used both in the humanities and social sciences and is considered more complex than either APA or MLA style.

If you prepare a research paper or report in APA or MLA style, format your document according to the following general guidelines: Use standard-sized paper (8.5 × 11 inches); set 1-inch top, bottom, left, and right margins; set text in a 12-point serif typeface (such as Cambria or Times New Roman); double-space text; indent the first line of each paragraph 0.5 inch; and insert page numbers in the upper right corners of pages.

When formatting a research paper or report according to MLA or APA standards, you need to follow certain guidelines for properly formatting the first page of the document. With MLA style, in the upper left corner of the first page, insert your name, your instructor's name, the course title, and the current date all double-spaced. Type the title of the document a double-space below the current date and then center the document title. Also, double-space between the title and first line of the text. Finally, insert a header in the upper right corner of the document that includes your last name followed by the current page number.

When using APA style, create a title page that is separate from the body of the document. On this page, include the title of your paper, your name, and your school's name, all double-spaced, centered, and located in the upper half of the page. Also, include a header with the text *Running Head:* followed by the title of your paper in uppercase letters at the left margin and the page number at the right margin.

1. Open **MobileSecurity.docx** and then save the document and name it **WL2-C5-P6-MobileSecurity**.
2. Format the first page of the document by completing the following steps:
   a. Press Ctrl + A to select the entire document.
   b. Change the font to Cambria and the font size to 12 points.
   c. Change the line spacing to 2.0.
   d. Remove extra spacing after paragraphs by clicking the PAGE LAYOUT tab, clicking in the *After* text box in the *Spacing* section in the Paragraph group, typing **0**, and then pressing the Enter key.
   e. Press Ctrl + Home to position the insertion point at the beginning of the document, type your first and last names, and then press the Enter key.
   f. Type your instructor's name and then press the Enter key.
   g. Type the title of your course and then press the Enter key.
   h. Type the current date and then press the Enter key.
   i. Type the document title **Mobile Security** and then center the title.

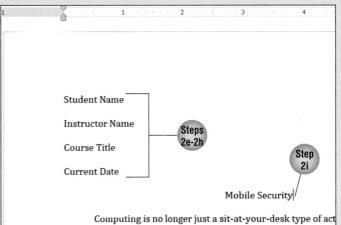

3. Insert a header in the document by completing the following steps:
   a. Click the INSERT tab.
   b. Click the Header button in the Header & Footer group and then click *Edit Header* at the drop-down list.
   c. Press the Tab key twice to move the insertion point to the right margin in the Header pane.
   d. Type your last name and then press the spacebar.
   e. Click the Page Number button in the Header & Footer group on the HEADER & FOOTER TOOLS DESIGN tab, point to *Current Position*, and then click the *Plain Number* option.

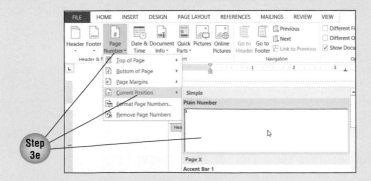

   f. Select the header text and change the font to 12-point Cambria.
   g. Double-click in the body of the document.
4. Save **WL2-C5-P6-MobileSecurity.docx**.

Inserting Source Citations

▼ **Quick Steps**

Insert a New Citation
1. Click REFERENCES tab.
2. Click Insert Citation button.
3. Click *Add New Source* at drop-down list.
4. Type necessary source information.
5. Click OK.

Insert a Citation Placeholder
1. Click REFERENCES tab.
2. Click Insert Citation button.
3. Click *Add New Placeholder* at drop-down list.
4. Type citation name.
5. Click OK.

When you create an in-text source citation, Word requires you to enter information about the source in fields at the Create Source dialog box. To insert a citation in a document, click the REFERENCES tab, click the Insert Citation button in the Citations & Bibliography group, and then click *Add New Source* at the drop-down list. At the Create Source dialog box, as shown in Figure 5.10, select the type of reference you want to cite—such as a book, journal article, or report—and then type the bibliographic information in the required fields. If you want to include more information than required in the displayed fields, click the *Show All Bibliography Fields* check box to insert a check mark and then type the additional bibliographic details in the extra fields. After filling in the necessary source information, click OK. The citation is automatically inserted in the document at the location of the insertion point.

Inserting Citation Placeholders

If you want to insert the information for an in-text source citation later, insert a citation placeholder. To do this, click the Insert Citation button in the Citations & Bibliography group and then click *Add New Placeholder* at the drop-down list. At the Placeholder Name dialog box, type a name for the citation placeholder and then press Enter or click the OK button. Insert the citation text later at the Edit Source dialog box, which contains the same options as the Create Source dialog box.

Insert
Citation

Figure 5.10 Create Source Dialog Box

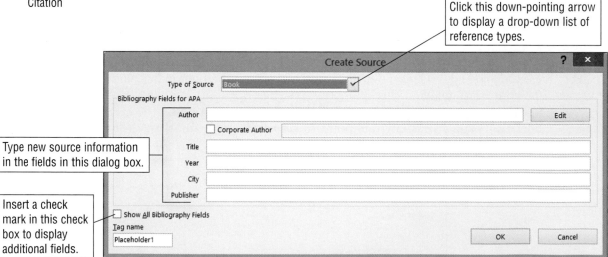

Project 6b | **Inserting Sources and a Citation Placeholder** | **Part 2 of 8**

1. With **WL2-C5-P6-MobileSecurity.docx** open, press Ctrl + End to move the insertion point to the end of the document and then type the text shown in Figure 5.11 on page 210 up to the first citation—the text *(Jefferson)*. To insert the citation, complete these steps:
   a. Press the spacebar once after typing the text *laptop*.

b. Click the REFERENCES tab.

c. Make sure the *Style* option box in the Citations & Bibliography group is set to *MLA*. If not, click the down-pointing arrow at the right of the *Style* option box and then click *MLA* at the drop-down list.

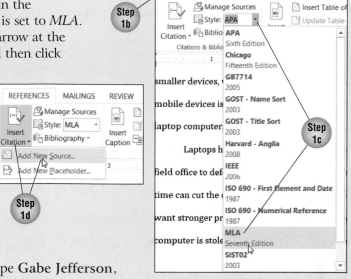

d. Click the Insert Citation button in the Citations & Bibliography group and then click *Add New Source* at the drop-down list.

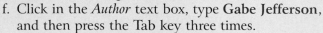

e. At the Create Source dialog box, click the down-pointing arrow at the right of the *Type of Source* option box and then click *Journal Article* at the drop-down list.

f. Click in the *Author* text box, type **Gabe Jefferson**, and then press the Tab key three times.

g. In the *Title* text box, type **Securing Laptops and Mobile Devices** and then press the Tab key.

h. In the *Journal Name* text box, type **Future Computing Technologies** and then press Tab.

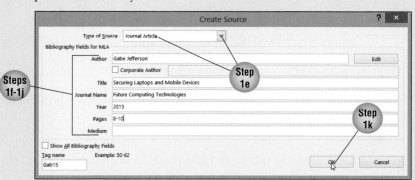

i. In the *Year* text box, type **2015** and then press the Tab key.

j. Type **8-10** in the *Pages* text box.

k. Click OK.

l. Type a period to end the sentence in the document.

2. Continue typing the text up to the next citation—the text *(Lopez)*—and insert the following source information for a book. (Click the down-pointing arrow at the right of the *Type of Source* option box and then click *Book* at the drop-down list.)

Author	**Rafael Lopez**
Title	**Technology World**
Year	**2015**
City	**Chicago**
Publisher	**Great Lakes Publishing House**

3. Continue typing the text up to the next citation—the text *(Nakamura)*—and then insert a citation placeholder by completing the following steps. (You will create the citation and fill in the source information in the next project.)

a. Click the Insert Citation button in the Citations & Bibliography group.

b. Click *Add New Placeholder* at the drop-down list.

c. At the Placeholder Name dialog box, type **Nakamura** and then press Enter.

4. Type the remaining text shown in Figure 5.11.

5. Save **WL2-C5-P6-MobileSecurity.docx**.

Figure 5.11 Project 6b

Laptops have a cable device you can use to tie them to an airport chair or desk in a field office to deter potential thieves from stealing them. The determined thief with enough time can cut the cable and get away with the laptop, so it is only a slight deterrent. If you want stronger protection, consider a service that allows you to remotely delete data if your computer is stolen and uses GPS to track your laptop (Jefferson).

Many newer laptops include fingerprint readers. Because fingerprints are unique to each individual, being able to authenticate yourself with your own set of prints to gain access to your computer is a popular security feature. If somebody without a fingerprint match tries to get into the computer data, the system locks up. If you travel with a laptop, activating password protection and creating a secure password is a good idea. If somebody steals your laptop and cannot get past the password feature, he or she cannot immediately get at your valuable data (Lopez).

Stopping thieves is one concern when you are on the road, but stopping employees from making costly mistakes regarding company data is another area where companies must take precautions. Making sure that employees who take company laptops outside of the office are responsible for safe and secure storage offsite is vital to company security (Nakamura). Policies might require them to keep backups of data on physical storage media or to back up data to a company network.

Editing a Source

After inserting information about a source into a document, you may need to edit the source to correct errors or change data. One method for editing a source is to click the citation in the document, click the Citation Options arrow that displays at the right side of the selected citation, and then click *Edit Source* at the drop-down list. This displays the Edit Source dialog box, which contains the same options as the Create Source dialog box. Make the desired changes at this dialog box and then click OK.

Inserting a Citation with an Existing Source

Once you insert source information at the Create Source dialog box, Word automatically saves it. To insert a citation in a document for source information that has already been saved, click the Insert Citation button in the Citations & Bibliography group and then click the desired source at the drop-down list.

▼ Quick Steps

Insert a Citation with an Existing Source
1. Click REFERENCES tab.
2. Click Insert Citation button.
3. Click desired source at drop-down list.

Project 6c   Edit an Existing Source and Inserting a Citation with an Existing Source   **Part 3 of 8**

1. With **WL2-C5-P6-MobileSecurity.docx** open, add the Nakamura source information by completing the following steps:

   a. Click the *Nakamura* citation in the document.

   b. Click the Citation Options arrow that displays at the right side of the selected citation.

   c. Click *Edit Source* at the drop-down list.

   d. At the Edit Source dialog box, click the *Type of Source* option box arrow and then click *Journal Article*.

   e. Type the following information in the specified text boxes:

Author	**Janet Nakamura**
Title	**Computer Security**
Journal Name	**Current Technology Times**
Year	**2015**
Pages	**20-28**
Volume	**VI**

   (Display the *Volume* field by clicking the *Show All Bibliography Fields* check box and then scroll down the options list.)

   f. Click the OK button to close the Edit Source dialog box.

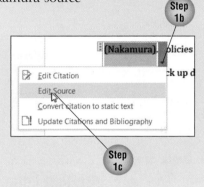

2. Press Ctrl + End to move the insertion point to the end of the document and then press the Enter key once. Type the text shown in Figure 5.12 up to the citation text *(Jefferson)* and then insert a citation from an existing source by completing the following steps:

   a. If necessary, click the REFERENCES tab.

   b. Click the Insert Citation button in the Citations & Bibliography group.

   c. Click the *Jefferson, Gabe* reference at the drop-down list.

   d. Type the remaining text in Figure 5.12.

3. Save **WL2-C5-P6-MobileSecurity.docx**.

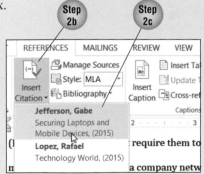

Figure 5.12 Project 6c

> If you travel and access the Internet using a public location, you have to be very careful not to expose private information (Jefferson). Anything you send over a public network can be accessed by malicious hackers and cybercriminals. Limit your use of online accounts to times when it is essential.

Managing Sources

▼ Quick Steps

Manage Sources
1. Click REFERENCES tab.
2. Click Manage Sources button.
3. Edit, add, and/or delete sources.
4. Click Close.

Manage
Sources

Click the Browse button in the Source Manager dialog box to select another master list.

▼ Quick Steps

Insert a Page Number in a Citation
1. Click citation to display placeholder.
2. Click Citation Options arrow.
3. Click *Edit Citation*.
4. Type page number(s).
5. Click OK.

All sources for the current document and sources created in previous documents display in the Source Manager dialog box, as shown in Figure 5.13. Display this dialog box by clicking the REFERENCES tab and then clicking the Manage Sources button in the Citations & Bibliography group. The *Master List* list box in the Source Manager dialog box displays all of the citations you have created in Word. The *Current List* list box displays all of the citations included in the currently open document.

Use options at the Source Manager dialog box to copy a source from the master list to the current list, delete a source, edit a source, and create a new source. To copy a source from the master list to the current list, click the desired source in the *Master List* list box and then click the Copy button that displays between the two list boxes. Click the Delete button to delete a source. Edit a source by clicking the source, clicking the Edit button, and then making changes at the Edit Source dialog box that displays. Click the New button to create a new source at the Create Source dialog box.

If the *Master List* list box contains a large number of sources, search for a specific source by typing keywords in the *Search* text box. As you type text, the list narrows to sources that match the text you are typing. When you are finished making changes at the Source Manager dialog box, click the Close button.

Inserting Page Numbers in a Citation

If you include a direct quote from a source, be sure to include quotation marks around all of the text used from that source and insert in the citation the page number(s) of the quoted material. To insert specific page numbers into a citation, click the citation in the document to select the citation placeholder. Click the Citation Options arrow and then click *Edit Citation* at the drop-down list. At the Edit Citation dialog box, type in the page number or numbers of the source from which the quote was borrowed and then click OK.

Figure 5.13 Source Manager Dialog Box

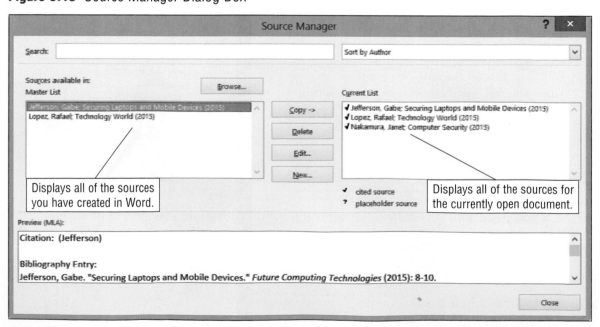

1. With **WL2-C5-P6-MobileSecurity.docx** open, edit a source by completing the following steps:
   a. If necessary, click the REFERENCES tab.
   b. Click the Manage Sources button in the Citations & Bibliography group.
   c. At the Source Manager dialog box, click the *Jefferson, Gabe* source entry in the *Master List* list box.
   d. Click the Edit button.
   e. At the Edit Source dialog box, delete the text in the *Author* text box and then type **Gabriel Jackson**.

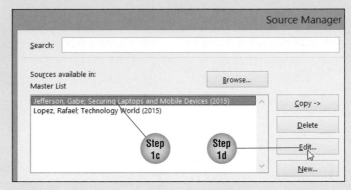

   f. Click OK to close the Edit Source dialog box.
   g. At the message asking if you want to update both the master list and current list with the changes, click Yes.
   h. Click the Close button to close the Source Manager dialog box. (Notice that the last name changed in both of the Jefferson citations to reflect the edit.)
2. Delete a source by completing the following steps:
   a. Select and then delete the last sentence in the fourth paragraph in the document (the sentence beginning *If somebody steals your laptop*), including the citation.
   b. Click the Manage Sources button in the Citations & Bibliography group.
   c. At the Source Manager dialog box, click the *Lopez, Rafael* entry in the *Current List* list box. (This entry will not contain a check mark because you deleted the citation from the document.)
   d. Click the Delete button.
   e. Click the Close button to close the Source Manager dialog box.

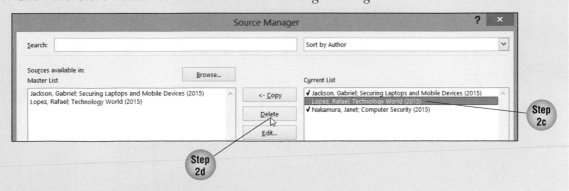

3. Create and insert a new source in the document by completing the following steps:
   a. Click the Manage Sources button in the Citations & Bibliography group.
   b. Click the New button in the Source Manager dialog box.
   c. Type the following book information in the Create Source dialog box. (Change the *Type of Source* option to *Book*.)

Author	**Georgia Miraldi**
Title	**Evolving Technology**
Year	**2015**
City	**Houston**
Publisher	**Rio Grande Publishing**

d. Click OK to close the Create Source dialog box.

e. Click the Close button to close the Source Manager dialog box.

f. Position the insertion point one space after the period that ends the last sentence in the document and then type this sentence: "**Be especially on guard when accessing your bank accounts, investment accounts, and retail accounts that store your credit card for purchases, and avoid entering your social security number**" (Press the spacebar once after typing the quotation mark that follows the word *number*.)

g. Insert a citation at the end of the sentence for Georgia Miraldi by clicking the Insert Citation button in the Citations & Bibliography group and then clicking *Miraldi, Georgia* at the drop-down list.

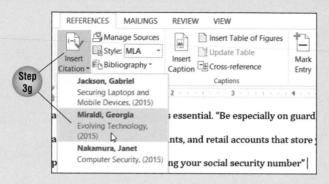

h. Type a period to end the sentence.

4. Because you inserted a direct quote from Georgia Miraldi, you will need to include the page number of the book in which you found the quote. Insert the page number within the citation by completing the following steps:

a. Click the *Miraldi* citation in the document.

b. Click the Citation Options arrow that displays at the right of the citation placeholder and then click *Edit Citation* at the drop-down list.

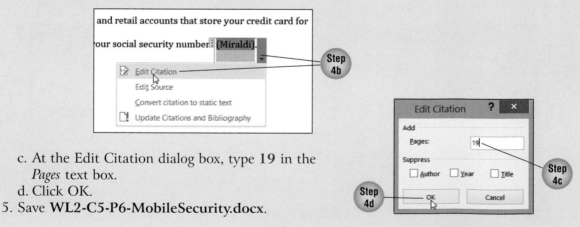

c. At the Edit Citation dialog box, type **19** in the *Pages* text box.

d. Click OK.

5. Save **WL2-C5-P6-MobileSecurity.docx**.

Inserting a Sources List

If you include citations in a report or research paper, you need to insert a sources list as a separate page at the end of the document. A sources list is an alphabetical list of the books, journal articles, reports, and other sources referenced in the report or paper. Depending on the reference style applied to a document, a sources list may be a bibliography, a references page, or a works cited page.

When you type source information for citations, Word automatically saves information from all of the fields and compiles a sources list, alphabetized by the authors' last names and/or the titles of the works. Insert a works cited page for a document formatted in MLA style, insert a references page for a document formatted in APA style, and insert a bibliography for a document formatted in Chicago style.

To insert a works cited page, move the insertion point to the end of the document and then insert a new page. Click the REFERENCES tab and make sure the *Style* option box is set to *MLA*. Click the Bibliography button in the Citations & Bibliography group and then click the desired works cited option. Complete similar steps to insert a bibliography in an APA-style document, except click the desired bibliography option.

▼ Quick Steps

Insert a Sources List
1. Insert new page at end of document.
2. Click REFERENCES tab.
3. Click Bibliography button.
4. Click desired works cited, reference, or bibliography option.

Bibliography

Project 6e | **Inserting a Works Cited Page** | **Part 5 of 8**

1. With **WL2-C5-P6-MobileSecurity.docx** open, insert a works cited page at the end of the document by completing these steps:
   a. Press Ctrl + End to move the insertion point to the end of the document.
   b. Press Ctrl + Enter to insert a page break.
   c. If necessary, click the REFERENCES tab.
   d. Click the Bibliography button in the Citations & Bibliography group.
   e. Click the *Works Cited* option in the *Built-In* section of the drop-down list.
2. Save **WL2-C5-P6-MobileSecurity.docx**.

Modifying and Updating a Sources List

If you insert a new source at the Source Manager dialog box or modify an existing source, Word automatically inserts the source information in the sources list. If you insert a new citation that requires you to add a new source, Word will not automatically update the sources list. To update the sources list, click anywhere in list and then click the Update Citations and Bibliography tab. The updated sources list will reflect any changes made to the citations and source information in the document.

▼ Quick Steps

Update a Sources List
1. Click anywhere in sources list.
2. Click Update Citations and Bibliography tab.

1. With **WL2-C5-P6-MobileSecurity.docx** open, create a new source and citation by completing the following steps:
   a. Position the insertion point immediately left of the period that ends the last sentence in the first paragraph of the document (after the word *safer*).
   b. Press the spacebar once.
   c. If necessary, click the REFERENCES tab.
   d. Click the Insert Citation button in the Citations & Bibliography group and then click *Add New Source* at the drop-down list.
   e. At the Create Source dialog box, insert the following source information for a website. (Change the *Type of Source* option to *Web site* and click the *Show All Bibliography Fields* check box to display all fields.)

Author	**Chay Suong**
Name of Web Page	**Securing and Managing Mobile Devices**
Year	**2014**
Month	**April**
Day	**20**
Year Accessed	(type current year in numbers)
Month Accessed	(type current month in letters)
Day Accessed	(type current day in numbers)
URL	**www.emcp.net/publishing**

   f. Click OK to close the Create Source dialog box.
2. Update the works cited page to include the new source by completing the following steps:
   a. Press Ctrl + End to move the insertion point to the end of the document.
   b. Click anywhere in the works cited text.
   c. Click the Update Citations and Bibliography tab located above the heading Works Cited. (Notice that the updated works cited includes the Suong reference.)
3. Save **WL2-C5-P6-MobileSecurity.docx**.

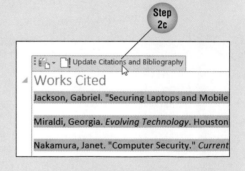

Step 2c

Formatting a Sources List

You may need to change formatting applied by Word to the sources list to meet the specific guidelines of MLA, APA, or Chicago reference style. For example, MLA and APA styles require the following formatting guidelines for sources list:

- Begin the sources list on a separate page after the last page of text in the report.
- Include the title *Works Cited*, *References*, or *Bibliography* at the top of the page and center it on the width of the page.
- Use the same font for the sources list as the font in the main document.
- Double-space between and within entries.
- Begin each entry at the left margin and format second and subsequent lines in each entry with a hanging indent.
- Alphabetize the entries.

The general formatting requirements for Chicago style are similar except that single spacing is applied within entries and double spacing is applied between entries.

1. With **WL2-C5-P6-MobileSecurity.docx** open, make the following formatting changes to the works cited page:

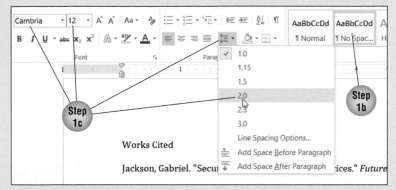

a. Select the *Works Cited* title and the entries below the title.
b. Click the HOME tab and then click the *No Spacing* style thumbnail in the Styles group.
c. With the text still selected, change the font to Cambria, the font size to 12 points, and the line spacing to 2.0.
d. Click anywhere in the title *Works Cited* and then click the Center button in the Paragraph group.
e. Select only the works cited entries and then press Ctrl + T. (Doing this formats the entries with a hanging indent.)
2. Press Ctrl + Home to move the insertion point to the beginning of the document.
3. Save and then print **WL2-C5-P6-MobileSecurity.docx**.

Choosing a Citation Style

Different subjects and different instructors or professors may require different forms of citation or reference styles. You can change the citation or reference style before beginning a new document or while working in an existing document. To do this, click the REFERENCES tab, click the down-pointing arrow at the right of the *Style* option box, and then click the desired style at the drop-down list.

▼ Quick Steps

Change the Citation Style
1. Click REFERENCES tab.
2. Click down-pointing arrow at right of *Style* option box.
3. Click desired style.

1. With **WL2-C5-P6-MobileSecurity.docx** open, change the document and works cited page from MLA style to APA style by completing the following steps:

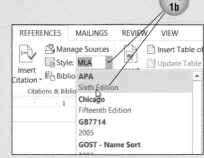

a. With the insertion point positioned at the beginning of the document, click the REFERENCES tab.
b. Click the down-pointing arrow at the right of the *Style* option box in the Citations & Bibliography group and then click *APA* at the drop-down list.
c. Scroll to the last page in the document (notice the changes to the citations), change the title *Works Cited* to *References*, select the four references, change the font to 12-point Cambria, change the spacing after paragraphs to 0, and then change the line spacing to 2.0.
2. Save the document and then print only the references page.
3. Close **WL2-C5-P6-MobileSecurity.docx**.
4. Display a blank document, click the REFERENCES tab, change the style to *MLA*, and then close the document without saving it.

Chapter Summary

- You can sort text in paragraphs, columns, and tables and sort records in a data source file. You can also select specific records in a data source file for merging with a main document.

- Use the Sort button in the Paragraph group on the HOME tab to sort text in paragraphs, columns, and tables.

- When sorting text set in columns, Word considers the left margin *Field 1*, text typed at the first tab *Field 2*, and so on.

- Sort on more than one field with the *Sort by* and *Then by* options at the Sort dialog box.

- Use the *Header row* option in the *My list has* section in the Sort Text dialog box to sort all text in columns except the first row.

- Sort records in a data source file at the Mail Merge Recipients dialog box. Sort by clicking the column heading or with options at the Filter and Sort dialog box with the Sort Records tab selected.

- Select specific records in a data source file with options at the Filter and Sort dialog box with the Filter Records tab selected.

- When nonbreaking spaces are inserted between words, Word considers these words as one unit and will not divide them when breaking and wrapping text to the next line. Insert a nonbreaking space with the keyboard shortcut Ctrl + Shift + spacebar.

- Use the Find and Replace feature to find special formatting, characters, and nonprinting elements and then replace them with nothing or other special text.

- Save a document as a template by changing the *Save as type* option at the Save As dialog box to *Word Template (*.dotx)* or display the Export backstage area, click the *Change File Type* option, click the *Template (*.dotx)* option, and then click the Save As button. At the Save As dialog box, save the template in the Custom Office Templates folder.

- Word adds the file extension *.dotx* to a template.

- Open a template located in the Custom Office Templates folder by displaying the New backstage area, clicking the *PERSONAL* option, and then clicking the desired template.

- Footnotes and endnotes provide explanatory notes and source citations. Footnotes are inserted and printed at the bottom of pages and endnotes are printed at the end of the document.

- By default, footnotes are numbered with arabic numbers and endnotes are numbered with lowercase roman numerals.

- Move, copy, or delete a footnote/endnote reference number in a document and all of the other footnotes/endnotes automatically renumber.

- Delete a footnote or endnote by selecting the reference number and then pressing the Delete key.

- Consider using in-text citations to acknowledge sources in a paper. Commonly used citation and reference styles include American Psychological Association (APA), Modern Language Association (MLA), and *Chicago Manual of Style* (Chicago).

- Insert a citation using the Insert Citation button in the Citations & Bibliography group on the REFERENCES tab. Specify source information at the Create Source dialog box.

- Insert a citation placeholder in a document if you want to type the source information at a later time.

- Edit a source at the Edit Source dialog box. Display this dialog box by clicking the source citation in the document, clicking the Citation Options arrow, and then clicking *Edit Source* at the drop-down list. Another option is to display the Source Manage dialog box, click the source you want to edit, and then click the Edit button.

- Manage sources—such as copying, deleting, editing, and inserting a new source—with options at the Source Manager dialog box. Display this dialog box by clicking the Manage Sources button in the Citations and Bibliography group on the REFERENCES tab.

- Insert a sources list, such as a works cited page, references page, or bibliography at the end of the document on a separate page. To do so, use the Bibliography button in the Citations & Bibliography group on the REFERENCES tab.

- To update a sources list, click anywhere in list text and then click the Update Citations and Bibliography tab.

- Change the reference style with the *Style* option box in the Citations & Bibliography group on the REFERENCES tab.

Commands Review

FEATURE	RIBBON TAB, GROUP	BUTTON, OPTION	KEYBOARD SHORTCUT
bibliography	REFERENCES, Citations & Bibliography		
citation style	REFERENCES, Citations & Bibliography		
Create Source dialog box	REFERENCES, Citations & Bibliography		
Filter and Sort dialog box with Select Records tab selected	MAILINGS, Start Mail Merge	, Filter	
Filter and Sort dialog box with Sort Records tab selected	MAILINGS, Start Mail Merge	, Sort	
Find and Replace dialog box	HOME, Editing		Ctrl + H
endnote	REFERENCES, Footnotes		Alt + Ctrl + D
footnote	REFERENCES, Footnotes		Alt + Ctrl + F
nonbreaking space			Ctrl + Shift + spacebar
Sort Options dialog box	HOME, Paragraph	, Options	
Sort Text dialog box	HOME, Paragraph		
Source Manager dialog box	REFERENCES, Citations & Bibliography		

Concepts Check   Test Your Knowledge

Completion: In the space provided at the right, indicate the correct term, symbol, or command.

1. The Sort button is located in this group on the HOME tab. _____

2. When sorting text in columns, Word considers the first tab this field number. _____

3. Click this option at the Sort Text dialog box to tell Word not to include the column headings in the sort. _____

4. Click the <u>Filter</u> hyperlink at this dialog box to display the Filter and Sort dialog box with the Filter Records tab selected. _____

5. Use this keyboard shortcut to insert a nonbreaking space. _____

6. Click this button at the expanded Find and Replace dialog box to display a pop-up list of special characters and nonprinting elements. _____

7. Word saves template documents with this file extension. _____

8. Click this option at the New backstage area to display templates saved in the Custom Office Templates folder. _____

9. Word numbers footnotes with this type of number. _____

10. Word numbers endnotes with this type of number. _____

11. Three of the most popular reference styles are APA (American Psychological Association), Chicago (*Chicago Manual of Style*), and this. _____

12. Click this tab to display the Citations & Bibliography group. _____

13. Create a new source for a document with options at this dialog box. _____

14. Click this button in the Citations & Bibliography group to display the Source Manager dialog box. _____

15. To update a bibliography, click anywhere in the bibliography and then click this tab. _____

Skills Check   Assess Your Performance

Assessment

1   SORT TEXT AND CREATE KEYBOARD SHORTCUTS WITH NONBREAKING SPACES

1. Open **SFSSorting.docx** and then save the document and name it **WL2-C5-A1-SFSSorting**.
2. Select the nine lines of text below the *Executive Team* heading and then sort the text alphabetically by last name.
3. Sort the three columns of text below the title *New Employees* by date of hire in ascending order.
4. Sort the text in the *First Qtr.* column in the table numerically in descending order.
5. Press Ctrl + End to move the insertion point to the end of the document and then type the text shown in Figure 5.14. Insert nonbreaking spaces within all of the keyboard shortcuts.
6. Save, print, and then close **WL2-C5-A1-SFSSorting.docx**.

Figure 5.14 Assessment 1

Keyboard Shortcuts

Word includes keyboard shortcuts you can use for creating, viewing, and saving documents. Press Ctrl + N to display a new blank document or press Ctrl + F12 to open a document. Use the shortcut Ctrl + W to close the currently open document. Additional keyboard shortcuts include pressing Alt + Ctrl + S to split the document window and pressing Alt + Shift + C to remove the document window split.

Assessment

2   INSERT FOOTNOTES IN DESIGNING A NEWSLETTER REPORT

1. Open **DesignNwsltr.docx** and then save the document and name it **WL2-C5-A2-DesignNwsltr**.
2. Create the first footnote shown in Figure 5.15 at the end of the first paragraph in the *Applying Guidelines* section.
3. Create the second footnote shown in Figure 5.15 at the end of the third paragraph in the *Applying Guidelines* section.
4. Create the third footnote shown in Figure 5.15 at the end of the last paragraph in the *Applying Guidelines* section.
5. Create the fourth footnote shown in Figure 5.15 at the end of the only paragraph in the *Choosing Paper Size and Type* section.
6. Create the fifth footnote shown in Figure 5.15 at the end of the only paragraph in the *Choosing Paper Weight* section.
7. Save and then print **WL2-C5-A2-DesignNwsltr.docx**.
8. Select the entire document and then change the font to Constantia.
9. Select all of the footnotes and change the font to Constantia.

Figure 5.15 Assessment 2

James Habermann, "Designing a Newsletter," *Desktop Designs* (2015): 23-29.

Shirley Pilante, "Adding Pizzazz to Your Newsletter," *Desktop Publisher* (2014): 32-39.

Arlita Maddock, "Guidelines for a Better Newsletter," *Business Computing* (2015): 9-14.

Monica Alverso, "Paper Styles for Newsletters," *Design Technologies* (2014): 45-51.

Keith Sutton, "Choosing Paper Styles," *Design Techniques* (2015): 8-11.

10. Delete the third footnote.
11. Save, print, and then close **WL2-C5-A2-DesignNwsltr.docx**.

Assessment

3 INSERT SOURCES AND CITATIONS IN A PRIVACY RIGHTS REPORT

1. Open **PrivRights.docx** and then save the document and name it **WL2-C5-A3-PrivRights**.
2. Make sure that MLA style is selected in the Citations & Bibliography group on the REFERENCES tab.
3. Format the title page to meet MLA requirements with the following changes:
   a. Select the entire document, change the font to 12-point Cambria, change the line spacing to 2.0, and remove the extra spacing after paragraphs.
   b. Move the insertion point to the beginning of the document, type your name, press the Enter key, type your instructor's name, press the Enter key, type the title of your course, press the Enter key, type the current date, and then press the Enter key.
   c. Type the title **Privacy Rights** at the top of the page and centered on the width of the page.
   d. Insert a header that displays your last name and the page number at the right margin and change the font to 12-point Cambria.
4. Press Ctrl + End to move the insertion point to the end of the document and then type the text shown in Figure 5.16 up to the first citation—the text *(Hartley)*. Insert the source information for a journal article written by Kenneth Hartley using the following information:

Author	**Kenneth Hartley**
Title	**Privacy Laws**
Journal Name	**Business World**
Year	**2015**
Pages	**24-46**
Volume	**XII**

5. Continue typing the text up to the next citation—the text *(Ferraro)*—and insert the following source information for a book:

Author	**Ramona Ferraro**
Title	**Business Employee Rights**
Year	**2014**
City	**Tallahassee**
Publisher	**Everglades Publishing House**

Figure 5.16 Assessment 3

An exception to the ability of companies to monitor their employees does exist. If the company has pledged to respect any aspect of employee privacy, it must keep that pledge. For example, if a business states that it will not monitor employee email or phone calls, by law, it must follow this stated policy (Hartley). However, no legal requirement exists mandating that companies notify their employees when and if monitoring takes place (Ferraro). Therefore, employees should assume they are always monitored and act accordingly.

Privacy advocates are calling for this situation to change. "They acknowledge that employers have the right to ensure that their employees are doing their jobs, but they question the need to monitor employees without warning and without limit" (Aldrich 20). The American Civil Liberties Union has, in fact, proposed a Fair Electronic Monitoring Policy to prevent abuses of employee privacy.

6. Continue typing the text up to the next citations—the text *(Aldrich)*—and insert the following information for an article in a periodical:

Author	**Kelly Aldrich**
Title	**What Rights Do Employees Have?**
Periodical Title	**Great Plains Times**
Year	**2015**
Month	**May**
Day	**6**
Pages	**18-22**

7. Insert the page number in the Kelly Aldrich citation using the Edit Citation dialog box.
8. Type the remaining text shown in Figure 5.16.
9. Edit the Kenneth Hartley source title to read *Small Business Privacy Laws* in the *Master List* section of the Source Manager dialog box (update both the Master List and Current List).
10. Select and delete the last two sentences in the second paragraph and then delete the Ramona Ferraro source in the *Current List* section of the Source Manager dialog box.
11. Insert a works cited page on a separate page at the end of the document.

12. Create a new source in the document using the Source Manager dialog box and include the following source information for a website:

Author	**Harold Davidson**
Name of Web Page	**Small Business Policies and Procedures**
Year	**2014**
Month	**December**
Day	**12**
Year Accessed	**2015**
Month Accessed	**February**
Day Accessed	**23**
URL	**www.emcp.net/policies**

13. Insert a citation for Harold Davidson at the end of the last sentence in the first paragraph.
14. Update the works cited page.
15. Format the works cited page to meet MLA requirements with the following changes:
    a. Select the *Works Cited* heading and all of the entries and click the *No Spacing* style thumbnail.
    b. Change the font to 12-point Cambria and change the spacing to 2.0.
    c. Center the title *Works Cited*.
    d. Format the works cited entries with a hanging indent.
16. Save and then print **WL2-C5-A3-PrivRights.docx**.
17. Change the document and works cited page from MLA style to APA style. Make sure you change the title of the sources list to *References*, select the references in the list, and then change the spacing after paragraphs to 0, the line spacing to 2.0, and the font to 12-point Cambria.
18. Save, print page 2, and then close **WL2-C5-A3-PrivRights.docx**.

Visual Benchmark   Demonstrate Your Proficiency

FORMAT A REPORT IN MLA STYLE

1. Open **SecurityDefenses.docx** and then save the document and name it **WL2-C5-VB-SecurityDefenses**.
2. Format the document so it displays as shown in Figure 5.17 with the following specifications:
    a. Change the document font to 12-point Cambria.
    b. Use the information from the works cited page when inserting citations into the document. The Hollingsworth citation is for a journal article, the Montoya citation is for a book, and the Gillespie citation is for a website.
    c. Format the works cited page to meet MLA requirements.
3. Save, print, and then close **WL2-C5-VB-SecurityDefenses.docx**.

Figure 5.17 Visual Benchmark

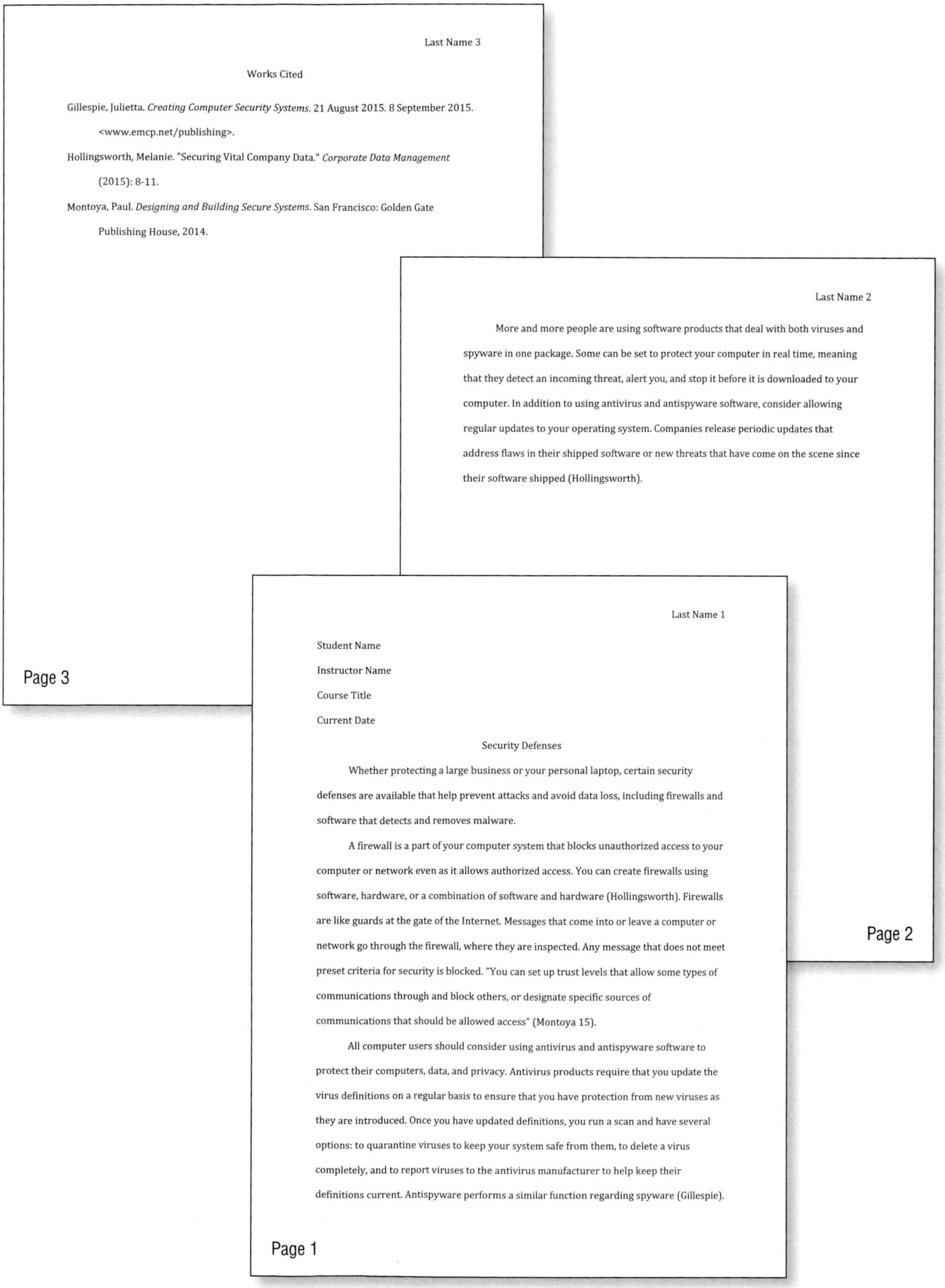

Last Name 3

Works Cited

Gillespie, Julietta. *Creating Computer Security Systems.* 21 August 2015. 8 September 2015.

    <www.emcp.net/publishing>.

Hollingsworth, Melanie. "Securing Vital Company Data." *Corporate Data Management*

    (2015): 8-11.

Montoya, Paul. *Designing and Building Secure Systems.* San Francisco: Golden Gate

    Publishing House, 2014.

Page 3

Last Name 2

More and more people are using software products that deal with both viruses and spyware in one package. Some can be set to protect your computer in real time, meaning that they detect an incoming threat, alert you, and stop it before it is downloaded to your computer. In addition to using antivirus and antispyware software, consider allowing regular updates to your operating system. Companies release periodic updates that address flaws in their shipped software or new threats that have come on the scene since their software shipped (Hollingsworth).

Page 2

Last Name 1

Student Name

Instructor Name

Course Title

Current Date

Security Defenses

Whether protecting a large business or your personal laptop, certain security defenses are available that help prevent attacks and avoid data loss, including firewalls and software that detects and removes malware.

A firewall is a part of your computer system that blocks unauthorized access to your computer or network even as it allows authorized access. You can create firewalls using software, hardware, or a combination of software and hardware (Hollingsworth). Firewalls are like guards at the gate of the Internet. Messages that come into or leave a computer or network go through the firewall, where they are inspected. Any message that does not meet preset criteria for security is blocked. "You can set up trust levels that allow some types of communications through and block others, or designate specific sources of communications that should be allowed access" (Montoya 15).

All computer users should consider using antivirus and antispyware software to protect their computers, data, and privacy. Antivirus products require that you update the virus definitions on a regular basis to ensure that you have protection from new viruses as they are introduced. Once you have updated definitions, you run a scan and have several options: to quarantine viruses to keep your system safe from them, to delete a virus completely, and to report viruses to the antivirus manufacturer to help keep their definitions current. Antispyware performs a similar function regarding spyware (Gillespie).

Page 1

Case Study   Apply Your Skills

Part 1

You are the office manager for Lincoln Freelance Services and have been compiling information on keyboard shortcuts for an employee training manual. Using the Help feature, find information on keyboard shortcuts for finding, replacing, and browsing through text as well as keyboard shortcuts for creating works cited/references, footnotes, and endnotes. Type the information you find on the keyboard shortcuts in a Word document. Use nonbreaking spaces within all of the keyboard shortcuts. Provide a title for the document and insert any other formatting to improve the appearance of the document. Save the document and name it **WL2-C5-CS-Shortcuts**. Print and then close the document.

Part 2

Lincoln Freelance Services provides freelance employees for businesses in Baltimore and surrounding communities. A new industrial park has opened in Baltimore and you need to fill a number of temporary positions. You decide to send a letter to current clients living in Baltimore to let them know about the new industrial park and the temporary jobs that are available. Create a letter main document and include in the letter the information that a new industrial park is opening in a few months, the location of the park (you determine a location), and that Lincoln Freelance Services will be providing temporary employees for many of the technology jobs. Include a list of at least five technology jobs (find job titles on the Internet) for which you will be placing employees. Include any additional information in the letter that you feel is important. Merge the letter main document only with those clients in the **LFSClients.mdb** data source file who live in Baltimore. Save the merged letters and name the document **WL2-C5-CS-LFSLtrs**. Print and then close **WL2-C5-CS-LFSLtrs.docx**. Save the letter main document and name it **WL2-C5-CS-LFSMD** and then close the document.

Part 3

Your supervisor has given you a report on newsletter guidelines and asked you to reformat it using APA reference style. Open the **WL2-C5-A2-DesignNwsltr.docx** document and then save it and name it **WL2-C5-CS-DesignNwsltr**. Remove the title *CREATING NEWSLETTER LAYOUT* and add 6 points of space before the heading *Choosing Paper Size and Type*. Remove the footnotes and insert the information as in-text journal article citations and then add a references page on a separate page. Center the title *References* and then select the entire document and change the font to Cambria. Save **WL2-C5-CS-DesignNwsltr.docx**.

Part 4

Your supervisor has asked you to include some additional information on newsletter guidelines. Using the Internet, look for websites that provide information on desktop publishing and/or newsletter design. Include in the **WL2-C5-CS-DesignNwsltr.docx** report document at least one additional paragraph with information you found on the Internet and include a citation for each source from which you have borrowed information. Save, print, and then close the report.

WORD
MICROSOFT®

Creating Specialized Tables and Indexes

PERFORMANCE OBJECTIVES

Upon successful completion of Chapter 6, you will be able to:
- Create, insert, and update a table of contents
- Create, insert, and update a table of figures
- Create, insert, and update an index

Tutorials

6.1 Inserting a Table of Contents

6.2 Customizing and Updating a Table of Contents

6.3 Assigning Levels to Table of Contents Entries

6.4 Inserting a Table of Figures

6.5 Creating and Customizing Captions

6.6 Marking Index Entries and Inserting an Index

6.7 Creating a Concordance File

6.8 Updating and Deleting an Index

A book, textbook, report, or manuscript often includes sections such as a table of contents, index, and table of figures. Creating these sections can be tedious when prepared manually. With Word, these sections can be created quickly and easily using automated functions. In this chapter, you will learn the steps to mark text for a table of contents, table of figures, and index and then insert the table or index. Model answers for this chapter's projects appear on the following pages.

Note: Before beginning the projects, copy to your storage medium the WL2C6 subfolder from the WL2 folder on the CD that accompanies this textbook and then make WL2C6 the active folder.

CONTENTS

Project 1 Create a Table of Contents for a Computer Interface Report WL2-C6-P1-AIReport.docx

TABLE OF CONTENTS

Project 2 Mark Text for and Insert a Table of Contents in a Company Handbook WL2-C6-P2-CompEval.docx

TABLE OF FIGURES

Page 1

Project 3 Create a Table of Figures for a Technology Report and a Travel Document Project 3b, WL2-C6-P3-TechRpt.docx

Productivity Software

Productivity software includes software that people typically use to complete work, such as word processing software (working with words), spreadsheet software (working with data, numbers, and calculations), database software (organizing and retrieving data records), or presentation software (creating slide shows with text and graphics).

WORD PROCESSING SOFTWARE

With word processing software, you can create documents that include sophisticated formatting; change text fonts; add special effects such as bold, italics, and underlining; add shadows, background colors, and other effects to text and objects; and include tables, photos, drawings, and links to online content.

Figure 1 Word Document

With a mail merge feature, you can take a list of names and addresses and print personalized letters and envelopes or labels. Figure 1 shows the application of some of the word processing features and tools Microsoft Word offers.

SPREADSHEET SOFTWARE

Using spreadsheet software, such as Microsoft Excel, you can perform calculations that range from simple (adding, averaging, and multiplying) to complex (estimating standard deviations based on a range of numbers, for example). In addition, spreadsheet software offers

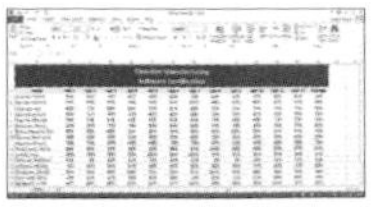

Figure 2 Excel Worksheet

sophisticated charting and graphing capabilities. Formatting tools help you create polished looking documents such as budgets, invoices, schedules, attendance records, and purchase orders. Figure 2 shows a typical Excel spreadsheet making use of several key features.

Page 2

Page 3

Output Devices

To get information into a computer, a person uses an input device. To get information out, a person uses an output device. Some common output devices include monitors and printers.

MONITOR

A monitor, or screen, is the most common output device used with a personal computer. The most common monitors use either a thin film transistor (TFT) active matrix liquid crystal display (LCD) or a plasma display. Plasma displays have a true level of color reproduction compared with LCDs. Emerging display technologies include surface-conduction electron-emitter displays (SED) and organic light emitting diodes (OLED).

Figure 3 Monitor

PRINTERS

After monitors, printers are the most important output devices. The print quality produced by these devices is measured in dpi, or dots per inch. As with screen resolution, the greater the number of dots per inch, the better the quality. The earliest printers for personal computers were dot matrix printers that used perforated computer paper. These impact printers worked something like typewriters, transferring the image of a character by using pins to strike a ribbon.

Figure 4 Laser Printer

A laser printer uses a laser beam to create points of electrical charge on a cylindrical drum. Toner, composed of particles of ink with a negative electrical charge, sticks to the charged points on the positively charged drum. As the page moves past the drum, heat and pressure fuse the toner to the page. Inkjet printers use a print head that moves across the page that sprays a fine mist of ink when an electrical charge moves through the

Page 3

Page 4

cartridge. An inkjet printer can use color cartridges and so provides affordable color printing suitable for home and small office use.

Developing Software

Through the years, some software products have become incredibly sophisticated as new features are added in each version. The *software development life cycle* (SDLC) has evolved over time. This procedure dictates the general flow of creating a new software product as shown in the figure below. The SDLC involves performing market research to ensure that a need or demand for the product exists; completing a business analysis to match the solution to the need; creating a plan for implementing the software, which involves creating a budget and schedule for the project; writing the software program; testing the software; deploying the software to the public, either by selling the product in a package or online; and performing maintenance and bug fixes to keep the product functioning optimally.

Figure 5 Developing Software

Page 4

Page 1

TABLES

Page 1

Page 2

TERRA TRAVEL SERVICES

Antarctic Zenith Adventures

Travel with our Antarctic experts, cruise on our state-of-the-art ships, and experience Antarctica in all of its grandeur. We use ice-rated expedition ships custom-designed for your comfort and safety. Each ship can carry up to 100 passengers and provides excellent viewing for watching whales, seabirds, and icebergs as well as facilities for educational presentations by our Antarctic experts. For our more adventurous clients, we offer additional activities such as snowshoeing, sea-kayaking, and camping on the Antarctic ice. Plan on a shore excursion where you can view penguin rookeries, seal colonies, and places of historical and scientific interest. To carry you to the Antarctic shore, we use inflatable boats that can carry 12 to 15 people. After a thrilling day on shore, we will take you back to the ship where you can enjoy a delicious meal prepared by our gourmet chefs. Our Antarctic travel experts are naturalists, historians, and adventurers committed to providing you with a fabulous Antarctic adventure.

Zenith Adventures	Length	Price
Antarctic Exploration	7 days	$4,399
Weddell Sea Adventure	10 days	$6,899
Falkland Islands	14 days	$7,699
Sailing Spectacular	14 days	$8,999

Adventure 1 Antarctic Zenith Adventures

Upcoming Adventures

Beginning next year, Zenith Adventures, together with Terra Travel Services, will offer volunteer vacation opportunities. Tentative volunteer adventures include building village and mountain paths, building homes, and helping the families of trail porters improve village facilities. Our volunteer adventures will provide you with an exciting vacation and a rewarding volunteer experience. The group size will be limited to a maximum of 15 and participants will be required to raise a minimum amount of money to contribute to the program and local charities. All charities have been carefully screened to ensure that funds are well-managed and distributed fairly. Look for more information in our next newsletter and consider a rewarding volunteer adventure.

Page 2

Project 3c, WL2-C6-P3-TTSAdventures.docx

Bicycling Adventure

A bicycle is the perfect form of transportation for a travel adventure. Sign up for one or our bicycle tours and travel at your own pace, interact with village residents, stay healthy and fit, and know that your adventure has a minimal effect on the environment. We offer bicycle tours ranging from a leisurely trip through the Loire Valley of France to a mountain-bike expedition in the Atlas Mountains in Morocco. Our Zenith Adventures bicycle guides provide you with historical and educational information about the region in which you are traveling. They also take care of luggage and transportation needs and maintain your bicycle. We are confident that we can provide the bicycle adventure of a lifetime!

Zenith Adventure	Length	Price
Loire Valley Tour	7 days	$1,999
Tuscan Village Tour	8 days	$2,499
Atlas Trek Extreme	9 days	$2,899
Great Wall of Chin	14 days	$3,299

Adventure 2 Tall-Ship Adventures

Page 3

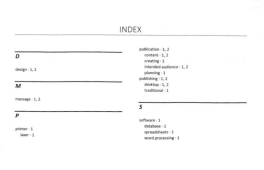

INDEX

D

design · 1, 2

M

message · 1, 2

P

printer · 1
   laser · 1

publication · 1, 2
   content · 1, 2
   creating · 1
   intended audience · 1, 2
   planning · 1
publishing · 1, 2
   desktop · 1, 2
   traditional · 1

S

software · 1
   database · 1
   spreadsheets · 1
   word processing · 1

3

Project 4 Create an Index for a Desktop Publishing Report

WL2-C6-P4-DTP.docx

newsletters	Newsletters
Newsletters	Newsletters
Software	Software
Desktop publishing	Software: desktop publishing
word processing	Software: word processing
Printers	Printers
Laser	Printers: laser
Design	Design
Communication	Communication
Consistency	Design: consistency
Elements	Elements
Nameplate	Elements: nameplate
Logo	Elements: logo
Subtitle	Elements: subtitle
Folio	Elements: folio
Headlines	Elements: headlines
Subheads	Elements: subheads
Byline	Elements: byline
Body Copy	Elements: body copy
Graphics Images	Elements: graphics images
Audience	Newsletters: audience
Purpose	Newsletters: purpose
focal point	Newsletters: focal point

Project 5 Create an Index with a Concordance File for a Newsletter

WL2-C6-P5-CFile.docx

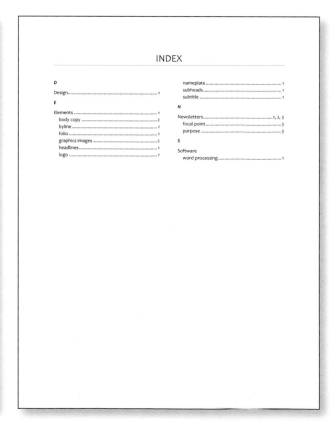

INDEX

D

Design...1

E

Elements...1
  body copy 2
  byline 1
  folio 1
  graphics images 2
  headlines 1
  logo 1

  nameplate 1
  subheads 1
  subtitle 1

N

Newsletters..1, 2, 3
  focal point 3
  purpose 3

S

Software
  word processing 1

WL2-C6-P5-PlanNwsltr.docx

Model Answers

Project 1   **Create a Table of Contents for a Computer Interface Report**   **2 Parts**

You will open a report on computer interfaces, mark text for a table of contents, and then insert the table of contents in the document. You will also make, customize, and update the table of contents.

Creating a Table of Contents

A *table of contents* appears at the beginning of a book, manuscript, or report and contains headings and subheadings with page numbers. In a previous chapter, you created a table of contents using the Quick Parts button in the Text group on the INSERT tab. You can also create a table of contents using the Table of Contents button in the Table of Contents group on the REFERENCES tab. Identify the text to be included in a table of contents by applying built-in heading styles or custom styles, assigning levels, or marking text.

HINT

You can use a table of contents to navigate quickly in a document and to get an overview of the topics it covers.

Applying Styles

To create a table of contents with built-in styles, open the document and then apply the desired styles. Word uses all text with the Heading 1 style applied for the first level of the table of contents, all text with the Heading 2 style applied for the second level, and so on. Apply built-in styles with options in the Styles group on the HOME tab.

HINT

If you apply heading styles to text in a document, you can easily insert a table of contents later.

Inserting a Table of Contents

After you have applied styles to the headings, insert the table of contents in the document. To do this, position the insertion point where you want the table of contents to appear, click the REFERENCES tab, click the Table of Contents button, and then click the desired option at the drop-down list.

Numbering the Table of Contents Page

Generally, the pages containing the table of contents are numbered with lowercase roman numerals (*i, ii, iii*). Change the format of the page number to lowercase roman numerals at the Page Number Format dialog box, shown in Figure 6.1. Display this dialog box by clicking the INSERT tab, clicking the Page Number button in the Header & Footer group, and then clicking *Format Page Numbers* at the drop-down list.

The first page of text in the main document, which usually comes immediately after the table of contents, should begin with the arabic number 1. To make it possible to change from roman to arabic page numbers within the same document, separate the table of contents from the first page of the document with a section break that begins a new page.

▼ **Quick Steps**

Insert a Table of Contents
1. Apply heading styles.
2. Click REFERENCES tab.
3. Click Table of Contents button.
4. Click desired option at drop-down list.

 Table of Contents

Number the Table of Contents Page
1. Click INSERT tab.
2. Click Page Number button.
3. Click *Format Page Numbers* at drop-down list.
4. Change number format to lowercase roman numerals at Page Number Format dialog box.
5. Click OK.

 Page Number

Figure 6.1 Page Number Format Dialog Box

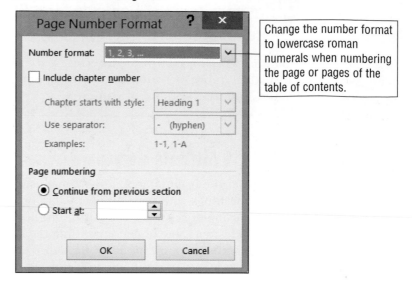

Change the number format to lowercase roman numerals when numbering the page or pages of the table of contents.

Navigating Using a Table of Contents

When you insert a table of contents into a document, you can use the headings it contains to navigate within the document. Table of contents headings are hyperlinks that are connected to the headings within the document.

To navigate in a document using table of contents headings, click in the table of contents to select it. Position the mouse pointer over the desired heading and a box will display with the path and file name as well as the text *Ctrl+Click to follow link*. Hold down the Ctrl key and click the left mouse button and the insertion point is positioned in the document at the location of the heading.

Project 1a **Inserting a Table of Contents**   **Part 1 of 2**

1. Open **AIReport.docx** and then save the document and name it **WL2-C6-P1-AIReport**. (This document contains headings with heading styles applied.)
2. Position the insertion point immediately left of the first *N* in *NATURAL INTERFACE APPLICATIONS* and then insert a section break by completing the following steps:
   a. Click the PAGE LAYOUT tab.
   b. Click the Breaks button in the Page Setup group.
   c. Click the *Next Page* option in the *Section Breaks* section.

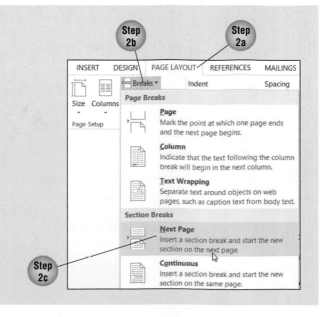

---

3. With the insertion point positioned below the section break, insert page numbers and change the beginning number to 1 by completing the following steps:
   a. Click the INSERT tab.
   b. Click the Page Number button in the Header & Footer group, point to *Bottom of Page*, and then click *Plain Number 2*.
   c. Click the Page Number button in the Header & Footer group on the HEADER & FOOTER TOOLS DESIGN tab and then click *Format Page Numbers* at the drop-down list.

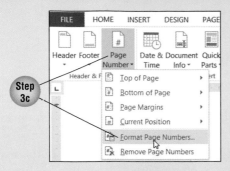

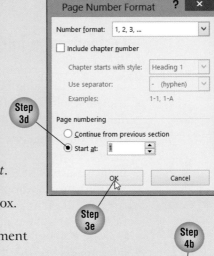

   d. At the Page Number Format dialog box, click *Start at*. (This inserts *1* in the *Start at* measurement box.)
   e. Click OK to close the Page Number Format dialog box.
   f. Double-click in the document to make it active.
4. Insert a table of contents at the beginning of the document by completing the following steps:
   a. Press Ctrl + Home to move the insertion point to the beginning of the document.
   b. Click the REFERENCES tab.
   c. Click the Table of Contents button in the Table of Contents group, and then click the *Automatic Table 1* option in the *Built-In* section of the drop-down list.

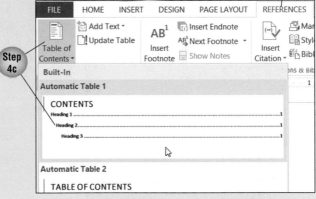

5. Insert page numbers in the table of contents page by completing the following steps:
   a. Scroll up the document and then click any character in the *CONTENTS* heading.
   b. Click the INSERT tab.
   c. Click the Page Number button in the Header & Footer group and then click *Format Page Numbers* at the drop-down list.
   d. At the Page Number Format dialog box, click the down-pointing arrow at the right side of the *Number format* option box and then click *i, ii, iii, …* at the drop-down list.
   e. Click OK to close the dialog box.

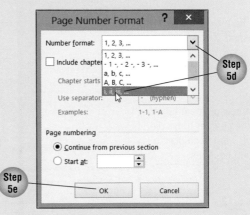

6. Navigate in the document using the table of contents by completing the following steps:
   a. Click on any character in the table of contents.
   b. Position the mouse pointer on the *Virtual Reality* heading, hold down the Ctrl key, click the left mouse button, and then release the Ctrl key. (This moves the insertion point to the beginning of the *Virtual Reality* heading in the document.)
   c. Press Ctrl + Home to move the insertion point to the beginning of the document.
7. Save **WL2-C6-P1-AIReport.docx** and then print only page 1 (the table of contents page).

Customizing a Table of Contents

Customize an existing table of contents in a document with options at the Table of Contents dialog box, as shown in Figure 6.2. Display this dialog box by clicking the Table of Contents button on the REFERENCES tab and then clicking *Custom Table of Contents* at the drop-down list.

At the Table of Contents dialog box, a sample table of contents displays in the *Print Preview* section. Change the table of contents format by clicking the down-pointing arrow at the right side of the *Formats* option box (located in the *General* section). At the drop-down list that displays, click the desired format. When you select a different format, that format displays in the *Print Preview* section. Page numbers in a table of contents will display after the text or aligned at the right margin, depending on what option is selected. You can also specify page number alignment with the *Right align page numbers* option. The number of levels that display depends on the number of heading levels specified in the document. Control the number of levels that display in a table of contents with the *Show levels* measurement box.

Figure 6.2 Table of Contents Dialog Box

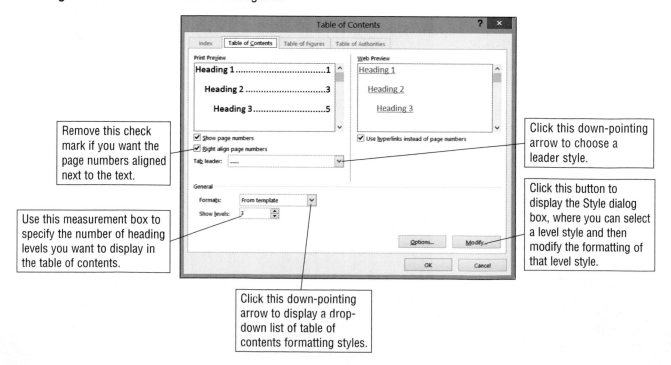

Remove this check mark if you want the page numbers aligned next to the text.

Click this down-pointing arrow to choose a leader style.

Use this measurement box to specify the number of heading levels you want to display in the table of contents.

Click this button to display the Style dialog box, where you can select a level style and then modify the formatting of that level style.

Click this down-pointing arrow to display a drop-down list of table of contents formatting styles.

Tab leaders help guide readers' eyes from the table of contents heading to the page number. The default tab leader is a period. To choose a different leader, click the down-pointing arrow at the right side of the *Tab leader* option box and then click the desired leader character from the drop-down list.

Word automatically identifies headings in a table of contents as hyperlinks and inserts page numbers. You can use these hyperlinks to move the insertion point to a specific location in the document. If you are going to post your document to the Web, consider removing the page numbers since readers will only need to click the hyperlink to view a specific page. Remove page numbering by removing the check mark from the *Show page numbers* check box in the Table of Contents dialog box.

If you make changes to the options at the Table of Contents dialog box and then click OK, a message will display asking if you want to replace the selected table of contents. At this message, click Yes.

Updating a Table of Contents

If you add, delete, move, or edit headings or other text in a document after inserting a table of contents, you need to update the table of contents. To do this, click anywhere within the current table of contents and then click the Update Table button or press the F9 key (the Update Field key). At the Update Table of Contents dialog box, shown in Figure 6.3, click *Update page numbers only* if changes occur only to the page numbers or click *Update entire table* if changes were made to headings or subheadings within the table. Click OK or press Enter to close the dialog box.

Removing a Table of Contents

Remove a table of contents from a document by clicking the Table of Contents button on the REFERENCES tab and then clicking *Remove Table of Contents* at the drop-down list. Another way to remove a table of contents is to click any character in the table of contents, click the Table of Contents tab located in the upper left corner of the table of contents (immediately left of the Update Table tab), and then click *Remove Table of Contents* at the drop-down list.

Figure 6.3 Update Table of Contents Dialog Box

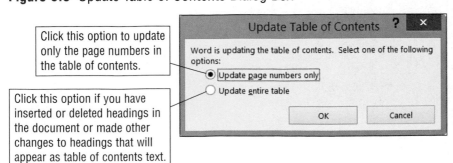

Click this option to update only the page numbers in the table of contents.

Click this option if you have inserted or deleted headings in the document or made other changes to headings that will appear as table of contents text.

▼ **Quick Steps**

Update a Table of Contents
1. Click in table of contents.
2. Click REFERENCES tab.
3. Click Update Table button.
4. Select *Update page numbers only* or *Update entire table*.
5. Click OK.

Remove a Table of Contents
1. Click REFERENCES tab.
2. Click Table of Contents button.
3. Click *Remove Table of Contents*..
OR
1. Click any character in table of contents.
2. Click Table of Contents tab.
3. Click *Remove Table of Contents*.

Update Table

1. With **WL2-C6-P1-AIReport.docx** open and the insertion point positioned at the beginning of the document, apply a different formatting style to the table of contents by completing the following steps:

   a. Click the REFERENCES tab, click the Table of Contents button, and then click *Custom Table of Contents* at the drop-down list.

   b. At the Table of Contents dialog box with the Table of Contents tab selected, click the down-pointing arrow at the right of the *Formats* option box in the *General* section and then click *Formal* at the drop-down list.

   c. Click the down-pointing arrow at the right of the *Tab leader* option box and then click the solid line option (bottom option) at the drop-down list.

   d. Click once on the down-pointing arrow at the right side of the *Show levels* measurement box to change the number to *2*.

   e. Click OK to close the dialog box.

   f. At the message asking if you want to replace the selected table of contents, click Yes.

2. Use the table of contents to move the insertion point to the beginning of the *NAVIGATION* heading located at the bottom of page 3.

3. Press Ctrl + Enter to insert a page break.

4. Update the table of contents by completing the following steps:

   a. Press Ctrl + Home and then click on any character in the table of contents.

   b. Click the Update Table tab.

   c. At the Update Table of Contents dialog box, make sure *Update page numbers only* is selected and then click OK.

5. Save the document, print only the table of contents page, and then close **WL2-C6-P1-AIReport.docx**.

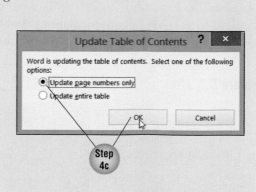

<table>
<tr><td>

Project 2 **Mark Text for and Insert a Table of Contents in a Company Handbook**

</td><td>

2 Parts

</td></tr>
</table>

> You will open a document that contains employee pay and evaluation information, mark text as table of contents fields, and then insert a table of contents in the document. You will also insert a file containing additional information on employee classifications and then update the table of contents.

Assigning Levels to Table of Contents Entries

Another method for identifying text for the table of contents is to use the Add Text button in the Table of Contents group on the REFERENCES tab. Click this button and a drop-down list of level options displays. Click the desired level for the currently selected text. After specifying levels, insert the table of contents by clicking the Table of Contents button and then clicking the desired option at the drop-down list.

Add Text

Marking Table of Contents Entries as Fields

Applying styles to text applies specific formatting. If you want to identify titles and/or headings for a table of contents but do not want heading style formatting applied, mark each title or heading as a field entry. To do this, select the text you want included in the table of contents and then press Alt + Shift + O. This displays the Mark Table of Contents Entry dialog box, shown in Figure 6.4.

In the dialog box, the text you selected in the document displays in the *Entry* text box. Specify the text level using the *Level* measurement box and then click the Mark button. This turns on the display of nonprinting symbols in the document and also inserts a field code immediately after the selected text.

For example, when you select the title in Project 2a, the following code is inserted immediately after the title: { TC "COMPENSATION" \f C \l "1" }. The Mark Table of Contents Entry dialog box also remains open. To mark the next entry for the table of contents, select the text and then click the Title bar of the Mark Table of Contents Entry dialog box. Specify the level and then click the Mark button. Continue in this manner until all of the table of contents entries have been marked.

If you mark table of contents entries as fields, you will need to activate the *Table entry fields* option when inserting the table of contents. To do this, display the Table of Contents dialog box and then click the Options button. At the Table of Contents Options dialog box, shown in Figure 6.5 on the next page, click the *Table entry fields* check box to insert a check mark and then click OK.

Figure 6.4 Mark Table of Contents Entry Dialog Box

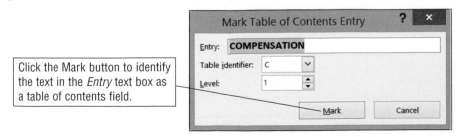

Figure 6.5 Table of Contents Options Dialog Box

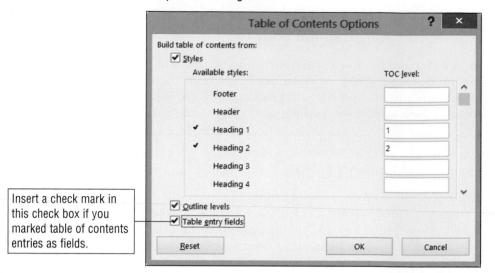

Insert a check mark in this check box if you marked table of contents entries as fields.

Project 2a **Marking Headings as Fields** Part 1 of 2

1. Open **CompEval.docx** and then save the document and name it **WL2-C6-P2-CompEval**.
2. Position the insertion point immediately to the left of the *C* in *COMPENSATION* and then insert a section break that begins a new page.
3. Mark the titles and headings as fields for insertion in a table of contents by completing the following steps:
   a. Select the title *COMPENSATION*.
   b. Press Alt + Shift + O.
   c. At the Mark Table of Contents Entry dialog box, make sure the *Level* measurement box is set at *1* and then click the Mark button. (This turns on the display of nonprinting characters.)
   d. Click in the document, scroll down, and then select the title *EVALUATION*.
   e. Click the dialog box Title bar and then click the Mark button.
   f. Click in the document, scroll up, and then select the heading *Rate of Pay*.
   g. Click the dialog box Title bar and then click the up-pointing arrow at the right of the *Level* measurement box in the Mark Table of Contents Entry dialog box until *2* displays.
   h. Click the Mark button.
   i. Mark the following headings as level 2:
      Direct Deposit Option
      Pay Progression
      Overtime
      Work Performance Standards
      Performance Evaluation
      Employment Records
   j. Click the Close button to close the Mark Table of Contents Entry dialog box.

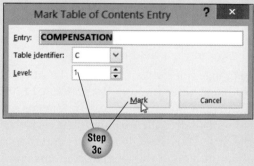

Step 3c

Step 3g   Step 3h

4. Position the insertion point at the beginning of the title *COMPENSATION* and then insert page numbers at the bottom center of each page of the section and change the starting number to 1. ***Hint: Refer to Project 1a, Step 3.***
5. Double-click in the document.
6. Insert a table of contents at the beginning of the document by completing the following steps:
   a. Position the insertion point at the beginning of the document (on the new page).
   b. Type the title **TABLE OF CONTENTS** and then press the Enter key.
   c. Click the REFERENCES tab.
   d. Click the Table of Contents button and then click *Custom Table of Contents* at the drop-down list.
   e. At the Table of Contents dialog box, click the Options button.
   f. At the Table of Contents Options dialog box, click the *Table entry fields* check box to insert a check mark.
   g. Click OK to close the Table of Contents Options dialog box.
   h. Click OK to close the Table of Contents dialog box.
   i. Apply bold formatting and center the heading *TABLE OF CONTENTS*.

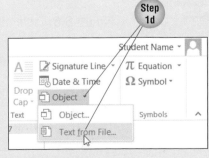

7. Insert a lowercase roman numeral page number on the table of contents page. ***Hint: Refer to Project 1a, Step 5.***
8. Click the Show/Hide ¶ button to turn off the display of nonprinting characters.
9. Save **WL2-C6-P2-CompEval.docx** and then print only page 1 (the table of contents page).

If you insert additional information in a document, you can easily update the table of contents. To do this, insert the text and then mark the text with options at the Mark Table of Contents Entry dialog box. Click anywhere in the table of contents and then click the Update Table tab. At the Update Table of Contents dialog box, click the *Update entire table* option and then click OK.

Project 2b   Updating the Entire Table of Contents   Part 2 of 2

1. With **WL2-C6-P2-CompEval.docx** open, insert a file into the document by completing the following steps:
   a. Press Ctrl + End to move the insertion point to the end of the document.
   b. Press Ctrl + Enter to insert a page break.
   c. Click the INSERT tab.
   d. Click the Object button arrow in the Text group and then click *Text from File* at the drop-down list.
   e. At the Insert File dialog box, navigate to the WL2C6 folder on your storage medium and then double-click *PosClassification.docx*.

2. Select and then mark text for inclusion in the table of contents by completing the following steps:
   a. Select the title *POSITION CLASSIFICATION*.
   b. Press Alt + Shift + O.
   c. At the Mark Table of Contents Entry dialog box, make sure that *1* displays in the *Level* measurement box and then click the Mark button.
   d. Click the Close button to close the Mark Table of Contents Entry dialog box.
3. Update the table of contents by completing the following steps:
   a. Select the entire table of contents (excluding the title).
   b. Click the REFERENCES tab.
   c. Click the Update Table button in the Table of Contents group.
   d. At the Update Table of Contents dialog box, click the *Update entire table* option.
   e. Click OK.
4. Turn off the display of nonprinting characters.
5. Save the document, print only the table of contents page, and then close **WL2-C6-P2-CompEval.docx**.

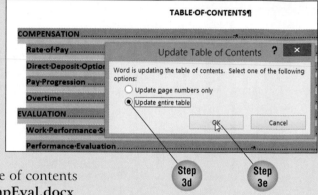

Step 3d

Step 3e

Project 3 **Create a Table of Figures for a Technology Report** **3 Parts**
and a Travel Document

You will open a report containing information on software, output devices, and the software development cycle, as well as images and a SmartArt diagram; insert captions; and then create a table of figures. You will also create and customize captions and insert a table of figures for an adventure document.

Creating a Table of Figures ■■■■■■■■■■■■■■■■■■■■■■■

A table of figures includes a list of all figures, tables, and equations in the document.

A document that contains figures should include a *table of figures* so readers can quickly locate specific figures. Figure 6.6 shows an example of a table of figures. You can create a table of figures by marking figures or images with captions and then using the caption names to create the table.

Figure 6.6 Table of Figures

TABLE OF FIGURES

FIGURE 1 SCANNED LINE ART 3
FIGURE 2 DIGITAL HALFTONE 8
FIGURE 3 BAR 12
FIGURE 4 LINE CHARTS 15
FIGURE 5 DETAIL VS. WEIGHT 18

Creating Captions

A *caption* is text that describes an item such as an image, table, equation, or chart. A caption generally displays below the item. Create a caption by selecting the figure text or image, clicking the REFERENCES tab, and then clicking the Insert Caption button in the Captions group. This displays the Caption dialog box, shown in Figure 6.7. At the dialog box, *Figure 1* displays in the *Caption* text box and the insertion point is positioned after *Figure 1*. Type a name for the figure and then press the Enter key. Word inserts *Figure 1* followed by the caption you typed below the selected text or image. If the insertion point is positioned in a table when you display the Caption dialog box, *Table 1* displays in the *Caption* text box instead of *Figure 1*.

Inserting a Table of Figures

After you have marked figures or images with captions within a document, insert the table of figures. A table of figures generally displays at the beginning of the document, after the table of contents and on a separate page. To insert the table of figures, click the Insert Table of Figures button in the Captions group on the REFERENCES tab. At the Table of Figures dialog box, shown in Figure 6.8 on the next page, make any necessary changes and then click OK.

The options at the Table of Figures dialog box are similar to the options available at the Table of Contents dialog box. For example, you can choose a format for the table of figures from the *Formats* option box, change the alignment of the page numbers, or add leaders before page numbers.

▼ Quick Steps

Create a Caption
1. Select text or image.
2. Click REFERENCES tab.
3. Click Insert Caption button.
4. Type caption name.
5. Click OK.

Insert
Caption

▼ Quick Steps

Insert a Table of Figures
1. Click REFERENCES tab.
2. Click Insert Table of Figures button.
3. Select desired format.
4. Click OK.

Insert Table
of Figures

Figure 6.7 Caption Dialog Box

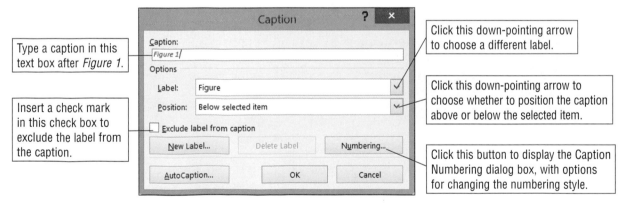

Type a caption in this text box after *Figure 1*.

Insert a check mark in this check box to exclude the label from the caption.

Click this down-pointing arrow to choose a different label.

Click this down-pointing arrow to choose whether to position the caption above or below the selected item.

Click this button to display the Caption Numbering dialog box, with options for changing the numbering style.

Figure 6.8 Table of Figures Dialog Box

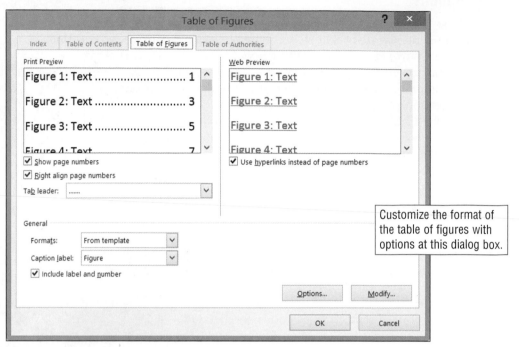

Customize the format of the table of figures with options at this dialog box.

Project 3a **Creating a List of Figures** Part 1 of 3

1. Open **TechRpt.docx** and then save the document and name it **WL2-C6-P3-TechRpt**.
2. Add the caption *Figure 1 Word Document* to an image by completing the following steps:
   a. Click the screen image that displays in the *WORD PROCESSING SOFTWARE* section.
   b. Click the REFERENCES tab.
   c. Click the Insert Caption button in the Captions group.
   d. At the Caption dialog box with the insertion point positioned after *Figure 1* in the *Caption* text box, press the spacebar once and then type **Word Document**.
   e. Click OK or press Enter.

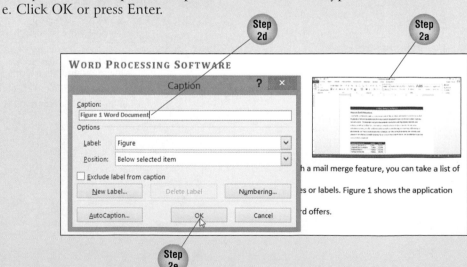

   f. Press Ctrl + E to center the caption in the text box.

3. Complete steps similar to those in Step 2 to create the caption *Figure 2 Excel Worksheet* for the image in the *SPREADSHEET SOFTWARE* section.

4. Complete steps similar to those in Step 2 to create the caption *Figure 3 Monitor* for the image in the *MONITOR* section.

5. Complete steps similar to those in Step 2 to create the caption *Figure 4 Software Life Cycle* for the SmartArt graphic in the *Developing Software* section.

6. Insert a table of figures at the beginning of the document by completing the following steps:

   a. Press Ctrl + Home to move the insertion point to the beginning of the document.

   b. Press Ctrl + Enter to insert a page break.

   c. Press Ctrl + Home to move the insertion point back to the beginning of the document and then type **TABLE OF FIGURES** bolded and centered.

   d. Press the Enter key, turn off bold formatting, and then change the paragraph alignment back to left alignment.

   e. If necessary, click the REFERENCES tab.

   f. Click the Insert Table of Figures button in the Captions group.

   g. At the Table of Figures dialog box, click the down-pointing arrow at the right side of the *Formats* option box and then click *Formal* at the drop-down list.

   h. Click OK.

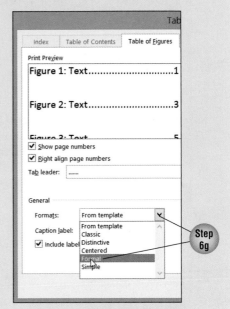

7. Save **WL2-C6-P3-TechRpt.docx**.

Updating or Deleting a Table of Figures

If you make changes to a document after inserting a table of figures, you can update the table of figures. To do this, click anywhere within the table of figures and then click the Update Table button in the Captions group on the REFERENCES tab or press the F9 key. At the Update Table of Figures dialog box, click *Update page numbers only* if the changes were made only to the page numbers or click *Update entire table* if changes were made to caption text. Click OK or press Enter to close the dialog box. To delete a table of figures, select the entire table using the mouse or keyboard and then press the Delete key.

▼ **Quick Steps**

Update a Table of Figures
1. Click in table of figures.
2. Click REFERENCES tab.
3. Click Update Table button or press F9.
4. Click OK.

Delete a Table of Figures
1. Select entire table of figures.
2. Press Delete key.

1. With **WL2-C6-P3-TechRpt.docx** open, insert an image of a laser printer by completing the following steps:
   a. Move the insertion point to the beginning of the second paragraph of text in the *PRINTERS* section.
   b. Click the INSERT tab and then click the Pictures button in the Illustrations group.
   c. At the Insert Picture dialog box, navigate to the WL2C6 folder on your storage medium and then double-click the file named **LaserPrinter.png**.
   d. Change the height of the clip art image to 1.5 inches.
   e. Change the text wrapping to *Square*.
2. Add the caption *Figure 4 Laser Printer* to the printer image and then center the caption.
3. Click on any character in the table of figures.
4. Press the F9 function key on your keyboard.
5. At the Update Table of Figures dialog box, click the *Update entire table* option and then click OK.
6. Save, print, and then close **WL2-C6-P3-TechRpt.docx**.
7. Close Word.

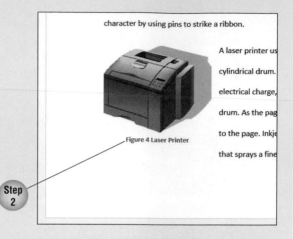

Step 2

Figure 4 Laser Printer

Customizing Captions

The Caption dialog box contains a number of options for customizing captions. Click the down-pointing arrow at the right of the *Label* option to specify the caption label. The default is *Figure*, which you can change to *Equation* or *Table*. A caption, by default, is positioned below the selected item. With the *Position* option, you can change the position of the caption so it is above the selected item. A caption contains a label, such as *Figure*, *Table*, or *Equation*. If you want only a caption number and not a caption label, insert a check mark in the *Exclude label from caption* check box.

Click the New Label button and the Label dialog box displays. At this dialog box, type a custom label for the caption. Word automatically inserts an arabic number (*1, 2, 3,* and so on) after each caption label. If you want to change the caption numbering style, click the Numbering button. At the Caption Numbering dialog box that displays, click the down-pointing arrow at the right side of the *Format* option box and then click the desired numbering style at the drop-down list. For example, you can change caption numbering to uppercase or lowercase letters or roman numerals.

If you insert items such as tables in a document on a regular basis, you can specify that you want a caption inserted automatically with each item. To do this, click the AutoCaption button. At the AutoCaption dialog box, insert a check mark before the item, such as *Microsoft Word Table* in the *Add caption when inserting* list box, and then click OK. Each time you insert a table in a document, Word inserts a caption above the table.

1. Open Word, open **TTSAdventures.docx**, and then save the document and name it **WL2-C6-P3-TTSAdventures**.
2. Insert a custom caption for the first table by completing the following steps:
   a. Click in any cell in the first table.
   b. Click the REFERENCES tab.
   c. Click the Insert Caption button.
   d. At the Caption dialog box, press the spacebar once and then type **Antarctic Zenith Adventures** in the *Caption* text box.

   Step 2e

   Step 2f

   e. Remove the label (*Table*) from the caption by clicking the *Exclude label from caption* check box to insert a check mark.
   f. Click the Numbering button.
   g. At the Caption Numbering dialog box, click the down-pointing arrow at the right side of the *Format* option box and then click the *A, B, C, …* option at the drop-down list.

   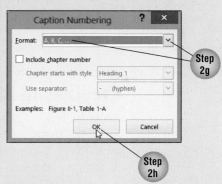

   Step 2g

   h. Click OK to close the Caption Numbering dialog box.
   i. At the Caption dialog box, click the down-pointing arrow at the right side of the *Position* option and then click *Below selected item* at the drop-down list.

   Step 2h

   j. Click OK to close the Caption dialog box.
3. After looking at the caption, you decide to add a custom label and change the numbering. Do this by completing the following steps:
   a. Select the *A Antarctic Zenith Adventures* caption.
   b. Click the Insert Caption button in the Captions group on the REFERENCES tab.
   c. At the Caption dialog box, click the *Exclude label from caption* check box to remove the check mark.
   d. Click the New Label button.
   e. At the New Label dialog box, type **Adventure** and then click OK.
   f. Click OK to close the Caption dialog box.
4. Format the caption by completing the following steps:
   a. Select the *Adventure 1 Antarctic Zenith Adventures* caption.
   b. Click the HOME tab.
   c. Click the Font Color button arrow.
   d. Click the *Dark Blue* color (ninth color in the *Standard Colors* section).
   e. Click the Bold button.
5. Insert a custom caption for the second table by completing the following steps:
   a. Click in any cell in the second table.
   b. Click the REFERENCES tab and then click the Insert Caption button.
   c. At the Caption dialog box, press the spacebar and then type **Tall-Ship Adventures**.
   d. Make sure *Below selected item* displays in the *Position* option box and then click OK to close the Caption dialog box.
6. Select the *Adventure 2 Tall-Ship Adventures* caption, apply the Dark Blue font color, and apply bold formatting.

7. Insert a table of figures by completing the following steps:
   a. Press Ctrl + Home and then press Ctrl + Enter to insert a page break.
   b. Press Ctrl + Home to move the insertion point above the page break.
   c. Turn on bold formatting, type **TABLES**, turn off bold formatting, and then press the Enter key.
   d. Click the REFERENCES tab and then click the Insert Table of Figures button in the Captions group.
   e. At the Table of Figures dialog box, click OK.
8. Save, print, and then close **WL2-C6-P3-TSSAdventures.docx**.

Project 4 · Create an Index for a Desktop Publishing Report · 2 Parts

You will open a report containing information on desktop publishing, mark specific text for an index, and then insert the index in the document. You will also make changes to the document and then update the index.

Creating an Index ■■■■■■■■■■■■■■■■■■■■■■■■■■■■■■■

An *index* is a list of topics contained in a publication that includes the page numbers on which those topics are discussed. Word lets you automate the process of creating an index in a manner similar to that used for creating a table of contents. When creating an index, you mark a word or words that you want included in the index.

Creating an index takes some thought and consideration. The author of the book, manuscript, or report must determine the main entries that will be included, as well as the subentries that will be added under main entries. An index may include such items as the main idea of a document, the main subject of a chapter or section, variations of a heading or subheading, and abbreviations. Figure 6.9 shows an example of an index.

Figure 6.9 Sample Index

INDEX

A
Alignment, 12, 16
ASCII, 22, 24, 35
    data processing, 41
    word processing, 39

B
Backmatter, 120
    page numbering, 123
Balance, 67-69
Banners, 145

C
Callouts, 78
Captions, 156
Color, 192-195
    ink for offset printing, 193
    process color, 195

D
Databases, 124-129
    fields, 124
    records, 124
Directional flow, 70-71

Marking Text for an Index

A selected word or words can be marked for inclusion in an index. Before marking words for an index, determine what main entries and subentries are to be included. Selected text is marked as an index entry at the Mark Index Entry dialog box.

To mark text for an index, select the word or words, click the REFERENCES tab, and then click the Mark Entry button in the Index group. You can also press Alt + Shift + X. At the Mark Index Entry dialog box, shown in Figure 6.10, the selected word or words appears in the *Main entry* text box. Make any necessary changes to the dialog box and then click the Mark button. (When you click the Mark button, Word automatically turns on the display of nonprinting symbols and displays the index field code.) Click the Close button to close the Mark Index Entry dialog box.

At the Mark Index Entry dialog box, the selected word or words displays in the *Main entry* text box. If the text is a main entry, leave it as displayed. If, however, the selected text is a subentry, type the main entry in the *Main entry* text box, click in the *Subentry* text box, and then type the selected text. For example, suppose a publication includes the terms *Page layout* and *Portrait*. The words *Page layout* are to be marked as a main entry for the index and *Portrait* is to be marked as a subentry below *Page layout*. To mark these words for an index, you would complete the following steps:

1. Select *Page layout*.
2. Click the REFERENCES tab and then click the Mark Entry button or press Alt + Shift + X.
3. At the Mark Index Entry dialog box, click the Mark button. (This turns on the display of nonprinting symbols.)
4. With the Mark Index Entry dialog box still displayed on the screen, click in the document to make the document active and then select *Portrait*.
5. Click the Mark Index Entry dialog box Title bar to make it active.
6. Select *Portrait* in the *Main entry* text box and then type **Page layout**.
7. Click in the *Subentry* text box and then type **Portrait**.
8. Click the Mark button.
9. Click the Close button.

▼ Quick Steps

Mark Text for an Index
1. Select text.
2. Click REFERENCES tab.
3. Click Mark Entry button.
4. Click Mark button.

Mark Entry

You can also mark text for an index using the keyboard shortcut Alt + Shift + X.

Figure 6.10 Mark Index Entry Dialog Box

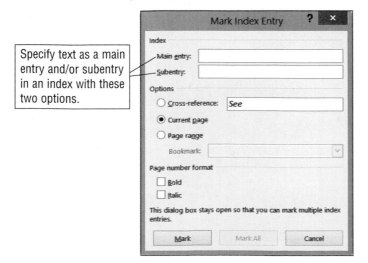

Specify text as a main entry and/or subentry in an index with these two options.

The main entry and subentry do not have to be the same as the selected text. You can select text for an index, type the text you want to display in the *Main entry* or *Subentry* text box, and then click the Mark button. At the Mark Index Entry dialog box, you can apply bold and/or italic formatting to the page numbers that will appear in the index. To apply formatting, click *Bold* and/or *Italic* to insert a check mark in the check box.

The *Options* section of the Mark Index Entry dialog box contains several options, with *Current page* the default. At this setting, the current page number will be listed in the index for the main entry and/or subentry. If you click *Cross-reference*, type the text you want to use as a cross-reference for the index entry in the *Cross-reference* text box. For example, you can mark the word *Serif* and cross reference it to *Typefaces*.

Click the Mark All button at the Mark Index Entry dialog box to mark all occurrences of the text in the document as index entries. Word marks only those entries whose uppercase and lowercase letters match the index entries.

Project 4a   Marking Words for an Index   Part 1 of 2

1. Open **DTP.docx** and then save the document and name it **WL2-C6-P4-DTP**.
2. Insert a page number at the bottom center of each page.
3. In the first paragraph, mark the word *software* for the index as a main entry and mark *word processing* in as a subentry below *software* by completing the following steps:
   a. Select *software* (located in the second sentence of the first paragraph).
   b. Click the REFERENCES tab and then click the Mark Entry button in the Index group.
   c. At the Mark Index Entry dialog box, click the Mark All button. (This turns on the display of nonprinting symbols.)
   d. With the Mark Index Entry dialog box still displayed, click in the document to make the document active and then select *word processing* (located in the last sentence of the first paragraph). (You may want to drag the dialog box down the screen so more of the document text is visible.)
   e. Click the Title bar of the Mark Index Entry dialog box to make the dialog box active.
   f. Select *word processing* in the *Main entry* text box and then type **software**.
   g. Click in the *Subentry* text box and then type **word processing**.
   h. Click the Mark All button.

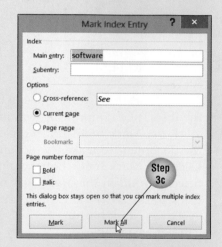

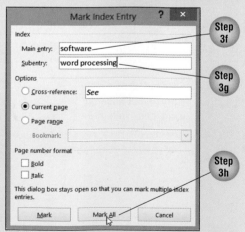

i. With the Mark Index Entry dialog box still displayed, complete steps similar to those in Steps 3d through 3h to select the first occurrence of each of the following words and then mark the word as a main entry or subentry for the index (click the Mark All button at the Mark Index Entry dialog box):

1) In the first paragraph in the *Defining Desktop Publishing* section:
   spreadsheets = subentry (main entry = *software*)
   database = subentry (main entry = *software*)

2) In the second paragraph in the *Defining Desktop Publishing* section:
   publishing = main entry
   desktop = subentry (main entry = *publishing*)
   printer = main entry
   laser = subentry (main entry = *printer*)

3) In the third paragraph in the *Defining Desktop Publishing* section:
   design = main entry

4) In the fourth paragraph in the *Defining Desktop Publishing* section:
   traditional = subentry (main entry = *publishing*)

5) In the only paragraph in the *Initiating the Process* section:
   publication = main entry
   planning = subentry (main entry = *publication*)
   creating = subentry (main entry = *publication*)
   intended audience = subentry (main entry = *publication*)
   content = subentry (main entry = *publication*)

6) In the third paragraph in the *Planning the Publication* section:
   message = main entry

j. Click Close to close the Mark Index Entry dialog box.
4. Turn off the display of nonprinting characters.
5. Save **WL2-C6-P4-DTP.docx**.

Inserting an Index

After you have marked all of the words that you want to include in an index as main entries or subentries, your next step is to insert the index. The index should appear at the end of a document, generally beginning on a separate page.

To insert the index, position the insertion point at the end of the document and then insert a page break. With the insertion point positioned below the page break, type *INDEX*, center it, apply bold formatting, and then press the Enter key. With the insertion point positioned at the left margin, click the REFERENCES tab and then click the Insert Index button in the Index group. At the Index dialog box, shown in Figure 6.11 on the next page, select the desired formatting and then click OK. Word inserts the index at the location of the insertion point with the formatting selected at the Index dialog box. Word also inserts section breaks above and below the index text.

At the Index dialog box, specify how the index entries will appear. The *Print Preview* section shows how the index will display in the document. The *Columns* measurement box has a default setting of *2*. At this setting, the index will display in two columns. You can increase or decrease this number.

By default, page numbers are right-aligned in the index. If you do not want the numbers right-aligned, click the *Right align page numbers* check box to remove the check mark. The *Tab leader* option is dimmed for all formats except *Formal*. If you click

▼ Quick Steps

Insert an Index
1. Click REFERENCES tab.
2. Click Insert Index button.
3. Select desired format.
4. Click OK.

Insert Index

Figure 6.11 Index Dialog Box

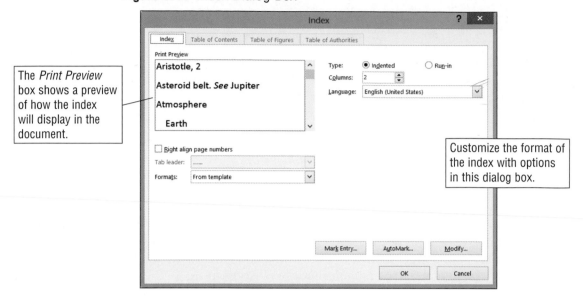

The *Print Preview* box shows a preview of how the index will display in the document.

Customize the format of the index with options in this dialog box.

Formal in the *Formats* option box, the *Tab leader* option displays in black. The default tab leader character is a period. To change to a different character, click the down-pointing arrow at the right of the option box and then click the desired character.

In the *Type* section, the *Indented* option is selected by default. At this setting, subentries will appear indented below main entries. If you click *Run-in*, subentries will display on the same lines as main entries.

Click the down-pointing arrow at the right side of the *Formats* option box and a list of formatting choices displays. At this list, click the desired formatting and the *Print Preview* box displays how the index will appear in the document.

Project 4b | **Inserting an Index** | Part 2 of 2

1. With **WL2-C6-P4-DTP.docx** open, insert the index into the document by completing the following steps:
   a. Press Ctrl + End to position the insertion point at the end of the document.
   b. Insert a page break.
   c. With the insertion point positioned below the page break, type **INDEX** and then press Enter.
   d. Click the REFERENCES tab.
   e. Click the Insert Index button in the Index group.
   f. At the Index dialog box, click the down-pointing arrow at the right side of the *Formats* option box and then click *Modern* at the drop-down list.
   g. Click OK to close the dialog box.
   h. Click in the title *INDEX*, apply the Heading 1 style, and then press Ctrl + E to center the title.
2. Save **WL2-C6-P4-DTP.docx** and then print the index page (the last page) of the document.
3. Close **WL2-C6-P4-DTP.docx**.

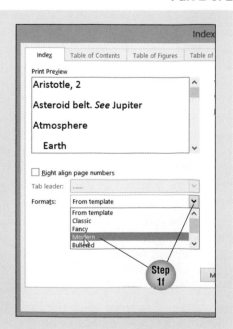

You will create and then save a concordance file. You will then open a report containing information on designing newsletters and use the concordance file to create an index.

Creating a Concordance File

Another method for creating an index is to create a concordance file and use the information in the file to create the index. Creating a concordance file saves you from having to mark each reference in a document.

A *concordance file* is a regular Word document containing a two-column table with no text outside the table. In the first column of the table, you enter the words you want to include in the index. In the second column, you enter the main entry and subentry that should appear in the index. To create a subentry, type the main entry followed by a colon, a space, and then the subentry. Figure 6.12 shows an example of a completed concordance file.

In the concordance file shown in Figure 6.12, the text as it appears in the document is inserted in the first column (such as *World War I*, *Technology*, and *technology*). The second column contains the text as it should appear in the index,

▼ Quick Steps

Create a
Concordance File
1. Click INSERT tab.
2. Click Table button and drag to create table.
3. In first column, type words you want in index.
4. In second column, type main entry and subentry.
5. Save document.

Figure 6.12 Concordance File

World War I	World War I
Technology	Technology
technology	Technology
Teletypewriters	Technology: teletypewriters
motion pictures	Technology: motion pictures
Television	Technology: television
Radio Corporation of America	Radio Corporation of America
coaxial cable	Coaxial cable
Telephone	Technology: telephone
Communications Act of 1934	Communications Act of 1934
World War II	World War II
radar system	Technology: radar system
Computer	Computer
Atanasoff Berry Computer	Computer: Atanasoff Berry Computer
Korean War	Korean War
Columbia Broadcasting System	Columbia Broadcasting System
Cold War	Cold War
Vietnam	Vietnam
artificial satellite	Technology: artificial satellite
Communications Satellite Act of 1962	Communications Satellite Act of 1962

specifying whether each item is a main entry or subentry. For example, the text *motion pictures* in the concordance file will appear in the index as a subentry under the main entry *Technology*.

After you have created a concordance file, you can use it to quickly mark text for an index in a document. To do this, open the document containing the text you want marked for the index, display the Index dialog box with the Index tab selected, and then click the AutoMark button. At the Open Index AutoMark File dialog box, double-click the concordance file name in the list box. Word turns on the display of nonprinting symbols, searches the document for text that matches the text in the concordance file, and then marks it accordingly. After marking text for the index, insert the index in the document as described earlier.

As you create the concordance file in Project 5a, Word's AutoCorrect feature will automatically capitalize the first letter of the first word entered in each cell. In Figure 6.12, you can see that several of the first words in the first column do not begin with capital letters. Before beginning the project, consider turning off this AutoCorrect capitalization feature. To do this, click the FILE tab and then click *Options*. At the Word Options dialog box, click *Proofing* in the left panel of the dialog box and then click the AutoCorrect Options button. At the AutoCorrect dialog box with the AutoCorrect tab selected, click the *Capitalize first letter of table cells* check box to remove the check mark. Click OK to close the dialog box and then click OK to close the Word Options dialog box.

Project 5a **Creating a Concordance File** Part 1 of 3

1. At a blank document, create the text shown in Figure 6.13 as a concordance file by completing the following steps:
   a. Click the INSERT tab.
   b. Click the Table button in the Tables group.
   c. Drag down and to the right until *2×1 Table* displays at the top of the grid and then click the left mouse button.
   d. Type the text in the cells as shown in Figure 6.13 on the next page. Press the Tab key to move to the next cell. (If you did not remove the check mark before the *Capitalize first letter of table cells* option at the AutoCorrect dialog box, the *n* in the first word in the first cell, *newsletters*, is automatically capitalized. Hover the mouse over the *N*, click the blue rectangle that displays below the *N*, and then click *Stop Auto-capitalizing First Letter of Table Cells*.)

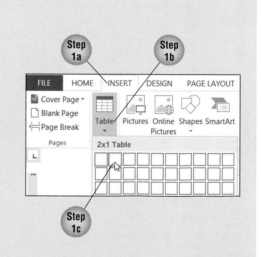

2. Save the document and name it **WL2-C6-P5-CFile**.
3. Print and then close **WL2-C6-P5-CFile.docx**.

Figure 6.13 Project 5a

newsletters	Newsletters
Newsletters	Newsletters
Software	Software
Desktop publishing	Software: desktop publishing
word processing	Software: word processing
Printers	Printers
Laser	Printers: laser
Design	Design
Communication	Communication
Consistency	Design: consistency
Elements	Elements
Nameplate	Elements: nameplate
Logo	Elements: logo
Subtitle	Elements: subtitle
Folio	Elements: folio
Headlines	Elements: headlines
Subheads	Elements: subheads
Byline	Elements: byline
Body Copy	Elements: body copy
Graphics Images	Elements: graphics images
Audience	Newsletters: audience
Purpose	Newsletters: purpose
focal point	Newsletters: focal point

If you removed the check mark before the *Capitalize first letter of table cells* option at the AutoCorrect dialog box, you may need to turn this feature back on. To do this, click the FILE tab and then click *Options*. At the Word Options dialog box, click *Proofing* in the left panel of the dialog box and then click the AutoCorrect Options button. At the AutoCorrect dialog box with the AutoCorrect tab selected, click the *Capitalize first letter of table cells* check box to insert a check mark. Click OK to close the dialog box and then click OK to close the Word Options dialog box.

1. Open **PlanNwsltr.docx** and then save the document and name it **WL2-C6-P5-PlanNwsltr**.
2. Mark text for the index using the concordance file by completing the following steps:
   a. Click the REFERENCES tab.
   b. Click the Insert Index button in the Index group.

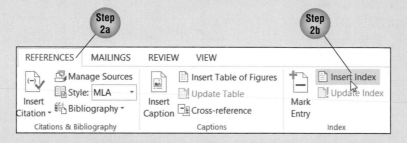

   c. At the Index dialog box, click the AutoMark button.
   d. At the Open Index AutoMark File dialog box, double-click **WL2-C6-P5-CFile.docx** in the Content pane. (This turns on the display of nonprinting symbols.)
3. Insert the index in the document by completing the following steps:
   a. Position the insertion point at the end of the document.
   b. Insert a page break.
   c. Type **INDEX**.
   d. Press the Enter key.
   e. Click the Insert Index button in the Index group.
   f. At the Index dialog box, click the down-pointing arrow at the right side of the *Formats* option box and then click *Formal* at the drop-down list.
   g. Click OK to close the dialog box.
4. Apply the Heading 1 style to the *INDEX* title and then center the title.
5. Turn off the display of nonprinting characters.
6. Save **WL2-C6-P5-PlanNwsltr.docx** and then print only the Index page.

Updating and Deleting an Index

▼ Quick Steps

Update an Index
1. Click in index.
2. Click Update Index button or press F9.

Delete an Index
1. Select entire index.
2. Press Delete key.

Update Index

If you make changes to a document after inserting an index, update the index. To do this, click anywhere within the current index and then click the Update Index button in the Index group or press the F9 key. To delete an index, select the entire index using the mouse or the keyboard and then press the Delete key.

1. With **WL2-C6-P5-PlanNwsltr.docx** open, insert a page break at the beginning of the title *PLANNING A NEWSLETTER*.

2. Update the index by clicking anywhere in the index, clicking the REFERENCES tab, and then clicking the Update Index button in the Index group.

3. Save **WL2-C6-P5-PlanNwsltr .docx** and then print only the index page.

4. Close **WL2-C6-P5-PlanNwsltr .docx**.

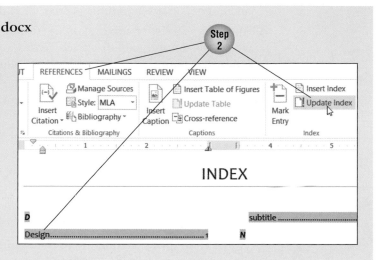

Chapter Summary

- Word provides options for automating the creation of a table of contents, table of figures, and index.

- Identify text to be included in a table of contents by applying a heading style, assigning a level, or marking text as a field entry.

- Mark text as a field entry at the Mark Table of Contents dialog box. Display this dialog box by pressing Alt + Shift + O.

- Creating a table of contents involves two steps: applying the appropriate styles to mark text that will be included and inserting the table of contents in the document.

- To insert the table of contents, position the insertion point where you want the table to appear, click the REFERENCES tab, click the Table of Contents button, and then click the desired option at the drop-down list.

- Generally the pages containing the table of contents are numbered with lowercase roman numerals.

- If you want the table of contents to print on a page separate from the document text, insert a section break that begins a new page between the table of contents and title of the document.

- If you make changes to a document after inserting a table of contents, update the table of contents by clicking anywhere in the table and then clicking the Update Table button on the REFERENCES tab or pressing the F9 key. Update a table of figures or index in a similar manner.

- Remove a table of contents by clicking the Table of Contents button on the REFERENCES tab and then clicking *Remove Table of Contents* at the drop-down list.

- Create a table of figures by marking specific text or images with captions and then using the caption names to create the table of figures. Mark captions at the Caption dialog box. Display this dialog box by clicking the Insert Caption button on the REFERENCES tab.

- Insert a table of figures in a document in a manner similar to that for inserting a table of contents. A table of figures generally displays at the beginning of the document, on a separate page after the table of contents.
- An index is a list of topics contained in a publication and the page numbers on which those topics are discussed. Word automates the process of creating an index in a manner similar to that for creating a table of contents.
- Mark text for an index at the Mark Index Entry dialog box. Display this dialog box by clicking the Mark Entry button on the REFERENCES tab or pressing Alt + Shift + X.
- After all of the necessary text has been marked as main entries and subentires for the index, insert the index, placing it on a separate page at the end of the document.
- Insert an index in a document by clicking the Insert Index button on the REFERENCES tab, making desired changes at the Index dialog box, and then clicking OK.
- Words that appear frequently in a document can be saved as a concordance file and used in creating an index. A concordance file is a regular document containing a two-column table. Using this table to create the index eliminates the need to mark each reference in a document.

Commands Review

FEATURE	RIBBON TAB, GROUP	BUTTON, OPTION	KEYBOARD SHORTCUT
Caption dialog box	REFERENCES, Captions		
Index dialog box	REFERENCES, Index		
Mark Index Entry dialog box	REFERENCES, Index		Alt + Shift + X
Mark Table of Contents Entry dialog box			Alt + Shift + O
Open Index AutoMark File dialog box	REFERENCES, Index	, AutoMark button	
Page Number Format dialog box	INSERT, Header & Footer	, *Format Page Numbers*	
Table of Contents dialog box	REFERENCES, Table of Contents	, *Custom Table of Contents*	
Table of Contents Options dialog box	REFERENCES, Table of Contents	, *Custom Table of Contents*, Options button	
Table of Figures dialog box	REFERENCES, Captions		
update table of contents	REFERENCES, Table of Contents		F9

Concepts Check   Test Your Knowledge

Completion: In the space provided at the right, indicate the correct term, symbol, or command.

1. A table of contents generally appears in this location in a document.   _____

2. In a built-in table of contents, Word uses text with this heading style applied as the first level.   _____

3. The pages of a table of contents are generally numbered with this type of number.   _____

4. Use this keyboard shortcut to update a table of contents.   _____

5. Use this keyboard shortcut to display the Mark Table of Contents Entry dialog box.   _____

6. If you mark table of contents entries as fields, you will need to activate this option at the Table of Contents Options dialog box.   _____

7. Create a table of figures by marking figures or images with these.   _____

8. Use this keyboard shortcut to display the Mark Index Entry dialog box.   _____

9. An index generally appears at this location in the document.   _____

10. Create this type of file and then use it to save time when marking text for an index.   _____

Skills Check   Assess Your Performance

Assessment

1   CREATE AND UPDATE A TABLE OF CONTENTS FOR A PHOTOGRAPHY REPORT    Grade It

1. Open **PhotoRpt.docx** and then save the document and name it **WL2-C6-A1-PhotoRpt**.
2. Move the insertion point to the beginning of the heading *Photography* and then insert a section break that begins a new page.
3. With the insertion point positioned below the section break, insert page numbers at the bottom center of pages and change the beginning number to 1.
4. Press Ctrl + Home to move the insertion point to the beginning of the document (on the blank page) and then create a table of contents with the *Automatic Table 1* option at the Table of Contents button drop-down list.

5. Display the Table of Contents dialog box, change the *Formats* option box to *Distinctive* and make sure a *3* displays in the *Show levels* measurement box.
6. Change the page number format on the table of contents page to lowercase roman numerals.
7. Save the document and then print only the table of contents page.
8. Insert a page break at the beginning of the heading *Camera Basics*.
9. Update the table of contents.
10. Save the document and then print only the table of contents page.
11. Close **WL2-C6-A1-PhotoRpt.docx**.

Assessment

2 INSERT CAPTIONS AND A TABLE OF FIGURES IN A REPORT

1. Open **InputDevices.docx** and then save the document and name it **WL2-C6-A2-InputDevices**.
2. Insert a caption for each of the three images in the document that uses *Figure* as the label, numbers (1, 2, 3, and so on) as the figure numbers, and displays below the image and is centered. Use *Keyboard* for the first figure caption, *Mouse* for the second, and *Laptop* for the third figure caption.
3. Move the insertion point to the beginning of the title COMPUTER INPUT DEVICES and then insert a section break that begins a new page.
4. Press Ctrl + Home, type **Table of Figures**, press the Enter key, and then insert a table of figures with the Formal format.
5. Apply the Heading 1 style to the title *Table of Figures*.
6. Move the insertion point to the title COMPUTER INPUT DEVICES and then insert a page number at the bottom center of each page and change the starting number to 1.
7. Move the insertion point to the title TABLE OF FIGURES and then change the page numbering style to lowercase roman numerals.
8. Insert a page break at the beginning of the MOUSE heading.
9. Update the table of figures.
10. Save, print, and then close **WL2-C6-A2-InputDevices.docx**.

Assessment

3 CREATE AND UPDATE AN INDEX FOR A NEWSLETTER

1. At a blank document, create the text shown in Figure 6.14 on the next page as a concordance file and then save the document and name it **WL2-C6-A3-CFile**.
2. Print and then close **WL2-C6-A3-CFile.docx**.
3. Open **DesignNwsltr.docx** and then save the document and name it **WL2-C6-A3-DesignNwsltr**.
4. Make the following changes to the document:
   a. Mark text for an index using the concordance file **WL2-C6-A3-CFile.docx**.
   b. Move the insertion point to the end of the document, insert a page break, type **INDEX**, press Enter, and then insert the index with the Classic format.
   c. Apply the Heading 1 style to the index title.

5. Add a page number at the bottom center of each page.
6. Change the line spacing to 2.0 for the entire document.
7. Insert a page break at the beginning of the title *CREATING NEWSLETTER LAYOUT*.
8. Update the index. (The index returns to the default line spacing.)
9. Save the document and then print the index page only.
10. Close **WL2-C6-A3-DesignNwsltr.docx**.

Figure 6.14 Assessment 3

NEWSLETTER	Newsletter
newsletter	Newsletter
consistency	Newsletter: consistency
element	Elements
margins	Elements: margins
column layout	Elements: column layout
nameplate	Elements: nameplate
location	Elements: location
logos	Elements: logos
color	Elements: color
ruled lines	Elements: ruled lines
Focus	Elements: focus
balance	Elements: balance
graphics	Graphics
images	Images
photos	Photos
Headlines	Newsletter: headlines
subheads	Newsletter: subheads
White space	White space
directional flow	Newsletter: directional flow
paper	Paper
Size	Paper: size
type	Paper: type
weight	Paper: weight
stock	Paper: stock
margin size	Newsletter: margin size

4 CUSTOMIZE AN INDEX

1. You can customize an index with options at the Index dialog box. At a blank document, display this dialog box by clicking the REFERENCES tab and then clicking the Insert Index button in the Index group. Look at the options offered at the dialog box and determine how to change leaders and number of columns. Close the blank document.
2. Open **WL2-C6-A3-DesignNwsltr.docx** and then save the document and name it **WL2-C6-A4-DesignNwsltr**.
3. Make the following changes to the index:
   a. Display the Index dialog box for the index.
   b. Change to a format that contains leaders.
   c. Change the leaders to hyphens (rather than periods).
   d. Specify three columns.
   e. Close the Index dialog box. When asked if you want to replace the selected index, click OK.
4. Save **WL2-C6-A4-DesignNwsltr.docx**.
5. Print only the index and then close the document.

Visual Benchmark   Demonstrate Your Proficiency

CREATE A TABLE OF CONTENTS AND TABLE OF FIGURES

1. Open **Networks.docx** and then save the document and name it **WL2-C6-VB-Networks**.
2. Format the document so it appears as shown in Figure 6.15 on pages 261–262 with the following specifications:
   a. Insert the captions for the figures as shown (see the third page of Figure 6.15).
   b. Insert the table of contents as shown (see the first page of Figure 6.15) using the From template format with hyphen leaders.
   c. Insert the table of figures as shown (see the second page of Figure 6.15) using the *From template* format with dot leaders.
   d. Insert page numbers at the right margins as shown (see the second and fourth pages of Figure 6.15).
3. Save, print, and then close **WL2-C6-VB-Networks.docx**.

Figure 6.15 Visual Benchmark

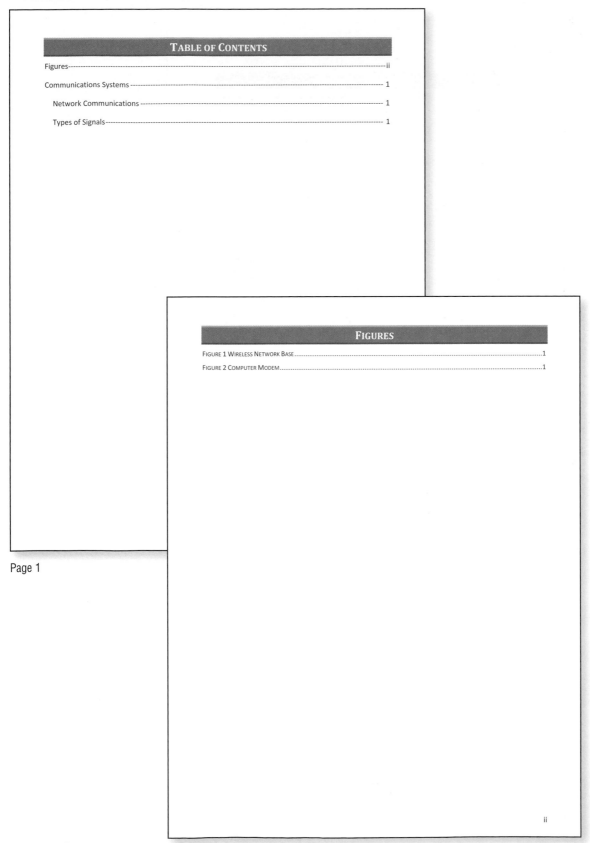

Page 1

Page 2

continues

Figure 6.15 Visual Benchmark—*Continued*

A computer network is one kind of communications system. This system includes sending and receiving hardware, transmission and relay systems, common sets of standards so all the equipment can "talk" to each other, and communications software.

NETWORK COMMUNICATIONS

You use such a networked communications system whenever you send/receive IM or email messages, pay a bill online, shop at an Internet store, send a document to a shared printer at work or at home, or download a file.

The world of computer network communications systems is made up of:

- Transmission media upon which the data travels to/from its destination.
- A set of standards and network protocols (rules for how data is handled as it travels along a communications channel). Devices use these to send and receive data to and from each other.
- Hardware and software to connect to a communications pathway from the sending and receiving ends.

Figure 1 Wireless Network Base

The first step in understanding a communications system is to learn the basics about transmission signals and transmission

TYPES OF SIGNALS

Two types of signals are used to tra digital. An analog signal is formed b voice is transmitted as an analog sig signal uses a discrete signal that is e 1, and low represents the digital bit

Telephone lines carry your voice usi

rather, the
signals. If
phone line

Figure 2 Computer Modem   (modulate

computer on the receiving end. The piece of hardware that sends and receives data from a transmission source such as your telephone line or cable television connection is a modem. The word modem comes from the combination of the words *mo*dulate and *dem*odulate.

Today, most new communications technologies simply use a digital signal, saving the trouble of converting transmissions. An example of this trend is the demise in 2009 of analog television transmissions as the industry switched to digital signals. Many people were sent scrambling to either buy a newer television set or buy a converter to convert digital transmissions back to analog to work with their older equipment. Newer computer networks, too, use a pure digital signal method of sending and receiving data over a network.

2

Case Study   Apply Your Skills

Part 1

You work in the Human Resources department at Brennan Distributors and are responsible for preparing an employee handbook. Open the **BDEmpHandbook.docx** document and then save the document and name it **WL2-C6-CS-BDEmpHandbook**. Apply the following specifications to the document:

- Insert page breaks before each centered title (except the first title, *Introduction*).
- Apply heading styles to the titles and headings.
- Change to a style set of your choosing.
- Apply a theme that makes the handbook easy to read.
- Insert a table of contents.
- Create a concordance file with a minimum of ten entries and then insert an index.
- Insert appropriate page numbering in the document.
- Insert a cover page.
- Add any other elements to improve the appearance of the document.

Save and then print **WL2-C6-CS-BDEmpHandbook.docx**.

Part 2

Open **NavigateWeb.docx** and then save the document and name it **WL2-C6-CS-NavigateWeb**. Apply the following specifications to the document:

- Move the insertion point to any cell in the first table in the document and then use the caption feature to create the caption *Table 1: Common Top-Level Domain Suffixes*.
- Move the insertion point to any cell in the second table and then create the caption *Table 2: Common Search Tools*.
- Move the insertion point to any cell in the third table and then create the caption *Table 3: Advanced Search Parameters*.
- Insert a table of contents.
- Insert a table of figures on the page following the table of contents.
- Insert appropriate page numbering in the document.
- Check the page breaks in the document. If a heading displays at the bottom of a page and the paragraph of text that follows displays at the top of the next page, format the heading so it stays with the paragraph of text that follows. ***Hint: Do this at the Paragraph dialog box with the Line and Page Breaks tab selected.***
- If necessary, update the entire table of contents and table of figures.

Save, print, and then close **WL2-C6-CS-NavigateWeb.docx**.

Part 3

Send an email to your instructor detailing the steps you followed to create table captions. Attach **WL2-C6-CS-NavigateWeb.docx** to the email.

WORD
MICROSOFT®

Working with Shared Documents

CHAPTER 7

PERFORMANCE OBJECTIVES

Upon successful completion of Chapter 7, you will be able to:

- Insert, edit, print, and delete comments
- Navigate between comments
- Distinguish comments from different users
- Track changes to a document
- Customize Track Changes
- Show markup
- Customize markup display
- Navigate to revisions
- Accept and reject revisions
- Compare documents
- Combine documents
- Show source documents
- Embed and link data between Excel and Word

Tutorials

7.1 Inserting and Editing Comments
7.2 Inserting Comments in the Reviewing Pane; Distinguishing Comments from Other Users
7.3 Tracking Changes in a Document
7.4 Displaying Changes for Review and Showing Markup
7.5 Customizing Track Changes Options
7.6 Comparing Documents
7.7 Combining Documents
7.8 Embedding and Linking Objects

In a company environment, you may need to share and distribute documents to other employees or associates. You may be part of a *workgroup*, which is a networked collection of computers that share files, printers, and other resources. As a member of a workgroup, you can collaborate with other members and distribute documents for review and/or revision. In this chapter, you will perform workgroup activities such as inserting comments, tracking changes from multiple users, comparing documents, and combining documents from multiple users. Model answers for this chapter's projects appear on the following pages.

If a Word 2013 document (in the .docx format) is located on a server running Microsoft SharePoint Server, multiple users can edit the document concurrently. Concurrent editing allows a group of users to work on a document at the same time or a single user to work on the same document from different computers. If a document is not located on a server running SharePoint Server, Word 2013 supports only single-user editing. Projects and assessments in this chapter assume that the files you are editing are not located on a server running SharePoint Server.

Note: Before beginning the projects, copy to your storage medium the WL2C7 subfolder from the WL2 folder on the CD that accompanies this textbook and then make WL2C7 the active folder.

WL2-C7-P1-OMSNewEmps.docx

Main document changes and comments		
Page 1: Commented	**Student Name**	1/6/2015 2:49:00 PM
Please include the total number of orientation hours.		
Page 1: Commented	**Taylor Stanton**	1/6/2015 3:15:00 PM
Check with Barb on the total number of orientation hours.		
Page 2: Commented	**Student Name**	1/6/2015 2:56:00 PM
Please include in this section the maximum probationary period, if any.		
Page 2: Commented	**Taylor Stanton**	1/6/2015 3:11:00 PM
Provide additional information on performance evaluation documentation.		

Header and footer changes
Text Box changes
Header and footer text box changes
Footnote changes
Endnote changes

Project 1 Insert Comments in a New Employees Document

WL2-C7-P1-OMSNewEmps.docx

BUILDING CONSTRUCTION AGREEMENT

THIS AGREEMENT made this _____ day of _____, 2015, by and between _____, hereinafter referred to as "builder," and _____, hereinafter referred to as "owner," the builder and the owner, for the considerations hereinafter named, agree as follows:

Construction Loan and Financing Arrangements: The owner either has or will obtain a construction loan to finance the work to be performed under this Agreement. If adequate financing has not been arranged within sixty (60) days of the date of this Agreement, or the owner cannot provide evidence to the builder of other financial ability to pay the full amount of the contract, then the builder at his option may treat this Agreement as null and void, and retain the down payment made on the execution of this Agreement.

Supervision of Work: Owner agrees that the direction and supervision of the working force including subcontractor, rests exclusively with the builder or his/her duly designated agent, and owner agrees not to issue any instructions to, or otherwise interfere with, same.

Start of Construction: The builder shall commence construction of the residence as soon as practical after signing of this Agreement and adequate financial arrangements satisfactory to the builder have been made.

Changes and Alterations: All changes in or departures from the plans and/or specifications shall be in writing. Where changes in or departures from plans and specifications requested in writing by owner will result in furnishing of additional labor and materials, the owner shall pay the builder for such extras at a price agreed upon in writing before commencement of said change. Where such change results in the omitting of any labor or materials, the builder shall allow the owner a credit therefore at a price agreed to in writing before commencement of said changes.

Possession of Residence: On final payment by owner and upon owner's request, builder will provide owner with affidavit stating that all labor, materials, and equipment used in the construction have been paid for or will be paid for in full by the builder unless otherwise noted. Builder shall not be required to give possession of the residence to the owner before final payment by owner. Final payment constitutes acceptance of the residence as being satisfactorily completed unless a separate escrow agreement is executed between the parties stipulating the unfinished items.

Exclusions: The owner is solely responsible for the purchase and installation of any septic tank or other individual subsurface sewage disposal system that may be required on the property.

Builder's Right to Terminate the Contract: Should the work be stopped by any public authority for a period of sixty (60) days or more, through no fault of the builder, or should the work be stopped through act or neglect of the owner for a period of seven days, or should the owner fail to pay the builder any payment within seven days after it is due, then the builder upon seven days written notice to the owner,

Page 1

---

may stop work or terminate the contract and recover from the owner payment for all work executed and any loss sustained and reasonable profit and damages.

The owner acknowledges that she/he has read and fully understands the provisions of this Agreement.

IN WITNESS WHEREOF, the builder and owner have hereunto set their hands this _____ day of _____, 20____.

_____   _____
BUILDER   OWNER

Page 2

Project 2 Track Changes in a Building Construction Agreement

WL2-C7-P2-Agreement.docx

Model Answers

COMMERCIAL LEASE AGREEMENT

This Commercial Lease Agreement ("Lease") is made by and between _____ ("Landlord") and _____ ("Tenant"). Landlord is the owner of land and improvements commonly known and numbered as _____ and legally described as follows (the "Building"): _____

_____. Landlord makes available for lease a portion of the Building designated as _____ (the "Leased Premises").

Landlord desires to lease the Leased Premises to Tenant, and Tenant desires to lease the Leased Premises from Landlord for the term at the rental, and upon the covenants, conditions, and provisions herein set forth.

THEREFORE, in consideration of the mutual promises herein contained, and other good and valuable consideration, it is agreed:

Term

A. Landlord hereby leases the Leased Premises to Tenant, and Tenant hereby leases the same from Landlord, for an "Initial Term" beginning _____ and ending _____. Landlord shall use his/her best efforts to give Tenant possession as nearly as possible at the beginning of the Lease term. If Landlord is unable to timely provide the Leased Premises, rent shall abate for the period of delay. Tenant shall make no other claim against Landlord for any such delay.

B. Tenant may renew the Lease for one extended term of _____. Tenant shall exercise such renewal option by giving written notice to Landlord not less than ninety (90) days prior to the expiration of the Initial Term. The renewal term shall be at the rental set forth below and otherwise upon the same covenants, conditions, and provisions as provided in this Lease.

Rental

A. Tenant shall pay to Landlord during the Initial Term rental of _____ per year, payable in installments of _____ per month. Each installment payment shall be due in advance on the first day of each calendar month during the lease term to Landlord at _____ or at such other place designated by written notice from Landlord or Tenant. The rental payment amount for any partial calendar months included in the lease term shall be prorated on a daily basis. Tenant shall also pay to Landlord a "Security Deposit" in the amount of _____.

B. The rental for any renewal lease term, if created as permitted under this Lease, shall be _____ per year payable in installments of _____ per month.

Page 1

Use

Notwithstanding the forgoing, Tenant shall not use the Leased Premises for the purposes of storing, manufacturing, or selling any explosives, flammables, or other inherently dangerous substance, chemical, item, or device.

Repairs

During the Lease term, Tenant shall make, at Tenant's expense, all necessary repairs to the Leased Premises. Repairs shall include such items as routine repairs of floors, walls, ceilings, and other parts of the Leased Premises damaged or worn through normal occupancy, except for major mechanical systems or the roof, subject to the obligations of the parties otherwise set forth in this Lease.

Sublease and Assignment

Tenant shall have the right, without Landlord's consent, to assign this Lease to a corporation with which Tenant may merge or consolidate, to any subsidiary of Tenant, to any corporation under common control with Tenant, or to a purchaser of substantially all of Tenant's assets. Except as set forth above, Tenant shall not sublease all or any part of the Leased Premises, or assign this Lease in whole or in part without Landlord's consent, such consent not to be unreasonably withheld or delayed.

Property Taxes

Landlord shall pay all general real estate taxes and installments of special assessments coming due during the Lease term on the Leased Premises, and all personal property taxes with respect to Landlord's personal property, if any, on the Leased Premises. Tenant shall be responsible for paying all personal property taxes with respect to Tenant's personal property at the Leased Premises.

_____

Landlord

_____

Tenant

Page 2

Project 3 Compare Lease Agreement Documents

WL2-C7-P3-ComAgrmnt.docx

LEASE AGREEMENT

THIS LEASE AGREEMENT (hereinafter referred to as the "Agreement") is made and entered into this ____ day of _____, 2015, by and between Lessor and Lessee.

Term

Lessor leases to Lessee and Lessee leases from Lessor the described Premises together with any and all appurtenances thereto, for a term of _____ year(s), such term beginning on _____, and ending at midnight on _____.

Damage Deposit

Upon the signing of this Agreement, Lessee shall deposit with Lessor the sum of _____ DOLLARS ($_____) receipt of which is hereby acknowledged by Lessor, as security for any damage caused to the Premises during the leasing term. Such deposit shall be returned to Lessee, without interest ,upon the termination of this leasing Agreement.

Rent

The total rent for the term hereof is the sum of _____ DOLLARS ($_____) less any reimbursements and payable on the _____ day of each month of the term. All such payments shall be made to Lessor at Lessor's address on or before the due date and without demand.

Use of Premises

The Premises shall be used and occupied by Lessee and Lessee's immediate family, exclusively, as a private, single-family dwelling, and no part of the Premises shall be used at any time during the term of this Agreement by Lessee for the purpose of carrying on any business, profession, or trade of any kind, or for any purpose other than as a private, single-family dwelling. Lessee shall not allow any other person, other than Lessee's immediate family or transient relatives and friends who are guests of Lessee, to use or occupy the Premises without first obtaining Lessor's written consent to such use.

Condition of Premises

Lessee stipulates, represents, and warrants that Lessee has examined the Premises, and that they are at the time of this Agreement in good order, repair, and in a safe, clean, and tenantable condition.

Alterations and Improvements

Lessee shall make no alterations to or improvements on the Premises without the prior written consent of Lessor. Any and all alterations, changes, and/or improvements built, constructed, or placed on the Premises by Lessee shall be and become the property of the Lessor and remain on the Premises at the expiration or earlier termination of this Agreement.

Page 1

Damage to Premises

In the event Premises are destroyed or rendered wholly unlivable by fire, storm, earthquake, or other casualty not caused by the negligence of Lessee, this Agreement shall terminate from such time except for the purpose of enforcing rights that may have accrued hereunder.

_____

LESSEE

_____

LESSOR

Page 2

Project 4 Combine Documents

WL2-C7-P4-CombinedLease.docx

Dearborn Industries

Revenues

Company revenues increased in 2015 as a result of development contracts with government entities focused on the design of flywheel technologies. Several development prototypes were produced and placed with potential customers and shipped and preproduction units have shipped. The increase in revenues is reflected in the following table:

Customer	1st Qtr	2nd Qtr	3rd Qtr	4th Qtr	Total
Lakeside Trucking	$ 69,450	$ 75,340	$ 88,224	$ 95,000	$ 328,014
Gresham Machines	25,210	28,340	33,400	43,199	130,149
Manchester County	30,219	28,590	34,264	40,891	133,964
Genesis Productions	35,290	51,390	59,334	72,190	218,204
Landower Company	12,168	19,355	25,209	262,188	318,920
Jewell Enterprises	24,329	21,809	33,490	49,764	129,392
Total	$ 196,666	$ 224,824	$ 273,921	$ 563,232	$ 1,258,643

Department Cost Percentages

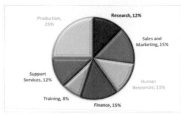

Project 5 Embed and Link Data between Excel and Word

WL2-C7-P5-DIRevs.docx

WL2-C7-P5-NSSCosts.docx

Project 1   Insert Comments in a New Employees Document   4 Parts

You will open a report containing company information for new employees and then insert and edit comments from multiple users.

Inserting and Managing Comments ▪▪▪▪▪▪▪▪▪▪▪▪▪▪▪

▼ Quick Steps

Insert a Comment
1. Select text.
2. Click REVIEW tab.
3. Click New Comment button.
4. Type comment.

New Comment

H I N T

Use comments to add notes, suggestions, or explanations, and to communicate with members of your workgroup.

You can provide feedback on and suggest changes to a document that someone else has written by inserting comments into it. Similarly, you can obtain feedback on a document that you have written by distributing it electronically to others and having them insert their comments into it.

To insert a comment in a document, select the text or item on which you want to comment or position the insertion point at the end of the text, click the REVIEW tab, and then click the New Comment button in the Comments group. This displays a comment balloon at the right margin, as shown in Figure 7.1.

Depending on any previous settings applied, clicking the New Comment button may cause the Reviewing pane to display at the left side of the document, rather than the comment balloon. If this happens, click the Show Markup button in the Tracking group on the REVIEW tab, point to *Balloons*, and then click *Show Only Comments and Formatting in Balloons* at the side menu. Also, check to make sure the Display for Review button in the Tracking group is set to *Simple Markup*. If it is not, click the Display for Review button arrow and then click *Simple Markup* at the drop-down list.

Figure 7.1 Comment Balloon

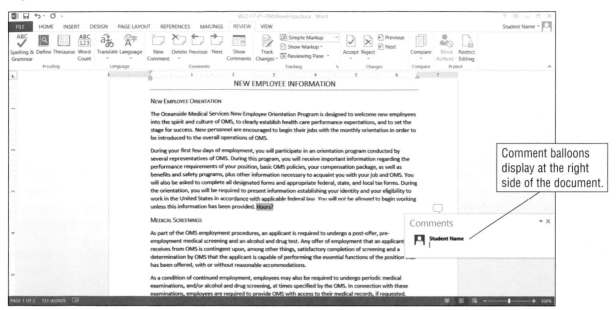

Comment balloons display at the right side of the document.

Project 1a **Inserting Comments** Part 1 of 4

1. Open **OMSNewEmps.docx** and then save the document and name it **WL2-C7-P1-OMSNewEmps**.
2. Insert a comment by completing the following steps:
   a. Position the insertion point at the end of the second paragraph in the *NEW EMPLOYEE ORIENTATION* section.
   b. Press the spacebar once and then type **Hours?**.
   c. Select *Hours?*.
   d. Click the REVIEW tab.
   e. If the Show Comments button in the Comments group is active (displays with a blue background), click the button to deactivate it.
   f. Click the New Comment button in the Comments group.
   g. Type **Please include the total number of orientation hours.** in the comment balloon.

Step 2d

Step 2f

Steps 2b-2c

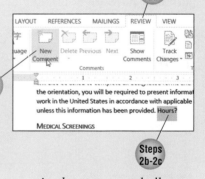

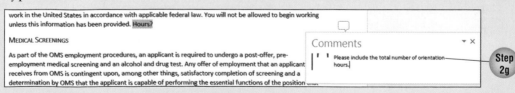

Step 2g

3. Insert another comment by completing the following steps:
   a. Move the insertion point to the end of the third (last) paragraph in the *MEDICAL SCREENINGS* section.
   b. Click the New Comment button in the Comments group.
   c. Type **Specify the locations where drug tests are administered.** in the comment balloon. (Since you did not have text selected when you clicked the New Comment button, Word selected the word immediately left of the insertion point).
   d. Click in the document to close the comment balloons.
4. Save **WL2-C7-P1-OMSNewEmps.docx**.

Inserting Comments in the Reviewing Pane

▼ **Quick Steps**

Insert a Comment in the Reviewing Pane
1. Click REVIEW tab.
2. Click Reviewing Pane button.
3. Click New Comment button.
4. Type comment.

Reviewing Pane

If your computer has a sound card and microphone, you can record voice comments.

You may prefer to insert comments with the Reviewing pane displayed on the screen. The Reviewing pane displays inserted comments as well as changes recorded with the Track Changes feature. (You will learn about Track Changes later in this chapter.)

To display the Reviewing pane, click the Reviewing Pane button in the Tracking group on the REVIEW tab. The Reviewing pane usually displays at the left side of the screen, as shown in Figure 7.2. Click the New Comment button in the Comments group and a comment icon and balloon displays in the right margin and the reviewer's name followed by "Commented" displays in the Reviewing pane. Type your comment and the text displays in the comment balloon as well as the Reviewing pane. (The Reviewing pane might display along the bottom of the screen, rather than at the left side. To specify where you want the pane to display, click the Reviewing Pane button arrow in the Tracking group on the REVIEW tab and then click *Reviewing Pane Vertical* or *Reviewing Pane Horizontal*.)

A summary displays toward the top of the Reviewing pane and provides counts of the number of comments inserted and the types of changes that have been made to the document. After typing your comment in the Reviewing pane, close the pane by clicking the Reviewing Pane button in the Tracking group or by clicking the Close button (marked with an X) located in the upper right corner of the pane.

Figure 7.2 Vertical Reviewing Pane

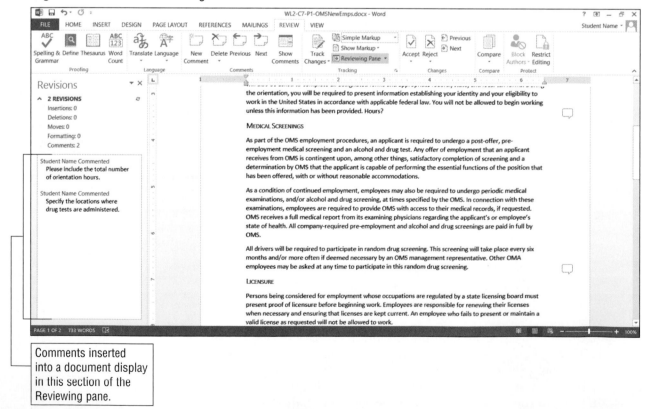

Comments inserted into a document display in this section of the Reviewing pane.

1. With **WL2-C7-P1-OMSNewEmps.docx** open, show the comments in the Reviewing pane by completing the following steps:
   a. If necessary, click the REVIEW tab.
   b. Click the Reviewing Pane button in the Tracking group.
   c. Click the Show Markup button in the Tracking group.
   d. Point to *Balloons* at the drop-down list.
   e. Click *Show All Revisions Inline* at the side menu.

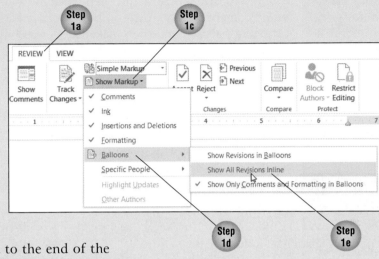

2. Insert a comment by completing the following steps:
   a. Move the insertion point to the end of the paragraph of text in the *INTRODUCTORY PERIOD* section.
   b. Press the spacebar once, type **Maximum?**, and then select *Maximum?*.
   c. Click the New Comment button in the Comments group on the REVIEW tab.
   d. With the insertion point positioned in the Reviewing pane, type **Please include in this section the maximum length of the probationary period.**

3. Click the Reviewing Pane button in the Tracking group to turn off the display of the Reviewing pane.

4. Save **WL2-C7-P1-OMSNewEmps.docx**.

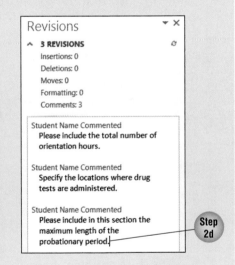

Navigating between Comments

When working in a long document with many comments, use the Previous and Next buttons in the Comments group on the REVIEW tab to move easily from comment to comment. Click the Next button to move the insertion point to the next comment or click the Previous button to move the insertion point to the preceding comment.

Previous   Next

Editing Comments

You can edit a comment in the Reviewing pane or in a comment balloon. To edit a comment in the Reviewing pane, click the Reviewing Pane button to turn on the pane and then click in the comment that you want to edit. Make the desired changes to the comment and then close the Reviewing pane. To edit a comment in a comment balloon, turn on the display of comment balloons, click in the comment balloon, and then make the desired changes.

Showing Comments

The Comments group on the REVIEW tab contains a Show Comments button. Click this button and comments display at the right side of the document. The Show Comments button is available only when the Display for Review button in the Tracking group is set to *Simple Markup*.

Project 1c Editing Comments

Part 3 of 4

1. With **WL2-C7-P1-OMSNewEmps.docx** open, navigate from one comment to another by completing the following steps:
   a. Press Ctrl + Home to move the insertion point to the beginning of the document.
   b. If necessary, click the REVIEW tab.
   c. Click the Next button in the Comments group. (This moves the insertion point to the first comment reference, opens the Reviewing pane, and inserts the insertion point in the pane.)
   d. Click the Next button to display the second comment.
   e. Click the Next button to display the third comment.
   f. Click the Previous button to display the second comment.
2. With the insertion point positioned in the Reviewing pane, edit the second comment to read: *Specify the locations within OMS where drug tests are administered as well as any off-site locations.*
3. Click the Reviewing Pane button to close the pane.
4. Edit a comment in a comment balloon by completing the following steps:
   a. Click the Show Markup button in the Tracking group, point to *Balloons*, and then click *Show Only Comments and Formatting in Balloons* at the side menu.
   b. Click the Show Comments button in the Comments group to display the balloons at the right side of the document.
   c. Display the paragraph of text in the *INTRODUCTORY PERIOD* section and then click in the comment balloon that displays at the right.
   d. Edit the comment so it displays as follows: *Please include in this section the maximum probationary period, if any.*

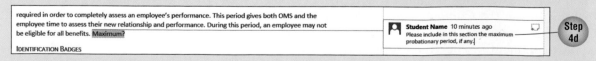

   e. Click in the document and then click the Show Comments button to turn off the display of comment balloons.
   f. Click the Show Markup button, point to *Balloons*, and then click *Show All Revisions Inline*.
5. Save **WL2-C7-P1-OMSNewEmps.docx**.

Distinguishing Comments from Different Users

More than one user can make comments in the same document. Word uses different colors to distinguish comments made by different users, generally displaying the first user's comments in red and the second user's comments in blue. (These colors may vary.)

You can change the user name and initials at the Word Options dialog box with *General* selected, as shown in Figure 7.3. To change the user name, select the name that displays in the *User name* text box and then type the desired name. Complete similar steps to change the user initials in the *Initials* text box. You may also need to insert a check mark in the *Always use these values regardless of sign in to Office.* check box.

Replying to Comments

When reviewing a document, you may want to reply to other people's comments. To reply to a comment, open the comment balloon, hover the mouse over the comment text, and then click the Reply button that displays to the right of the reviewer's name. Type the reply in the window that opens below the comment. You can also click in a comment and then click the New Comment button in the Comments group or right-click in a comment and then click *Reply to Comments* at the shortcut menu.

Printing Comments

To print a document with the comments, display the Print backstage area and then click the first gallery in the *Settings* category (which is the gallery containing the text *Print All Pages*). At the drop-down list, insert a check mark before the *Print Markup* option if you want to print the document with the comments. If you want to print the document without the comments, click *Print Markup* to remove the check mark. If you want to print only the comments and not the document, click *List of Markup* at the drop-down list. This prints the contents of the Reviewing pane, which may include comments, tracked changes, and changes to headers, footers, text boxes, footnotes, and endnotes.

▼ **Quick Steps**

Change the User Name and Initials
1. Click FILE tab.
2. Click *Options*.
3. Type desired name in *User name* text box.
4. Type desired initials in *Initials* text box.
5. Click OK.

Reply to a Comment
1. Open comment balloon.
2. Hover mouse over comment text.
3. Click Reply button.
4. Type reply in reply window.

Print a Document with the Comments
1. Click FILE tab, *Print* option.
2. Click first gallery in *Settings* category.
3. If necessary, click *Print Markup* to insert check mark.
4. Click Print button.

Print Only the Comments
1. Click FILE tab, *Print* option.
2. Click first gallery in *Settings* category.
3. Click *List of Markup*.
4. Click Print button.

Figure 7.3 Word Options Dialog Box with *General* Selected

Insert a check mark in this check box if you want Word to use the values you enter in this section regardless of the account used to sign in to Office.

Change the user name and initials with these options.

Deleting Comments

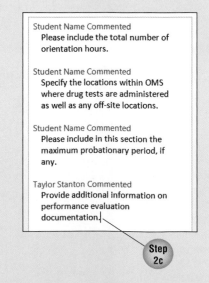

Quick Steps

Delete a Comment
1. Click REVIEW tab.
2. Click Next button until desired comment is selected.
3. Click Delete button.

Delete

Delete a comment by clicking the Next button in the Comments group on the REVIEW tab until the desired comment is selected and then clicking the Delete button in the Comments group. If you want to delete all of the comments in a document, click the Delete button arrow and then click *Delete All Comments in Document* at the drop-down list. A comment can also be dimmed in a document without being deleted. To dim a comment, right-click the comment and then click *Mark Comment Done* at the shortcut menu.

Project 1d **Changing User Information and Inserting and Deleting Comments** **Part 4 of 4**

1. With **WL2-C7-P1-OMSNewEmps.docx** open, change the user information by completing the following steps:
   a. Click the FILE tab.
   b. Click *Options*.
   c. At the Word Options dialog box, make sure *General* is selected in the left panel.
   d. Make a note of the current name and initials in the *Personalize your copy of Microsoft Office* section.
   e. Select the name displayed in the *User name* text box and then type **Taylor Stanton**.
   f. Select the initials displayed in the *Initials* text box and then type **TS**.
   g. Click the *Always use these values regardless of sign in to Office* check box to insert a check mark.
   h. Click OK to close the Word Options dialog box.

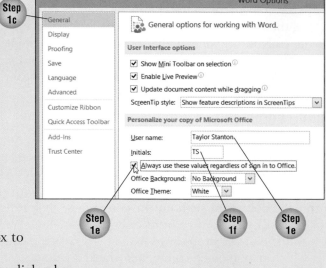

2. Insert a comment by completing the following steps:
   a. Move the insertion point to the end of the first paragraph of text in the *PERFORMANCE REVIEW* section.
   b. Click the New Comment button in the Comments group on the REVIEW tab.
   c. Type **Provide additional information on performance evaluation documentation.** in the Reviewing pane.
   d. Click the Reviewing Pane button to close the pane.
3. Respond to a comment by completing the following steps:
   a. Press Ctrl + Home to move the insertion point to the beginning of the document.
   b. Click the Show Markup button, point to *Balloons*, and then click *Show Only Comments and Formatting in Balloons* at the drop-down list.
   c. Click the Next button in the Comments group. (This opens the comment balloon for the first comment.)

> Student Name Commented
> Please include the total number of orientation hours.
>
> Student Name Commented
> Specify the locations within OMS where drug tests are administered as well as any off-site locations.
>
> Student Name Commented
> Please include in this section the maximum probationary period, if any.
>
> Taylor Stanton Commented
> Provide additional information on performance evaluation documentation.

Step 2c

d. Click the Reply button that displays to the right of the reviewer's name in the comment balloon.

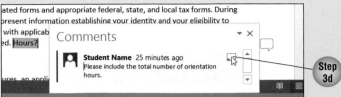

Step 3d

e. Type **Check with Barb on the total number of orientation hours.**

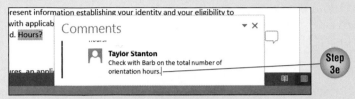

Step 3e

   f. Click in the document to close the comment balloon.

4. Print only the information in the Reviewing pane by completing the following steps:

   a. Click the FILE tab and then click the *Print* option. (You can also display the Print backstage area by pressing Ctrl + P.)

   b. At the Print backstage area, click the first gallery in the *Settings* category and then click *List of Markup* in the *Document Info* section of the drop-down list.

   c. Click the Print button.

5. Delete a comment by completing the following steps:

   a. Press Ctrl + Home.

   b. If necessary, click the REVIEW tab.

   c. Click the Next button in the Comments group.

   d. Click the Next button again.

   e. Click the Next button again.

   f. Click the Delete button in the Comments group.

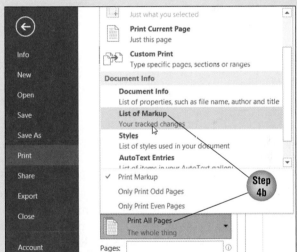

Step 4b

6. Print only the information in the Reviewing pane by completing Step 4.

7. Change the user information back to the default settings by completing the following steps:

   a. Click the FILE tab and then click *Options*.

   b. At the Word Options dialog box with *General* selected, select *Taylor Stanton* in the *User name* text box and then type the original name.

   c. Select the initials *TS* in the *Initials* text box and then type the original initials.

   d. Click the *Always use these values regardless of sign in to Office* check box to remove the check mark.

   e. Click OK to close the dialog box.

8. Save and then close **WL2-C7-P1-OMSNewEmps.docx**.

You will open a building construction agreement, turn on Track Changes, and then make changes to the document. You will also customize Track Changes and accept and reject changes.

Tracking Changes in a Document ■■■■■■■■■■■■■■

If more than one person in a work group needs to review and edit a document, consider using the Track Changes feature in Word. When Track Changes is turned on, Word tracks each deletion, insertion, and formatting change made in a document. Turn on Track Changes by clicking the REVIEW tab and then clicking the Track Changes button in the Tracking group or by pressing the keyboard shortcut Ctrl + Shift + E. Turn off Track Changes by completing the same steps.

Displaying Changes for Review

Track Changes

The Display for Review button in the Tracking group on the REVIEW tab has a default setting of *Simple Markup*. At this setting, any changes you make to the document display in the document and Word inserts a vertical change line in the left margin next to the line of text in which the change was made. To see the changes, click the Display for Review button and then click the *All Markup* option.

Display for Review

With *All Markup* selected, all of the changes display in the document. For example, if you delete text, it stays in the document but displays in a different color with a line through it. You can also turn on the display of all markup by clicking one of the vertical change lines that display in at the left margin next to changes that have been made or by clicking a comment balloon.

If you have made tracked changes to a document, you can preview what the final document will look like with the changes applied by clicking the Display for Review button and then clicking *No Markup* at the drop-down list. This displays the document with the changes made but does not actually make the changes to the document. If you want to see the original document without any changes marked, click the Display for Review button and then click *Original* at the drop-down list.

Showing Markup

Show Markup

With the display of all markup turned on, specify what tracking information displays in the body of the document with options at the Balloons side menu. To show all of the revisions in balloons in the right margin, click the Show Markup button, point to *Balloons*, and then click *Show Revisions in Balloons* at the side menu. Click *Show All Revisions Inline* to display all of the changes in the document with vertical change lines in the left margin next to the lines of text in which changes have been made. Click the *Show Only Comments and Formatting in Balloons* option at the side menu and insertions and deletions display in the text while comments and formatting changes display in balloons in the right margin.

1. Open **Agreement.docx** and then save the document and name it **WL2-C7-P2-Agreement**.
2. Turn on Track Changes by clicking the REVIEW tab and then clicking the Track Changes button in the Tracking group.

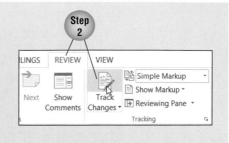

3. Type the word **BUILDING** between the words *THIS* and *AGREEMENT* in the first paragraph of text in the document.

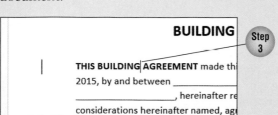

4. Show all markup by clicking the Display for Review button in the Tracking group on the REVIEW tab and then clicking *All Markup* at the drop-down list. (Notice that the text *BUILDING* is underlined and displays in red in the document.)

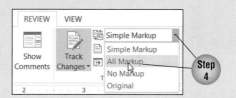

5. Select and then delete *thirty (30)* in the second paragraph. (The deleted text displays with a strikethrough in the document.)
6. Type **sixty (60)**.
7. Move a paragraph of text by completing the following steps:
   a. Select the paragraph of text that begins *Supervision of Work*, including the blank line below the paragraph.
   b. Press Ctrl + X to cut the text. (The text stays in the document and displays in red with strikethroughs across it.)
   c. Position the insertion point immediately before the word *Start* (in the paragraph that begins *Start of Construction and Completion:*).
   d. Press Ctrl + V to paste the cut text in the new location. The inserted text displays in green with a double underline. Notice that the text in the original location changes to green with double-strikethrough characters.)
8. Turn off Track Changes by clicking the Track Changes button in the Tracking group.
9. Display revisions in balloons by clicking the Show Markup button, pointing to *Balloons*, and then clicking *Show Revisions in Balloons* at the side menu.

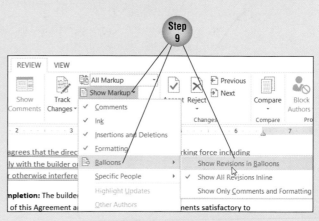

10. After looking at the revisions in balloons, click the Show Markup button, point to *Balloons,* and then click *Show All Revisions Inline* at the side menu.
11. Save **WL2-C7-P2-Agreement.docx**.

Displaying Information about Tracked Changes

Display information about a tracked change by hovering the mouse pointer over the change. After approximately one second, a box containing the author's name and the date, time, and type of change (for example, whether it was a deletion or insertion) displays above the change. You can also display information on tracked changes by displaying the Reviewing pane. Each change is listed separately in the Reviewing pane.

Changing User Information

Word uses a different color for each person (up to eight) who makes changes to a document. This color coding allows anyone looking at the document to identify which user made which changes. In the *Distinguishing Comments from Different Users* section earlier in this chapter, you learned how to change the user name and initials at the Word Options dialog box. In Project 2b, you will change the user name and initials and then make additional tracked changes.

Locking Track Changes

▼ Quick Steps

Lock Track Changes
1. Click REVIEW tab.
2. Click Track Changes button arrow.
3. Click *Lock Tracking*.
4. Type password.
5. Press Tab.
6. Type password.
7. Click OK.

If you want to ensure that all changes to a document will be tracked, lock tracking so that it cannot be turned off. To do this, click the Track Changes button arrow and then click *Lock Tracking* at the drop-down list. At the Lock Tracking dialog box, type a password, press the Tab key, type the password again, and then click OK. Unlock tracking by clicking the Track Changes button arrow and then clicking *Lock Tracking*. At the Unlock Tracking dialog box, type the password and then click OK.

Customizing Markup Display

Customize which tracked changes display in a document with options at the Show Markup button drop-down list. If you want to show only one particular type of tracked change, remove the check marks before all of the options except the desired one. For example, if you want to view only formatting changes and not other types of changes, such as insertions and deletions, remove the check mark before each option except *Formatting*. In addition to the Show Markup button drop-down list, you can customize which tracked changes display with options at the Track Changes Options dialog box, shown in Figure 7.4. Display this dialog box by clicking the Tracking group dialog box launcher.

If the changes of more than one reviewer have been tracked in a document, you can choose to view only the changes of a particular reviewer. To do this, click the Show Markup button, point to *Specific People* at the drop-down list, then click the *All Reviewers* check box to remove the check mark. Click the Show Markup button, point to *Reviewers*, and then click the check box of the desired reviewer.

Figure 7.4 Track Changes Options Dialog Box

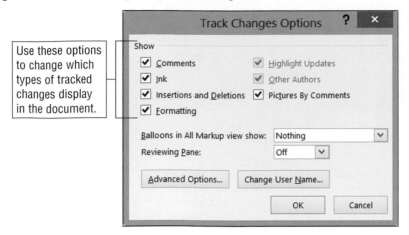

Use these options to change which types of tracked changes display in the document.

Project 2b | **Changing User Information and Tracking Changes** | Part 2 of 4

1. With **WL2-C7-P2-Agreement.docx** open, change the user information by completing the following steps:
   a. Click the FILE tab and then click *Options*.
   b. At the Word Options dialog box with *General* selected, select the current name in the *User name* text box and then type **Julia Moore**.
   c. Select the initials in the *Initials* text box and then type **JM**.
   d. Click in the *Always use these values regardless of sign in to Office.* check box to insert a check mark.
   e. Click OK to close the dialog box.
2. Make additional changes to the contract and track the changes by completing the following steps:
   a. Click the Track Changes button on the REVIEW tab to turn on tracking.
   b. Select the title *BUILDING CONSTRUCTION AGREEMENT* and then change the font size to 14 points.
   c. Delete the text *at his option* (located in the second sentence in the second paragraph).
   d. Delete the text *and Completion* (which displays near the beginning of the fourth paragraph).

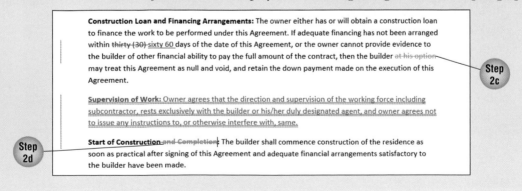

e. Delete *thirty (30)* in the paragraph that begins *Builder's Right to Terminate the Contract:* (located on the second page).

f. Type **sixty (60)**.

g. Select the text *IN WITNESS WHEREOF* that displays near the bottom of the document and then turn on bold formatting.

3. Click the REVIEW tab and then click the Track Changes button to turn off tracking.

4. Click the Reviewing Pane button to turn on the display of the Reviewing pane and then use the vertical scroll bar at the right side of the Reviewing pane to review the changes.

5. View the changes in balloons by clicking the Show Markup button, pointing to *Balloons*, and then clicking *Show Revisions in Balloons*.

6. Click the Reviewing Pane button to turn off the display of the pane.

7. Scroll through the document and view the changes in the balloons.

8. Click the Show Markup button, point to *Balloons*, and then click *Show All Revisions Inline* at the side menu.

9. Change the user information back to the information that displayed before you typed *Julia Moore* and the initials *JM* by completing the following steps:

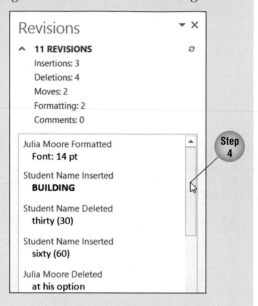

Step 4

a. Click the FILE tab and then click *Options*.

b. At the Word Options dialog box, select *Julia Moore* in the *User name* text box and then type the original name.

c. Select the initials *JM* in the *Initials* text box and then type the original initials.

d. Click in the *Always use these values regardless of sign in to Office.* check box to remove the check mark.

e. Click OK to close the dialog box.

10. Display only those changes made by Julia Moore by completing the following steps:

a. Click the Show Markup button in the Tracking group and then point to *Specific People*.

b. Click *All Reviewers* at the side menu.

c. Click the Show Markup button, point to *Specific People*, and then click *Julia Moore*.

d. Scroll through the document and notice that only changes made by Julia Moore display in the document.

Step 10a

Step 10b

e. Return the display to all of the reviewers by clicking the Show Markup button, pointing to *Specific People*, and then clicking *All Reviewers*.

11. Print the document with the markup by completing the following steps:
    a. Click the FILE tab and then click the *Print* option.
    b. At the Print backstage area, click the first gallery in the *Settings* category and then make sure a check mark displays before the *Print Markup* option. (If the *Print Markup* option is not preceded by a check mark, click the option.)
    c. Click the Print button.
12. Save **WL2-C7-P2-Agreement.docx**.

Customizing Track Changes Options

Default settings determine how tracked changes display in a document. For example, with all of the markup showing, inserted text displays in red with an underline below it and deleted text displays in red with strikethrough characters running through it. Moved text displays in the original location in green with double-strikethrough characters running through it and the text in the new location displays in green with double-underlining below the text.

Customize these options, along with others, at the Advanced Track Changes Options dialog box, shown in Figure 7.5. Use options at this dialog box to customize the display of markup text, moved text, table cell highlighting, formatting, and balloons. Display this dialog box by clicking the Tracking group dialog box launcher. At the Track Changes Options dialog box, click the Advanced Options button.

Figure 7.5 Advanced Track Changes Options Dialog Box

Change the display of markup with options in this section.

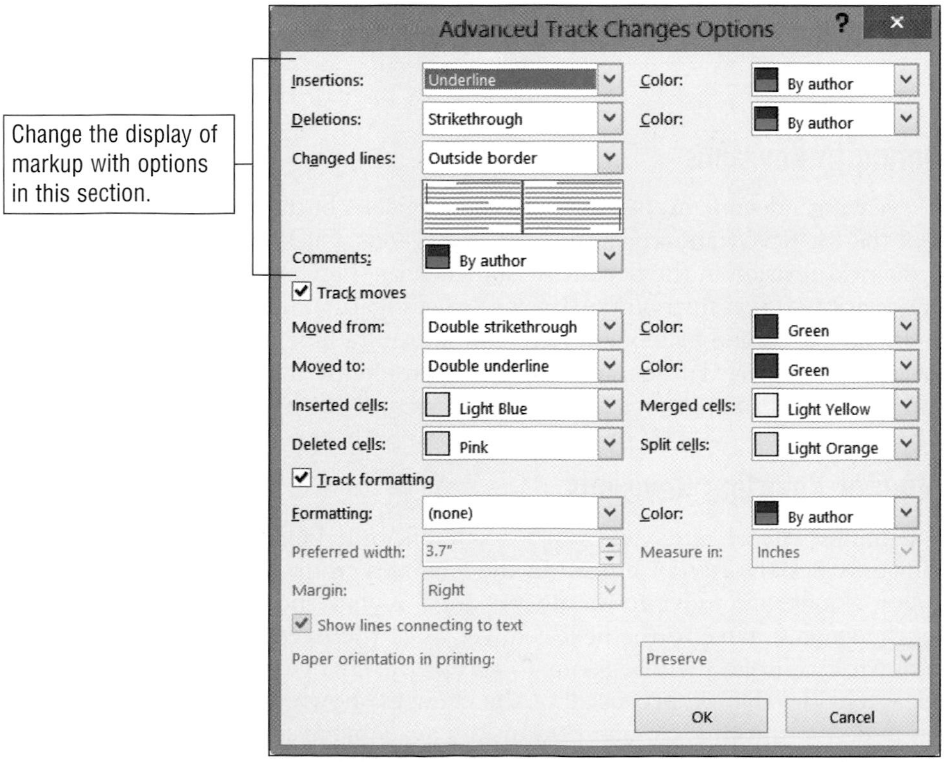

1. With **WL2-C7-P2-Agreement.docx** open, customize the Track Changes options by completing the following steps:
   a. If necessary, click the REVIEW tab.
   b. Click the Tracking group dialog box launcher.
   c. Click the Advanced Options button at the Track Changes Options dialog box.
   d. At the Advanced Track Changes Options dialog box, click the down-pointing arrow at the right side of the *Insertions* option box and then click *Double underline* at the drop-down list.

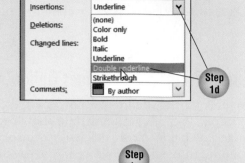

   e. Click the down-pointing arrow at the right side of the *Insertions Color* option box and then click *Green* at the drop-down list. (You will need to scroll down the list to display this color.)
   f. Click the down-pointing arrow at the right side of the *Moved from Color* option box and then click *Dark Blue* at the drop-down list.
   g. Click the down-pointing arrow at the right side of the *Moved to Color* option box and then click *Violet* at the drop-down list. (You will need to scroll down the list to display this color.)

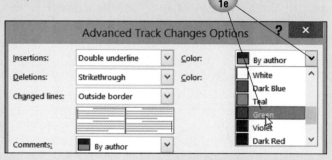

   h. Click OK to close the dialog box.
   i. Click OK to close the Track Changes Options dialog box.
2. Save **WL2-C7-P2-Agreement.docx**.

Navigating to Revisions

Next

Previous

When reviewing a document, use the Next and Previous buttons in the Changes group on the REVIEW tab to navigate among revisions. Click the Next button to review the next revision in the document and click the Previous button to review the previous revision. If you turn on the Track Changes feature, move text, and then turn on the display of revision balloons, a small Go button (a blue, right-pointing arrow) will display in the lower right corner of any balloon identifying moved text. Click the Go button in one of the balloons to move the insertion point to the other balloon.

Accepting or Rejecting Revisions

Accept

Reject

Tracked changes can be removed from a document only by accepting or rejecting the changes. Click the Accept button in the Changes group on the REVIEW tab to accept a change and move to the next change or click the Reject button to reject a change and move to the next change. Click the Accept button arrow and a drop-down list displays with options to accept the change and move to the next change, accept the change, accept all of the changes shown, and accept all of the changes and stop tracking. Similar options are available at the Reject button arrow drop-down list.

1. With **WL2-C7-P2-Agreement.docx** open, display all of the tracked changes *except* formatting changes by completing the following steps:
   a. Click the Show Markup button in the Tracking group and then click *Formatting* at the drop-down list. (This removes the check mark before the option.)
   b. Scroll through the document and notice that the vertical change line in the left margin next to the two formatting locations has been removed.
   c. Click the Show Markup button and then click *Formatting* at the drop-down list. (This inserts a check mark before the option.)
2. Navigate to review tracked changes by completing the following steps:
   a. Press Ctrl + Home to move the insertion point to the beginning of the document.
   b. Click the Next button in the Changes group to select the first change.
   c. Click the Next button again to select the second change.
   d. Click the Previous button to select the first change.
3. Navigate between the original and new locations of the moved text by completing the following steps:
   a. Press Ctrl + Home to move the insertion point to the beginning of the document.
   b. Click the Show Markup button, point to *Balloons*, and then click *Show Revisions in Balloons*.
   c. Click the Go button (a small, right-pointing arrow) that displays in the lower right corner of the Moved balloon. (This selects the text in the Moved up balloon.)
   d. Click the Go button in the lower right corner of the Moved up balloon. (This selects the text in the Moved balloon.)
   e. Click the Show Markup button, point to *Balloons*, and then click *Show All Revisions Inline*.

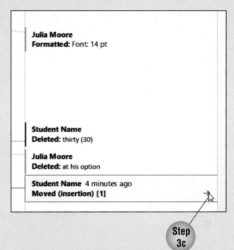

Step 3c

4. Press Ctrl + Home to move the insertion point to the beginning of the document.
5. Display and then accept only formatting changes by completing the following steps:
   a. Click the Tracking group dialog box launcher.
   b. At the Track Changes Options dialog box, click in the *Comments* check box to remove the check mark.
   c. Click the *Ink* check box to remove the check mark.
   d. Click the *Insertions and Deletions* check box to remove the check mark.
   e. Click OK to close the Track Changes Options dialog box.

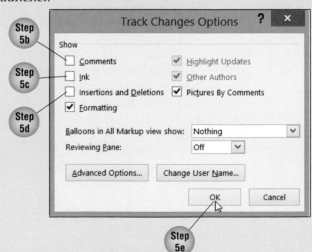

Step 5b

Step 5c

Step 5d

Step 5e

f. Click the Accept button arrow and then click *Accept All Changes Shown* at the drop-down list. (This accepts only the formatting changes in the document, because those are the only changes showing.)

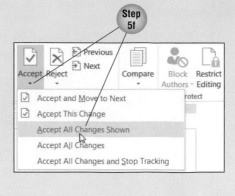

6. Redisplay all of the changes by completing the following steps:
   a. Click the Tracking group dialog box launcher.
   b. Click in the *Comments* check box to insert a check mark.
   c. Click in the *Ink* check box to insert a check mark.
   d. Click in the *Insertions and Deletions* check box to insert a check mark.
   e. Click OK to close the Track Changes Options dialog box.
7. Press Ctrl + Home to move the insertion point to the beginning of the document.
8. Reject the change inserting the word *BUILDING* by clicking the Next button in the Changes group and then clicking the Reject button. (This rejects the change and moves to the next revision in the document.)

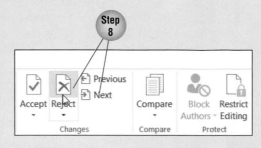

9. Click the Accept button to accept the change deleting *thirty (30)*.
10. Click the Accept button to accept the change inserting *sixty (60)*.
11. Click the Reject button to reject the change deleting the words *at his option*.
12. Accept all of the remaining changes by clicking the Accept button arrow and then clicking *Accept All Changes* at the drop-down list.

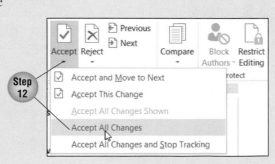

13. Return Track Changes options to the default settings by completing the following steps:
    a. If necessary, click the REVIEW tab.
    b. Click the Tracking group dialog box launcher.
    c. At the Track Changes Options dialog box, click the Advanced Options button.
    d. At the Advanced Track Changes Options dialog box, click the down-pointing arrow at the right side of the *Insertions* option and then click *Underline* at the drop-down list.
    e. Click the down-pointing arrow at the right side of the *Insertions Color* option box and then click *By author* at the drop-down list. (You will need to scroll up the list to display this option.)
    f. Click the down-pointing arrow at the right side of the *Moved from Color* option box and then click *Green* at the drop-down list. (You may need to scroll down the list to display this color.)
    g. Click the down-pointing arrow at the right side of the *Moved to Color* option box and then click *Green* at the drop-down list.
    h. Click OK to close the dialog box.
    i. Click OK to close the Track Changes Options dialog box.

14. Check to make sure all tracked changes are accepted or rejected by completing the following steps:
     a. Click the Reviewing Pane button in the Tracking group.
     b. Check the summary information that displays at the top of the Reviewing pane and make sure that zeros follow all of the options.
     c. Close the Reviewing pane.
15. Save, print, and then close **WL2-C7-P2-Agreement.docx**.

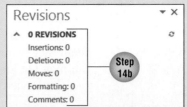

Project 3   Compare Lease Agreement Documents   2 Parts

You will compare the contents of a lease agreement and an edited version of the lease agreement. You will then customize compare options and then compare the documents again.

Comparing Documents ■■■■■■■■■■■■■■■■■■■■■■

Word contains a Compare feature that will compare two documents and display the differences as tracked changes in a third document. To use this feature, click the REVIEW tab, click the Compare button in the Compare group, and then click *Compare* at the drop-down list. This displays the Compare Documents dialog box, shown in Figure 7.6. At this dialog box, click the Browse for Original button. At the Open dialog box, navigate to the folder that contains the first of the two documents you want to compare and then double-click the document. Click the Browse for Revised button in the Compare Documents dialog box, navigate to the folder containing the second of the two documents you want to compare, and then double-click the document.

Quick Steps

Compare Documents
1. Click REVIEW tab.
2. Click Compare button.
3. Click *Compare* at drop-down list.
4. Click Browse for Original button.
5. Double-click desired document.
6. Click Browse for Revised button.
7. Double-click desired document.

Compare

HINT
Word does not change the documents you are comparing.

Figure 7.6 Compare Documents Dialog Box

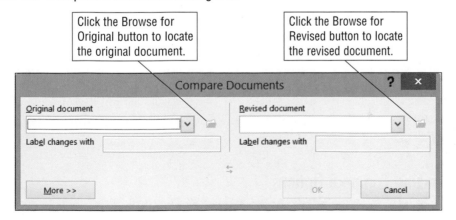

Click the Browse for Original button to locate the original document.

Click the Browse for Revised button to locate the revised document.

Viewing Compared Documents

When you click OK at the Compare Documents dialog box, the compared document displays with the changes tracked. Other windows may also display, depending on the option selected at the Show Source Documents side menu. Display this side menu by clicking the Compare button and then pointing to *Show Source Documents*. You may see just the compared document or you may see the compared document plus the Reviewing pane, original document, and/or revised document.

1. Close any open documents.
2. Click the REVIEW tab.
3. Click the Compare button and then click *Compare* at the drop-down list.
4. At the Compare Documents dialog box, click the Browse for Original button.

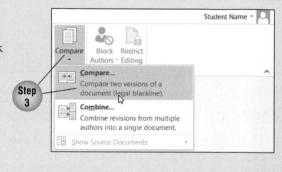

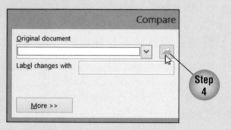

5. At the Open dialog box, navigate to the WL2C7 folder on your storage medium and then double-click **ComAgrmnt.docx**.
6. At the Compare Documents dialog box, click the Browse for Revised button.
7. At the Open dialog box, double-click **EditedComAgrmnt.docx**.
8. Click OK.
9. If the original and revised documents display along with the compared document, click the Compare button, point to *Show Source Documents* at the drop-down list, and then click *Hide Source Documents* at the side menu.
10. With the compared document active, print the document with markup.
11. Click the FILE tab and then click the *Close* option. At the message asking if you want to save changes, click the Don't Save button.

Customizing Compare Options

By default, Word compares the original document with the revised document and displays the differences as tracked changes in a third document. Change this default along with others by expanding the Compare Documents dialog box. Expand the dialog box by clicking the More button and additional options display, as shown in Figure 7.7.

Figure 7.7 Expanded Compare Documents Dialog Box

Control the level of comparisons made between the original and revised documents with options in this section.

Use options in this section to specify whether you want to show changes at the character or word level and where you want to show the changes.

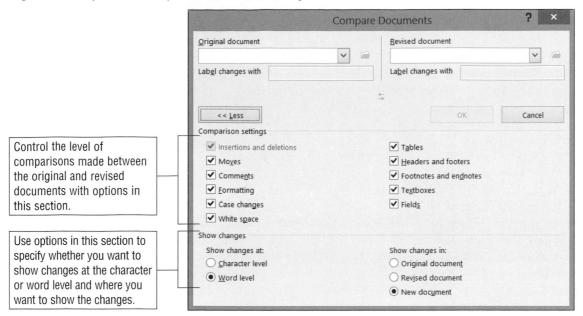

Control the level of comparison that Word makes between the original and revised documents with options in the *Comparison settings* section of the dialog box. The *Show changes at* option in the *Show changes* section of the dialog box has a default setting of *Word level*. At this setting, Word shows changes to whole words rather than individual characters within the word. For example, if you deleted the letters *ed* from the end of a word, Word would display the entire word as a change rather than just the *ed*. If you want to show changes by character, click the *Character level* option.

By default, Word displays differences between compared documents in a new document. With options in the *Show changes in* section, you can change this to *Original document* or *Revised document*. If you change options in the expanded Compare Documents dialog box, the selected options will be the defaults the next time you open the dialog box.

Project 3b | **Customizing Compare Options and Comparing Documents** | Part 2 of 2

1. Close any open documents.
2. Click the REVIEW tab.
3. Click the Compare button and then click *Compare* at the drop-down list.
4. At the Compare Documents dialog box, click the Browse for Original button.
5. At the Open dialog box, navigate to the WL2C7 folder on your storage medium and then double-click *ComAgrmnt.docx*.
6. At the Compare Documents dialog box, click the Browse for Revised button.
7. At the Open dialog box, double-click *EditedComAgrmnt.docx*.
8. At the Compare Documents dialog box, click the More button. (Skip this step if the dialog box displays expanded and a Less button displays above the *Comparison settings* section.)

9. Click the *Moves* check box and then click the *Formatting* check box to remove the check marks.
10. Click OK.
11. Print the document with markup.
12. Close the document without saving it.
13. Return the options to the default settings by completing the following steps:
    a. Close any open documents.
    b. Click the REVIEW tab.
    c. Click the Compare button and then click *Compare* at the drop-down list.
    d. At the Compare Documents dialog box, click the Browse for Original button.
    e. At the Open dialog box, double-click ***ComAgrmnt.docx***.
    f. At the Compare Documents dialog box, click the Browse for Revised button.
    g. At the Open dialog box, double-click ***EditedComAgrmnt.docx***.
    h. At the Compare Documents dialog box, click the *Moves* check box to insert a check mark and then click the *Formatting* check box to insert a check mark.
    i. Click the Less button.
    j. Click OK.
14. At the new document, accept all of the changes.
15. Save the document and name it **WL2-C7-P3-ComAgrmnt**.
16. Print and then close the document.

Step 9

Compare

Original document
ComAgrmnt.docx

Label changes with

<< Less

Comparison settings
☑ Insertions and deletions
☐ Moves
☑ Comments
☐ Formatting
☑ Case changes
☑ White space

Project 4   Combine Documents   2 Parts

You will open a lease agreement document and then combine edited versions of the agreement with the original document.

Combining Documents ■■■■■■■■■■■■■■■■■■■■■■■■■■

▼ **Quick Steps**

Combine Multiple Versions of a Document
1. Click REVIEW tab.
2. Click Compare button.
3. Click *Combine* at drop-down list.
4. Click Browse for Original button.
5. Double-click desired document.
6. Click Browse for Revised button.
7. Double-click desired document.
8. Click OK.

If several people have made changes to a document, you can combine their changed versions with the original document. You can combine each person's changed document with the original until you have incorporated all of the changes into the original document. To do this, open the Combine Documents dialog box, shown in Figure 7.8 on the next page, by clicking the Compare button on the REVIEW tab and then clicking *Combine* at the drop-down list. The Combine Documents dialog box contains many of the same options as the Compare Documents dialog box.

To combine documents at the Combine Documents dialog box, click the Browse for Original button, navigate to the desired folder, and then double-click the original document. Click the Browse for Revised button, navigate to the desired folder, and then double-click one of the documents containing revisions. You can also click the down-pointing arrow at the right side of the *Original document* option box or the *Revised document* option box and a drop-down list displays with the most recently selected documents.

Figure 7.8 Combine Documents Dialog Box

Click the Browse for Original button to locate the original document.

Click the Browse for Revised button to locate the revised document.

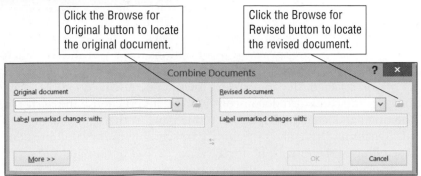

Combining and Merging Documents

Control how changes are combined with options in the expanded Combine Documents dialog box. This dialog box contains many of the same options as the expanded Compare Documents dialog box. By default, Word merges the changes in the revised document into the original document. Change this default setting with options in the *Show changes in* section. You can choose to merge changes into the revised document or a new document.

Project 4a **Combining Documents**   Part 1 of 2

1. Close all open documents.
2. Click the REVIEW tab.
3. Click the Compare button in the Compare group and then click *Combine* at the drop-down list.

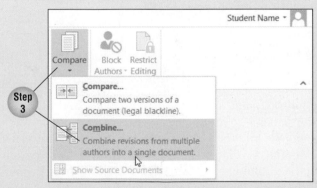

4. At the Combine Documents dialog box, click the More button to expand the dialog box.
5. Click the *Original document* option in the *Show changes in* section.
6. Click the Browse for Original button.
7. At the Open dialog box, navigate to the WL2C7 folder on your storage medium and then double-click *OriginalLease.docx*.
8. At the Combine Documents dialog box, click the Browse for Revised button.
9. At the Open dialog box, double-click *LeaseReviewer1.docx*.
10. Click OK.
11. Save the document and name it **WL2-C7-P4-CombinedLease**.

Showing Source Documents

Use options in the Show Source Documents side menu to specify which source documents to display. Display this side menu by clicking the Compare button and then pointing to *Show Source Documents*. Four options display at the side menu: *Hide Source Documents*, *Show Original*, *Show Revised*, and *Show Both*. With the *Hide Source Documents* option selected, the original and revised documents do not display on the screen; only the combined document displays. If you choose the *Show Original* option, the original document displays in a side pane at the right side of the document. Synchronous scrolling is selected, so scrolling in the combined document results in scrolling in the other. Choose the *Show Revised* option and the revised document displays in the panel at the right. Choose the *Show Both* option to display the original document in a panel at the right side of the screen and the revised document in a panel below the original document panel.

Project 4b | **Combining and Showing Documents** | Part 2 of 2

1. With **WL2-C7-P4-CombinedLease.docx** open, click the Compare button, point to *Show Source Documents*, and then click *Hide Source Documents* at the side menu if necessary. (This displays the original document with the combined document changes shown as tracked changes.)
2. Click the Compare button, point to *Show Source Documents*, and then click *Show Original* at the side menu. (This displays the original document at the right, the original document with tracked changes in the middle, and the Reviewing pane at the left side of the screen.)

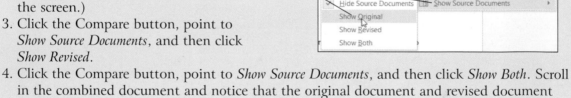

3. Click the Compare button, point to *Show Source Documents*, and then click *Show Revised*.
4. Click the Compare button, point to *Show Source Documents*, and then click *Show Both*. Scroll in the combined document and notice that the original document and revised document also scroll simultaneously.
5. Click the Compare button, point to *Show Source Documents*, and then click *Hide Source Documents*.
6. Close the Reviewing pane.
7. Click the Compare button and then click *Combine* at the drop-down list.
8. At the Combine Documents dialog box, click the Browse for Original button.
9. At the Open dialog box, double-click **WL2-C7-P4-CombinedLease.docx**.
10. At the Combine Documents dialog box, click the Browse for Revised button.
11. At the Open dialog box, double-click **LeaseReviewer2.docx**.
12. At the Combine Documents dialog box, click OK.
13. Save **WL2-C7-P4-CombinedLease.docx**.
14. Print the document with markup.
15. Accept all of the changes to the document. (Look through the document and notice that the *Rent* heading displays in blue. Select *Rent* and then change the font color to *Dark Red*.)
16. Keep the heading *Damage to Premises* together with the next paragraph.
17. Save, print, and then close **WL2-C7-P4-CombinedLease.docx**.

Project 5   **Embed and Link Data between Excel and Word**   **3 Parts**

> You will copy and embed Excel data into a Word document and then update the embedded data. You will also copy and link an Excel chart into a Word document and then update the data in the chart.

Embedding and Linking Objects ■■■■■■■■■■■■■■■■■■

One of the reasons the Microsoft Office suite is used extensively in business is because it allows data from one program to be seamlessly integrated into another program. For example, a chart depicting sales projections created in Excel can easily be added to a corporate report prepared in Word.

Integration is the process of adding content from other sources to a file. Integrating content is different than simply copying and pasting it. While it makes sense to copy and paste objects from one application to another when the content is not likely to change, if the content is dynamic, the copy and paste method becomes problematic and inefficient. To illustrate this point, assume one of the outcomes from the presentation to the board of directors is a revision to the sales projections, which means that the chart originally created in Excel has to be updated to reflect the new projections. If the first version of the chart was copied and pasted into Word, it would need to be deleted and then the revised chart in Excel would need to be copied and pasted into the Word document again. Both Excel and Word would need to be opened and edited to reflect this change in projection. In this case, copying and pasting the chart would not be efficient.

To eliminate the inefficiency of the copy and paste method, you can integrate objects between programs. An *object* can be text in a document, data in a table, a chart, or picture, or any combination of data that you would like to share between programs. The program that was used to create the object is called the *source* and the program the object is linked or embedded to is called the *destination*.

Embedding and linking are two methods you can use to integrate data. *Embedding* an object means that the object is stored independently in both the source and the destination programs. When you edit an embedded object in the destination program, the source program opens to help you make the changes, but the changes will not be reflected in the version of the object stored in the source program. If the object is changed in the source program, the changes will not be reflected in the version of the object stored in the destination program.

Linking inserts a code into the destination file that connects the destination to the name and location of the source object. The object itself is not stored within the destination file. When an object is linked, changes made to the content in the source program are automatically reflected in the destination program. Your decision to integrate data by embedding or linking will depend on whether the data is dynamic or static. If the data is dynamic, then linking the object is the most efficient method of integration.

Embedding Objects

An object that is embedded is stored in both the source and the destination programs. The content of the object can be edited in *either* the source or the destination; however, a change made in one will not be reflected in the other.

The difference between copying and pasting and copying and embedding is that embedded objects can be edited with the source program's tabs and options.

Since embedded objects are edited within the source program, the source program must reside on the computer when the file is opened for editing. If you are preparing a Word document that will be edited on another computer, you may want to check before embedding any objects to verify that the other computer has the same programs.

To embed an object, open both programs and both files. In the source program, click the desired object and then click the Copy button in the Clipboard group on the HOME tab. Click the button on the Taskbar representing the destination program file and then position the insertion point at the location where you want the object embedded. Click the Paste button arrow in the Clipboard group and then click *Paste Special* at the drop-down list. At the Paste Special dialog box, click the source of the object in the *As* list box and then click OK.

Edit an embedded object by double-clicking the object. This displays the object with the source program tabs and options. Make any desired changes and then click outside the object to close the source program tabs and options.

Project 5a — Embedding Excel Data in a Document
Part 1 of 3

1. Open **DIRevs.docx** and then save the document and name it **WL2-C7-P5-DIRevs**.
2. Start Excel and then open **DISales.xlsx**, located in the WL2C7 folder on your storage medium.
3. Select cells A2 through F9.
4. Click the Copy button in the Clipboard group on the HOME tab.
5. Click the Word button on the Taskbar.
6. Press Ctrl + End to move the insertion point to the end of the document.
7. Click the Paste button arrow and then click *Paste Special* at the drop-down list.
8. At the Paste Special dialog box, click *Microsoft Excel Worksheet Object* in the *As* list box and then click OK.
9. Save **WL2-C7-P5-DIRevs.docx**.
10. Click the Excel button on the Taskbar, close the workbook, and then close Excel.
11. With **WL2-C7-P5-DIRevs.docx** open, double-click in any cell in the Excel data. (This displays the Excel tabs and options for editing the data.)
12. Click in cell E3 (contains the amount *$89,231*), type **95000**, and then press Enter.
13. Click in cell F9 and then double-click the AutoSum button in the Editing group on the HOME tab. (This inserts the total *$1,258,643* in the cell.)
14. Click outside the Excel data to remove the Excel tabs and options.
15. Save, print, and then close **WL2-C7-P5-DIRevs.docx**.

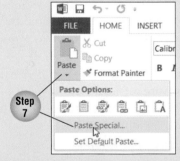

Step 7

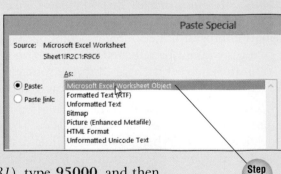

Step 8

Linking Objects

If the content of the object that you will integrate between programs is likely to change, you can link the object from the source program to the destination program. Linking the object establishes a direct connection between the source and destination programs. The object is stored in the source program only, and the destination program contains a code that indicates the name and location of the source of the object. Whenever the document containing the link is opened, a message displays to indicate that the document contains links and asking if you want to update them.

To link an object, open both programs and program files. In the source program file, click the desired object and then click the Copy button in the Clipboard group on the HOME tab. Click the button on the Taskbar representing the destination program file and then position the insertion point in the desired location. Click the Paste button arrow in the Clipboard group on the HOME tab and then click *Paste Special* at the drop-down list. At the Paste Special dialog box, click the source program for the object in the *As* list box, click the *Paste link* option located at the left side of the *As* list box, and then click OK.

▼ **Quick Steps**

Link an Object
1. Open source and destination programs and files.
2. Click desired object in source program.
3. Click Copy button.
4. Click Taskbar button for destination program file.
5. Position insertion point where desired.
6. Click Paste button arrow.
7. Click *Paste Special*.
8. Click source file format in *As* list box.
9. Click *Paste link* option.
10. Click OK.

Project 5b   **Linking an Excel Chart to a Document**   Part 2 of 3

1. Open **NSSCosts.docx** and then save the document and name it **WL2-C7-P5-NSSCosts**.
2. Open Excel and then open **NSSDept%.xlsx** located in the WL2C7 folder on your storage medium.
3. Save the workbook and name it **WL2-C7-P5-NSSDept%**.
4. Copy and link the chart to the Word document by completing the following steps:
   a. Click the chart to select it.
   b. Click the Copy button in the Clipboard group on the HOME tab.
   c. Click the Word button on the Taskbar.
   d. Press Ctrl + End to move the insertion point to the end of the document.
   e. Click the Paste button arrow and then click *Paste Special* at the drop-down list.
   f. At the Paste Special dialog box, click the *Paste link* option.
   g. Click *Microsoft Excel Chart Object* in the *As* list box.

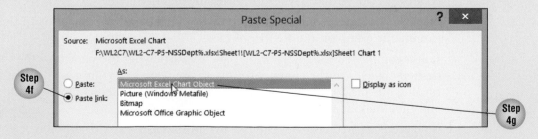

   h. Click OK.
5. Click the Excel button on the Taskbar, close **WL2-C7-P5-NSSDept%.xlsx**, and then close Excel.
6. With **WL2-C7-P5-NSSCosts.docx** open on the screen, save, print, and then close the document.

Editing a Linked Object

Edit linked objects in the source program in which they were created. Open the file containing the object, make the changes as required, and then save and close the file. If both the source and destination programs are open at the same time, the changed content is reflected immediately in both programs.

Project 5c   **Linking an Excel Chart to a Document**   **Part 3 of 3**

1. Open Excel and then open **WL2-C7-P5-NSSDept%.xlsx**.
2. Make the following changes to the data:
   a. In cell B4, change *18%* to *12%*.
   b. In cell B6, change 10% to *13%*.
   c. In cell B8, change 5% to 8%.
3. Click the Save button on the Quick Access toolbar to save the edited workbook.
4. Close **WL2-C7-P5-NSSDept%.xlsx** and then close Excel.
5. In Word, open **WL2-C7-P5-NSSCosts.docx**.
6. At the message telling you that the document contains links, click the Yes button. (Notice the changes to the chart data.)
7. Save, print, and then close **WL2-C7-P5-NSSCosts.docx**.

Chapter Summary

- Insert a comment in a document by clicking the New Comment button in the Comments group on the REVIEW tab. When you click the New Comment button, a comment balloon displays at the right margin. If any previous settings have been applied, the Reviewing pane, rather than a comment balloon, may display.

- Turn the display of the Reviewing pane on and off with the Reviewing Pane button in the Tracking group on the REVIEW tab.

- You can insert comments in the Reviewing pane. The summary section of the Reviewing pane provides a count of the number of comments inserted and a count of changes that have been made to the document.

- Navigate to review comments using the Previous and Next buttons in the Comments group on the REVIEW tab.

- Edit a comment in the Reviewing pane by displaying the pane and then making desired changes to the comment. Edit a comment in a comment balloon by turning on the display of balloons, clicking in the desired comment balloon, and then making the desired changes.

- If changes are made to a document by another person with different user information, the changes display in a different color. Change the user name and initials at the Word Options dialog box with *General* selected.

- Reply to a comment by clicking the Reply button that displays to the right of the reviewer's name in the comment balloon and then typing the reply.

- Print a document along with the inserted comments or choose to print only the comments and not the document.

- Delete a comment by clicking the Next button in the Comments group on the REVIEW tab until the desired comment is selected and then clicking the Delete button in the Comments group.

- Use the Track Changes feature when more than one person is reviewing a document and making changes to it. Turn on Tracked Changes by clicking the Track Changes button in the Tracking group on the REVIEW tab.

- Display information about tracked changes—such as the author's name, date and time, and type of change—by positioning the mouse pointer on a change. After approximately one second, a box displays with the information. You can also display information about tracked changes by displaying the Reviewing pane.

- Control how markup displays in a document with the Display for Review button in the Tracking group on the REVIEW tab. Control the markup that Word displays in a document with options at the Show Markup button drop-down list.

- Change Track Changes default settings with options at the Advanced Track Changes Options dialog box. Display this dialog box by clicking the Tracking group dialog box launcher and then clicking the Advanced Options button at the Track Changes Options dialog box.

- Move to the next change in a document by clicking the Next button in the Changes group on the REVIEW tab and move to the previous change by clicking the Previous button.

- Use the Accept and Reject buttons in the Changes group on the REVIEW tab to accept and reject changes made in a document.

- Use the Compare button in the Compare group on the REVIEW tab to compare two documents and display the differences between them as tracked changes in a third document.

- Customize options for comparing documents at the expanded Compare Documents dialog box. Click the More button to expand the dialog box.

- If several people review a document, you can combine their changed versions with the original document. Combine documents with options at the Combine Documents dialog box.

- Customize options for combining documents at the expanded Combine Documents dialog box. Click the More button to expand the dialog box.

- Specify which source documents to display by clicking the Compare button in the Compare group on the REVIEW tab, pointing to *Show Source Documents*, and then clicking the desired option at the side menu.

- An object created in one program in the Microsoft Office suite can be copied, linked, or embedded into another program in the suite. The program containing the original object is called the source program and the program in which it is inserted is called the destination program.

- An embedded object is stored in both the source and the destination programs. A linked object is stored in the source program only. Link an object if you want the contents in the destination program to reflect any changes made to the object stored in the source program.

Commands Review

FEATURE	RIBBON TAB, GROUP	BUTTON, OPTION	KEYBOARD SHORTCUT
accept changes	REVIEW, Changes		
Advanced Track Changes Options dialog box	REVIEW, Tracking	, *Advanced Options*	
balloons	REVIEW, Tracking	, *Balloons*	
Combine Documents dialog box	REVIEW, Compare	, *Combine*	
Compare Documents dialog box	REVIEW, Compare	, *Compare*	
delete comment	REVIEW, Comments		
display for review	REVIEW, Tracking		
new comment	REVIEW, Comments		
next comment	REVIEW, Comments		
next revision	REVIEW, Changes		
Paste Special dialog box	HOME, Clipboard	, *Paste Special*	
previous comment	REVIEW, Comments		
previous revision	REVIEW, Changes		
reject changes	REVIEW, Changes		
Reviewing pane	REVIEW, Tracking		
show markup	REVIEW, Tracking		
show source documents	REVIEW, Compare	, *Show Source Documents*	
Track Changes	REVIEW, Tracking		Ctrl + Shift + E
Track Changes Options dialog box	REVIEW, Tracking		

Concepts Check

Test Your Knowledge

Completion: In the space provided at the right, indicate the correct term, command, or number.

1. Insert a comment into a document by clicking this button in the Comments group on the REVIEW tab.

   _____

2. Navigate to review comments by using these two buttons in the Comments group on the REVIEW tab.

   _____

3. Change user information with options at this dialog box.

   _____

4. If a document contains comments, print only the comments by displaying the Print backstage area, clicking the first gallery in the *Settings* category, clicking this option, and then clicking the Print button.

   _____

5. Turn on the Track Changes feature by clicking the Track Changes button in this group on the REVIEW tab.

   _____

6. Use this keyboard shortcut to turn on Track Changes.

   _____

7. Show all markup in a document by clicking this button in the Tracking group on the REVIEW tab and then clicking *All Markup* at the drop-down list.

   _____

8. Display information on tracked changes in this pane.

   _____

9. With Track Changes turned on, text that has been moved displays in this color by default.

   _____

10. Customize options for tracking changes at the Track Changes Options dialog box and this dialog box.

    _____

11. Click the *Combine* option at the Compare button drop-down list and this dialog box displays.

    _____

12. Specify which source document to display by clicking the Compare button, pointing to this option, and then clicking the desired option at the side menu.

    _____

13. Do this to an object if you want the contents in the destination program to reflect any changes made to the object stored in the source program.

    _____

Skills Check   Assess Your Performance

Assessment

1   INSERT COMMENTS IN A WEB REPORT

1. Open **NavigateWeb.docx** and then save the document and name it **WL2-C7-A1-NavigateWeb**.
2. Delete the only comment in the document.
3. Position the insertion point at the end of the first paragraph in the *IPs and URLs* section and then insert a comment with the following text: *Please identify what the letters ICANN stand for.*
4. Position the insertion point at the end of the third paragraph in the *IPs and URLs* section and then insert a comment with the following text: *Insert a caption for the following table and the two other tables in the document.*
5. Position the insertion point at the end of the last paragraph in the document (above the table) and insert a comment with the following text: *Include in the following table additional examples of methods for narrowing a search.*
6. Save the document and then print only the comments.
7. Close **WL2-C7-A1-NavigateWeb.docx**.

Assessment

2   TRACK CHANGES IN A COMPUTER VIRUSES REPORT

1. Open **CompChapters.docx** and then save the document and name it **WL2-C7-A2-CompChapters**.
2. Turn on Track Changes and then make the following changes:
   a. Edit the first sentence in the document so it displays as follows: *The computer virus is one of the most familiar forms of risk to computer security.*
   b. Type **computer's** between *the* and *motherboard* in the last sentence in the first paragraph of the document.
   c. Delete the word *real* in the second sentence of the *Types of Viruses* section and then type **significant**.
   d. Select and then delete the last sentence in the *Methods of Virus Operation* section (which begins *A well-known example of the logic bomb was the*).
   e. Turn off Track Changes.
3. Display the Word Options dialog box with *General* selected and then change the user name to *Stacey Phillips* and the initials to *SP*. Insert a check mark in the *Always use these values regardless of sign in to Office.* check box.
4. Turn on Track Changes and then make the following changes:
   a. Delete the words *or cracker* located in the seventh sentence in the *Types of Viruses* section.
   b. Delete the word *garner* in the first sentence in the *CHAPTER 2: SECURITY RISKS* section and then type **generate**.
   c. Select and then move the *Employee Theft* section after the *Cracking Software for Copying* section.
   d. Turn off Track Changes.

5. Display the Word Options dialog box with *General* selected. Change the user name back to the original name and the initials back to the original initials. Also remove the check mark from the *Always use these values regardless of sign in to Office.* check box.
6. Print the document with the markup.
7. Accept all of the changes in the document *except* reject the change moving the *Employee Theft* section after the *Cracking Software for Copying* section.
8. Save, print, and then close **WL2-C7-A2-CompChapters.docx**.

Assessment

3 COMPARE ORIGINAL AND REVISED SECURITY STRATEGIES DOCUMENT

1. Compare **Security.docx** with **EditedSecurity.docx** and insert the changes into a new document. ***Hint: Choose* New document *at the expanded Compare Documents dialog box.***
2. Save the compared document and name it **WL2-C7-A3-Security.docx**.
3. Print only the list of markup (not the document).
4. Reject the changes made to the bulleted text and the last paragraph in the *Disaster Recovery Plan* section and accept all of the other changes.
5. Add a page number at the bottom center of each page.
6. Save the document, print only the document, and then close **WL2-C7-A3-Security.docx**.

Assessment

4 COMBINE ORIGINAL AND REVISED LEGAL DOCUMENTS

1. Open **LegalSummons.docx** and then save the document and name it **WL2-C7-A4-LegalSummons**.
2. Close **WL2-C7-A4-LegalSummons.docx**.
3. At a blank screen, combine **WL2-C7-A4-LegalSummons** (the original document) with **Review1-LegalSummons.docx** (the revised document) into the original document. ***Hint: Choose* Original document *at the Combine Documents expanded dialog box.***
4. Accept all of the changes to the document.
5. Save and then close **WL2-C7-A4-LegalSummons.docx**.
6. At a blank screen, combine **WL2-C7-A4-LegalSummons.docx** (the original document) with **Review2-LegalSummons.docx** (the revised document) into the original document.
7. Print only the list of markup.
8. Accept all of the changes to the document.
9. Save the document, print only the document, and then close **WL2-C7-A4-LegalSummons.docx**.

Assessment

5 LINKING AN EXCEL CHART WITH A WORD DOCUMENT

1. Open **WESales.docx** and then save it and name it **WL2-C7-A5-WESales**.
2. Open Excel and then open the workbook named **WESalesChart.xlsx**.
3. Save the Excel worksheet and name it **WL2-C7-A5-WESalesChart**.

4. Link the Excel chart to the end of **WL2-C7-A5-WESales.docx**. (Make sure you use the Paste Special dialog box.)
5. Save, print, and then close **WL2-C7-A5-WESales.docx**.
6. With Excel the active program, make the following changes to the data in the specified cells:
   a. Change the amount in cell F3 from *$500,750* to *$480,200*.
   b. Change the amount in cell E4 from *$410,479* to *$475,500*.
7. Save and close **WL2-C7-A5-WESalesChart.xlsx** and then close Excel.
8. Open **WL2-C7-A5-WESales.docx** and click Yes at the message asking if you want to update the document.
9. Save, print, and then close **WL2-C7-A5-WESales.docx**.

Assessment

 6 ### TRACK CHANGES IN A TABLE

1. Open **SalesTable.docx** and then save the document and name it **WL2-C7-A6-SalesTable**.
2. You can track changes made to a table and customize the Track Changes options for a table. Display the Advanced Track Changes Options dialog box and then make the following changes:
   a. Change the color for inserted cells to *Light Purple*.
   b. Change the color for deleted cells to *Light Green*.
3. Turn on Track Changes and then make the following changes:
   a. Insert a new row at the beginning of the table.
   b. Merge the cells in the new row. (At the message saying the action will not be marked as a change, click OK.)
   c. Type **Clearline Manufacturing** in the merged cell.
   d. Delete the *Fanning, Andrew* row.
   e. Insert a new row below *Barnet, Jacqueline* and then type **Montano, Neil** in the first cell, **$530,678** in the second cell, and **$550,377** in the third cell.
   f. Turn off Track Changes.
4. Save and then print the document with markup.
5. Accept all of the changes.
6. Display the Advanced Track Changes Options dialog box and then return the inserted cells color back to *Light Blue* and the deleted cells color back to *Pink*.
7. Save, print, and then close **WL2-C7-A6-SalesTable.docx**.

Visual Benchmark Demonstrate Your Proficiency

TRACK CHANGES IN AN EMPLOYEE PERFORMANCE DOCUMENT

1. Open **NSSEmpPerf.docx** and then save the document and name it **WL2-C7-VB-NSSEmpPerf**.
2. Turn on Track Changes and then make the changes shown in Figure 7.8 on the next page. (Make the editing changes before you move the *Employment Records* section after the *Performance Evaluation* section.)
3. Turn off Track Changes and then print only the list of markup.

4. Accept all changes to the document.
5. Save the document, print only the document, and then close **WL2-C7-VB-NSSEmpPerf.docx**.
6. At a blank screen, combine **WL2-C7-VB-NSSEmpPerf.docx** (the original document) with **EditedNSSEmpPerf.docx** (the revised document) into the original document.
7. Accept all of the changes to the document.
8. Save, print, and then close **WL2-C7-VB-NSSEmpPerf.docx**.

Figure 7.8 Visual Benchmark

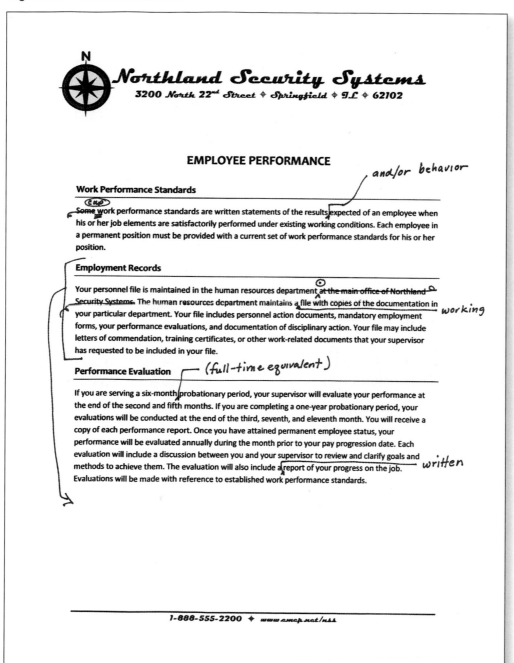

Case Study   Apply Your Skills

Part 1

You work in the training department at Hart International. Your department is responsible for preparing training material and training employees on how to use software applications within the company. Your supervisor, Nicole Sweeney, has asked you to help her prepare a Microsoft Word training manual. She has written a portion of the manual and has had another employee, Gina Singh, review the contents and make tracked changes. Ms. Sweeney has asked you to combine Gina's revised version with the original document. To do this, combine **HITraining.docx** with **HITrainingGS.docx**. Go through the original document with the tracked changes and accept and/or reject each revision. Not all of Gina's changes are correct, so check each one before accepting it. Save the combined document and name it **WL2-C7-CS-HITraining**.

Part 2

Ms. Sweeney has asked you to prepare training materials on how to check the spelling and grammar in a document and how to customize spelling and grammar options. Using the **WL2-C7-CS-HITraining.docx** document as a guideline, write information (including steps) on how to complete a spelling and grammar check in a document and how to change spelling and grammar options at the Word Options dialog box with *Proofing* selected. Include in the document a table that presents the names of the buttons available at the Spelling task pane and Grammar task pane and a brief description of what task each button completes. Save the completed document and name it **WL2-C7-CS-HISpelling**.

Part 3

If possible, send a copy of your document to one or two classmates and have them edit the document with Track Changes turned on. Combine their edited documents with your original **WL2-C7-CS-HISpelling** document. Save, print, and then close the document.

Part 4

Open **WL2-C7-CS-HITraining.docx**, move the insertion point to the end of the document, and then insert **WL2-C7-CS-HISpelling.docx**. Apply at least the following elements to the document:

- Heading styles
- Style set
- Theme
- Table style
- Table of contents
- Page numbering
- Cover page

Save, print, and then close the document.

WORD
MICROSOFT®

CHAPTER 8

Protecting and Preparing Documents

PERFORMANCE OBJECTIVES

Upon successful completion of Chapter 8, you will be able to:

- Restrict formatting and editing in a document and allow exceptions to restrictions
- Protect a document with a password
- Open a document in different views
- Modify document properties
- Inspect and encrypt a document
- Restrict permission to a document
- Mark a document as final
- Check a document for accessibility and compatibility issues
- Manage versions

Tutorials

8.1 Restricting Formatting and Editing in a Document

8.2 Protecting a Document with a Password and Opening Documents in Different Views

8.3 Managing Document Properties

8.4 Restricting and Inspecting a Document

8.5 Checking the Accessibility and Compatibility of a Document

8.6 Managing Versions

In Chapter 7, you learned to perform workgroup activities such as inserting comments into a document, tracking changes made by other users, comparing documents, and combining documents from multiple users. In this chapter, you will learn how to protect the integrity of shared documents, limit the formatting or editing changes that other users can make, and prepare documents for distribution. Model answers for this chapter's projects appear on the following pages.

Note: Before beginning the projects, copy to your storage medium the WL2C8 subfolder from the WL2 folder on the CD that accompanies this textbook and then make WL2C8 the active folder.

TANDEM ENERGY CORPORATION

Overview

Tandem Energy Corporation is a development stage company that was incorporated on May 1, 2009. The corporation and its subsidiary (collectively referred to as the "Company") designs, develops, configures, and offers for sale power systems that provide highly reliable, high-quality, environmentally friendly power. The Company has segmented the potential markets for its products into two broad categories: high-energy, high-power, uninterruptible power system (UPS), and high-power distributed generation and utility power-grid energy storage system. We have available for sale several high-energy products that deliver a low level of power over a long period of time (typically measured in hours). These products are tailored to the telecommunications, cable systems, computer networks, and Internet markets.

We are developing a new high-energy product for potential applications in the renewable energy market for both photovoltaic and wind turbine uses. As part of exploring these markets, we have committed to invest $2 million in Clear Sun Energies and we have purchased the inverter electronics technology of Technology Pacific[SN1].

We have taken significant actions over the last eighteen months to reduce our expenditures for product development, infrastructure, and production readiness. Our headcount, development spending, and capital expenditures have been significantly reduced. We have continued the preliminary design and development of potential products for markets under consideration and with specific approval by the Company's board of directors.

Research and Development

We believe that our research and development efforts are essential to our ability to successfully design and deliver our products to our targeted customers, as well as to modify and improve them to reflect the evolution of markets and customer needs. Our research and development team has worked closely with potential customers to define product features and performance to address specific needs. Our research and development expenses, including engineering expenses, were approximately $8,250,000 in 2011, $15,525,000 in 2010, and $7,675,000 in 2009. We expect research and development expenses in 2011 to be lower than in 2012. As we determine market opportunities, we may need to make research and development expenditures in the future. As of December 31, 2011, we employed twenty-five engineers and technicians who were engaged in research and development.

Manufacturing

Historically, our manufacturing has consisted of the welding and assembly of our products. We have previously contracted out the manufacture of our high-energy flywheel components, using our design drawings and processes to facilitate more rapid growth by taking advantage of third-party installed manufacturing capacity. For a limited number of non-proprietary components, we generate performance specifications and obtain either standard or custom components.

Our facility is underutilized as a result of reductions in development work and customer orders for production. We are maintaining a limited manufacturing staff, many of whom are skilled in quality-control techniques. We expect to continue to utilize contract manufacturing and outside suppliers in the future based on our estimate of product demand from potential customers. The suppliers of the mechanical flywheel and the control electronics for our high-power UPS product are both single-source suppliers, and the

---

WL2-C8-P1-TECRpt.docx

Main document changes and comments		
Page 1: Commented	**Student Name**	1/12/2015 11:34:00 AM

Include additional information on the impact of this purchase.

Header and footer changes

Text Box changes

Header and footer text box changes

Footnote changes

Endnote changes

Project 1 Restrict Formatting and Editing in a Company Report

WL2-C8-P1-TECRpt.docx

1

REAL ESTATE SALE AGREEMENT

The Buyer, BUYER, and Seller, SELLER, hereby agree that SELLER will sell and BUYER will buy the following property, with such improvements as are located thereon, and is described as follows: All that tract of land lying and being in Land Lot _____ of the _____ District, Section _____ of _____ County, and being known as Address:

City:_____ State: _____ Zip:_____, together with all light fixtures, electrical, mechanical, plumbing, air-conditioning, and any other systems or fixtures as are attached thereto; all plants, trees, and shrubbery now a part thereof, together with all the improvements thereon, and all appurtenances thereto, all being hereinafter collectively referred to as the "Property." The full legal description of said Property is the same as is recorded with the Clerk of the Superior Court of the County in which the Property is located and is made a part of this Agreement by reference.

SELLER will sell and BUYER will buy upon the following terms and conditions, as completed or marked. On any conflict of terms or conditions, that which is added will supersede that which is printed or marked. It is understood that the Property will be bought by Warranty Deed, with covenants, restrictions, and easements of record.

Financing: The balance due to SELLER will be evidenced by a negotiable Promissory Note of Borrower, secured by a Mortgage or Deed to Secure Debt on the Property and delivered by BUYER to SELLER dated the date of closing.

New financing: If BUYER does not obtain the required financing, the earnest money deposit shall be forfeited to SELLER as liquidated damages. BUYER will make application for financing within five days of the date of acceptance of the Agreement and in a timely manner furnish any and all credit, employment, financial, and other information required by the lender.

Closing costs: BUYER will pay all closing costs to include: Recording Fees, Intangibles Tax, Credit Reports, Funding Fees, Loan Origination Fee, Document Preparation Fee, Loan Insurance Premium, Title Insurance Policy, Attorney's Fees, Courier Fees, Overnight Fee, Appraisal Fee, Survey, Transfer Tax, Satisfaction and Recording Fees, Wood Destroying Organism Report, and any other costs associated with the funding or closing of this Agreement.

Prorations: All taxes, rentals, condominium or association fees, monthly mortgage insurance premiums, and interest on loans will be prorated as of the date of closing.

Title insurance: Within five (5) days of this Agreement SELLER will deliver to BUYER or closing attorney: Title insurance commitment for an owner's policy in the amount of the purchase price. Any expense of securing title, including but not limited to legal fees, discharge of liens, and recording fees will be paid by SELLER.

WL2-C8-P3-REAgrmnt.docx

2

Survey: Within ten (10) days of acceptance of this Agreement, BUYER or closing attorney, may, at BUYER's expense, obtain a new staked survey showing any improvements now existing thereon and certified to BUYER, lender, and the title insurer.

Default and attorney's fees: Should BUYER elect not to fulfill obligations under this Agreement, all earnest monies will be retained by SELLER as liquidated damages and fund settlement of any claim, whereupon BUYER and SELLER will be relieved of all obligations under this Agreement. If SELLER defaults under this agreement, the BUYER may seek specific performance in return of the earnest money deposit. In connection with any litigation arising out of this Agreement, the prevailing party shall be entitled to recover all costs including reasonable attorney's fees.

IN WITNESS WHEREOF, all of the parties hereto affix their hands and seals this _____ day of _____, 20_____.

WL2-C8-P3-REAgrmnt.docx

Project 3 Prepare a Real Estate Agreement for Distribution

WL2-C8-P3-REAgrmnt.docx

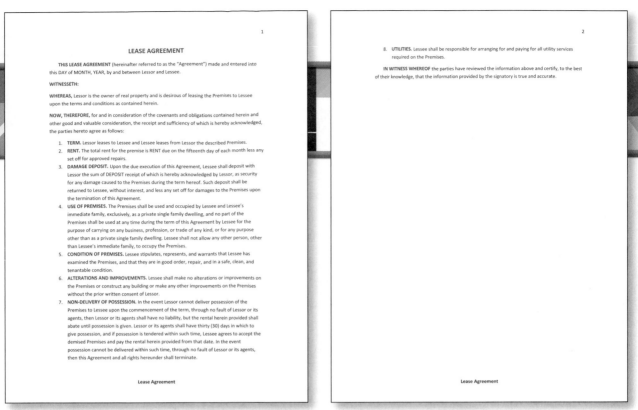

Project 4 Prepare and Inspect a Lease Agreement

WL2-C8-P4-Lease.docx

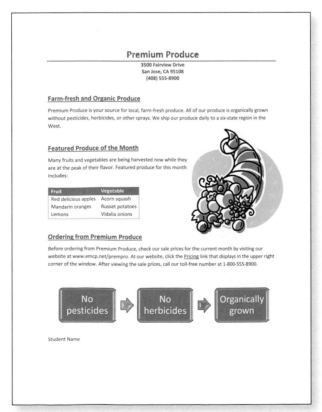

Project 5 Check the Accessibility and Compatibility of a Produce Document

WL2-C8-P5-PremPro.docx

Restrict Formatting and Editing in a Company Report

You will open a company report document, restrict formatting and editing in the document, insert a password, and allow exceptions to restrictions for specific users.

Protecting Documents ■■■■■■■■■■■■■■■■■■■■■■■■

Within your organization, you may want to distribute copies of a document among members of a group. In some situations, you may want to protect your document and limit the changes that others can make to it. If you create a document containing sensitive, restricted, or private information, you should consider protecting it by saving it as a read-only document or securing it with a password.

With options at the Restrict Editing task pane, you can limit what formatting and editing users can perform on the text in a document. Limiting formatting and editing is especially useful in a workgroup environment, in which a number of people in an organization will review and edit the same document.

For example, suppose you are responsible for preparing the yearly corporate report for your company. This report contains information from a variety of departments, such as finance, human resources, and sales and marketing. You can prepare the report and then specify what portions of the document given individuals are allowed to edit. You might specify that a person in the finance department can edit only that portion of the report containing information on finances. Similarly, you might specify that someone in human resources can edit only data pertinent to the human resources department. By limiting others' options for editing, you can protect the integrity of the document.

Restrict Editing

To protect a document, display the Restrict Editing task pane, shown in Figure 8.1, by clicking the REVIEW tab and then clicking the Restrict Editing button in the Protect group. Use options in the *Formatting restrictions* section to

Figure 8.1 Restrict Editing Task Pane

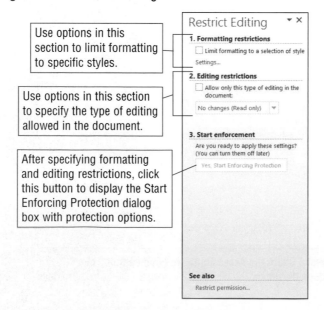

limit formatting to specific styles and use options in the *Editing restrictions* section to specify the type of editing allowed in the document.

The Protect group on the REVIEW tab contains a Block Authors button. This button is available only when a document is saved to a Microsoft SharePoint Foundation site that supports workspaces. If the button is active, select the portion of the document you want to block from editing and then click the Block Authors button. To unblock authors, click in the locked section of the document and then click the Block Authors button.

Restricting Formatting

With options in the *Formatting restrictions* section of the Restrict Editing task pane, you can lock specific styles used in a document, thus allowing the use of only those styles and prohibiting users from making other formatting changes. Click the <u>Settings</u> hyperlink in the *Formatting restrictions* section and the Formatting Restrictions dialog box displays, as shown in Figure 8.2.

Insert a check mark in the *Limit formatting to a selection of styles* check box and the styles become available in the *Checked styles are currently allowed* list box. In this list box, insert check marks in the check boxes preceding the styles you want to allow and remove check marks from the check boxes preceding the styles you do not want to allow. Limit formatting to a minimum number of styles by clicking the Recommended Minimum button. This allows formatting with styles that Word uses for certain features, such as bulleted and numbered lists. Click the None button to remove all of the check marks and prevent all styles from being used in the document. Click the All button to insert check marks in all of the check boxes and allow all styles to be used in the document.

Use options in the *Formatting* section of the dialog box to allow or not allow AutoFormat to make changes in a document and to allow or not allow users to switch themes or style sets.

▼ **Quick Steps**

Display the Formatting Restrictions Dialog Box
1. Click REVIEW tab.
2. Click Restrict Editing button.
3. Click <u>Settings</u> hyperlink.

Figure 8.2 Formatting Restrictions Dialog Box

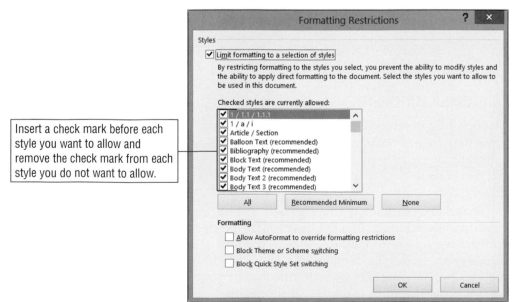

Insert a check mark before each style you want to allow and remove the check mark from each style you do not want to allow.

1. Open **TECRpt.docx** and then save the document and name it **WL2-C8-P1-TECRpt**.
2. Restrict formatting to the Heading 1 and Heading 2 styles by completing the following steps:
   a. Click the REVIEW tab.
   b. Click the Restrict Editing button in the Protect group.

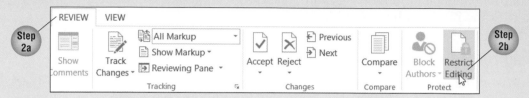

c. At the Restrict Editing task pane, click the *Limit formatting to a selection of styles* check box to insert a check mark. (Skip this step if the check box already contains a check mark.)
d. Click the <u>Settings</u> hyperlink.
e. At the Formatting Restrictions dialog box, click the None button.
f. Scroll down the list box and then click to insert check marks in the *Heading 1* check box and *Heading 2* check box.
g. Click OK.
h. At the message telling you that the document may contain direct formatting or styles that are not allowed and asking if you want to remove them, click Yes.
3. Save **WL2-C8-P1-TECRpt.docx**.

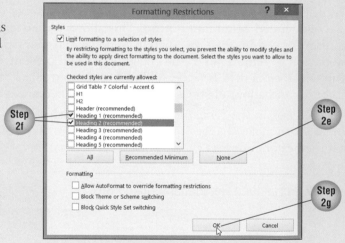

Enforcing Restrictions

The first step in protecting your document is to specify formatting and editing restrictions and any exceptions to those restrictions. The second step is to start enforcing the restrictions. Click the Yes, Start Enforcing Protection button in the task pane to display the Start Enforcing Protection dialog box, as shown in Figure 8.3.

At the Start Enforcing Protection dialog box, the *Password* option is automatically selected. To add a password, type the desired password in the *Enter new password (optional)* text box. Click in the *Reenter password to confirm* text box and then type the same password again. Choose the *User authentication* option if you want to use encryption to prevent any unauthorized changes. If Word does not recognize the password you type when opening a password-protected document, check to make sure Caps Lock is off and then try typing the password again.

Figure 8.3 Start Enforcing Protection Dialog Box

Type the same password in both of these text boxes. The characters in the password will display as bullets.

Project 1b **Protecting a Document**   **Part 2 of 3**

1. With **WL2-C8-P1-TECRpt.docx** open, click the Yes, Start Enforcing Protection button (located near the bottom of the task pane).
2. At the Start Enforcing Protection dialog box, type **formatting** in the *Enter new password (optional)* text box. (Bullets will display in the text box, rather than the letters you type.)
3. Press the Tab key (which moves the insertion point to the *Reenter password to confirm* text box) and then type **formatting**. (Bullets will display in the text box, rather than the letters you type.)
4. Click OK to close the dialog box.
5. Read the information in the task pane telling you that the document is protected and that you may format text only with certain styles. Click the <u>Available styles</u> hyperlink. (This displays the Styles task pane with only four styles in the list box: *Clear All*, *Normal*, *Heading 1*, and *Heading 2*.)
6. Apply the Heading 1 style to the title *TANDEM ENERGY CORPORATION* and apply the Heading 2 style to the following headings: *Overview*, *Research and Development*, *Manufacturing,* and *Sales and Marketing*.
7. Close the Styles task pane.
8. Apply the Lines (Simple) style set.
9. At the message indicating that some of the styles could not be updated, click OK.
10. Save the document.
11. Remove the password protection from the document by completing the following steps:
    a. Click the Stop Protection button located at the bottom of the task pane.
    b. At the Unprotect Document dialog box, type **formatting** in the Password text box.
    c. Click OK.
12. Save **WL2-C8-P1-TECRpt.docx**.

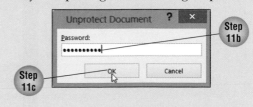

Restricting Editing

Use the *Editing restrictions* option at the Restrict Editing task pane to limit the types of changes users can make to a document. Insert a check mark in the *Allow only this type of editing in the document* check box and the drop-down list below the option becomes active. Click the down-pointing arrow at the right of the option box and the following options become available: *Tracked changes*, *Comments*, *Filling in forms*, and *No changes (Read only)*.

If you do not want users to be able to make any changes to a document, choose the *No changes (Read only)* option. Choose the *Tracked changes* option if you want users to be able to make tracked changes in a document and choose the *Comments* option if you want users to be able to make comments in a document. These two options are useful in a workgroup environment, in which a document is routed to various members of the group for review. Choose the *Filling in forms* option and users will be able to fill in the fields in a form but will not be able to make any other changes.

Project 1c   **Restricting Editing of a Document**   **Part 3 of 3**

1. With **WL2-C8-P1-TECRpt.docx** open, restrict editing only to comments by completing the following steps:
   a. Make sure the Restrict Editing task pane displays.
   b. Click the *Allow only this type of editing in the document* check box to insert a check mark.
   c. Click the down-pointing arrow at the right of the option box below *Allow only this type of editing in the document* and then click *Comments* at the drop-down list.

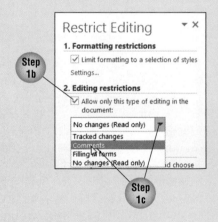

2. Click the Yes, Start Enforcing Protection button located near the bottom of the task pane.
3. At the Start Enforcing Protection dialog box, click OK. (Adding a password is optional.)
4. Read the information in the task pane telling you that the document is protected and that you may only insert comments.
5. Click each ribbon tab and notice the buttons and options that are dimmed and unavailable.
6. Insert a comment by completing the following steps:
   a. Move the insertion point immediately to the right of the period that ends the last sentence in the second paragraph of the *Overview* section.
   b. Click the REVIEW tab (if necessary), click the Show Markup button in the Tracking group, point to *Balloons*, and then click the *Show All Revisions Inline* option.
   c. Click the Reviewing Pane button to turn on the display of the Reviewing pane.
   d. Click the New Comment button in the Comments group on the REVIEW tab.

e. Type the following text in the Reviewing pane:
   Include additional information on the impact of this purchase.
   f. Close the Reviewing pane.
   g. Click the Stop Protection button located at the bottom of the Restrict Editing task pane.
   h. Close the Restrict Editing task pane.
7. Save the document and then print only page 1.
8. Print only the comment. (To do this, display the Print backstage area, click the first gallery in the *Settings* category, click the *List of Markup* option, and then click the Print button.)
9. Close **WL2-C8-P1-TECRpt.docx**.

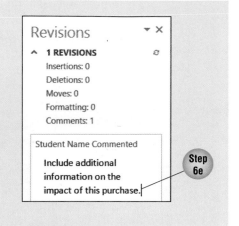

Revisions

^ **1 REVISIONS** ⟳
   Insertions: 0
   Deletions: 0
   Moves: 0
   Formatting: 0
   Comments: 1

Student Name Commented

Include additional information on the impact of this purchase.

Step 6e

Project 2 **Protect a Contract Document and Identify a Training Document as Read-Only**   **2 Parts**

You will open a contract document and then protect the document with a password. You will also open documents in different views.

Protecting a Document with a Password

In the previous section of this chapter, you learned how to protect a document with a password using options at the Start Enforcing Protection dialog box. You can also protect a document with a password using options at the General Options dialog box, shown in Figure 8.4 on the next page. To display this dialog box, press the F12 key to display the Save As dialog box, click the Tools button located near the bottom of the dialog box next to the Save button, and then click *General Options* at the drop-down list.

At the General Options dialog box, you can assign a password to open the document, modify the document, or both. To insert a password to open the document, click in the *Password to open* text box and then type the password. Passwords can contain up to 15 characters, should be 8 characters or more in length, and are case sensitive. Consider combining uppercase letters, lowercase letters, numbers, and/or symbols in your password to make it secure. Use the *Password to modify* option to create a password that a person must enter before he or she can make edits to the document.

At the General Options dialog box, insert a check mark in the *Read-only recommended* check box to save a document as a read-only document. If you open a document that is saved as a read-only document and then make changes to it, you have to save the document with a new name. Use this option if you do not want the contents of the original document changed.

▼ **Quick Steps**

Add a Password to a Document
1. Press F12.
2. Click Tools button.
3. Click *General Options*.
4. Type password in *Password to modify* text box.
5. Press Enter.
6. Type same password again.
7. Press Enter.

A strong password contains a mix of uppercase and lowercase letters as well as numbers and symbols.

Figure 8.4 General Options Dialog Box

Protect your document with a password by typing a password in this text box.

Click this check box to identify the document as read-only.

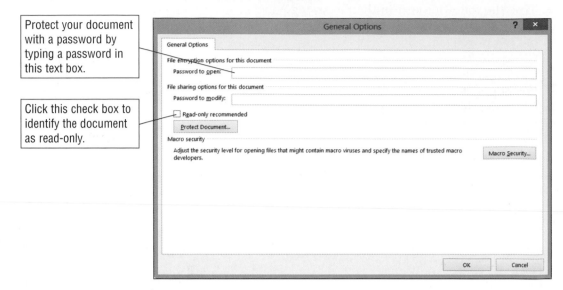

Project 2a Protecting a Document with a Password   Part 1 of 2

1. Open **TECContract.docx**.
2. Save the document and name it **WL2-C8-P2-TECContract**.
3. Save the document and protect it with a password by completing the following steps:

   Step 3c

   a. Press F12 to display the Save As dialog box.
   b. Click the Tools button located near the bottom of the dialog box (next to the Save button) and then click *General Options* at the drop-down list.
   c. At the General Options dialog box, type your first name in the *Password to open* text box. (If your name is longer than 15 characters, abbreviate it. You will not see your name; Word inserts bullets in place of the letters.)
   d. After typing your name, press the Enter key.
   e. At the Confirm Password dialog box, type your name again in the Reenter password to open text box. (Be sure to type it exactly as you did in the *Password to open* text box, including uppercase or lowercase letters.) Press the Enter key.
   f. Click the Save button at the Save As dialog box.
4. Close **WL2-C8-P2-TECContract.docx**.
5. Open **WL2-C8-P2-TECContract.docx** and type your password when prompted in the *Enter password to open file* text box.
6. Close the document.

Opening a Document in Different Views

Use the Open button in the Open dialog box to open a document in different views. At the Open dialog box, click the Open button arrow and a drop-down list of options displays. Click the *Open Read-Only* option and the document opens in Read Mode view and Read-Only mode. In Read-Only mode, you can make changes to the document but you cannot save the document with the same name. Exit Read Mode view and display the document in Print Layout view by pressing the Esc key on the keyboard.

Click the *Open as Copy* option and a copy of the document opens and the text *Copy (1)* displays at the beginning of the document name in the Title bar. Click the *Open in Protected View* option and the document opens with the text *(Protected View)* after the document name in the Title bar. A message bar displays above the document telling you that the file was opened in Protected view. To edit the document, click the Enable Editing button in the message bar. Open a document with the *Open and Repair* option and Word will open a new version of the document and attempt to repair any issues.

▼ **Quick Steps**

Open a Document in Different Views
1. Display Open dialog box.
2. Click desired document name.
3. Click Open button arrow.
4. Click desired option at drop-down list.

Project 2b **Opening a Document in Different Views** Part 2 of 2

1. Open **TECTraining.docx** and then save the document and name it **WL2-C8-P2-TECTraining**.
2. Close **WL2-C8-P2-TECTraining.docx**.
3. Open a document as a read-only document by completing the following steps:
   a. Press Ctrl + F12 to display the Open dialog box and then navigate to the WL2C8 folder on your storage medium.
   b. Click once on the document name *WL2-C8-P2-TECTraining.docx*.
   c. Click the Open button arrow (located near the bottom right corner of the dialog box) and then click *Open Read-Only* at the drop-down list.
   d. The document opens in Read Mode view. Press the Esc key to exit Read Mode and display the document in Print Layout view. Notice that *[Read-Only]* displays after the name of the document in the Title bar.

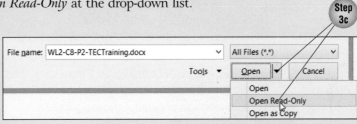

   e. Close the document.
4. Open a document in Protected view by completing the following steps:
   a. Press Ctrl + F12 to display the Open dialog box.
   b. Click once on the document name *PremPro.docx*.
   c. Click the Open button arrow and then click *Open in Protected View* at the drop-down list.
   d. Press the Esc key to exit Read Mode view and display the document in Print Layout view. Notice the message bar that displays with information telling you that the file was opened in Protected view.
   e. Click each tab and notice that most of the formatting options are dimmed.
   f. Click in the document and then click the Enable Editing button in the message bar. This removes *(Protected View)* after the document name in the Title bar and makes available the options in the tabs.

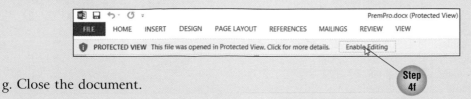

   g. Close the document.

Project 3 Prepare a Real Estate Agreement for Distribution   3 Parts

You will open a real estate agreement and then prepare it for distribution by inserting document properties, marking it as final, and encrypting it with a password.

Managing Document Properties ■■■■■■■■■■■■■■■■

▼ Quick Steps

Display Document Information Panel
1. Click FILE tab.
2. Click Properties button.
3. Click *Show Document Panel.*

Each document you create has properties associated with it, such as the type of document, the location in which it has been saved, and when it was created, modified, and accessed. You can view and modify document properties at the Info backstage area. You can also modify document properties at the document information panel. To display information about the open document, click the FILE tab. Document property information displays at the right side of the Info backstage area, as shown in Figure 8.5.

The document property information that displays in the Info backstage area includes the file size, number of pages and words, total editing time, and any tags or comments that have been added. Add or update a document property by hovering your mouse over the information that displays at the right of the property (a rectangular text box with a light blue border displays), clicking in the text box, and then typing the desired information. In the *Related Dates* section, dates display for when the document was created and when it was last modified and printed. The *Related People* section displays the name of the author of the document and provides options for adding additional author names. Display additional document properties by clicking the Show All Properties hyperlink.

Properties ▾

Properties

You also can add information to a document's properties at the document information panel, shown in Figure 8.6. Display this panel by clicking the Properties button that displays above the document property information in the Info backstage area and then clicking *Show Document Panel* at the drop-down list.

Figure 8.5 Info Backstage Area

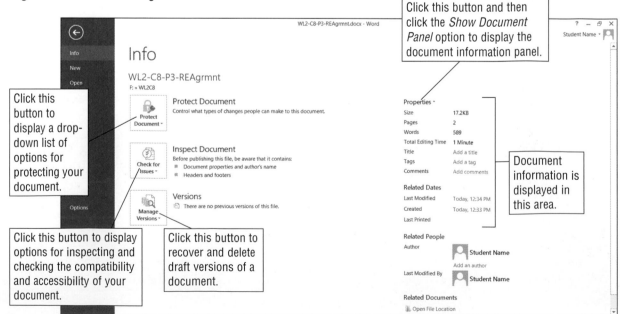

Click this button to display a drop-down list of options for protecting your document.

Click this button to display options for inspecting and checking the compatibility and accessibility of your document.

Click this button to recover and delete draft versions of a document.

Click this button and then click the *Show Document Panel* option to display the document information panel.

Document information is displayed in this area.

314   Word Level 2 ■ Unit 2

Figure 8.6 Document Information Panel

Type document information in the text boxes in the document information panel.

ⓘ Document Properties ▼					Location: F:\WL2C8\WL2-C8-P3-REAgrmnt.docx		✳ Required field ✕
Author:	Title:	Subject:	Keywords:	Category:	Status:		
Student Name							
Comments:							

By typing specific information in each text box in the document information panel, you can describe a document. Inserting text in some of the text boxes can help you organize and identify your documents. For example, insert specific keywords contained in the document in the *Keywords* text box, and you can search for all documents containing those keywords. Text you type in the document information panel is saved with the document. Print the document properties for a document by displaying the Print backstage area, clicking the first gallery in the *Settings* category, clicking *Document Info* at the drop-down list, and then clicking the Print button.

In addition to inserting information about a document in the document information panel, you can insert specific information with options at the Properties dialog box, shown in Figure 8.7. The name of the dialog box reflects the currently open document. Display this dialog box by clicking the Document Properties button that displays in the upper left corner of the document information panel and then clicking *Advanced Properties* at the drop-down list. You can also display this dialog box by displaying the Info backstage area, clicking the Properties button, and then clicking *Advanced Properties* at the drop-down list. Another method for displaying the Properties dialog box is to display the Open dialog box, click the desired document, click the Organize button, and then click *Properties* at the drop-down list. You can also right-click on the desired file name and then click *Properties* at the shortcut menu.

▼ **Quick Steps**

Display the Properties Dialog Box
1. Click FILE tab.
2. Click Properties button.
3. Click *Advanced Properties*.

Figure 8.7 Properties Dialog Box with General Tab Selected

The Properties dialog box displays information about the document. Click each tab to display additional document information.

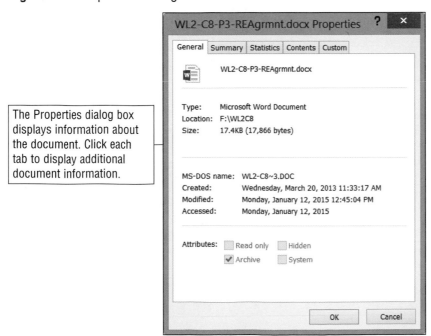

WL2-C8-P3-REAgrmnt.docx Properties ? ✕

General | Summary | Statistics | Contents | Custom

WL2-C8-P3-REAgrmnt.docx

Type: Microsoft Word Document
Location: F:\WL2C8
Size: 17.4KB (17,866 bytes)

MS-DOS name: WL2-C8~3.DOC
Created: Wednesday, March 20, 2013 11:33:17 AM
Modified: Monday, January 12, 2015 12:45:04 PM
Accessed: Monday, January 12, 2015

Attributes: ☐ Read only ☐ Hidden
            ☑ Archive   ☐ System

OK   Cancel

The Properties dialog box with the General tab selected displays information about the document type, size, and location. Click the Summary tab to view fields such as title, subject, author, company, category, keywords, and comments. Some fields may contain data and others may be blank. You can insert, edit, or delete text in the fields. With the Statistics tab selected, information displays such as the number of pages, paragraphs, lines, words, and characters and with the Contents tab active, the dialog box displays the document title.

Click the Custom tab to add custom properties to the document. For example, you can add a property that displays the date the document was completed, information on the department in which the document was created, and much more.

Project 3a   Inserting Document Properties   **Part 1 of 3**

1. Open **REAgrmnt.docx** and then save the document and name it **WL2-C8-P3-REAgrmnt**.
2. Make the following changes to the document:
   a. Insert page numbers that print at the top of each page at the right margin.
   b. Insert the footer *WL2-C8-P3-REAgrmnt.docx* centered on each page.
3. Insert document properties by completing the following steps:
   a. Click the FILE tab. (Make sure the Info backstage area displays.)
   b. Hover your mouse over the text *Add a title* that displays at the right of the *Title* document property, click in the text box that displays, and then type **Real Estate Sale Agreement**.
   c. Display the document information panel by clicking the Properties button that displays above the document property information and then clicking *Show Document Panel* at the drop-down list.

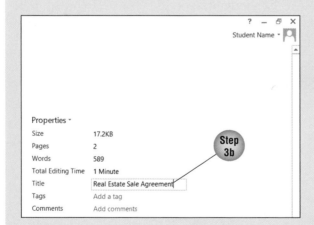
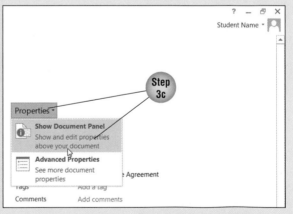

d. Select any text that appears in the *Author* text box and then type your first and last names.

e. Press the Tab key twice (which makes the *Subject* text box active) and then type **Real Estate Sale Agreement**.

f. Press the Tab key and then type the following words, separated by commas, in the *Keywords* text box: **real estate, agreement, contract, purchasing**.

g. Press the Tab key and then type **Agreement** in the *Category* text box.

h. Press the Tab key twice and then type the following text in the *Comments* text box: **This is a real estate sale agreement between two parties.**

4. Click the Close button that displays in the upper right corner of the document information panel.

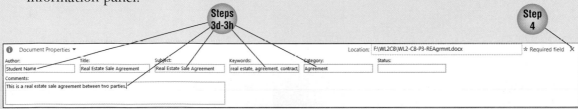

5. Save **WL2-C8-P3-REAgrmnt .docx** and then print only the document properties by completing the following steps:

a. Click the FILE tab and then click the *Print* option.

b. At the Print backstage area, click the first gallery in the *Settings* category and then click *Document Info* at the drop-down list.

c. Click the Print button.

6. Save **WL2-C8-P3-REAgrmnt .docx**.

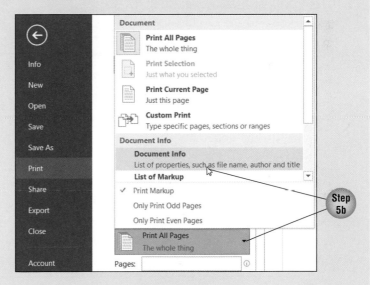

Restricting Documents ■■■■■■■■■■■■■■■■■■■

The middle panel in the Info backstage area contains buttons for protecting a document, checking for issues in a document, and managing versions of a document. Click the Protect Document button in the middle panel and a drop-down list displays with the following options: *Mark as Final, Encrypt with Password, Restrict Editing, Restrict Access,* and *Add a Digital Signature*.

Protect Document

Marking a Document as Final

Click the *Mark as Final* option to save the document as a read-only document. When you click this option, a message displays telling you that the document will be marked and then saved. At this message, click OK. This displays another message telling you that the document has been marked as final, which indicates that editing is complete and that this is the final version of the document. The message further indicates that when a document is marked as final, the status property is set to *Final*; typing, editing commands, and proofing marks are turned off; and the document can be identified by the Mark as Final icon, which displays toward the left side of the Status bar. At this message, click OK. After a document is marked as final, the message *This document has been marked as final to discourage editing.* displays to the right of the Protect Document button in the Info backstage area.

Project 3b **Marking a Document as Final**   **Part 2 of 3**

1. With **WL2-C8-P3-REAgrmnt.docx** open, mark the document as final by completing the following steps:
   a. Click the FILE tab.
   b. Click the Protect Document button at the Info backstage area and then click *Mark as Final* at the drop-down list.
   c. At the message telling you that the document will be marked and saved, click OK.
   d. At the next message that displays, click OK. Notice the message that displays to the right of the Protect Document button.
   e. Click the Back button to return to the document.

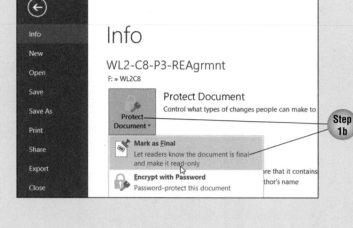

2. At the document, notice the message bar that displays near the top of the screen and then close the document.
3. Open **WL2-C8-P3-REAgrmnt.docx** and then click the Edit Anyway button on the yellow message bar.

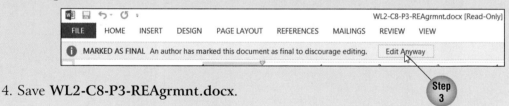

4. Save **WL2-C8-P3-REAgrmnt.docx**.

Encrypting a Document

▼ Quick Steps

Encrypt a Document
1. Click FILE tab.
2. Click Protect Document button.
3. Click *Encrypt with Password*.
4. Type password and then press Enter.
5. Type password again and then press Enter.

Word provides a number of methods for protecting a document with a password. Previously in this chapter, you learned how to protect a document with a password using options at the Start Enforcing Protection dialog box and the General Options dialog box. In addition to these two methods, you can protect a document with a password by clicking the Protect Document button at the Info backstage area and then clicking the *Encrypt with Password* option at the drop-down list. At the Encrypt Document dialog box that displays, type your password in the text box (the text will display as bullets) and then press the Enter key or click OK. At the Confirm Password dialog box, type your password again (the text will display as bullets) and then press the Enter key or click OK. When you apply a password, the message *A password is required to open this document.* displays to the right of the Protect Document button.

Restricting Editing

Click the Protect Document button at the Info backstage area and then click the *Restrict Editing* option at the drop-down list and the document displays with the Restrict Editing task pane open. This is the same task pane you learned about previously in this chapter.

Restrict
Editing

Adding a Digital Signature

Use the *Add a Digital Signature* option at the Protect Document button drop-down list to insert an invisible digital signature in a document. A *digital signature* is an electronic stamp that verifies a document's authenticity. Before adding a digital signature, you must obtain one. You can obtain a digital signature from a commercial certification authority.

Project 3c   **Encrypting a Document with a Password**   **Part 3 of 3**

1. With **WL2-C8-P3-REAgrmnt.docx** open, encrypt the document with a password by completing the following steps:
   a. Click the FILE tab, click the Protect Document button at the Info backstage area, and then click *Encrypt with Password* at the drop-down list.
   b. At the Encrypt Document dialog box, type your initials in uppercase letters in the Password text box. (The text will display as bullets.)
   c. Press the Enter key.
   d. At the Confirm Password dialog box, type your initials again in uppercase letters in the *Reenter password* text box (your text will display as bullets) and then press the Enter key.
2. Click the Back button to return to the document.
3. Save and then close the document.
4. Open **WL2-C8-P3-REAgrmnt.docx**. At the Password dialog box, type your initials in uppercase letters in the *Enter password to open file* text box and then press the Enter key.
5. Save, print, and then close **WL2-C8-P3-REAgrmnt.docx**.

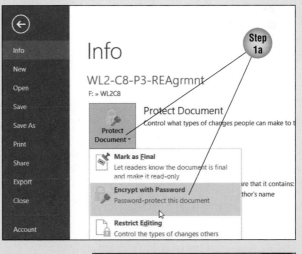

Project	4	**Prepare and Inspect a Lease Agreement**	1 Part

You will open a lease agreement document, make tracked changes, hide text, and then inspect the document.

Inspecting Documents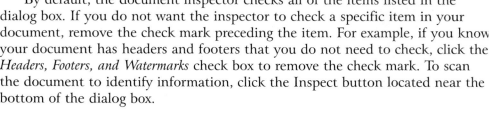

Use options from the Check for Issues button drop-down list at the Info backstage area to inspect a document for personal and hidden data along with compatibility and accessibility issues. When you click the Check for Issues button, a drop-down list displays with the following options: *Inspect Document*, *Check Accessibility*, and *Check Compatibility*.

Using the Document Inspector

Check for
Issues

Word includes a document inspector that will inspect your document for personal data, hidden data, and **metadata**, which is data that describes other data, such as document properties. You may want to remove some personal or hidden data before you share a document with other people. To check your document for personal or hidden data, click the FILE tab, click the Check for Issues button at the Info backstage area, and then click the *Inspect Document* option at the drop-down list. This displays the Document Inspector dialog box, shown in Figure 8.8.

By default, the document inspector checks all of the items listed in the dialog box. If you do not want the inspector to check a specific item in your document, remove the check mark preceding the item. For example, if you know your document has headers and footers that you do not need to check, click the *Headers, Footers, and Watermarks* check box to remove the check mark. To scan the document to identify information, click the Inspect button located near the bottom of the dialog box.

Figure 8.8 Document Inspector Dialog Box

Remove the
check marks
from those
options you
do not want
the Document
Inspector to
check.

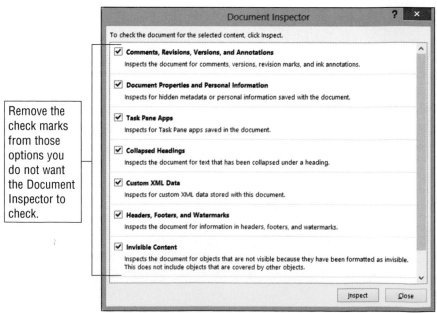

When the inspection is complete, the results display in the dialog box. A check mark before an option indicates that the inspector did not find the specific items. If an exclamation point displays before an option, it means that the inspector found items and a list of the items displays. If you want to remove the found items, click the Remove All button that displays at the right of the desired option. Click the Reinspect button to ensure that the specific items were removed and then click the Close button.

Project 4 **Inspecting a Document** **Part 1 of 1**

1. Open **Lease.docx** and then save the document and name it **WL2-C8-P4-Lease.docx**.
2. Make the following changes to the document:
   a. Turn on the Track Changes feature.
   b. Select the title *LEASE AGREEMENT* and then change the font size to 14 points.
   c. Delete the word *first* that displays in the second numbered paragraph (the *RENT* paragraph) and then type **fifteenth**.
   d. Move the insertion point to the beginning of the text *IN WITNESS WHEREOF* (located on page 2) and then press the Tab key.
   e. Turn off Track Changes.
3. Hide text by completing the following steps:
   a. Move the insertion point to the end of the first paragraph of text in the document (one space after the period at the end of the sentence).
   b. Type **The entire legal description of the property is required for this agreement to be valid.**
   c. Select the text you just typed.
   d. Click the HOME tab.
   e. Click the Font group dialog box launcher.
   f. At the Font dialog box, click the *Hidden* option in the *Effects* section.
   g. Click OK to close the dialog box.
4. Click the Save button on the Quick Access toolbar.
5. Inspect the document by completing the following steps:
   a. Click the FILE tab.
   b. Click the Check for Issues button at the Info backstage area and then click *Inspect Document* at the drop-down list.

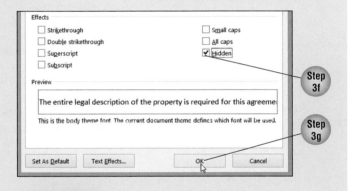

c. At the Document Inspector dialog box, tell the Document Inspector not to check the document for XML data by clicking the *Custom XML Data* check box to remove the check mark.

d. Click the Inspect button.

e. Read through the inspection results and then remove all of the hidden text by clicking the Remove All button that displays at the right side of the *Hidden Text* section. (Make sure that a message displays below *Hidden Text* indicating that the text was successfully removed.)

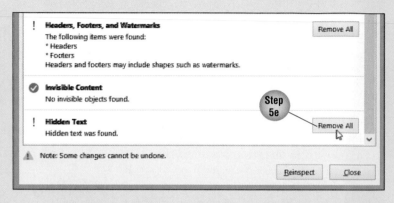

f. Click the Reinspect button.

g. To keep the header and footer text in the document, click the *Headers, Footers, and Watermarks* check box to remove the check mark.

h. Click the Inspect button.

i. Read through the inspection results and then remove all revisions by clicking the Remove All button that displays at the right side of the *Comments, Revisions, Versions, and Annotations* section.

j. Click the Reinspect button.

k. To leave the remaining items in the document, click the Close button.

6. Click the Back button to return to the document and then save the document.

7. Print and then close **WL2-C8-P4-Lease.docx**.

Project 5   **Check the Accessibility and Compatibility of a Produce Document**   **3 Parts**

You will open a document containing information on produce, check for accessibility issues, and check the compatibility of elements with previous versions of Word. You will also manage unsaved versions of the document.

Checking the Accessibility of a Document

Word includes the accessibility checker feature, which checks a document for content that a person with disabilities, such as a visual impairment, might find difficult to read. Check the accessibility of a document by clicking the Check for Issues button at the Info backstage area and then clicking *Check Accessibility*. The accessibility checker examines the document for the most common accessibility problems in Word documents and groups them into three categories: errors (content that is unreadable to a person who is blind); warnings (content that is difficult to read); and tips (content that may or may not be difficult to read). The accessibility checker examines the document, closes the Info backstage area, and displays the Accessibility Checker task pane.

At the Accessibility Checker task pane, passages of text that are unreadable are grouped in the *ERRORS* section, passages with content that is difficult to read are grouped in the *WARNINGS* section, and passages with content that may or may not be difficult to read are grouped in the *TIPS* section. Select an issue in one of the sections, and an explanation of why this is an issue and how you can fix it displays at the bottom of the task pane.

▼ Quick Steps

Check Accessibility
1. Click FILE tab.
2. Click Check for Issues button.
3. Click *Check Accessibility*.

Project 5a **Checking the Accessibility of a Document** Part 1 of 3

1. Open **PremPro.docx** and then save the document and name it **WL2-C8-P5-PremPro**.
2. Complete an accessibility check by completing the following steps:
   a. Click the FILE tab.
   b. At the Info backstage area, click the Check for Issues button and then click *Check Accessibility* at the drop-down list.
   c. Notice the Accessibility Checker task pane that displays at the right side of the screen. The task pane displays an *ERRORS* section and a *WARNINGS* section. Click *Picture 4* in the *ERRORS* section and then read the information that displays near the bottom of the task pane describing why you should fix the error and how to fix it.

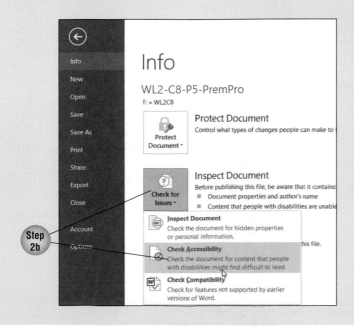

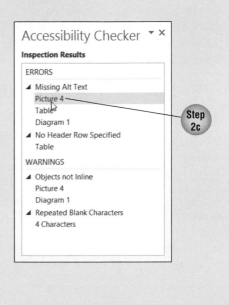

3. Add alternate text (which is a text-based representation of the clip art image) to the clip art by completing the following steps:

a. Right-click on the clip art image in the document and then click *Format Picture* at the shortcut menu.

b. At the Format Picture task pane, click the Layout & Properties icon and then click *ALT TEXT* to expand the options.

c. Click in the *Title* text box, type **Cornucopia**, and then press the Tab key. (This selects the default text in the *Description* text box.)

d. Type **Clip art image of a cornucopia of fruits and vegetables representing Premium Produce.**

e. Click the Close button to close the task pane.

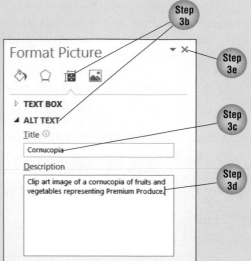

4. Click the first *Table* entry in the *ERRORS* section and then read the information that displays near the bottom of the task pane about creating alternate text for a table. Since the table contains text that is easily interpreted, you do not need to include alternate text.

5. Click the *Diagram 1* entry in the *ERRORS* section and then read the information about alternate text. Since this diagram contains text that is easily interpreted, you do not need to include alternate text.

6. Click *Picture 4* in the *WARNINGS* section and then read the information about objects that are not inline with text. You will not make the change suggested since the clip art would move to a different location on the page.

7. Click *Diagram 1* in the *WARNINGS* section and notice that it is the same information about objects that are not inline.

8. Close the Accessibility Checker task pane by clicking the Close button located in the upper right corner of the task pane.

9. Save **WL2-C8-P5-PremPro.docx**.

Checking the Compatibility of a Document

▼ **Quick Steps**

Check Compatibility
1. Click FILE tab.
2. Click Check for Issues button.
3. Click *Check Compatibility*.
4. Click OK.

Use one of the Check for Issues button drop-down options, *Check Compatibility*, to check your document and identify elements that are not supported or will act differently in previous versions of Word from Word 97 through Word 2010. To run the compatibility checker, open the desired document, click the Check for Issues button at the Info backstage area, and then click *Check Compatibility* at the drop-down list. This displays the Microsoft Word Compatibility Checker dialog box, which displays a summary of the elements in the document that are not compatible with previous versions of Word. This box also indicates what will happen when the document is saved and then opened in a previous version.

1. With **WL2-C8-P5-PremPro.docx** open, check the compatibility of elements in the document by completing the following steps:
   a. Click the FILE tab, click the Check for Issues button at the Info backstage area, and then click *Check Compatibility* at the drop-down list.
   b. At the Microsoft Word Compatibility Checker dialog box, read the information that displays in the *Summary* text box.
   c. Click the Select versions to show button and then click *Word 97-2003* at the drop-down list. (This removes the check mark from the option.) Notice that the information about SmartArt graphics being converted to a static object disappears from the *Summary* text box. This is because Word 2007 and Word 2010 support SmartArt graphics.
   d. Click OK to close the dialog box.

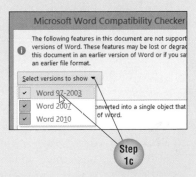

2. Save the document in Word 2003 format by completing the following steps:
   a. Press F12 to display the Save As dialog box with WL2C8 the active folder.
   b. At the Save As dialog box, click the *Save as type* option box and then click *Word 97-2003 Document (*.doc)* at the drop-down list.
   c. Select the text in the *File name* text box and then type **WL2-C8-P5-PremPro-2003format**.
   d. Click the Save button.
   e. Click the Continue button at the Microsoft Word Compatibility Checker dialog box.
3. Close **WL2-C8-P5-PremPro-2003format.doc**.

Managing Versions ■■■■■■■■■■■■■■■■■■■■■■■■

While you are working in a document, Word automatically saves the document every 10 minutes. This automatic backup feature can be very helpful if you accidentally close your document without saving it or if the power to your computer is disrupted. As Word automatically saves backups of your currently open document, the saved versions are listed to the right of the Manage Versions button in the Info backstage area, as shown in Figure 8.9 on the next page. Each autosave document displays with *Today*, followed by the time and *(autosave)*. When you save and then close your document, the autosave backup documents are deleted.

Manage
Versions

To open an autosave backup document, click the FILE tab and then click the backup document you want to open (backup documents display to the right of the Manage Versions button). The document opens as a read-only document and a

Figure 8.9 Autosave Documents in Info Tab Backstage View

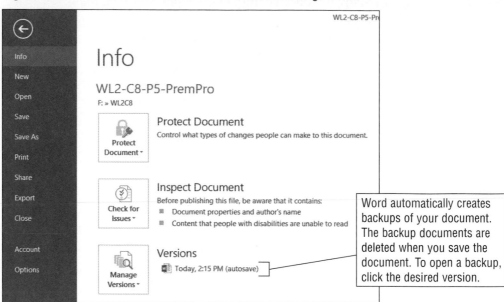

Word automatically creates backups of your document. The backup documents are deleted when you save the document. To open a backup, click the desired version.

Quick Steps

Display the UnsavedFiles Folder
1. Click FILE tab.
2. Click Manage Versions button.
3. Click *Recover Unsaved Documents*.
OR
1. Click FILE tab.
2. Click *Open* option.
3. Click Recover Unsaved Documents button.

Delete a Backup File
1. Click FILE tab.
2. Right-click backup file.
3. Click *Delete This Version* at shortcut menu.

Delete All Unsaved Files
1. Click FILE tab.
2. Click Manage Versions button.
3. Click *Delete All Unsaved Documents*.
4. Click Yes.

Change the AutoRecover Time
1. Click FILE tab.
2. Click *Options*.
3. Click *Save*.
4. Type desired minutes in *Save AutoRecover information every* measurement box.
5. Click OK.

yellow message bar displays with a Compare button and Restore button. Click the Compare button and the autosave document is compared to the original document. You can review the comparison to decide which changes you want to accept and reject. Click the Restore button and a message displays indicating that you are about to overwrite the last saved version with the selected version. At this message, click OK.

When you save a document, the autosave backup documents are deleted. However, if you close a document without saving (after 10 minutes) or the power is disrupted, Word keeps the backup file in the UnsavedFiles folder on the hard drive. Access this folder by clicking the Manage Versions button at the Info backstage area and then clicking *Recover Unsaved Documents*. At the Open dialog box that displays, double-click the desired backup file that you want to open. You can also display the UnsavedFiles folder by clicking the FILE tab, clicking the *Open* option, and then clicking the Recover Unsaved Documents button that displays below the Recent Documents list. Files in the UnsavedFiles folder are kept for four days after the creation of the document. After that, they are automatically deleted.

Manage each backup file by right-clicking on it. At the shortcut menu that displays, click the *Open Version* option to open the backup file, click the *Delete This Version* option to delete the backup file, or click the *Compare with Current* option to compare the backup file with the currently open file. If you want to delete all of the unsaved files, open a blank document, click the FILE tab, click the Manage Versions button, and then click the *Delete All Unsaved Documents* option. At the message asking if you are sure you want to delete the unsaved documents, click Yes.

As mentioned previously, by default, Word automatically saves a backup of an unsaved document every 10 minutes. To change this default setting, click the FILE tab and then click *Options*. At the Word Options dialog box, click *Save* in the left panel. Notice that the *Save AutoRecover information every* measurement box is set at 10 minutes. To change this number, click the up-pointing arrow to the right of *10* to increase the number of minutes between autosaves or click the down-pointing arrow to decrease the number of minutes between autosaves.

1. At a blank screen, decrease the autosave time by completing the following steps:
   a. Click the FILE tab and then click *Options*.
   b. At the Word Options dialog box, click *Save* in the left panel.
   c. Click the down-pointing arrow at the right of the *Save AutoRecover information every* measurement box until *1* displays.

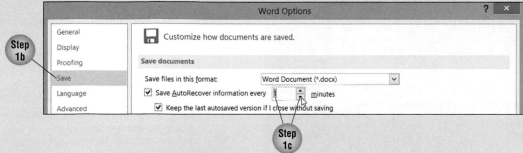

   d. Click OK to close the dialog box.
2. Open **WL2-C8-P5-PremPro.docx**.
3. Press Ctrl + End to move the insertion point to the end of the document and then type your first and last names.
4. Leave the document open for more than one minute without making any changes. After at least one minute has passed, click the FILE tab and then check to see if an autosave document displays to the right of the Manage Versions button. (If not, click the Back button to return to the document and wait a few more minutes.)
5. When an autosave document displays in the Info backstage area, click the Back button to return to the document.
6. Select the SmartArt graphic and then delete it.
7. Click the FILE tab and then click the autosave document that displays to the right of the Manage Versions button. If more than one autosave document displays, click the one at the bottom of the list. This opens the autosave document as read-only.

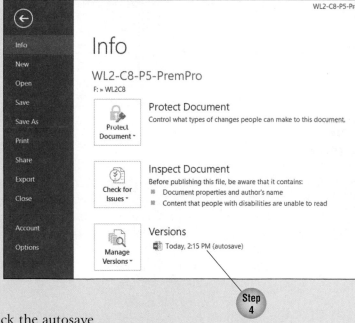

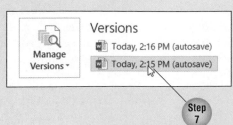

8. Restore the document to the autosave document by clicking the Restore button that displays in the yellow message bar.

9. At the message that displays indicating that you are about to overwrite the last saved version with the selected version, click OK. (This saves the document with the SmartArt.)

10. Press the Esc key to display the document in Normal view.

11. Check to see what versions of previous documents Word has saved by completing the following steps:

    a. Click the FILE tab.

    b. Click the Manage Versions button and then click *Recover Unsaved Documents* at the drop-down list.

    c. At the Open dialog box, check the documents that display in the Content pane.

    d. Click the Cancel button to close the Open dialog box.

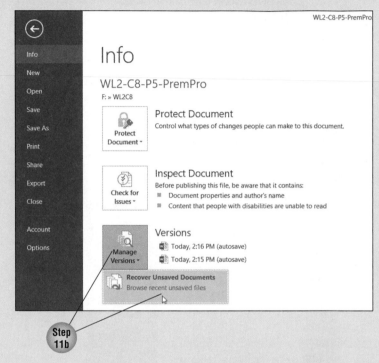

12. Delete a backup file by completing the following steps:

    a. Click the FILE tab.

    b. Right-click the first autosave backup file name that displays to the right of the Manage Versions button.

    c. Click *Delete This Version* at the shortcut menu.

    d. At the message that displays asking if you are sure you want to delete the selected version, click the Yes button.

13. Return the autosave time to 10 minutes by completing the following steps:

    a. At the Info backstage area, click *Options*.

    b. At the Word Options dialog box, click *Save* in the left panel.

    c. Click the up-pointing arrow at the right of the *Save AutoRecover information every* measurement box until *10* displays.

    d. Click OK to close the dialog box.

14. Save, print, and then close **WL2-C8-P5-PremPro.docx**.

15. Delete all of the unsaved backup files by completing the following steps:

    a. Press Ctrl + N to display a blank document.

    b. Click the FILE tab.

    c. Click the Manage Versions button and then click *Delete All Unsaved Documents*.

    d. At the message that displays, click Yes.

16. Click the Back button to return to the blank document.

Chapter Summary

- Restrict formatting and editing in a document and apply a password to it with options at the Restrict Editing task pane. Display this task pane by clicking the REVIEW tab and then clicking the Restrict Editing button in the Protect group.

- Restrict formatting by specifying styles that are allowed and not allowed in a document. Do this at the Formatting Restrictions dialog box. Display this dialog box by clicking the Settings hyperlink in the Restrict Editing task pane.

- To restrict editing in a document, insert a check mark in the *Allow only this type of editing in the document* check box at the Restrict Editing task pane, click the down-pointing arrow at the right of the option box, and then click the desired option.

- Enforce editing and formatting restrictions by clicking the Yes, Start Enforcing Protection button in the Restrict Editing task pane and make desired changes at the Start Enforcing Protection dialog box.

- Protect a document with a password using options at the Start Enforcing Protection dialog box or General Options dialog box.

- Open a document in different views with options at the Open button drop-down list in the Open dialog box.

- The Info backstage area displays information about document properties.

- Display the document information panel by clicking the Properties button at the Info backstage area and then clicking *Show Document Panel* at the drop-down list.

- You also can insert document information at the Properties dialog box. Display this dialog box by clicking the Properties button at the Info backstage area and then clicking *Advanced Properties* or by clicking the Document Properties button at the document information panel and then clicking *Advanced Properties*.

- When you mark a document as final, it is saved as a read-only document. Mark a document as final by clicking the Protect Document button at the Info backstage area and then clicking *Mark as Final* at the drop-down list. Typing, editing commands, and proofing marks are turned off when a document is marked as final.

- Protect a document with a password by clicking the Protect Document button at the Info backstage area and then clicking *Encrypt with Password*.

- Another method for displaying the Restrict Editing task pane is to click the Protect Document button at the Info backstage area and then click *Restrict Editing* at the drop-down list.

- Inspect a document for personal data, hidden data, and metadata with options at the Document Inspector dialog box. Display this dialog box by clicking the Check for Issues button at the Info backstage area and then clicking *Inspect Document* at the drop-down list.

- The accessibility checker checks a document for content that a person with disabilities might find difficult to read. Run the accessibility checker by clicking the Check for Issues button at the Info backstage area and then clicking *Check Accessibility* at the drop-down list.

- Run the compatibility checker to check your document and identify elements that are not supported or that will act differently in previous versions of Word. To determine the compatibility of the features in your document, click the Check for Issues button at the Info backstage area and then click *Check Compatibility* at the drop-down list.
- By default, Word automatically saves a backup of your unsaved document every 10 minutes. A list of backup documents displays to the right of the Manage Versions button at the Info backstage area. Click the document name to open the backup document.
- When you save a document, Word automatically deletes the backup documents. However, if you close a document without saving it or the power to your computer is disrupted, Word keeps a backup document in the UnsavedFiles folder on the hard drive. Display this folder by clicking the Manage Versions button at the Info backstage area and then clicking *Recover Unsaved Documents* at the drop-down list.
- Delete an autosave backup file by displaying the Info backstage area, right-clicking the desired autosave backup file, and then clicking *Delete This Version* at the shortcut menu.
- Delete all of the unsaved documents by displaying a blank document, clicking the FILE tab, clicking the Manage Versions button, and then clicking *Delete All Unsaved Documents*. At the message that displays, click Yes.
- You can change the 10-minute autosave default setting with the *Save AutoRecover information every* measurement at the Word Options dialog box with *Save* selected in the left panel.

Commands Review

FEATURE	RIBBON TAB, GROUP /OPTION	BUTTON, OPTION
accessibility checker	FILE, *Info*	, *Check Accessibility*
compatibility checker	FILE, *Info*	, *Check Compatibility*
document information panel	FILE, *Info*	Properties ▾ , *Show Document Panel*
Document Inspector dialog box	FILE, *Info*	, *Inspect Document*
Encrypt Document dialog box	FILE, *Info*	, *Encrypt with Password*
Formatting Restrictions dialog box	REVIEW, Protect	, *Settings*
General Options dialog box	FILE, *Save As*	Tools, *General Options*
Properties dialog box	FILE, *Info*	Properties ▾ , *Advanced Properties*
Restrict Editing task pane	REVIEW, Protect	
UnsavedFiles folder	FILE, *Info*	, *Recover Unsaved Documents*

Concepts Check Test Your Knowledge

Completion: In the space provided at the right, indicate the correct term, command, or number.

1. Limit what formatting users can perform on text in a document with options in this section of the Restrict Editing task pane. _____

2. Limit what types of changes users can make to a document with options in this section of the Restrict Editing task pane. _____

3. Click this button in the Restrict Editing task pane to display the Start Enforcing Protection dialog box. _____

4. Protect a document with a password using options at the Start Enforcing Protection dialog box or using options at this dialog box. _____

5. You can add or modify a document's properties at this panel. _____

6. Display the Properties dialog box by clicking the Properties button at the Info backstage area and then clicking this option at the drop-down list. _____

7. Use this feature to inspect your document for personal data, hidden data, and metadata. _____

8. Use this feature to check a document for content that a person with disabilities might find difficult to read. _____

9. Create alternate text for an image with *ALT TEXT* options at this task pane. _____

10. Use this feature to check your document and identify elements that are not supported in previous versions of Word. _____

11. Word keeps backup files in this folder on the hard drive. _____

Skills Check   Assess Your Performance

Assessment

1   RESTRICT FORMATTING AND EDITING OF A WRITING REPORT

1. Open **WritingProcess.docx** and then save the document and name it **WL2-C8-A1-WritingProcess**.
2. Display the Restrict Editing task pane and then restrict formatting to the Heading 2 and Heading 3 styles. (At the message asking if you want to remove formatting or styles that are not allowed, click No.)
3. Enforce the protection and include the password *writing*.
4. Click the <u>Available styles</u> hyperlink.
5. Apply the Heading 2 style to these two titles: *THE WRITING PROCESS* and *REFERENCES*.
6. Apply the Heading 3 style to the seven remaining headings in the document. (The Heading 3 style may not display until you apply the Heading 2 style to the first title.)
7. Close the Styles task pane and then close the Restrict Editing task pane.
8. Save the document and then print only page 1.
9. Close **WL2-C8-A1-WritingProcess.docx**.

Assessment

2   INSERT COMMENTS IN A SOFTWARE LIFE CYCLE DOCUMENT

1. Open **CommCycle.docx** and then save the document and name it **WL2-C8-A2-CommCycle**.
2. Display the Restrict Editing task pane, restrict editing to comments only, and then start enforcing the protection. (Do not include a password.)
3. Type the comment **Create a SmartArt graphic that illustrates the software life cycle.** at the end of the first paragraph in the document.
4. Type the comment **Include the problem-solving steps.** at the end of the paragraph in the *Design* section.
5. Type the comment **Describe a typical beta testing cycle.** at the end of the paragraph in the *Testing* section.
6. Print only the comments.
7. Close the Restrict Editing task pane.
8. Save and then close **WL2-C8-A2-CommCycle.docx**.

Assessment

3   INSERT DOCUMENT PROPERTIES, CHECK COMPATIBILITY, AND SAVE A PRESENTATION DOCUMENT IN A DIFFERENT FORMAT

1. Open **Presentation.docx** and then save the document and name it **WL2-C8-A3-Presentation**.
2. Make the following changes to the document:
   a. Apply the Heading 1 style to the title *Delivering a How-To Presentation*.
   b. Apply the Heading 2 style to the other three headings in the document.
   c. Change the style set to *Centered*.

d. Apply the View theme and apply the Green theme colors.

e. Change the color of the clip art image to *Green, Accent color 1 Light*.

3. Display the document information panel and then type the following in the specified text boxes:

Author	(Type your first and last names)
Title	**Delivering a How-To Presentation**
Subject	**Presentations**
Keywords	**presentation, how-to, delivering, topics**
Comments	**This document describes the three steps involved in developing a how-to presentation.**

4. Close the document information panel.

5. Save **WL2-C8-A3-Presentation.docx** and then print only the document properties.

6. Run the accessibility checker on the document and then create alternate text for the clip art image. Type the text **Presentation clip art image** for the title and type **Clip art image representing a person giving a presentation.** for the description. Close the accessibility checker.

7. Save and then print **WL2-C8-A3-Presentation.docx**.

8. Run the compatibility checker to determine what features are not supported by earlier versions of Word.

9. Save the document in the *Word 97-2003 Document (*.doc)* format and name it **WL2-C8-A3-Presentation-2003format**.

10. Save, print, and then close **WL2-C8-A3-Presentation-2003format.doc**.

Assessment

 4 ### CREATE A DOCUMENT ON INSERTING AND REMOVING A SIGNATURE

1. The Text group on the INSERT tab contains a Signature Line button for inserting a signature in a document. Use Word's Help feature to learn about inserting and removing a signature by typing **add or remove a digital signature** at the Word Help window and then clicking the <u>Add or remove a digital signature in Office files</u> hyperlink. Read the information in the article and then prepare a Word document with the following information:
   - An appropriate title
   - How to create a signature line in Word
   - How to sign a signature line in Word
   - How to remove a signature from Word
   - How to add an invisible digital signature in Word

2. Apply formatting to enhance the apearance of the document.

3. Save the document and name it **WL2-C8-A4-Signature**.

4. Print and then close **WL2-C8-A4-Signature.docx**.

Visual Benchmark   Demonstrate Your Proficiency

FORMAT A DOCUMENT, INSERT DOCUMENT PROPERTIES, CHECK COMPATIBILITY, AND SAVE A DOCUMENT IN A DIFFERENT FORMAT

1. Open **InfoSystem.docx** and then save the document and name it **WL2-C8-VB-InfoSystem**.
2. Format the document so it appears as shown in Figure 8.10 with the following specifications:
   a. Apply the Lines (Stylish) style set and then apply the Dividend theme.
   b. Insert the Integral footer and type your name as the author.
   c. Insert the SmartArt Continuous Cycle graphic and apply the Colorful - Accent Colors color and apply the Metallic Scene style.
   d. Recolor the clip art image as shown in the figure.
   e. Make any other changes needed so your document displays as shown in Figure 8.10.
3. Display the document information panel and then type the following in the specified text boxes:

Author	(Type your first and last names)
Title	**Developing an Information System**
Subject	**Software Development**
Keywords	**software, design, plan**
Category	**Software**
Status	**Draft**
Comments	**This document describes the four steps involved in developing an information system.**

4. Save the document and then print only the document properties.
5. Inspect the document and remove any hidden text.
6. Run the accessibility checker and then create alternate text for the clip art image.
7. Run the compatibility checker to determine what features are not supported by earlier versions of Word.
8. Save the document in the *Word 97-2003 Document (*.doc)* format and name it **WL2-C8-VB-InfoSystem-2003format**.
9. Save, print, and then close **WL2-C8-VB-InfoSystem-2003format.doc**.

Figure 8.10 Visual Benchmark

Developing an Information System

Identifying and assembling a team of employees with the required skills and expertise is a necessary first step in developing a new in-house information system. A management group may be involved in answering questions and providing information in the early planning phases of the project, but programmers and/or software engineers handle the design and implementation of any new system.

Programmers specialize in the development of new software, while software engineers are highly skilled professionals with programming and teamwork training. Their organized, professional application of the software development process is called software engineering.

Project Plan

The first step in the system development life cycle is planning. The planning step involves preparing a needs analysis and conducting feasibility studies. During this step, a company usually establishes a project team, and the team creates a project plan. The project plan includes an estimate of how long the project will take to complete, an outline of the steps involved, and a list of deliverables. Deliverables are documents, services, hardware, and software that must be finished and delivered by a certain time and date.

Project Team

Because of their large size, information systems require the creation of a project team. A project team usually includes a project manager, who acts as the team leader. Sometimes the project manager also functions as a systems analyst, responsible for completing the systems analysis and making design recommendations. Other project team members include software engineers and technicians. The software engineers deal with programming software, while technicians handle hardware issues. The comprehensive process software engineers initiate is called the system development life cycle (SDLC), a series of steps culminating in a completed information system.

Designing the System

A project is ready to move into the design stage once the project team has approved the plan, including the budget. The design process begins with the writing of the documentation, which covers functional and design specifications. In most cases, the project team creates the functional specifications, describing what the system must be able to do.

Implementation

The project can move into the next phase, implementation, once the development team and the systems house develop the design specification and approve the plans. This step is where the actual work of putting the system together is completed, including creating a prototype and completing the programming. In most cases, implementing the new system is the longest, most difficult step in the process.

STUDENT NAM

Support Stage

A system goes into the support stage after it has been accepted and approved. A support contract normally allows users to contact the systems house for technical support, training, and sometimes on-site troubleshooting. Even if the system was designed in-house, the responsible department often operates as an independent entity—sometimes even charging the department acquiring the system. The support stage continues until a new information system is proposed and developed, usually years later. At that point, the existing system is retired and no longer used.

STUDENT NAME 2

Case Study

Apply Your Skills

You work in the Training department at Hart International. Your department is responsible for preparing training material and training employees on how to use software applications within the company. Your supervisor asked you to help her prepare a Microsoft Word training manual. She had already written a portion of the manual and had you add training information and then format the manual.

If you completed Part 1 of the Case Study for Chapter 7, you should have a document saved in your WL2C7 folder named **WL2-C7-CS-HITraining.docx**. Open **WL2-C7-CS-HITraining.docx** from the WL2C7 folder on your storage medium and then save the document in your WL2C8 folder and name it **WL2-C8-CS-HITraining**. Move the insertion point to the end of the document and then insert the document named **HIManual.docx** located in your WL2C8 folder. (Insert the file with the Object button in the Text group on the INSERT tab.)

If you do not have **WL2-C7-CS-HITraining.docx** in your WL2C7 folder, open **HIManual.docx** from your WL2C8 folder and then save the document and name it **WL2-C8-CS-HITraining.docx**.

Add information to the document on how to insert the following buttons on the Quick Access toolbar: Quick Print, Open, Close, Spelling & Grammar, and Thesaurus. Apply formatting to the document and then save the completed document.

Your supervisor has decided that options on company computers should be modified and wants you to determine the steps for making the modifications and then include the steps in the training manual. Open the Word Options dialog box and then determine how to make the following modifications:

- Change the Office background to *Geometry* and the Office theme to *Light Gray*. (General)
- Change the grammar writing style to *Grammar & Style*. (Proofing)
- Change the minutes for saving AutoRecover information to 5 minutes. (Save)
- Change the number of documents that display in the Recent Documents list to 15. (Advanced) ***Hint: The option is located in the* Display *section of the dialog box. You will need to scroll down the dialog box to display this section.***

With **WL2-C8-CS-HITraining.docx** open, write the steps involved in making each customization listed above. If your document contains a table of contents, you will need to update the entire table. Save the document.

Prepare the document for distribution by inspecting the document and then restricting editing to comments only. Save, print, and then close **WL2-C8-CS-HITraining.docx**.

WORD
MICROSOFT®

Performance Assessment

Note: Before beginning the unit assessments, copy to your storage medium the WL2U2 subfolder from the WL2 folder on the CD that accompanies this textbook and then make WL2U2 the active folder.

Word
WL2U2

Assessing Proficiency ▪▪▪▪▪▪▪▪▪▪▪▪▪▪▪

In this unit, you learned how to use features for citing sources in a document, such as footnotes, endnotes, in-text citations, and bibliographies; how to insert tables of contents, tables of figures, and indexes; and how to use features for sharing and distributing documents, such as inserting comments, tracking changes, comparing and combining documents, linking and embedding files between programs, and restricting access to documents.

Assessment 1 Sort Text

1. Open **SHSSort.docx** and then save the document and name it **WL2-U2-A01-SHSSort**.
2. Select the five clinic names, addresses, and telephone numbers below *SUMMIT HEALTH SERVICES* and then sort the text alphabetically in ascending order by clinic name.
3. Sort the three columns of text below *EXECUTIVE TEAM* by the extension number in ascending order.
4. Sort the text in the table in the *First Half Expenses* column numerically in descending order.
5. Save, print, and then close **WL2-U2-A01-SHSSort.docx**.

Assessment 2 Select Records and Create Mailing Labels

1. At a blank document, use the mail merge feature to create mailing labels with Avery US Letter, 5160 Easy Peel Address Labels and the **SHS.mdb** data source file (located in the WL2U2 folder). Before merging the data source file with the mailing labels document, sort the records alphabetically in ascending order by last name.
2. Merge the sorted data source file with the labels document.
3. Save the merged labels document and name it **WL2-U2-A02-Lbls1**.
4. Close the document and then close the labels main document without saving it.
5. Use the mail merge feature to create mailing labels using the **SHS.mdb** data source file (use the same label option as in Step 1). Select records from the data source file of clients living in the city of Greensboro and then merge those records with the labels document.

6. Save the merged labels document and name it **WL2-U2-A02-Lbls2**.
7. Close the document and then close the labels main document without saving it.

Assessment 3 Insert Footnotes in a Desktop Publishing Report

1. Open **DTP.docx** and then save the document and name it **WL2-U2-A03-DTP**.
2. Insert the first footnote shown in Figure U2.1 at the end of the second paragraph in the *Defining Desktop Publishing* section.
3. Insert the second footnote shown in Figure U2.1 at the end of the fourth paragraph in the *Defining Desktop Publishing* section.
4. Insert the third footnote shown in Figure U2.1 at the end of the second paragraph in the *Planning the Publication* section.
5. Insert the fourth footnote shown in Figure U2.1 at the end of the last paragraph in the document.
6. Keep the heading *Planning the Publication* together with the paragraph of text that follows it.
7. Save and then print **WL2-U2-A03-DTP.docx**.
8. Select the entire document and then change the font to Constantia.
9. Select all of the footnotes and then change the font to Constantia.
10. Delete the third footnote.
11. Save, print, and then close **WL2-U2-A03-DTP.docx**.

Figure U2.1 Assessment 3

Laurie Fellers, *Desktop Publishing Design* (Dallas: Cornwall & Lewis Publishing, 2015), 67-72.

Joel Moriarity, "The Desktop Publishing Approach," *Desktop Publishing* (2015): 3-6.

Chun Man Wong, *Desktop Publishing with Style* (Seattle: Monroe-Ackerman Publishing, 2014), 89-93.

Andrew Rushton, *Desktop Publishing Tips and Tricks* (Minneapolis: Aurora Publishing House, 2015), 103-106.

Assessment 4 Create Citations and Prepare a Works Cited Page for a Report

1. Open **DesignWebsite.docx** and then save the document and name it **WL2-U2-A04-DesignWebsite**.
2. Format the title page to meet MLA requirements with the following changes:
   a. Make sure the document's reference style is set to MLA.
   b. Select the entire document, change the font to 12-point Cambria, change the line spacing to 2.0, and remove the space after paragraphs.
   c. Move the insertion point to the beginning of the document, type your name, press the Enter key, type your instructor's name, press the Enter key, type the title of your course, press the Enter key, and then type the current date.
   d. Insert a header that displays your last name and the page number at the right margin and then change the font to 12-point Cambria.

3. Press Ctrl + End to move the insertion point to the end of the document and then type the text shown in Figure U2.2 (in MLA style) up to the first citation—the text (*Mercado*). Insert the source information from a journal article written by Claudia Mercado using the following information:

Author	**Claudia Mercado**
Title	**Connecting a Web Page**
Journal Name	**Connections**
Year	**2015**
Pages	**12-21**
Volume	**IV**

4. Continue typing the text up to the next citation—the text *(Holmes)*—and insert the following source information from a website:

Author	**Brent Holmes**
Name of Web Page	**Hosting Your Web Page**
Year	**2014**
Month	**September**
Day	**28**
Year Accessed	*(type current year)*
Month Accessed	*(type current month)*
Day Accessed	*(type current day)*
URL	**www.emcp.net/webhosting**

5. Continue typing the text up to the next citation—the text *(Vukovich)*—and insert the following information from a book:

Author	**Ivan Vukovich**
Title	**Computer Technology in the Business Environment**
Year	**2015**
City	**San Francisco**
Publisher	**Gold Coast Publishing**

6. Insert the page number in the citation by Ivan Vukovich using the Edit Citation dialog box.
7. Type the remaining text shown in Figure U2.2 on the next page.
8. Edit the Ivan Vukovich source by changing the last name to *Vulkovich* in the *Master List* section of the Source Manager dialog box. Click Yes at the message asking if you want to update the source in both the Master List and the Current List.
9. Create a new source in the document using the Source Manager dialog box and include the following source information for a journal article:

Author	**Sonia Jaquez**
Title	**Organizing a Web Page**
Journal Name	**Design Techniques**
Year	**2015**
Pages	**32-44**
Volume	**IX**

10. Type the following sentence at the end of the last paragraph in the document: **Browsers look for pages with these names first when a specific file at a website is requested, and index pages display by default if no other page is specified.**
11. Insert a citation for Sonia Jaquez at the end of the sentence you just typed.
12. Insert a citation for Claudia Mercado following the second sentence in the first paragraph of the document.
13. Insert a works cited page at the end of the document on a separate page.

Figure U2.2 Assessment 4

One of the first tasks in website development is finding a good host for the site. Essentially, a web host lets you store a copy of your web pages on the hard drive of a powerful computer connected to the Internet with a fast connection that can handle thousands of users (Mercado). Hosting your own website is possible but is feasible only if you own an extra computer that can be dedicated to the role of a web server, have a high-speed Internet connection, and feel confident about handling the job of network security and routing (Holmes). Most people's situations do not fit those criteria. Fortunately, several free and fee-based web hosting services are available.

As you plan a website, decide what types of content you will include and then think about how all of the pages should link together. Most websites consist of a home page that provides the starting point for users entering the site. "Like the top of a pyramid or the table of contents of a book, the home page leads to other web pages via hyperlinks" (Vukovich 26). Most home pages have the default name index.html (or sometimes index.htm).

14. Format the works cited page as follows to meet MLA requirements:
    a. Select the *Works Cited* title and all of the entries and then click the *No Spacing* style thumbnail.
    b. Change the font to 12-point Cambria and change the spacing to 2.0.
    c. Center the title *Works Cited*.
    d. Format the works cited entries with a hanging indent. ***Hint: Use Ctrl + T to create a hanging indent.***
15. Save and then print **WL2-U2-A04-DesignWebsite.docx**.
16. Change the document and works cited page from MLA style to APA style. Change the title *Works Cited* to *References* and apply 12-point Cambria font formatting to the references in the list.
17. Save, print page 3, and then close **WL2-U2-A04-DesignWebsite.docx**.

Assessment 5 Create an Index and Table of Contents for a Desktop Publishing Report

1. At a blank document, create the text shown in Figure U2.3 as a concordance file.
2. Save the document and name it **WL2-U2-A05-CF**.
3. Print and then close **WL2-U2-A05-CF.docx**.
4. Open **DTPDesign.docx** and then save the document and name it **WL2-U2-A05-DTPDesign**.
5. Make the following changes to the document:
   a. Apply the Heading 1 style to the title and apply the Heading 2 style to the two headings in the report.
   b. Apply the Minimalist style set.
   c. Mark text for an index using the concordance file **WL2-U2-A05-CF.docx**.
   d. Insert the index (choose the Formal format style) at the end of the document on a separate page.
   e. Apply the Heading 1 style to the title of the index.

Figure U2.3 Assessment 5

message	Message
publication	Publication
design	Design
flier	Flier
letterhead	Letterhead
newsletter	Newsletter
intent	Design: intent
audience	Design: audience
layout	Design: layout
thumbnail	Thumbnail
principles	Design: principles
Focus	Design: focus
focus	Design: focus
balance	Design: balance
proportion	Design: proportion
contrast	Design: contrast
directional flow	Design: directional flow
consistency	Design: consistency
color	Design: color
White space	White space
white space	White space
Legibility	Legibility
headline	Headline
subheads	Subheads

f. Insert a section break that begins a new page at the beginning of the title *DESKTOP PUBLISHING DESIGN*.

g. Move the insertion point to the beginning of the document and then insert the *Automatic Table 1* table of contents.

h. Number the table of contents page with a lowercase roman numeral at the bottom center of the page.

i. Number the other pages in the report with arabic numbers at the bottom center of the page and start the numbering with 1 on the page containing the report title.

j. Insert a page break at the beginning of the heading *Creating Focus*.

6. Update page numbers for the index and the table of contents.

7. Save, print, and then close **WL2-U2-A05-DTPDesign.docx**.

Assessment 6 Create Captions and Insert a Table of Figures in a Report

1. Open **SoftwareCareers.docx** and then save the document and name it **WL2-U2-A06-SoftwareCareers**.

2. Click in any cell in the first table and then insert the caption *Table 1 Software Development Careers* so it displays above the table. (Change the paragraph spacing after the caption to 3 points.)

3. Click in any cell in the second table and then insert the caption *Table 2 Application Development Careers*. (Change the paragraph spacing after the caption to 3 points.)

4. Move the insertion point to the beginning of the heading *SOFTWARE DEVELOPMENT CAREERS* and then insert a section break that begins a new page.

5. With the insertion point below the section break, insert a page number at the bottom center of each page and change the starting page number to 1.

6. Move the insertion point to the beginning of the document and then insert the *Automatic Table 1* table of contents.

7. Press Ctrl + Enter to insert a page break.

8. Type **Tables**, press the Enter key, and then insert a table of figures using the Formal format.

9. Apply the Heading 1 style to the title *Tables*.

10. Move the insertion point to the beginning of the document and then change the numbering format to lowercase roman numerals.

11. Update the entire table of contents.

12. Save, print, and then close **WL2-U2-A06-SoftwareCareers.docx**.

Assessment 7 Insert Comments and Track Changes in an Online Shopping Report

1. Open **OnlineShop.docx** and then save the document and name it **WL2-U2-A07-OnlineShop**.

2. Move the insertion point to end of the first paragraph in the report and then insert the comment **Include the source where you found this definition.**

3. Move the insertion point to the end of the paragraph in the *Online Shopping Venues* section and then insert the comment **Include at least two of the most popular online shopping stores.**

4. Click the Display for Review button arrow and then click *All Markup* at the drop-down list.

5. Turn on Track Changes and then make the following changes:
   a. Delete the comma and the words *and most are eliminating paper tickets altogether*, which display at the end of the last sentence in the second paragraph (do not delete the period that ends the sentence).
   b. Edit the heading *Advantages of Online Shopping* so it displays as *Online Shopping Advantages*.
   c. Bold the first sentence of each of the bulleted paragraphs on the first page.
   d. Turn off Track Changes.
6. Display the Word Options dialog box with *General* selected and then type **Trudy Holmquist** as the user name and **TH** as the user initials. (Make sure you insert a check mark in the *Always use these values regardless of sign in to Office.* check box.)
7. Turn on Track Changes and then make the following changes:
   a. Delete the words *the following* in the first paragraph in the *Online Shopping Advantages* section.
   b. Type the following bulleted text between the third and fourth bulleted paragraphs on the second page: **Keep thorough records of all transactions.**
   c. Turn off Track Changes.
8. Print the document with markup.
9. Display the Word Options dialog box with *General* selected and then change the user name back to the original name and the initials back to the original initials. (Remove the check mark from the *Always use these values regardless of sign in to Office.* check box.)
10. Accept all of the changes in the document *except* the change deleting the comma and the text *and most are eliminating paper tickets altogether*. (Leave the comments in the document.)
11. Save, print, and then close **WL2-U2-A07-OnlineShop.docx**.

Assessment 8 Combine Documents

1. Open **Software.docx** and then save the document and name it **WL2-U2-A08-Software**.
2. Close **WL2-U2-A08-Software.docx**.
3. At a blank screen, combine **WL2-U2-A08-Software.docx** (the original document) with **Software-AL.docx** (the revised document) into the original document.
4. Save **WL2-U2-A08-Software.docx**.
5. Print the document with markup.
6. Accept all of the changes to the document.
7. Make the following changes to the document:
   a. Apply the Basic (Stylish) style set.
   b. Apply the Wisp theme.
   c. Apply the Red theme colors.
   d. Insert the Austin footer.
8. Save, print, and then close **WL2-U2-A08-Software.docx**.

Assessment 9 Linking Excel Data with a Word Document

1. Open **NCUHomeLoans.docx** and then save the document and name it **WL2-U2-A09-NCUHomeLoans**.
2. Open Excel and then open **NCUMortgages.xlsx**.
3. Save the Excel workbook with Save As and name it **WL2-U2-A09-NCUMortgages**.

4. Select cells A2 through G14 and then link the cells to the **WL2-U2-A09-NCUHomeLoans** Word document as a Microsoft Excel Worksheet Object. (Use the Paste Special dialog box.)
5. Save, print, and then close **WL2-U2-A09-NCUHomeLoans.docx**.
6. With Excel the active program, make the following changes to the data:
a. Click in cell A3, type **200000**, and then press Enter.
b. Position the mouse on the small green square (the fill handle) that displays in the lower right corner of cell A3 until the pointer displays as a black plus symbol. Hold down the left mouse button, drag down to cell A6, and then release the mouse button. (This inserts *$200,000* in the cells.)
7. Save and then close **WL2-U2-A09-NCUMortgages.xlsx**.
8. Open **WL2-U2-A09-NCUHomeLoans.docx** and click Yes at the message asking if you want to update the document.
9. Save, print, and then close **WL2-U2-A09-NCUHomeLoans.docx**.

Assessment 10 Restrict Formatting in a Report

1. Open **InterfaceApps.docx** and then save the document and name it **WL2-U2-A10-InterfaceApps**.
2. Display the Restrict Editing task pane and then restrict formatting to the Heading 1 and Heading 2 styles. (At the message that displays asking if you want to remove formatting or styles that are not allowed, click No.)
3. Enforce the protection and include the password *report*.
4. Click the <u>Available styles</u> hyperlink in the Restrict Editing task pane.
5. Apply the Heading 1 style to the title of the report and apply the Heading 2 style to the four headings in the report.
6. Close the Styles task pane.
7. Close the Restrict Editing task pane.
8. Save the document and then print only page 1.
9. Close **WL2-U2-A10-InterfaceApps.docx**.

Assessment 11 Insert Document Properties and Save a Document in a Previous Version of Word

1. Open **KLHPlan.docx** and then save the document and name it **WL2-U2-A11-KLHPlan**.
2. Make the following changes to the document:
a. Apply the Heading 1 style to the three headings in the document: *Plan Highlights*, *Quality Assessment*, and *Provider Network*.
b. Change the style set to Centered.
c. Apply the Blue II theme colors.
3. Move the insertion point to the end of the document and then insert the document named **KLHPlanGraphic.docx**.
4. Display the document information panel and then type the following information in the specified text boxes:

Author	(Insert your first and last names.)
Title	**Key Life Health Plan**
Subject	**Company Health Plan**
Keywords	**health, plan, network**
Category	**Health Plan**
Comments	**This document describes highlights of the Key Life Health Plan.**

5. Close the document information panel.

6. Save the document and then print only the document properties.
7. Inspect the document and remove any hidden text.
8. Save and then print **WL2-U2-A11-KLHPlan.docx**.
9. Assume that the document will be read by a colleague with Word 2003 and run the compatibility checker to determine what features are not supported by earlier versions of Word.
10. Save the document in the *Word 97-2003 Document (*.doc)* format and name it **WL2-U2-A11-KLHPlan-2003format**.
11. Save, print, and then close **WL2-U2-A11-KLHPlan-2003format.doc**.

Writing Activities ■■■■■■■■■■■■■■■■■■■

The following writing activities give you the opportunity to practice your writing skills and demonstrate an understanding of some of the important Word features you have mastered in this unit.

Activity 1 Prepare an APA Guidelines Document

You work for a psychiatric medical facility and many of the psychiatrists and psychiatric nurses you work with submit papers to journals that require formatting in APA style. Your supervisor has asked you to prepare a document that describes the APA guidelines and then provides the steps on how to format a Word document in APA style. Find a website that provides information on APA style and include the hyperlink in your document. (Consider websites for writing labs at colleges and universities.) Apply formatting to enhance the appearance of the document. Save the document and name it **WL2-U2-Act1-APA**. Print and then close **WL2-U2-Act1-APA.docx**.

Activity 2 Create a Rental Form Template

You work in a real estate management company that manages rental houses. You decide to automate the standard rental form that is normally filled in by hand. Open **LeaseAgreement.docx** and then save the document and name it **WL2-U2-Act2-LeaseAgreement**. Look at the lease agreement document and determine how to automate it so it can be filled in using the Find and Replace feature in Word. Change the current *Lessor* and *Lessee* names to *LESSOR* and *LESSEE*. Save the document as a template named **LeaseForm** to the Custom Office Templates folder. Open the **LeaseForm.dotx** template (from the New backstage area) and then complete the following find and replaces. Use your judgment about which occurrences should be changed and which should not.

DAY	24th
MONTH	February
YEAR	2015
RENT	$950
DEPOSIT	$500
LESSOR	Samantha Herrera
LESSEE	Daniel Miller

Save the document and name it **WL2-U2-Act2-Lease1**. Use the **LeaseForm.dotx** template to create another rental document. You determine the text to replace with the standard text. Save the completed rental document and name it **WL2-U2-Act2-Lease2**.

Internet Research ▪■■■■■■■■■■■■■■■■■■

Create a Job Search Report

Use a search engine to search for companies offering employment opportunities. Search for companies offering jobs in a field in which you are interested in working. Locate at least three websites that interest you and then create a report in Word that includes the following information about the sites:

- Site name, address, and URL
- A brief description of the site
- Employment opportunities available at the site

Create a hyperlink from your report to each site and include any additional information pertinent to the site. Apply formatting to enhance the document. Save the document and name it **WL2-U2-Act3-JobSearch**. Print and then close **WL2-U2-Act3-JobSearch.docx**.

Job Study ▪■■■■■■■■■■■■■■■■■■■■■■■■■■

Format a Guidelines Report

As a staff member of a computer e-tailer, you are required to maintain cutting-edge technology skills, including being well versed in the use of new software programs such as those in the Office 2013 suite. Recently, your supervisor asked you to develop and distribute a set of strategies for reading technical and computer manuals that the staff will use as they learn new programs. Use the concepts and techniques you learned in this unit to edit the guidelines report as follows:

1. Open **Strategies.docx** and then save the document and name it **WL2-U2-JS-Strategies**.
2. Turn on Track Changes and then make the following changes:
   a. Change all occurrences of *computer manuals* to *technical and computer manuals*.
   b. Format the document with appropriate heading styles.
   c. Insert at least two comments about the content and/or formatting of the document.
   d. Print the list of markup.
   e. Accept all of the tracked changes.
3. Turn off Track Changes.
4. Insert a table of contents.
5. Number the pages in the document.
6. Create a cover page.
7. Save, print, and then close **WL2-U2-JS-Strategies.docx**.

Index

Comparison option box, 193–194
compatibility check, 324–325
concordance file, to create index, 251–255
Create Custom Dictionary dialog box, 65
Create New Building Block dialog box, 95
Create New Document button, 159
Create New Theme Colors dialog box, 133, 134
Create Source dialog box, 208
cross-reference
    defined, 162
    for index, 248
    inserting and navigating with, 162–163
Cross-reference button, 162
custom bullets, defining and inserting, 11–13
Custom Dictionaries dialog box, 65
Customize Keyboard dialog box, 150
Customize Quick Access Toolbar button, 109, 111
customizing
    AutoCorrect, 85–91
    AutoFormatting, 89–91
    building blocks, 99–103
    captions in table of figures, 244–246
    compared document options, 286–288
    images, 16–21
    markup display, 278–279
    photograph, 20–21
    Quick Access toolbar, 109–113
    ribbon, 113–117
    spelling checker, 58
    table of contents, 234–236
    text box, 22–23
    themes, 132–140
    Track Changes options, 281–282
custom numbers, inserting, 6–8
Custom Office Templates folder, 200

D

data source, sorting records in, 190–196
Date & Time button, 24
Define button, 70
Define New Bullet dialog box, 11
Define New Multilevel List dialog box, 14
Define New Number Format dialog box, 9
deleting
    AutoCorrect text, 89–91
    bookmark, 156

building blocks, 103–104
comments, 274–275
custom themes, 138–140
index, 254
macros, 148–149
table of figures, 243
DESIGN tab, 133
destination program, 291
DEVELOPER tab, 144
dictionary
    changing default, 65–67
    creating custom, 65–67
    defining words, 70–71
    removing, 65
digital signature, adding, 319
Display for Review button, 276
Document Formatting group, 132, 133
document information panel, 314–315
document inspector, 320–322
Document Inspector dialog box, 320
document properties
    inserting, 105–106
    managing, 314–317
documents
    accessibility check, 323–324
    combining, 288–290
    comments, inserting and managing, 268–275
    comparing documents, 285–288
    compatibility check, 324–325
    creating based on template, 201
    embedding objects, 291–292
    encrypting, 318–319
    grammar check, 61–63
    inserting properties, 105–106
    inspecting, 320–325
    linking
        to new, 159–161
        objects in, 293–294
        to place in, 158
    managing
        properties for, 314–317
        versions of, 325–328
    marking as final, 317–318
    merging, 289
    navigating, 154–163
    opening in different views, 312–313
    protecting, 306–313
    readability statistics of, 63–64
    restricting, 317–319
    saving
        macro-enabled document/ template, 152–153
        as template, 200
    spell check, 57–60
    Track Changes, 276–285
    word count for, 67, 69

Don't Capitalize after text box, 86
Don't Correct text box, 86
DRAWING TOOLS FORMAT tab, 22

E

editing
    building block properties, 98–99
    comments, 272
    custom themes, 137–138
    footnotes and endnotes, 204–206
    linked object, 294
    Restrict Editing task pane, 306
    restricting, 310–311, 319
    sources, 210
    during spelling and grammar check, 58
Edit Theme Colors dialog box, 137
email address, linking to, 160
E-Mail Address button, 160
embedding
    defined, 291
    Excel data in document, 292
    objects, 291–292
em dash, 198
Encrypt Document dialog box, 318–319
en dash, 198
endnotes
    creating, 203
    defined, 202
    note reference number, 202
    printing, 203
    viewing and editing, 204–206
Excel
    embedding data in document, 292
    entering data in worksheet to create chart, 34–35
    linking chart to document, 293
    linking to file in, from Word, 159
Export backstage area, 200

F

Field dialog box, 106–107
fields
    Comparison option box, 193–194
    inserting, 106–108
    marking table of contents entries as, 237–239
    sorting on more than one, 188
    updating, 108
figures. *See* table of figures
files, linking to file in another program, 159–161
Filter and Sort dialog box, 190–191
    clear current options, 195